History as Performance

This study analyzes history as performance: as the interaction of actors, plays, stages, and enactments. By this, it examines women's politics in Habsburg Galicia around 1900: a Polish woman active in the peasant movement, a Ukrainian feminist, and a Jewish Zionist. It shows how the movements constructed essentialistically regarded collectives, experience as a medially comprehensible form of credibility, and a historically based inevitability of change, and legitimized participation and intervention through social policy and educational practices. Traits shared by the movements included the claim to interpretive sovereignty, the ritualization of participation, and the establishment of truths about past and future.

Dietlind Hüchtker is Professor for Historical Transregional Studies at Vienna University.

Routledge Studies in Cultural History

87 Russia's French Connection
   A History of the Lasting French Imprint on Russian Culture
   Adam Coker

88 Transatlantic Encounters in History of Education
   Translations and Trajectories from a German-American Perspective
   Edited by Fanny Isensee, Andreas Oberdorf, and Daniel Töpper

89 The Humanities in Transition from Postmodernism into the Digital Age
   Nigel A. Raab

90 Negotiating Memory from the Romans to the Twenty-First Century
   Damnatio Memoriae
   Edited by Øivind Fuglerud, Kjersti Larsen, and Marina Prusac-Lindhagen

91 Cultures and Practices of Coexistence from the Thirteenth Through the Seventeenth Centuries
   Multi-Ethnic Cities in the Mediterranean World, Volume 1
   Edited by Marco Folin and Antonio Musarra

92 Controversial Heritage and Divided Memories from the Nineteenth Through the Twentieth Centuries
   Multi-Ethnic Cities in the Mediterranean World, Volume 2
   Edited by Marco Folin and Heleni Porfyriou

93 History as Performance
   Political Movements in Galicia Around 1900
   Dietlind Hüchtker

For more information about this series, please visit: https://www.routledge.com/Routledge-Studies-in-Cultural-History/book-series/SE0367

History as Performance
Political Movements in
Galicia Around 1900

Dietlind Hüchtker

TRANSLATED BY CHRIS ABBEY

NEW YORK AND LONDON

First published in English 2021
by Routledge
52 Vanderbilt Avenue, New York, NY 10017

and by Routledge
2 Park Square, Milton Park, Abingdon, Oxon, OX14 4RN

Routledge is an imprint of the Taylor & Francis Group, an informa business

© 2021 Taylor & Francis

The right of Dietlind Hüchtker to be identified as author of this work has been asserted in accordance with sections 77 and 78 of the Copyright, Designs and Patents Act 1988.

All rights reserved. No part of this book may be reprinted or reproduced or utilised in any form or by any electronic, mechanical, or other means, now known or hereafter invented, including photocopying and recording, or in any information storage or retrieval system, without permission in writing from the publishers.

Trademark notice: Product or corporate names may be trademarks or registered trademarks, and are used only for identification and explanation without intent to infringe.

Published in German as *Geschichte als Performance. Politische Bewegungen in Galizien um 1900* by Campus Verlag (2014).

Library of Congress Cataloging-in-Publication Data
Names: Hüchtker, Dietlind, author.
Title: History as performance : political movements in Galicia around 1900 / Dietlind Hüchtker ; translated by Chris Abbey.
Other titles: Geschichte als Performance. English
Description: First edition. | New York : Routledge Taylor & Francis Group, 2021. | Series: Routledge studies in cultural history ; 93 | Includes bibliographical references and index.
Identifiers: LCCN 2020026053 (print) |
LCCN 2020026054 (ebook) | ISBN 9780367545710 (hardback) |
ISBN 9781003089759 (ebook) | ISBN 9781000175608
(adobe pdf) | ISBN 9781000175639 (mobi) |
ISBN 9781000175660 (epub)
Subjects: LCSH: Galicia (Poland and Ukraine)—Politics and government—19th century. | Galicia (Poland and Ukraine)—History—19th century. | Women—Political activity—Galicia (Poland and Ukraine) | Feminism—Galicia (Poland and Ukraine)—History—19th century. | Social movements—Galicia (Poland and Ukraine)—History—19th century. | Peasant uprisings—Galicia (Poland and Ukraine)
Classification: LCC DK4600.G3475 H8313 2021 (print) |
LCC DK4600.G3475 (ebook) | DDC 322.4082/094779—dc23
LC record available at https://lccn.loc.gov/2020026053
LC ebook record available at https://lccn.loc.gov/2020026054

ISBN: 978-0-367-54571-0 (hbk)
ISBN: 978-1-003-08975-9 (ebk)

Typeset in Sabon
by codeMantra

Contents

List of Figures vii
Acknowledgments ix
List of Abbreviations xi

Introduction 1
Arenas: Politics in Galicia 3
Tools: Performance, Performativity, Ritual, and Space 9
Rules: Research Contexts 15
Strategies: Approaches 22

1 **Finding Roles: The Participants** 33
 Heroic Narrating, or: Maria Wysłouchowa and Love 35
 Dramatic Directing, or: Natalja Kobryns'ka and Books 54
 Theatrical Enacting, or: Rosa Pomeranz and Charisma 75

2 **Propagating: The Plays** 119
 Writing Collectives into Existence 122
 Composing Experience 133
 Enacting History 141

3 **Organizing: The Stages** 155
 Ritualizing Education 157
 Rehearsing Nation 170
 Designing Society 180

4 **Mobilizing: The Enactments** 199
 Recitations about Role Models 200
 Monologues about Competition 212
 Dialogues about Practice 223

Conclusion 240
The Participants: Author, Artistic Director and Actor 241
The Plays: Collectives, Experience, and History 243
The Stages: Education, Nation, and Society 244
The Enactments: Role Models, Competition and Practice 246
The Performance 247

Appendix of Names 251
Bibliography 259
Index 311

Figures

1.1 Maria Wysłouchowa. Beskid Museum in Wisła, before 1905, Wikimedia Commons/User:Piotrus/CC BY-SA (https://creativecommons.org/licenses/by-sa/3.0)   36
1.2 Natalja Kobryns'ka, Gazeta Den', 1900, Wikimedia Commons/Unknown author/Public domain   55
1.3 Rosa Pomeranz. 1936. In Pamięci Róży Melzerowej, [edited by Sabina Feuersteinowa, Berta Jegerowa, and Henryka Schreiberowa], n.p. L'viv: printed by Koło Kobiet Żydowskich, by kind permission of the National Library of Israel   76
2.1 Przodownica, detail of the front page, Podkarpacie Biblioteka Cyfrowa, public domain   122
2.2 Zorza, detail of the front page, Polona, public domain   123

Acknowledgments

This book is a translation of my habilitation thesis published in 2014. I would especially like to thank Michael G. Müller for discussions and encouragement spanning many years. My thanks to Chris Abbey for his translation as well as Laura Loew for proofreading and copy editing. The Campus publishing house generously allowed the book to be republished in English, and I am indebted to Max Novick from academic publisher Routledge for his patience and persistence. Moreover, I am most grateful to Christian Lübke, director of the Leibniz Institute for the History and Culture of Eastern Europe, for approving the translation, which the German Federal Ministry of Education and Research kindly funded.

Dietlind Hüchtker
Berlin, February 2020

Abbreviations

AHMT	Archiv der Hochschule für Musik und Theater "Felix Mendelssohn Bartholdy" (Archive of Felix Mendelssohn Bartholdy University of Music and Theatre), Leipzig
AOB	Archiwum Odon Bujwid (Odon Bujwid Archive), Kraków
BJ	Biblioteka Jagiellońska (Jagiellonian Library), Kraków
BN	Biblioteka Narodowa (National Library of Poland), Warsaw
BO	Biblioteka Ossolineum (Ossolineum Library), Wrocław
BS	L'vivs'ka nacional'na naukova biblioteka Ukraïny imeni V. Stefanyka (Stefanyk National Science Library, L'viv)
CDIA	Central'nyj deržavnyj istoryčnyj archiv Ukraïny (Central State Archives of Ukraine), L'viv
CZA	Central Zionist Archives, Jerusalem
IlŠ	Instytut literatury im. T. H. Ševčenka nacional'na akademija nauk Ukraïny (T. H. Ševčenko Institute of Literature of the National Academy of Sciences of Ukraine), Kiev
PAN KRAKÓW	Polska Akademia Nauk (Polish Academy of Sciences), Kraków
PAN WARSZAWA	Polska Akademia Nauk, Instytut literacki (Polish Academy of Sciences, Institute of Literature), Warsaw
PNP	Památník národního písemnictví (Monument of National Literature), Prague

Introduction

"We tell ourselves that Lemberg, Léopol, Lvov, Lviv, and Lwów are all different names for the same city ... but in fact each is a distinct city of its own, with very precise rules of transition from one to the other."[1] At the end of Thomas Pynchon's novel *Against the Day*, with the First World War over, the algebraist E. Percy Movay tells the "old Vectorial hand" Kit of "a fabled group of mathematicians in Lwów, out at the wild frontier of the now-defunct Austro-Hungarian Empire."[2] After coming across a series of amazing mathematical theories there, Kit travels west and east from the railway station, landing up in the hidden city of Shambala before unexpectedly reappearing in Paris. Being a Vectorist he searches for mathematical formulae that can be used to measure the dimensions of space and time. Being a researcher, he knows about different types of theories. And being the son of a miner and union leader, he also experiences other dimensions of reality. He is forced to acknowledge the limited scope of mathematical laws, their confines imposed by other rules, emotions, interests, and natural events.

The characters in Pynchon's novel walk, ride on horseback, and fly by airship between the 1893 World's Fair in Chicago and the years shortly after the First World War, between Colorado, Europe, and Siberia. They experience and observe the different perceptions and interpretations of history, including the exclusivity people attach to their own views and the parallelism of different exclusivities. They consider the search for laws and accept their interpretations, the importance of social bonds and their violent destruction, the failure of goals and ideas, and the changes that nevertheless occur. The novel could be read as a search for the rules of change, rules governing the numerous transitions from one place and time to another. For example, the different names of the city of L'viv in the Polish–Lithuanian Commonwealth, in the Austrian partition, in the Habsburg crownland of Galicia, in the Jewish diaspora, in the eras of Russian and Soviet rule, in Western Ukraine, and in the southeast of the Second Polish Republic are more than mere translations. In fact, various names engender different geographical and temporal reference spaces with successive, opposing, mutually exclusive, and overlapping political and historical narratives. Switching between times, spaces, and histories is not easy; it entails knowing the rules, to say nothing of formulating and breaking them. Well, just as *Against the Day* develops translocal and transtemporal references, this study on the history of political movements in Galicia focuses on the diversity of reference spaces and rules of transition.

Being politically active means more than drawing up demands or developing arguments. It also means formulating narratives and choreographing practices. Only then do events become visions of society that are recorded and then manifested physically (i.e. by taking action) and modified. The political movements of the nineteenth-century forged links between past, present, and future based on experience and which turned historical interpretations into truths. In other words (and this is the starting point of my observations), they constituted identity politics—and its views and practices continue to characterize the perception and presentation of history, historiography, and politics to this day.

The historicization of knowledge was crucial to political causes, such as national, labor, peasant, and women's movements. These movements formed collectives whose shared history of oppression or deprivation prompted them to act and gave them hope for a better future.[3] They established narratives by means of historicity and experience as well as practices of participation and change. This enabled them to translate their goals into practical work and develop interpretations of society. To propagate and constitute change, all movements made use of educational and social work projects, which formed a code that could be interpreted and understood beyond political differences, national narratives, and regional specifics. This code—comprising education, knowledge, modernity, and progress—was both a weapon used to fight with and the proposal brought to the table by the various actors in the political struggle for a better society. But in order to be able to debate and compete, an agreement had to be reached concerning the nature and rules of the struggle. Therefore, the codes were clear and communicable to contemporaries, no matter how antagonistic the positions and currents described with them sometimes were, with progress and tradition irreconcilably opposed, and with no holds barred in a struggle whose weapons included national inclusion and exclusion as well as accusations of loss of nationhood and culture or even betrayal.

History is not simply a chronological sequence of events. Events occur diachronically, sometimes complementing, sometimes contradicting each other, and sometimes merely alongside each other. The job of history is to weave them together—and the job of historiography is to analyze them and highlight these links. Beyond the epistemological and philosophical debates about whether historical science ought to or does indeed operate inductively or deductively, hermeneutically or analytically, the problem of depicting the contingency and dependency of historical logics remains.[4] The essence of both history and the science of history is to present historical phenomena—structures and events—with attention paid to the logic of reasoning and the plausibility of the plot as well as emotions and practices. Above all, however, history is a practice of change—change in the way events are perceived and presented. Even in analytical and structural studies, historiography examines characteristic examples of change such as political turning points and exceptional circumstances as well as differences between epochs and regions. This means that in both history and historiography, narratives are developed.

Narrativity is a concept, an approach that can be used to examine the concepts of the world, i.e. the *how* of changes, the negotiation of new rules, the mechanisms by which they gain acceptance, and dependency and independence. In addition, narrativity implies roles: instances of narrative and perception, narrators, and listeners. Narrativity, therefore, means practices, their interpretations and changes, instead of fixed discourses or hegemonic explanations.[5] Like fictional stories, the narration of history (and histories) follows rules. Consequently, a simple distinction between fiction (narrative literature) and factuality (analytical historiography) does not go far enough. That is not to say that "the right of veto of sources," and thus, the falsifiability or verifiability of the narrative is suspended.[6] How historical actors narrate history and practice change, and how narration and change simultaneously enter another narrative, that of this author, are the subject of this study.

Allow me to begin with three observations about the writing of history in a double sense, i.e. both political movements that made history by shaping social change, and historiography integrating divergent spatial and temporal constructions. First, the study provides an example of how history can be written beyond master narratives confined to national or political history. Second, it presents the relationality between direction and effectiveness. Third, it develops a method of presentation weaving together different levels of political engagement, subjectivity, narrativity and performativity, narration and action, and motives and contexts. It shows history as performance—and historiography as the practice of narration.

Arenas: Politics in Galicia

The starting point of the study is the politics of three women in Galicia around 1900: Maria Wysłouchowa, Natalja Kobryns'ka and Rosa Pomeranz. All three came from families who were involved in specific movements: the Polish uprisings, the spread of Ruthenian literature and culture,[7] and nurturing awareness of Jewish history and heritage. All three received support during their education and became active in causes themselves: the peasant movement, the women's movement, and the Zionist movement. They put social work at the center of their activity and focused on women's politics in a dual sense: women who were politically active and policy aimed at women. Wysłouchowa's goal was to mobilize peasant women for the peasant movement, Kobryns'ka initiated an autonomous women's movement associated with the Ruthenian movement influenced by contemporary socialist ideas, while Pomeranz sought to carve out a role for women in Zionism.

Maria Wysłouchowa corresponded with the Polish writer Eliza Orzeszkowa.[8] They both came from the Eastern Borderlands (*Kresy Wschodnie*), the areas of the Polish–Lithuanian Commonwealth which after the partitions were incorporated into the Russian Empire. Maria Wysłouchowa lived in L'viv from 1885; Eliza Orzeszkowa resided in Grodno on the border with the Kingdom of Poland. In 1890, Wysłouchowa described to Orzeszkowa the peasant deputies elected to the *Sejm*, the Galician diet, as follows:

> For example, a few weeks ago, the highlanders of Żywiec county, despite the wild agitation of the "elder" brothers and pressure from the government, voted by an overwhelming majority to elect a younger brother of the highlanders as a deputy to the *Sejm*. This is already the fourth deputy from the Polish peasants (I do not count the Ruthenians), the fourth sincere defender of peasant rights. Last Tuesday, I attended the annual opening of the diet. In the black room full of black frock coats and even blacker cassocks, the colorful, picturesque folk costumes shone like pansies of the new day. Their [the peasants'] strikingly tanned faces stood out from the faces covered with various masks imposed by "civilization" and expressed the most intense attention and passion for the solemnity of the moment. In their tough hands, they held pencils and eagerly noted the main issues addressed by the debate for several hours without showing any signs of fatigue.[9]

Wysłouchowa painted a vivid picture of the deputies in her description. The peasants' efforts to conduct themselves properly in the diet, their concentration, and the solemnity of the historical moment can be clearly imagined. The contrast between their colorful costumes and other deputies' dark, stiff suits emphasized the unusual nature of the occasion. Despite their unusual attire, the peasant deputies proved with their tireless writing that they mastered the necessary cultural techniques. Nonetheless, the use of the adverb "eagerly" adds a childish touch to the description.

Wysłouchowa knew how to tell a story, and she successfully inserted her worldview into this little episode. She described the participation of the peasants in the peasant movement as successful politics, first because peasants had managed to be elected despite curia suffrage and second, because the "younger brothers" represented a political current which in her eyes was new and forward-looking.[10] Their colorful clothing promised a livelier, more original society, the black contrast referring back to the idea of a conservative, privileged noble and spiritual elite. Literacy implied that education was a prerequisite while fighting for and claiming participation was a key element of the program of Wysłouchowa's movement.

The description constructs a paternalistic relationship between the narrator as one of the intellectual leaders of the movement, and the peasants, the intended beneficiaries of social work. Why the Ruthenians did not count is uncertain. Perhaps Wysłouchowa equated "Polish" with "progressive"; maybe she considered the Polish peasants' enactment worth emphasizing because it constituted a victory over the conservative Polish-speaking elite. The need to mention the Ruthenian peasants, however, indicates that the national pattern of order "Ruthenian" versus "Polish"—as opposed to, for example, a social pattern such as "peasantry" versus "gentry"—was not yet taken for granted. In addition, the remark "already the fourth" peasant deputy implies that peasants had only recently been elected to the diet, thanks to the support of the peasant movement. However, this was not the case. In 1848, and then again in 1861, after the introduction of curia suffrage, peasants had been represented in both the *Sejm* and the Imperial Council (*Reichsrat*), where they had articulated their interests against the landed Polish elite. For a while, there had even been a Polish-Ruthenian peasants' club set up to defend their rights to use forestland and pasture, a move that had prompted the elite to force the peasants out of the diet again, one of the main arguments cited being their poor literacy.[11]

The account also mentions other aspects. It describes politics as something requiring narration and which is carried out, a form of behavior—in fact an enactment. Orzeszkowa was unfamiliar with the enactment since there was neither a diet nor deputies in the Russian Empire or the Kingdom of Poland at the time. She was, therefore, simply a spectator of the scene directed by Wysłouchowa, the letter's writer. But it was not just two political systems which constituted the scenery for the letter, and not just Orzeszkowa who made up the audience, for Wysłouchowa herself was disenfranchised despite her education and political activity merely by virtue of her gender. However, this fact was not included in her description. Evidently, her gender did not hinder the construction of intellectual leadership over a peasant base as a constituent of the movement. In this sense, Wysłouchowa's letter about the peasants in the *Sejm* is itself politics, while her account can be regarded as a speech act whose writing strategies were consisted of differences and power relations.

Starting in the second half of the nineteenth century, movements emerged in Galicia which demanded political, social, and economic rights and participated in the latest pan-European projects and debates on education and reform. They were based on societies and associations with cultural ambitions hosting activities ranging from literacy courses to a series of lectures on Darwinism or the position of women in history, religion, and society. Some of these associations set up schools, kindergartens, and adult education centers, dealt with much-discussed approaches to reform such as Froebel's educational principles, and organized holiday camps for poor children and training courses. Others demanded access to high school and higher education for women as well as equal suffrage regardless of origin and gender, entered the debate on morality and marriage reform, and campaigned against the trafficking in women and girls. These movements regarded themselves as progressive, a key concept in the political discussions of the time and an adjective indicating a goal, a pledge, namely a better society and the possibilities of historical development towards desired objectives.

It was in this context that the three women served the peasant, women's, and Zionist movements. They combined their activities in these associations with the writing of literary and journalistic texts. They moved in circles that were opposed to the ruling elites—not just imperial power but also institutionalized aristocratic politics, Polish domination, religious orthodoxy, and male hegemony. In these spheres, social criticism, new aesthetic paths of artistic creation, the shaping of everyday life, and political organization augmented each other. The time around 1900 can be seen as a "symbol and construct" representing "the gender politics and state politics" of classical modernity, or as a period at the turn of the century that was perceived as an ambivalent entanglement of tradition and modernity, a period of high expectations and deep disappointments—and not just in Kraków and L'viv, but likewise in Vienna and Berlin.[12]

Galicia was by no means a political utopia for any of the women or the movements they served. In fact, it was more like a negative point of reference denoting "Galician conditions," namely a backwater associated with economic and social backwardness as well as corruption.[13] Nevertheless, all three women referred to Galicia, partly because the Habsburg Empire was a constitutional state where, despite censorship and repression, it was possible to publish and to found political parties and associations. I also will show that Galicia as a metonym for backwardness, on the one hand, and nationality as a metonym for progress on the other were mutually dependent.

Progress and tradition, equality and differences, the public and private sphere, new and old hierarchies were discussed, constituted, shifted, and re-established under the banner of women's politics, which came to symbolize the struggle for power and influence, the "battle of the sexes" being just one aspect.[14] On the one hand, starting in the Enlightenment, gender had been elevated to a universal organizational category of society, the construction of a gender dichotomy serving to justify the exclusion of women from institutions. On the other hand, it was precisely this universality that paved the way for the demand for equal rights for women, while institutionalization made it possible to demand standardized rights. While the family was invented as a haven of tradition and an ahistorical constant of society (and connoted with femininity), education and other areas of society were professionalized, implying a change in family affairs.

The progressiveness of a movement or society was measured by women's political demands and their political situation.[15] Women's movements considered the gender issue an essential factor in a progressive society and campaigned among women. The peasant movement regarded the family as the basic unit of society, but also fought for kindergartens and the right for women to attend higher education. Zionism, too, extolled the importance of mothers for the Jewish nation and gave women the right to vote and stand for election at the Second Zionist Congress in 1898. Moreover, the socialist movements emphasized the role of the mother in the family and the nation and put women's suffrage on their agenda. Some of them attacked marriage as a bourgeois institution and propagated "free love," just as the Ruthenian socialist movement, the Radicals, in Galicia at the turn of the century did.

Political activity and political orientation were not always easy and repeatedly failed. For example, Kobryns'ka clashed with her "socialist sisters" over her attempts to organize women by gender, Pomeranz lamented the "indifference" of Jewish intellectual women (and men) towards Zionism, while Wysłouchowa and others regarded Galicia as a stronghold of Catholic and noble "traditionalism" and "conservatism" and tried to identify the female heroes of history.

The movements regarded themselves as national. The peasant and women's movements in which Wysłouchowa was involved saw themselves as Polish, even though the program of the Peasant Party (*Stronnictwo Ludowe*) drawn up in 1895 with the key involvement of her husband Bolesław Wysłouch propagated a multi-ethnic Poland and their home became an intellectual center for both Polish and Ruthenian activists with democratic and socialist leanings. Kobryns'ka appealed to Ruthenian women and operated alongside the Radicals identifying with a Ruthenian nation. Her activities were aimed at bringing about a gender-equitable Ruthenian society. In Zionism, in which Pomeranz was active, it was necessary to gain the support of the Jewish population for the Jewish nation. The Zionist movement competed with a national policy focusing on the diaspora, not to mention non-Jewish movements: the socialist and women's movements.

The nation was as ubiquitous as gender and just as closely associated with reform. As well as being an "imagined community" (as emphasized by nationalism research),[16] it was also omnipresent and yet ambiguous, a symbol of progress *and* order, of inclusion *and* exclusion, of participation, education, domination, *and* competition. For example, Wysłouchowa praised the rural culture of Polish-speaking peasants in general as the basis of a Polish nation, especially in Cieszyn Silesia. Kobryns'ka aspired to autonomous organizations for Ruthenian women independent of male-dominated party politics but was skeptical about joint petitions by Polish, Ruthenian, and Jewish women. And Pomeranz considered assimilation into a non-Jewish culture to be the greatest enemy of Jewry, which is why she only campaigned for education and equal rights in Zionism.

Neither gender nor nation was clear and exclusive. Politics for the nation emerged through transnational connections, in international organizations, and through local orientations; the space of the nation was by no means unique. For women, politics also meant allying themselves with supporters from the opposite sex, repeatedly reconfirming the dominant gender dichotomy and repeatedly dissolving it—and thus transgressing borders. The transnationality of the nation and the transgression of gender boundaries were (and still are) central requirements of identity politics.[17] None of the movements confined themselves to a national space, despite regarding themselves as national.

In their struggle for a better society, despite championing different goals, the three protagonists shared basic political practices. They wrote literary and political texts and organized educational and reform projects. Wysłouchowa participated in educational associations, Kobryns'ka propagated kindergartens and communal kitchens, and Pomeranz set up reform centers combining social work and education projects. All three made speeches with the aims of mobilization and propagation. They were all intellectual women campaigning for the sovereignty of interpretation and opportunities.

However, these three women are not meant to draw attention to a particular, feminine form of politics. Making gender an integral part of historical analysis means deconstructing masculinity as a norm-setting paradigm.[18] The women's political activity is, therefore, examined as an example of acting in movements, not as an example of femininity. If the political activities of the women and the movements are to be analyzed in their complexity, the peripheral Habsburg province of Galicia, viewed by researchers and contemporaries alike as socially, politically, and economically backward, needs to be considered beyond paradigms of modernization history such as politicization, participation, and middle classes. Accordingly, the peasant movement, Zionism, and the women's movement are not defined in advance but examined in terms of their narratives and practices.[19] Above all, the structural parallels between the different movements are highlighted. Thus, this entails analyzing the dichotomies of political activity, the divisions into tradition and modernity, as well as East and West in their workings, and discursive strategies are already self-evident given the linguistic turn. What is less self-evident, however, is the consequence of studying the movements' practices as performative acts, i.e. as practices of cultural change.[20] It is from these observations that the key questions of the study are derived: How do narratives come to constitute reality? How do practices become habitual? How do they shape and change relations between the sexes, between activists and addressees? In short: how is politics *produced?*

Tools: Performance, Performativity, Ritual, and Space

Much attention has already been paid in socio-scientific and historical research to the conditions under which political movements emerge, with the result that assuming a direct correlation between objective inequality and protest is just as rash as extending this model to include subjectively perceived disadvantage. Opportunity, a specific context, and the availability of resources are also crucial to turn inequality and disadvantage into protest.[21] Furthermore, ideas, knowledge, and representations have to provide or enable such interpretations of collective deprivation, too. The interpretations require understandable language and comprehensible practices, i.e. sensemaking and rehearsals in specific places.

A metaphor frequently used for political events is "arena": "When Pomeranz... moved to L'viv, she was able to continue her national activity in a broader arena."[22] "Arena" refers to an area, both concrete and abstract space for political action. This space is associated with struggle: "One arena where the battle for the forests and pastures took place was the Galician diet."[23] An arena is a scene with edges and borders.[24] The term has become a concept in political science. As Theodore Lowi emphasizes: "*Arena* is for politics as *market* is for economics. In the real world, there is no 'pure market' just as there is no 'pure power arena.'" And there is more than just one arena: "[T]here is a different arena, field of play, process, and power structure in each of the department categories."[25]

An arena is the place of direction to which corresponding relevance is attached by actors and audience. It is limited by a topic and by a specific range. The struggles or directed action in an arena follow rules that are repeatable and performative. Although the rules may be changed, the practices used must be comprehensible to the participants and the audience. They need not be accepted by everyone—in fact rule changes always attract the opponents' attention—but they must make sense, even if only the sense of the opposite position. There are many different, partly overlapping arenas in which different rules apply, creating a stream of new, different senses and contradictions.[26] Jean-François Lyotard used the concept of the "language-game" for his analysis of *The Postmodern Condition,* in which he draws attention (among other things) to adherence to rules, yet also to the fact that these rules change when the games are changed. Different institutions, such as the church, army, school, or family, obey different language-games, i.e. rules of what to say and how to say it. In addition, Lyotard emphasizes the changeability of how the game is played depending on location and context. In institutions, the rules are stricter than, for example, in social relationships.[27] Thinking of politics as an arena takes into account both aspects of political activity, namely narrativity and practices, and refers to the interplay between actors, modes of action and interpretation, sensemaking, institutions, places, and traditions.[28] The concept of the game is based on the changeable rules of these narratives and practices.

Consideration of performance, performativity and ritual is useful in order to make the aspects of a rule-based struggle involving multiple participants in specific places analyzable and, above all, representable.[29] In dramatics, a performance is understood as an event, an action with an unknown outcome rather than a directed play:

[Spectators] no longer represent distanced or empathetic observers and interpreters of the actors' actions onstage; nor do they act as intellectual decoders of messages conveyed by the actions of the actors.[30]

This means that in a performance the signifier and signified lose their polarity and selectivity:

> [This] does not imply a subject–object relationship in which spectators turn actors into objects of their observation, while the actors (as subjects) cease to confront the audience (as objects) with non-negotiable messages. Instead, their bodily co-presence creates a relationship between co-subjects. Through their physical presence, perception, and response, the spectators become co-actors that generate the performance by participating in the "play." The rules that govern the performance correspond to the rules of a game, negotiated by all participants—actors and spectators alike; they are followed and broken by all in equal measure.[31]

This means that the performance takes place between the actors and audiences, and is produced by them together. Performance is governed by rules that may be broken during the performance or created through interaction among the participants. Like narration, it boils down to the relationality of representation, interpretation, and verification. The performance also addresses the theatricality, the spectacle of political activity. A movement refers back to a narrative of inequality and injustice, of suffering and oppression, which must be narrated spectacularly and with rhetorical proficiency. An association or a magazine that wants to achieve political goals requires an audience (grassroots or readership) willing to provide not just passive but also active support, for example by spreading the word and becoming personally involved by, say, attending lectures, classes, and rallies, voting, subscribing, or even as examples of its educational success.

A performance tied to the participants' forms of communication and knowledge can and is intended to alter, shift, and emphasize them, but must still address them in order to be understood. According to

Wysłouchowa's description, the appearance of the peasant deputies in their colorful garb not only changed the atmosphere in the *Sejm,* but also represented a new form of politics geared to participation.[32] Then again, the peasants wore their traditional costumes, their "Sunday best," and tried to live up to the new requirements precisely because they accepted the rules of parliament, the seriousness of the occasion, the practice of making notes, and the attention paid to deputies' speeches. Similarly, an educational organization in a rural location keen sign up new members for the peasant movement provided information about hygiene or the nation in an attempt to boost the movement's appeal, yet implicitly also addressed rural knowledge formations and power relations. However, it was only the interplay of lectures, agitation, and the involvement of the audience appropriating symbolic capital which shifted the emphasis from experiential to institutional knowledge; it was only the audience who turned the performance by the organization's activists into politics; and only the event's virtual networking (by being reported in a publication) that made it part of the movement.

Performance is usually presented as being freely chosen. It is assumed that the artists decide to address and perform a subject of their own choosing and adopt various roles, all the while retaining their own characters behind the scenes. This school of thought accommodates political activity in that there are many different ways to, say, strengthen the nation or build up a viable women's movement. However, it is not just a freedom of choice and changing roles that make the concept interesting for an analysis of political activity but also the aspect of representation, interpretation, and changing meaning. To strengthen this aspect, let me cite some observations regarding performativity.

Performativity denotes self-referential, reality-constituting speech acts.[33] Judith Butler regards identity as the result of cultural constitutional performance, as performativity rather than expressivity, as production or continuous materialization (of the body) rather than an expression. The conditions of this embodiment—Butler is concerned with gender—are neither freely selectable nor fully determined by society. They embody historical possibilities.[34] Against the background of the extent to which performativity can be understood independently of structures, Alf Lüdtke emphasizes the fluid boundaries between *"intentional actions* and [on the other hand] *events that befall one or unintended circumstances."*[35] Rosi Braidotti introduced the concept of "nomadic subjects" or "nomadic conditions" as a "new figuration of subjectivity in a multidifferentiated non-hierarchical way."[36] The subject is understood as relational and as a product of social relationships, as local rather than universal, fluid, and contradictory rather than consistent, a factor of permanent differentiation and performative acts.

Braidotti's observations on the nomadic constitution of a subject suggest pursuing the paths of the protagonists from personal relationships to literary works, from political slogans to their perceptions of themselves and back again, without making connections by applying a given cause-and-effect logic. Being a performative speech act similar to doing gender,[37] the constitution of national collectives in Galicia can be understood as doing nation. This is only to be expected. Instead of asserting the constructivist character of national identities for the umpteenth time or unmasking identity politics as essentialist, the study explores the formation of national and gender collectives and how they operate.[38]

In contrast to the aesthetic intention of art, politics is more concerned with shifts in power relations and seizing the prerogative of interpretation. How ideas and views about the world gain relevance is a question that has been addressed by research into the imagined communities of nations as well as other fields. How did people come to believe in a collective (including its agency) that had never been truly visible and could only be imagined? And why did the nation acquire more importance than other communities and collectives? Philipp Sarasin explored the mechanisms of imagining. He started from Benedict Anderson's view that the symbols of a nation are simultaneously empty and overdetermined. There is no signified before the signifier; instead, a permanent process of differentiation takes place within a field of meanings between the signified and the not or differently signified.[39] In this field, the meanings (of nation, for example) become apparent within this permanence. Identity emerges when a signifier in a (historical) moment becomes completely different, a limitation: "In the field of political discourse, it is the privileged signifiers which can stop the sliding of the signifieds in society's field of differences for a while."[40] These signifieds represent everything the nation can mean. The political ability of narratives, therefore, results from the "fixation" of differentiation as something central and significant.[41] The narratives constitute the emptiness and overdetermination of the differentiation, the "fixation" act as strategies. They determine dominance and marginality, the prerogative of interpretation, and design competencies. All political movements were constantly engaged in making specific distinctions—gender, class, nation, and ethnicity—central and meaningful in order to distinguish themselves from other movements.

The "fixation" of differentiation is a process that can be analyzed by considering aspects of ritual.[42] In ethnology and the social sciences, rituals are understood to be performances in which strategies and rules of direction are followed, although distinguishing between ritual, ceremony, custom, use, and habit in empirical research is often difficult.[43] Catherine Bell criticizes the long-standing distinction drawn in ritual research between thought and action as well as intention and ritual. She refers to ritualization as a way of acting strategically and understands strategy to mean not just the intention of individual actors but also cultural changes. According to Bell, processuality suspends the contrast between thought and action. Ritualization is "situational, strategic, embedded in a misrecognition of what it is in fact doing; and able to reproduce or reconfigure a vision of the order of power in the world."[44] It is understood as a strategy for constructing limited and limiting power relations, and which at the same time means consent and resistance, misunderstanding, and appropriation.[45] The strategy is to keep ascertaining a hierarchized difference rather than performing a fixed ritual. "The continuity, innovation, and oppositional contrasts established in each case are strategies that arise from the 'sense of ritual' played out under particular conditions—not in a fixed ritual structure, a closer grammar, or an embalmed historical model."[46] Ritualization as defined by Bell and differentiation as defined by Sarasin, therefore, do not mean given practices, but a specific view of the entanglement between repetition and change in action. They reveal the interplay of latent and manifest sensemaking and above all shifts in meaning. Wysłouchowa implied in her letter a connection between the peasant movement and the election of peasant representatives; she propagated a participatory model of politics and established a hierarchical difference between herself and the peasant deputies. This explains why she did not address the fact that her gender ruled her out from being elected to the diet.

Ritualization is strategic, but it amounts to more than the intention of the actors. For example, the reason why the peasant deputies wrote in the diet was not just to confirm their mastery of this necessary parliamentary cultural technique, but also simply in order to make notes. Intentions are linked to traditions; they are an endless echo of rites of power and influence. If political activity is considered a form of ritualization, our attention is also directed to the gradual, occasionally sudden shifts in modes of acting and thinking.[47] As far as the political movements are concerned, this means asking about the *how* of their construction, about the ideas and practices involved in the construction of their genesis and their representation. Their narrative can be understood as one of permanent competition over main signifiers, over gender, class, and nation, yet also over reality and fiction, over knowledge and experience. At different times and in different contexts, some of the signifiers became more important than others, but even then, the signifiers were both empty and overdetermined. They reduced complex reality and championed it at the same time. Analyzing observations on ritualizations is interesting because the aim of political movements is to affirm and shift power relations. A political performance implicitly or explicitly formulates demands and thus goals. It can, therefore, succeed or fail due to institutional and social conditions, which it always does and must do simultaneously, for if it were to succeed, the demands would become superfluous. In this sense, like the middle phase of a ritual, it is liminal, i.e. it is in a transitional stage.

A performance is conducted in a place; it requires a stage. It is claimed that movements are often seen in terms of the appropriation of spaces, both concrete and metaphorical: the appropriation of streets and squares, parliaments and universities, as well as opportunities for participation. This idea results from the assumption of historical-empirical exclusion on the basis of gender (or class). Women (workers and peasants) were motivated by structural disadvantage to take up activities in which they claimed spaces they were barred from. Women were bound to domesticity, for example, and so the women's movement appropriated public spaces or fought for access to them. In this line of argument, both the spaces and the actors are viewed as static.

In the following, by contrast, it is assumed that political movements have to create spaces in the first place, and that conversely spaces establish a collective. One of the central areas of women's politics was social work projects, as they gave the female participants an opportunity to demonstrate their skills in organizing society. They created concrete spaces for the acceptance of new female professions (carer, kindergarten teacher), and at the same time, these spaces as the basis of the collective construed the women's movement. Therefore, a relational constructivist concept of space is useful.[48] Instead of analyzing the politics of the three women as the appropriation of closed spaces, following on from Arjun Appaduraj, their projects should be understood as mobile geographies, as practices of the construction of concrete and abstract spaces, as the creation of halls and buildings, as well as the design of relationships and hierarchies, centers and peripheries, and thus of gender and society.[49] This also means examining the transnationality of national movements, their cross-border networks, and local competitors.

The conceptual ideas presented here provide a mental framework to develop a view that simultaneously accommodates structure, discourse and agency, or in other words, which integrates the relevance of multiple levels.[50] This study uses a performance concept to analyze the politics of the three women and is based on observations about ritualization and performativity. In doing so, it focuses on the contextual and historical links between space and politics. Space is understood as a relational concept that arises during the action and shapes the action. Politics is regarded as a communicative process, as a way of shaping society, of rehearsing new social (power) structures and generating their meaning or creating sense. Gender history and, in many cases, the history of everyday life, too, long ago proposed an expanded notion of politics and raised the question of language, symbolism, rituals, media, communication, debate, and power relations.[51] The combination of performance and performativity is intended to highlight the creation or ritualization of political identities and the construction of politics as identification, cause and effect, or oppression and rebellion, yet also the inevitability of these constructions, their historical foundation.[52] Construction does not mean free choice or invention, but differential displacement and redefinition—a new move in Lyotard's terminology. Part of this move is historiography. It could be put this way: "culture as text" becomes "history as performance."[53]

Rules: Research Contexts

The idea of examining the parallels in the politics of three women active in different movements was stimulated by debate about the deconstruction of national historical master narratives. For a long time, research into the history of Galicia and the political movements in question was determined by the paradigms of Polish, Ukrainian, and Jewish national history. In the meantime, however, holistic concepts, such as nation, modernization, and the notion of clear directions of development, have been discussed for Galicia, too.[54] To elucidate the starting points of the study, there follows a concise overview of how transnational and transpolitical approaches, the relationality of collective formation, identity, and alterity discussed in postcolonial studies and cultural studies, as well as equality and difference have found their way into research on Galicia and political movements.

A number of studies have examined two or three nationalities in Galicia in parallel by posing a joint question and addressing an overarching subject. Harald Binder addressed the Galician Imperial Council deputies in Vienna, party politics, and electoral practice in Galicia, pointing out aspects of party structure and politics extending beyond the national competition.[55] Angelique Leszczawski-Schwerk uses space as a category shaping structures of power and dominance to analyze boundaries and cooperation between Polish and Ukrainian feminist politics.[56] Others focus on links between their subject and unrelated contexts. Moshe Rosman suggested that instead of imagining Jewish and non-Jewish history as two magnetic fields attracting or repelling each other, it should be seen as recombinant DNA arising from a vast repertoire of building blocks and constantly being rearranged.[57] He called for Jewish history to be interpreted intertextually since it cannot be explained solely by a solely Jewish history of ideas or a Jewish history of socio-economic change, nor by specifically Jewish reactions to general or non-Jewish phenomena like industrialization, urbanization or anti-Semitism. Instead, the contemporary ways and possibilities of advancement and participation, the construction of collective identities, and emancipatory demands are also building blocks that are constantly being rearranged.[58] The relationality of nation-building has been addressed by, for instance, Yaroslav Hrytsak, now one of the most famous historians in Ukraine, in his study of Ivan Franko, a trilingual literary and publicist as well as a socialist and Ruthenian activist in Galicia.[59] Hrytsak pursues the thesis that nation-building depends on international contexts, by which he means not only imperial politics but also transnational relations, such as the importance of German and Polish culture for intellectual advancement and the initial influence of Ukrainophiles from Eastern Ukraine on the Galician intelligentsia. Furthermore, he refers to the theatrical and acting analogy and emphasizes the role of the audience, although not the rule changes.[60]

Delphine Bechtel continued the entanglement approach with her analysis of the dichotomy between "eastern" and "western" Jewry:

> The innovative thesis I propose in this work is based on the idea that German Jewish culture and east European Jewish culture, far from being two separate and opposite discourses, met, influenced, and fertilized *each other, jointly* engendering a vast Jewish cultural renaissance movement in both west and east that was to characterize Central and Eastern Europe throughout the first third of the twentieth century.[61]

In her view, neither the concept of the mirror nor that of reception, influence, or image reflects the entanglement of mutual construction. Instead, it needs to be understood as a continuous process of interaction taking into account both the actors and the media as well as not just central, canonical texts, but equally popular distributive practices. Applied to political movements, this means not starting from clearly defined entities, but instead analyzing their confrontation and competition as interaction, as practice and interpretation—or, one might say, as performance.

Since the advent of the cultural turn in research, (East-) Central Europe and Galicia have moved into focus as literary, intellectual, and mythical places of multiculturalism. Stefan Simonek recently demonstrated the parallelism between hybridity concepts in postcolonial studies and the concepts of interference developed in (East-) Central European literary studies, pointing out that the view is guided not just by the subject "Galicia" but also by methodological and theoretical problems.[62] Occasionally, Galicia is stylized as a prime example of a reversal of perspective, the polyethnic nature of the periphery being viewed as the European norm instead of national-state homogeneity.[63] In his study *The Idea of Galicia*, Larry Wolff examined legends and fantasies of Galician political culture and substantiated his thesis that the idea of the province was fundamentally "non-national," understanding "non-national" as another construct like "national."[64] His study benefits from its examination of intellectual culture beyond national paradigms. However, Wolff devoted hardly any attention to the Galician women active in politics or literature, regardless of whether they were feminist, socialist, or nationalist. This is regrettable, partly because women contributed to the myth of Galicia and were not just literary objects, but above all because analyzing their politics and literature increases awareness of ambivalences. After all, in the course of postmodernism, the ethnic and linguistic diversity, specifically close linguistic and cultural cooperation and competition between Galicia, (East-) Central Europe, the Habsburg Empire, Vienna, and Prague became a new paradigm.[65] It functions in several studies on Galicia as an essential, practically unhistorical requirement of modern cultural diversity. Just how important a transnational perspective on the Galician and East-Central European region remains is shown by various research in the field of Global History in which no conceptual role is played by Central or Eastern Europe.[66] The aim is not to "rescue the reputation" of the region but to achieve a praxeological, situational perspective.[67]

Therefore, food for thought for a performance-based account is provided by not only the discussions about breaking up *a single* holistic model (the national historical model) but also by the debates about the master narratives of the historiography of political movements: the constituents oppression and politicization, the essentialized differentiation of political currents. Additional assistance is provided by studies taking a transpolitical and transnational view of political movements with their diverging, competing goals. Studies of the Ruthenian and Polish socialist movements in Galicia have pointed to their interpersonal networking and shared debates.[68] Oksana Malančuk-Rybak drew parallels between the Ukrainian and Polish women's movements; what they had in common was the romantic-national tradition of the concept of liberation and the high prestige of women, probably meaning femininity. She explained that the motherland and the Mother of God played a prominent role and were assigned religious and patriotic values. Their activity was based on the socio-political program of positivism, which discussed and called for gender equality.[69]

Malančuk-Rybak distinguishes between movements in existing nation-states, such as Great Britain, France, and the German Empire, and stateless nations, especially in East-Central Europe, and assumes that the latter would have been more focused on collective demands. From this, she derives different concepts of freedom. While individual feminism placed the rights of the subject to the fore, the collective feminism formulated community-oriented demands, including for national liberation.[70] Malančuk-Rybak combines the argument repeatedly found in the historiography of East-Central Europe—namely, that the lack of statehood was central to shaping political demands—with the geographical distinction that whereas collective feminism dominated in the east of Europe, individual feminism did so in the west. Although it is normally emphasized that women's movements combined individual and collective demands, structural-historical and geohistorical typologies are widespread. For example, Karen Offen, like Malančuk-Rybak, distinguishes between individual and relational feminism, although her geographical proviso from the more remote American perspective is somewhat shifted: she attributes the former above all to the Anglo-American region and collective feminism to continental Europe.[71] Her observations on typologies of feminism have helped to synthesize different processes and priorities beyond the respective national history on a transnational level. Nevertheless, the geographical shifts in categorical attributions indicate that such blanket typologization has limited explanatory value—and that the geographies of historical research are mobile and not "objective facts."

Natascha Vittorelli criticized attempts at typologization leading to polarization between a radical or progressive western feminism and a backward east European feminism.[72] Her proposal that the terms "feminism" and "women's politics" be understood in the context in order to avoid an implicit hierarchization into more or less antipatriarchal politics inherent in the definitions is directed against the normative function of definitions.[73] Vittorelli discusses the activities, networks, and publications of women in Southeastern Europe and compares them with the historiographical meanings of the term "women's movement."[74] Her observations encouraged women's politics to be examined in practice instead of being measured against the yardstick of "feminism."

Using the example of the politics of the French women's movement, Joan Scott drew attention to the constituent function of different approaches to politics in her study *Only Paradoxes to Offer*.[75] The movement defined itself by referring to not only the fundamental equality of the sexes (for example by demanding women's suffrage) but also to fundamental differences (for instance with its politicization of motherhood as a political contribution to a better society). According to Scott, this contradiction did not represent different directions or wings of the movement, or chronologically successive phases, but was a paradox resulting from the marginalization of femininity and the establishment of masculinity as a universal principle. Equality and difference were different strategic variants from which the teleology of cumulative progress had been developed to form a continuous history out of disparate, discontinuous actions of women. As well as deconstructing essentialized views of gender and politics, Scott also encouraged analysis of the political strategies and historical interpretations that conveyed thinking in dichotomies, implying that historiography should be regarded as part of interpretive acts.

Moreover, for a study seeking to analyze structural similarities in the thinking and action of movements from a transpolitical angle, studies are of interest that analyze feminism and women's policy in the context of other movements or cultural change instead of in their subtle differentiations.[76] Regarding the activities of Ukrainian women in Galicia and Eastern Ukraine, Martha Bohachevsky-Chomiak and others argue the existence of a form of feminism in the church.[77] This proposition is backed up by the agrarian structure of Ukrainian-speaking society and the origin of the intelligentsia in the clergy. Both factors favored community focus which, according to Bohachevsky-Chomiak, meant that confrontation between the sexes was comparatively low.[78] Mary Louise Robert's study of "the new women" in Paris around 1900 makes reference to disruptive acts that challenged societal norms: not just the women's movement, but also women's employment, cohabitation, the way women appeared in public, etc.[79]

Research into the peasant movement in Galicia concentrates on aspects of social and cultural change in rural areas. Jan Molenda and others emphasize that a process of integration into a national community is more complex to analyze than a top-down movement emanating from political parties. Molenda highlighted the importance of women's and youth activities for the social and cultural modernization of the village in the second half of the nineteenth century.[80] However, his main finding is that until the First World War, neither female nor male peasants felt they belonged to the nation in either the Kingdom of Poland or Galicia. Rejecting an inevitability of nation-building and increasing development towards nationality, Keely Stauter-Halsted emphasizes that notions of nationhood were enshrined on several levels in rural areas and could be understood as a process of negotiation.[81] Kai Struve's comparison of Polish and Ruthenian peasant movements shows the similarity of the means used by different, sometimes fiercely competing for imaginations of the nation referring to overlapping geographical constructions.[82]

The study by Maciej Janowski reports on the extent of association-led reform initiatives and the differences between political parties regarding their educational, cultural, and publishing activities. It examines the emergence of a modern public sphere and, based on the concept of multiple modernities,[83] puts forward the thesis that Galicia underwent "modernization without industrialization."[84] Janowski's central concern is the deconstruction of an unquestioned topos of backwardness which has long dominated the historiography of both the Habsburg crownland and the region of East-Central Europe in general.[85] In addition, he draws attention to the directing nature of politics as well as to the interplay of speeches and stirring songs, of an educational program and participation, and states:

> The similarity of Polish and Ruthenian political, social and cultural ideas is evident, their correspondence in the forms of social life being reflected in newspapers. Opposing each other, the publicists and politicians of both nations used the same examples and arguments and cited the same Latin proverbs that they had memorized in class at the same high schools. The advertisement pages in the newspapers are almost identical: they promoted the same preparations against insects (Zacherlin), the same remedies for hair loss (Anna Csillag) and the same spa.[86]

In contrast to his differentiated presentation of Polish and Ruthenian politics, Janowski analyzes the public sphere of women and of Jews each as part of an overall collective. Katrin Steffen, however, emphasized the diversity of Jewish lifestyles in her study of Polish Jews in the interwar period, "[b]etween acculturation or Yiddishkeit, between Zionism and socialism, between secularized identity and religious orthodoxy, between Jewish tenants and largely acculturated Jews, between luftmenschen, lawyers, teachers, and journalists."[87]

A similar conclusion is reached by comparative studies of the intelligentsia of Eastern and Western Europe, which emphasize that formulating a concise, general definition is next to impossible. The intelligentsia was not simply made up of specific professional groups or social formations, nor even members of the elite or the middle classes. Likewise, a definition proceeding from an irresolvable conflict between "educated society and the state as a concomitant of the transition to modernity"[88] is equally unconvincing since the relationship between the state and social ideals differed in terms of not just political orientations but also the state as an occupying power, national state, and empire. The notions of "subculture" or "counter-elite" sum up specific aspects and practices instead of constituting a consistent group.[89] The connection between transnational mindsets emphasizing the simultaneity of broad references as well as of local constellations and styles is hardly surprising for the nineteenth century either, for intellectuals attended the same universities, read the same books, and studied the same theories.[90]

Instead of seeking a social, cultural, or political definition of the intelligentsia, therefore, an approach will be discussed which starts from a multilayered context of the interpretation of society, power, and influence.[91] Accordingly, we need to ask how aesthetic dimensions determined political behavior,[92] and also how the intelligentsia constituted itself as the elite of a movement, or conversely, how power, prestige, and advancement were constituted, especially among groups that were excluded from conventional institutions of power and advancement, such as educated women.[93] Empowerment or advancement required communication and interpretation but also caused conflicts. The groups constituting the movements sometimes shared values and goals but differed in their access to resources, and above all only emerged in connection with the constitution of a political movement.[94] Research into education highlights its importance as a resource for social advancement; however, it usually analyzes it either in connection with a social formation such as the "intelligentsia" or "educated functional elites" or alternatively with a history of institutions.[95] By contrast, the fact that education was also a battle cry and a form of legitimization for the aspirations of political movements and that it only achieved its far-reaching significance through this connotation has so far played only a minor role in the discussion.

The "movement notions of... republicanism, democratism, liberalism, socialism" emerging in the wake of the political, social, economic and technical changes of the nineteenth century were described by Reinhart Koselleck as "a political-social field" that was "induced by the tension progressively torn open between experience and expectation."[96]

Using the example of the French women's movement, Joan Scott speaks of imagination and desire as the key motives instead of the horizon of expectation.[97] Scott and Koselleck regard the divergence of experience and future orientation as constitutive of nineteenth-century political movements.[98] Both of them discussed "experience" as a historically constructed category organized by language, both stressed that the past is connected to the future by the construction of experience, the "benefit" of experience consisting precisely in its focus on the future. They proposed that the relations between the space of experience and the horizon of expectation or imagination provided an impetus for overcoming the "given" forms of society and a glimpse of something "new." They regarded the experience as something historical, experience being constructed for the political movements from the nineteenth century onwards in a way that finally made "tradition" and "progress" or "given" and "new" categories of the perception of the world. Koselleck's and Scott's reflections encourage a transpolitical and transnational notion of movement, and above all combining the future orientation of political movements with the invention of historicity.

Discursive formations, mindsets, and practices beyond classification by political currents or national affiliations have been highlighted by microhistorical and biographical studies.[99] A perspective going beyond political classification—in this case, Zionist or national—was supported by François Guesnet with his analysis of Zionist Maccabean celebrations as being directed as bourgeois-based education.[100] Iris Schröder identified "belief in a better world" as the central motif of civic engagement.[101] At any rate, the value system[102] was shared by many political movements, even though or perhaps because in some cases they competed so fiercely with each other in terms of both their political objectives and national narratives. Several studies have highlighted the high importance of women's movements in the implementation of principles of social work and the institutionalization of the welfare state.[103] Local historical, microhistorical, and biographical studies encourage an examination of the intertextuality of concepts, the networks between projects and organizations established through personal relations or the transnational publication market, and focus on interpretations towards general developments. They can be transferred to various movements whose representatives, ideas, and practices traveled the world.[104]

All these observations on the relationality and contextuality of concepts, on how shared ideas are used, are taken up in the study and translated into an analysis of politics as the interaction of discursive and performative acts. The leitmotif of world improvement is a central starting point for the question of women's politics in Galicia, which below is not assumed to be tied to a specific social formation. How then could Wysłouchowa, despite her sex, claim leadership and interpretation position in the peasant movement?

Strategies: Approaches

Politics can only be analyzed as the interplay of discursive and performative acts with a wide variety of research material. The corpus is made up of published texts by the three women: their numerous articles in literary, movement, and political journals, as well as brochures and books. They include literary narratives, political pamphlets, contemporary analyses, popular historical texts, travelogues, a short autobiography, and ethnographic studies. In addition, texts linked to the movements are considered in order to emphasize the similarity of arguments and views across genres. The texts, interpreted as speech acts, are examined with respect to intertextuality and dialogicality, as well as the ways in which political power and influence were constituted and hierarchies were shifted and shaped. Political positions and goals result not only from content and style, from latent and manifest statements, but also from the place of publication, a literary newspaper, a women's almanac, or a movement's organ.

The women's ego-documents, especially their correspondence, is also revealing.[105] Correspondence between close acquaintances which is neither fictitious nor exclusively intended for publication is poised between intimate, "secret,"[106] personal relationships and political objects or contexts.[107] The letters switch between private and public; they privatize the political and politicize the private. They form a bridge to other genres or aestheticize views, feelings, and opinions, for example, by adopting writing conventions.[108] They are thus a medium of communication over time and space and between different text functions, between aesthetics and pragmatics.[109] Letters affirm and materialize friendships and constitute networks in which literary and political practices and goals are discussed.[110] They combine emotions, aesthetics, and rhetoric, which played an important role in friendships as a basis for political action. The networks span the central spheres of action. They express the tension between experience and discourse, norms and practice.[111]

Extensive correspondence between Wysłouchowa and Kobryns'ka has been consulted. In addition to the letters, they received and preserved in their own estates, others they wrote have been preserved as part of their recipients' estates at various libraries. The main sources are the manuscript departments of the T. H. Ševčenko Institute of Literature of the National Academy of Sciences of Ukraine (Instytut literatury im. T. H. Ševčenka NAN Ukraïny, IlŠ) in Kiev,[112] the Stefanyk National Science Library of Ukraine (L'vivs'ka nacional'na naukova biblioteka Ukraïny imeni V. Stefanyka, BS) in L'viv, the Jagiellonian Library (Biblioteka Jagiellońska, BJ) in Kraków, the Museum of Czech Literature (Památník národního písemnictví, PNP) in Prague, the Institute of Literature of the Polish Academy of Sciences Warsaw (Polska Akademia Nauk, Instytut literacki, PAN Warszawa), the Polish Academy of Sciences Kraków

(Polska Akademia Nauk, PAN Kraków), and the National Library (Biblioteka Narodowa, BN) in Warsaw. The estate of the Wysłouchs is preserved in the manuscript department of the Ossolineum Library (Biblioteka Ossolineum, BO) in Wrocław.[113] Supplementary material was found in the Central Historical Archives of Ukraine (Central'nyj deržavnyj istoryčnyj archiv Ukraïny, CDIA) in L'viv, the Central Zionist Archives (CZA) in Jerusalem, and the private Odo Bujwid Archive (Archiwum Odo Bujwid, AOB) in Kraków, as well as in the Archive of the Felix Mendelssohn Bartholdy University of Music and Theatre (Archiv der Hochschule für Musik und Theater "Felix Mendelssohn Bartholdy," AHMT) in Leipzig.

The search for Pomeranz's correspondence was fruitless. Even so, information about her role in the history of the Zionist movement can be gleaned not only from her publications but also by analyzing Zionist journals, such as the international *Die Welt: Zentralorgan der Zionistischen Bewegung* (The World: Central Organ of the Zionist Movement)[114] and the Galician magazines *Przyszłość: Organ narodowej partyi żydowskiej. Dwutygodnik poświęcony politycznym, społecznymi, umysłowym sprawom żydostwa* (The Future: Organ of the National Jewish Party—Biweekly journal of political, social and spiritual affairs of Judaism) founded in 1892, which from 1898 bore the subtitle *Organ Syonistów* (Organ of Zionists), and which was succeeded from 1900 by the Zionist *Wschód: Tygodnik poświęcony sprawom żydostwa* (The East—A weekly devoted to Jewish affairs).

The magazines represented two crownland and one international recruitment, discussion, and contact publications.[115] In addition to substantial articles, they contained several sections with anonymous reports documenting the tireless agitation by the movement: societies, events, and festivities in all sorts of places large and small. These reports were sent to the journal by local representatives or the respective regional organizations in order to document their activities and to shore up their position in the movement. Conversely, movements' organs needed such reports in order to constitute a far-reaching geographical network. Reports about organizations are, therefore, typical of publications of political parties and movements, as is the mix of political, historical, fictional, and educational texts, bearing out their aim of conducting both political *and* cultural work. These reports contain some information about Pomeranz's activities. However, they did not simply describe events, they also shaped them; they did not mirror the interests or events that preoccupied the Zionist movement, but instead constructed (sub-) communities, readerships, and modes of communication.[116] These short reports are evaluated not only in terms of the events mentioned, the founding of societies and the organization of festivities, projects and speeches, but also with regard to their style of presentation and place of publication. What matters is not whether Pomeranz really spoke as enthusiastically as reported but what the report mentioned about her and how the speech was contextualized.

I have also made use of commemorative volumes and obituaries written by friends and associates. These initially fulfilled the function of a temporary or, as Jan Assmann put it, communicative memory.[117] Over time they became—and this was implied because they were published for this purpose—part of collective memory, a "document trail."[118] Such commemorative writings, therefore, allow several interpretations: as well as keeping the memory of the deceased alive for relatives, friends, and associates, they also have journalistic and historical functions. Like autobiographical texts, this makes them interesting regarding strategies of linking individual and collective levels as well as across times and spaces.

The study examines women's politics using three women from different political movements as examples. The women barely had anything to do with each other. My aim is not to highlight connections or competition between them personally. The parallel examination of a Polish, a Ruthenian, and a Jewish female is intended to show the structural and discursive circumstances of political movements in the nineteenth century. Just as microhistory and ethnology do not conduct research about but in rural areas,[119] the biographies of the three women are not investigated for their own sake; instead, the world is analyzed in their biographies.[120]

The mode of presentation is derived from the objective of connecting the various levels of politics—not just identifying different rules, but also including the changeability and the "inventiveness of the players."[121] The women's political activity is regarded as a performance involving rule-based, comprehensible debate about women's politics. The starting points of the accounts are the lives, texts, societies, and conflicts of the three women. The biographical connection allows the entanglement of the different levels to be shown. Based on their biographies, the women's actions and possibilities are presented. Their texts can be analyzed in terms of the constitution of rhetoric, knowledge, emotions, or possible interpretations. The practices of the movements come to the fore in their organizations and projects, the rehearsal of courses of action. Conflicts and discussions highlight the concurrence of actors, enforcement strategies, changes, or shifts. This approach benefits from an eclectic use of different concepts and notions as proposed by Mieke Bal: identity, space, narrative, collective.[122]

Performance includes the performers with their different responsibilities or roles, the plays to be performed and their direction, and the audience's participation in the enactments. The ritualizations, the permanent choreography of differences and their shifts, the relationships between meaning and reference are explored. The biographies, publications, projects, and conflicts are analyzed. All these aspects taken together make up politics. All three women were involved in writing, organization, conceptual work and enactment, and examples of their activities are discussed in all chapters (although the attention devoted to each of them varies depending on the context and their activity). Rather than the women or similarities in their biographies, the focus is on the connections between their views of life and politics.

The political activity of the three women is analyzed in four chapters. All chapters are divided into three levels. On the first level, the examples are shaped by the three women's different abilities and interests. Their life stages, texts, associations, and communication are dealt with in the chapters. On the second level, the objects are interpreted in the context of the women's respective movements. The interpretations make up the subchapters: collectives, experience, and history, education, nation, and society, as well as role models, competition, and practice. The third level examines aspects of performance, including participants, plays, stage, and enactment forming the structure of the study.

Chapter 1 "Finding roles" concentrates on the biographies of the three women. It sheds light on their origins, activities, and connections. One sought to educate Polish women in rural areas, the second to unite all Ruthenian women, and the third to organize Jewish women in the Zionist movement. This chapter analyzes the various levels of political activity, networks, friendships, and conflicts, literary and feuilleton contexts, contemporary political debates, and projects.[123] Political movements require different abilities: narrating, directing, enacting. It is shown that the women are examples of these abilities: Maria Wysłouchowa stands for narrating, Natalja Kobryns'ka for directing, Rosa Pomeranz for enacting. These interpretations are not intended to produce a new or even final interpretation of their biographies, nor is it implied that the women each had only one ability. Their varied activities from writing (including didactic plays, letters, reports, analyses, and demands) to speechmaking are presented in their respective contexts, hence revealing the complexity of social circumstances. The following chapters are structured by women's political activities: writing, organizing, and (conflict-ridden) communicating.

Chapter 2 "Propagating" examines their writings (plays) and how they were made politically relevant. The literary and historical narrative is examined because this is something that the three women felt to be particularly effective. The impact strategies of the texts, the connection between interpretation, place of publication, and plot are analyzed. The subject of the chapter comprises two magazines for peasant women published by Wysłouchowa, several stories by Kobryns'ka and Pomeranz, and Pomeranz's novel about Galicia. It is argued that three themes are central to the "plays" of political movements: first, a narrative establishment of a collective community; second, the construction of experience; and third, narrative strategies for their historicization.

Chapter 3 "Organizing" examines the stages, the construction, and the design of concrete and abstract spaces. I have selected from the women's extensive activities reading rooms, kindergartens, and reform centers because these are examples of the movements' educational and social work practice, they make the performative clear, and are also typical of the three women; they can be used to show individual and contextual connections. Of course, the projects presented have different backgrounds: socialist, democratic, feminist, moderate, and radical. Nevertheless, performative similarities are shown in which social practices for the implementation of societal models are carried out. It is argued that central themes of the movements, namely the need for education, the progressiveness of the nation, and the malleability of society, are presented on these stages. They represent the stage sets for the plays dealing with the collectives, experience, and history.

Chapter 4 "Mobilizing" focuses on the enactments. It concentrates on the interaction of all participants, including opponents and the audience. This chapter is based mainly on the writings of the women, on published debates, political analyses, and historiographical texts. An analysis of the self-historicization of movements focusing on intertextuality, i.e. the interaction of plots, begins with an autobiographical episode recounted by Wysłouchowa. Kobryns'ka's polemics against her socialist environment, the Radicals, are analyzed in terms of the creative power of a monologue intended to set out the stakeholders' positions. Central to this are the persuasion strategies of "progress" and "backwardness," which are examined as part of a political code. Starting with an intra-Zionist conflict over the question of practice, at the end Pomeranz is analyzed in dialogue. It is shown how the truths of the movements were forged in competition with different positions, emphases, or fractions. The themes of "education," "nation," and "society" are combined with "collectives," "experience," and "history," and then placed in a broader intertextual context. This chapter develops the transnationality of the movements in question and the networks of the protagonists operated not only with regard to the imagined collectives and mutual support but also with respect to the productivity of competition and difference. Change, competition, and practice are central aspects that determined the modes of interpretation and operation of the movements studied.

Feminist research has deconstructed the consistent autonomous first-person narrator of an autobiography or biography as the norm of a male, white middle-class subject.[124] For instance, the "autobiographical pact" introduced by Philippe Lejeune into the debate, intended to assure the readership of the identity between the depicted self and the author,[125] presupposes an autonomous legal entity—a category from which women were long time excluded.[126] Even the continuity of name as a proof of identity does not apply to married women. This is especially striking for Rosa Pomeranz, later Melzer (the Polish form being Melcerowa), who published under both her maiden name and her married name. In addition, there are alternative spellings in different languages or language codifications. In German, we find Rosa Pomeranz/Pomeranz-Melzer/Melzer, in Polish Róża/Różia Pomeranz-Melzerowa and Pomeranc-Melcerowa, while Kobryns'ka's first name is written Natalija, Natalïja or Natalja. Although the names reflect different contexts and divergent rules, to simplify matters I have nevertheless decided to write the names with a uniform spelling: Rosa Pomeranz, Maria Wysłouchowa, and Natalja Kobryns'ka. However, literature is cited with the name and spelling used in the original.

As is clearly apparent in the opening quote from Pynchon's novel, places (like people) can also have different names. They obey different principles and may belong to different contexts. For the sake of readability, I have decided to use the popular English spelling (if there is one). Additional place names are spelled depending on the context and are added to the index. For the Cyrillic alphabet, I use a scientific transliteration. The many personal names inevitable in a biographical approach are listed in the appendix of names. The details included are relevant to the politics and political activities of the three women.

Notes

1. Pynchon, *Day*, 1079.
2. Pynchon, *Day*, 1077–78.
3. See also Hölscher, *Entdeckung*, especially 129–31.
4. Munslow, *Narrative*, especially 123–29.
5. Munslow, *Narrative*, 9–25, 39.
6. Koselleck, "Fiktion," 51–54; Koschorke, *Fact*, 275–76.
7. In the 19th century, language and nationality were an object and means in the debate about collective formation, advancement, and policymaking. Their descriptors changed their meanings while the rules of their use also changed. "Ruthenian" was used for the Ruthenian-speaking population in Galicia, and "Ukrainian" for Eastern Ukraine, the region with a Ukrainian-speaking population which was part of the Russian Empire. However, "Ukrainian" also became a political concept of the Ukrainophiles, who sought joint nation-building by the Galician Ruthenians with the Eastern Ukrainians. In addition, there were other options such as assimilation into the Polish or Russian elite, and Ukrainophile or Russophile language policy. Only in the twentieth century did "Ukrainian" prevail as a nationality descriptor. Here, I have adopted the rule applied (although not always consistently) by Kobryns'ka and use "Ruthenian" for the Ruthenian-speaking population in Galicia and "Ukrainian" for Eastern Ukraine. See also Himka, "Construction"; Rudnytsky, "Ukrainians"; Magocsi, *Roots*, 83–98.
8. Regarding Orzeszkowa, see Jankowski, "Orzeszkowa"; Chapter 4, Recitations.
9. Translations of quotations, unless otherwise stated, by the author and translator. Wysłouchowa to Orzeszkowa, October 27, 1890, PAN Warsaw,

28 Introduction

800. Wysłouchowa was presumably referring to the election in 1889, in which a number of peasants were voted into the *Sejm*, causing consternation among landowners. Regarding the *Sejm* election in 1889, see Struve, *Bauern*, 220–22; Dunin-Wąsowicz, "Bewegungen," 57.

10 Echoing the Old and Young Ruthenians or the Old and Young Czechs, the younger brothers (in contrast to the elder ones) signify a change of generation and direction in a movement (in this case the peasant movement). The use of the word "brothers" reflects Wysłouchowa's view of a movement and nation involving the peasant population. She used "sisters" in a similar way. Regarding her use of language, see also Chapter 2, Writing collectives.

11 Struve, *Bauern*, 115–21; Stauter-Halsted, *Nation*, 68–77.

12 Hacker, *Gewalt*, 17, 20; see also Vittorelli, *Frauenbewegung um 1900*, 191, footnote 1; similarly Andrzej Mencwel, who analyzed the play *Wesele, Dramat w 3 aktach* ("The Wedding—Drama in 3 acts") by Stanisław Wyspiański, which premiered in Kraków in 1901 and is still considered part of the canon of Polish literature today, as a chronotope. Mencwel, "Poza 'weselem,'" 145; Wolff, *Idea*, 280–307; see also "Die Jahrhundertwende."

13 The term "Galician elections" had a similar connotation. See Binder, *Galizien*, 13.

14 Scott, Introduction to *Gender*.

15 Kinnunen, "Feminismus."

16 Benedict Anderson, *Communities*. Regarding criticism of an essentialist concept of ethnicity in research to Eastern Europe, see also Müller, "Nation."

17 Stalleybrass and White, *Politics*, 1–26; Hacker, *Gewalt*, 279–83; regarding the policymaking potential of transgression, see also Ebrecht and Bettinger, "Einleitungsessay," especially 10–13; regarding transnationality, see Marung and Naumann, "Einleitung"; for an introduction, see also Marung, Middell, and Müller, "Territorialisierung."

18 Hausen, "Nicht-Einheit."

19 Regarding "productive fuzziness" (*produktive Unschärfen*), see also Gehmacher, "Frauenrechtlerinnen," 136–37. The protagonists mainly use terms like "women's movement" and "women's affairs" or "women's issues," occasionally also "feminist" (as both an adjective and a noun). I use the latter term as a heuristic description of an autonomous women's policy—as opposed to the umbrella term 'women's politics', which also refers to other movements. This does not imply political categorization, not to mention anything about the level of radicalism. See also Vittorelli, "Wie Frauenbewegung geschrieben wird."

20 Roberts, *Acts*, 8, 15.

21 Klandermans, "Movements."

22 Schreiber, "Wspomnienia," 13.

23 Dunin-Wąsowicz, "Bewegungen," 53.

24 Shimoni, *Ideology*, 19.

25 Lowi, *Arenas*, 9. Emphasis in the original. See also Linz and Stepan, *Problems*, 13.

26 Lowi, *Arenas*, 33.

27 Lyotard, *Condition*, 9–11, 16–17.

28 Holste, Hüchtker, and Müller, "Aufsteigen."

29 Regarding the benefits of dramatic and theatrical metaphors in historical research, see also Krischer, "Verfahren," 220; Martschukat and Patzold, "Geschichtswissenschaft."

30 Fischer-Lichte, *Power*, 32.

31 Fischer-Lichte, *Power*, 32, see also 25.

Introduction 29

32 Regarding the Imperial Council in Vienna, see Buszko, "Ludowcy," 111–13, which also addresses the active role of peasant deputies.
33 Regarding terminology confusion and explanations, see Snoek, "Performance."
34 Butler, *Bodies*, 1–23; see also Fischer-Lichte, *Power*, 26–27.
35 Lüdtke, "Alltagsgeschichte—ein Bericht," 293. Emphasis in the original.
36 Braidotti, *Subjects*, 146. See also Braidotti, "Identity."
37 Ethnomethodological concepts were contributed to Gender Studies by for example Gesa Lindemann. Lindemann, "Konstruktion." Regarding the nation as a ubiquitous leitmotif, see also Porter, *Nationalism*, 3–9.
38 See Geulen, "Nation."
39 See Sarasin, "Wirklichkeit," 150–51; Benedict Anderson, *Communities*, 10.
40 Sarasin, "Wirklichkeit," 171.
41 See Wagner, "Fest-Stellungen."
42 See for instance Hettling, "Erlebnisraum."
43 Fischer-Lichte, "Performance"; see also Turner, *Ritual*.
44 Bell, *Theory*, 81; see also Wulf and Zirfas, "Anthropologie."
45 Bell, *Theory*, 7–8.
46 Bell, *Theory*, 124.
47 Raphael, "Strukturwandel."
48 Regarding the social and symbolic space, see Bourdieu, *Reason*, 1–13; de Certeau, *Practice*, 91–130; Schenk, "Paradigma"; Löw, *Raumsoziologie*, 179–91.
49 Appadurai, "Disjuncture."
50 The emphasis here is on presentation. A number of theoretical concepts on the link between discourse and agency have been discussed. Some time ago, Linda Alcoff proposed the concept of "positionality" while Donna Haraway suggested "situated knowledges." Alcoff, "Feminism"; Haraway, "Knowledges"; see also Hüchtker, "Deconstruction."
51 Scott, Introduction to *Gender*; more recently also Frevert, "Politikgeschichte," 21; Frevert, "Kommunikation"; Stollberg-Rilinger, "Kulturgeschichte."
52 Regarding the performance of performativity, see Bal, *Concepts*, 212.
53 Similar to Braungart, "Authentizität," 363.
54 Velychenko, "Narratives"; Müller-Funk, "Kakanien"; see also the website *Kakanien revisited*; from the perspective of cultural and literary studies, see Weismann, *Potenzial*; from the perspective of the empire see Judson, *Habsburg Empire*.
55 Binder, *Galizien*, 23. See also Binder, "Öffentlichkeit"; Wendland, "Galizien."
56 Leszczawski-Schwerk, "Frauenbewegungen"; Leszczawski-Schwerk, *Tore*. See also Kaps, "Peripherisierung"; Kosyk, "Geschichte."
57 Rosman, "Prolegomenon."
58 See also the concept of examining Zionism in the context of the national movements of the nineteenth century: Hroch, "Zionism"; Shimoni, *Ideology*, 3–51. Stanislawski, *Zionism*, XIII–XXI, argues that instead of being a turning point, a break with previous modernization efforts in Judaism (i.e. a reaction to the rise of anti-Semitism at the end of the nineteenth century), Zionism was in fact a genuine further development of contemporary ideas, concepts and currents in the European context.
59 Hrytsak, *Ivan Franko*; Hrytsak, "Space."
60 Hrytsak, *Ivan Franko*, XIV–XVII.
61 Bechtel, *Renaissance*, 12. Emphasis in the original.
62 Simonek, "'Raum.'"
63 Magocsi, "Galicia." Hoff, "Badania," deplores the lack of a synthesis of research on Galician history.

30 Introduction

64 Wolff, *Idea.*
65 Csáky, Feichtinger, Karoshi, and Munz, "Pluralitäten"; see also Simonek, "Franko"; Bechtel and Galmiche, Introduction to *Les villes* 10.
66 The mental maps become apparent when Western hegemony is primarily compared to the non-European trans-oceanic regions. See Berger and Nehring, *History*; Stefan Berger, "Movements."
67 Krzoska, Lichy, and Rometsch, "Ostmitteleuropa"; for a general view, see Landwehr, *Abwesenheit.*
68 Himka, *Socialism;* Jobst, *Nationalismus.*
69 Malančuk-Rybak, "Ukraïns'kyj ta pol's'kyj žinočyj ruch"; see also Malančuk-Rybak, *Ideolohija.*
70 See also Smolyar, "Experiment," 397.
71 Offen, *Feminisms*, 19–25. Offen's distinction dates back to 1988 and has since been frequently attacked. She did not want relational and individual feminism to be understood as separate strategies or tactics, explaining that they had been intertwined in historical argumentation, and instead related them more generally to socio-political goals and the history of political ideas. In my view, however, this is precisely where the often implicit and occasionally explicit geopolitical localizations result from. See Offen, "Criticism," 24.
72 Vittorelli, "Wie Frauenbewegung geschrieben wird."
73 See also Loutfi, "Politics," 85; de Haan, Daskalova, and Loutfi, Introduction to *Dictionary*, 4–5.
74 Vittorelli, *Frauenbewegung um 1900.*
75 Scott, *Paradoxes.* See the summary of the debate by Paletschek and Pietrow-Ennker, "Emancipation," 304–05.
76 Regarding the debate about feminism in the context of research on social movements, see also Ferree and Mueller, "Feminism."
77 Bohachevsky-Chomiak, *Feminists*, XXIV; Bohachevsky-Chomiak, "Nationalism"; see also Zhurzhenko, "Women."
78 Lyudmyla Smolyar talks of "pragmatic feminism." Smolyar, "Experiment," 398.
79 Roberts, *Acts*, 1–17.
80 Molenda, *Chłopi*, 36, 78–94. Freidenreich, *Politics*, 59, emphasizes that Zionism's rural policy was bolstered by women and young people in particular.
81 Stauter-Halsted, *Nation*, 208–15; regarding the Ruthenian-speaking peasant population, see also Himka, "Transformation."
82 Struve, *Bauern*, 438–39.
83 Eisenstadt, "Modernities."
84 Janowski, "Galizien," see also Haid, Weismann, and Wöller, Einleitung to *Galizien.*
85 See Müller, "Historisierung," for a critical rejection of the category of backwardness.
86 Janowski, "Galizien," 843.
87 Steffen, *Polonität*, 13.
88 Sdvižkov, *Zeitalter*, 209.
89 The difficulties are explained by Brower, *Nihilists*, 33–36.
90 Konstantinovič and Rinner, *Literaturgeschichte*, 249.
91 Regarding the connection between the intelligentsia, advancement and education, see also Lyons, "Leser," 489. Kennedy and Suny, "Introduction," 22–23, draw attention to the women's movement with regard to the growing importance of education and self-education. Regarding Galicia and national movements, see for instance Pacholkiv, *Emanzipation.*

Introduction 31

92 Kennedy and Suny, "Introduction," 20.
93 Regarding the German women's movement, see Klausmann, "Frauenbewegung."
94 See Goldman, "Intellectuals," 298–300; see also Kennedy and Suny, "Introduction," 18–25. A compromise between discourse analysis and socio-historical approaches is called for by Jedlicki, "Wiek."
95 See for instance the overview by Gaus, "Dimensionen"; Kusber, Bildungskonzepte; Vierhaus, "Bildung."
96 Koselleck, "'Space,'" 264.
97 Scott, "Phantasie."
98 Gerhard, "Kommentar."
99 See praxeological approaches questioning what makes actors perceive the world as ordered, i.e. understanding diverse practices as movements, Reckwitz, "Grundelemente." On the other hand, more recent anthologies are still trying to find an overarching definition. See for instance Rucht, "Movements."
100 Guesnet, "Chanukah."
101 Schröder, Welt, 2, 23, 328–34.
102 Hettling and Hoffmann, "Wertehimmel." Whether the value system of the Galician activists was bourgeois is subject to debate.
103 Regarding German examples, see Nitsch, Wohltätigkeitsvereine; Meyer-Renschhausen, Kultur; Klausmann, Politik; regarding biographical studies Dormus, Kazimiera Bujwidowa; Hecht, Feminismus; Schaser, Helene Lange.
104 Schüler, Frauenbewegung; regarding Zionism, see also for instance Berkowitz, "'Tzimmes'"; Shimoni, Ideology.
105 Von Hammerstein, "Selbst."
106 See Hausen, "Öffentlichkeit," 82.
107 Hämmerle and Saurer, "Frauenbriefe," 25–27.
108 For the example of the gallant letter, see Anton, Authentizität, 27–32.
109 Nickisch, Brief, especially 1–28; Hébrard, "La correspondence."
110 Hoock-Demarle, Europe, 7–15. Jansen, "Briefe," stresses the importance of letter networks for the political culture of the nineteenth century.
111 Hämmerle and Saurer, "Frauenbriefe," 11.
112 The T. H. Ševčenko Institute of Literature contains estates and correspondence of various Ukrainian writers and publicists, including the estate of Ivan Franko and numerous letters written by and to Kobryns'ka. See Nacional'na akademija nauk Ukraïny, Putivnyk.
113 Including her correspondence and material from her editorial work; see the description of the collection Lutman, Bonarska, and Kruczkiewicz, "Papiery"; Turska, Inwentarz; Fastnacht, Inwentarz.
114 Die Welt was founded in 1897 by Theodor Herzl. Various well-known figures of the Zionist movement were involved in it, such as Max Nordau and Saul Raphael Landau. See Schenker, "Press."
115 Binder, "Das polnische Pressewesen," 2088. Rachel Manekin notes that the Zionist press in the Habsburg Empire appeared largely in German and Polish in order to reach a broad readership. Manekin, "Presse," 2341. She does not mention Di yidishe froyenvelt (The Jewish Women's World), which was however only published in 1902 in Kraków.
116 Steffen, Polonität, 32–39; see also Requate, "Öffentlichkeit." Jörg Requate emphasizes the complexity of the interrelations between society and media as well as the importance of communication structures.
117 Assmann, "Gedächtnis."
118 Ricœur, Rätsel, 119.

32 Introduction

119 Geertz, "Description," 22; Levi, "Microhistory," 93.
120 Hrytsak, *Ivan Franko*, VII; similarly, Schaser, *Helene Lange*, 23.
121 Lyotard, *Condition*, 17.
122 Bal, *Concepts*, 3–21.
123 Regarding the link between different perspectives and levels in socio-historical biographical research, see also Gestrich, "Einleitung," 20–23.
124 Gilmore, "Mark"; see also Groag and Yalom, *Lifes;* Swindells, *Uses;* Brodzki and Schenck, *Life/Lines*.
125 Lejeune, "Pakt."
126 Bernhold and Gehmacher, *Auto/Biographie*, 62–63; Hahn, *Namen*, especially 7; see also Hecht, *Feminismus*, 19–20.

1 Finding Roles
The Participants

From a multitude of interpretations and self-interpretations, various narratives are crystallized about the three women's understanding of themselves and the world—narratives in which different aspects of life are united, defiantly oppose, or even stand alongside each other without being connected. Maria Wysłouchowa can be interpreted as a Polish women's campaigner or a Galician peasant activist, the wife of famous peasant politician Bolesław Wysłouch, as a journalist, and a lecturer in adult education. Natalja Kobryns'ka can be presented as a lone feminist campaigner, a Ruthenian socialist, an underrated literary figure, and Rosa Pomeranz as a charismatic speaker and pianist, a convinced Zionist, a Jewish woman, one of the first female delegates at the Zionist World Congress in Basel, and one of the first female members of the Polish *Sejm*. The geographical references of their political activities are just as diverse: the Habsburg Empire and the Imperial Council, the Galician *Sejm*, Galician misery, East European Judaism, Palestine, Poland, the Ukrainian-speaking population in Galicia and the Russian Empire, the European women's movements, and reform projects. There are several ways to bring about coherence: stories from their lives could be told in which their experiences of deprivation and oppression, their acquaintance with other intellectuals or with literature prompted the protagonists to enter politics. Alternatively, their biographies could be typified as Polish, Jewish, or Ruthenian and their dedication explained with the respective national narrative. Instead, the women could be introduced as representatives of the peasant, women's, and Zionist movements.

Researchers largely agree that biographies, far from being an accurate reflection of a "lived life," are constructions by their authors.[1] Rather than simply recreating reality, they take material and transform it into a narrative.[2] If, however, the biographies of political activists are considered, their engagement often becomes the coherent, essential meaning of the subject's life.[3] The narrated persons become heroes in a dual sense, their lives consisting in political representation while they simultaneously sacrifice themselves to it. Biographies about marginalized persons are frequently intended to be mirrors of a "lived life" and to reconstruct reality in order to overcome fragmentary information and sparse coverage.

34 Finding Roles: The Participants

The reference to marginality legitimizes writing and publishing, and is comparable to the gesture of modesty found time and again in women's autobiographies.[4] For example, the introduction to a number of sketches of Jewish female *Rebels & Radicals* begins with the sentence: "There is no history of Jewish women."[5] Although the construction of life stories is discussed in research on biographies, the writing strategies of the texts themselves often serve exactly the opposite purpose: they attempt to create coherence where fragmentation prevails. By being "snatched from oblivion," the protagonists become consistent subjects whose existence is disputed and whose associated sacralization as victims and heroes is criticized.

The specific characteristic of biographical texts is the identificatory offering of the genre—for both author and readers.[6] The scholarly analyses at the beginning, the introductory gesture of modesty, and the marginality could be regarded as a ritualized act of writing, for the gesture of writing now no longer legitimizes its subject as a biography about heroes who were marginalized, suffering, or putting up resistance, but as an analysis of historical and biographical research. The references to gaps in the narrative included in the preface of biographies published in recent decades is not only based on the assumption that a consistent biography is an illusion (despite its importance for the interpretations and changing levels of interpretation), but also reflects or should reflect the fact that the view of an author or researcher is subject to inconsistencies. The portrayal itself depends on historical and individual perspectives, while the manner of portrayal is tied to the context of the author.[7]

Below, we consider heroes by snatching them from oblivion, something which certainly applies to Pomeranz in particular. This means a change in significance, a *mise-en-scène* of the marginalized subject, be it women or Galicia. And last but not least, the aim is to highlight the narrative quality of their biographies, not truths about their lives. The narrative aspect, however, refers not to fiction, but to the diversity of consistency and logic in narrated life. Biographies, it is suggested, like autobiographies, can be understood as intertextual and dialogical,[8] as an interaction between subject, the narrator's self, author, and reader.[9]

Using autobiographical texts by Polish feminists, Natali Stegmann revealed the diversity of life plans and the simultaneous possible "patterns" of interpretation—for example, setting the narrative in the rebellious milieu of Polish noble families, the transfiguration of fathers as role models and mentors in the world of education and the public sphere—patterns that paved the way to becoming a feminist.[10] In her biography of Natalja Kobryns'ka, Martha Bohachevsky-Chomiak also emphasizes such a pattern, a close bond between father and daughter as a route into politics.[11] "Pattern" is a very apt term for biographical narratives since it expresses a dual level as a strategy for life and for writing.[12] Seeing fathers as role models, for instance, opened up to young women a world with male connotations. As a topos in the narrative, it highlighted the achievements of women who had managed to gain a foothold in areas viewed by them as different. A close relationship between fathers and daughters indicates the permeability of normative gender constructions, the relationship simultaneously renewing, confirming, and reifying gender segregation—the separate spheres—as the central ordering principle of the nineteenth century.[13]

Adopting Stegmann's approach, the lives of the three women are told according to the patterns of their political engagement. The patterns are taken from the model of performance and represent different aspects of engagement: writing, directing, enacting. These activities are linked to the roles played by the three women, author, artistic director, and actor. All three roles were necessary for political action, and all three women played different roles throughout their lives. Therefore, the roles do not explain the lives of the women; instead, the patterns developed in the biographical narrative serve to bring these roles to life. The main phases of their lives are presented and contextualized. Their presentation can be understood as a dialogue with the narrated persons, with their first-person narratives, with other biographers as well as with the readers.

This chapter has two objectives. Firstly, the complexity and interpretation possibilities of the lives and biographies are shown, and secondly, the patterns shedding light on the roles of political action are revealed. The presentation combines contingency with context, conditions, and structures. This also includes the painstaking reconstruction of activities and details, such as in the case of Pomeranz. And despite extensive material about and by Kobryns'ka and Wysłouchowa, many gaps still remain about them too, even regarding their political engagement, their participation in associations and rallies, and their correspondence.[14] These gaps may be accidental or intentional, since they contradict their self-representation.[15] This is another reason why the aim of this chapter is not necessarily to map out three lives. Instead, emphasis is placed on the patterns denoting the possibilities of political roles.

Heroic Narrating, or: Maria Wysłouchowa and Love

Maria Wysłouchowa was born Maria Bouffałówna in 1858, and died of heart disease in L'viv in 1905. She worked as a teacher in Warsaw and was involved in women's circles set up to provide education and support families affected by repression in the Russian Empire. In 1885, she married Bolesław Wysłouch and moved with him to L'viv, where they became involved in the Galician peasant movement, both in an organizational capacity and through journalism. In addition, she was associated with the Polish women's movement and published magazines and booklets devoted to nationalist and feminist politics (Figure 1.1).

Figure 1.1 Maria Wysłouchowa. Beskid Museum in Wisła, before 1905, Wikimedia Commons/User:Piotrus/CC BY-SA (https://creativecommons.org/licenses/by-sa/3.0).

Wysłouchowa conducted extensive correspondence over many years in which she discussed and commented on political and journalistic work (her own and others'), described events and decisions of the peasant and women's movement, organized meetings and trips, cultivated friendships, and kept in touch with her family. Among others, she corresponded with Czech women's movement activist and writer Vilma Sokolová-Seidlová,[16] whom she had met in 1891 at a meeting of the Czech gymnastics organization The Falcon (*Sokol*), as well as with rural writer Władysław Orkan,[17] who for her was akin to a model demonstrating the educational advancement of the peasant population and the patriotism of the people.[18] Wysłouchowa and Sokolová-Seidlová shared their commitment to women's and nationalist politics. They both wrote political and literary texts, which they exchanged, commented on, and above all translated for their respective readerships.[19] The letters connected two women who lived far apart and met very rarely (presumably only once or twice). With Orkan, Wysłouchowa exchanged information about sensitivities and working conditions. Occasionally she reminded him to write and referred to herself as a motherly advisor.[20] She corresponded with both of them about political projects and literary matters, cultivating a working and friendship relationship,[21] a kind of virtual conversation.[22] To both of them, she commented on the female hero of the story "Dwa bieguny" (Two Poles) by Eliza Orzeszkowa shortly after its publication. The letter to Sokolová-Seidlová written in 1894 sounds very enthusiastic:

> Among the latest works, a one-volume novel published last year under the title "Dwa bieguny" is wonderful. Its hero is the most ideal type of woman I have ever encountered in a book or in real life. After the death of her brother, who perished as a martyr in Siberia after the 1863 uprising..., the female hero of "Dwa bieguny" devotes herself to social work on her large estate in Lithuania she has inherited from him. She teaches the village children, allows poor girls and young men to live in her house, where the former develop under her wing into exemplary citizens, the latter into clever, energetic people; she saves poorer neighbors threatened by the liquidation of their country. (You probably know, my dear, but perhaps you don't know either that in Lithuania no Pole or basically no Catholic has the right to buy land, while the government, with the aim of Russifying the country, grants very high interest-free loans to Russians who acquire property there—actually gifts since it never demands repayment. Any Pole who sells land must emigrate because he has no right to hold office in his homeland, not even as a watchman or postman.) But allow me to return from horrible reality to the beautiful novel. Our hero meets a handsome, educated young man with whom she falls in love and who loves her. But she sacrifices her love to duty because her chosen native of Warsaw is accustomed to entertainment of the kind offered by civilization in European capitals, and cannot live in a godforsaken, quiet backwater, yet she doesn't want to leave her post, doesn't want perhaps the only little candle that she has managed to light in the gloomy country forced into chains to go out. Those are the bare bones of the novel, written in an outstanding style with the full mastery of the art.[23]

Through educational work, the hero of the novel persuades the villagers to resist the policy of Russification in the parts of the Polish–Lithuanian Commonwealth annexed by the Russian Empire. Even more remarkable is her sacrifice. The hero sacrifices her love to duty, her personal happiness to the needs of the nation. For Wysłouchowa, the hero is the "most ideal type of woman"—not only in the novel, but also in real life. Life and novel complement each other. The fact that such a connection exists is made clear by the description of the Russian policy of repression,[24] separated by brackets from the plot as reality. In the letter, this insertion serves to concretize the constellation of the novel. Wysłouchowa read Orzeszkowa's story as a contribution to positivism. Although with its literary treatment of political and social questions, positivism corresponded to realism, in the Polish context, it could also be viewed as a political and social response to the failure of the uprisings.[25] It encouraged the reader to consider society and to take up practical reform projects, what was called "organic work" (*praca organiczna*).[26]

In her letter to Orkan, however, Wysłouchowa's comments on the hero of "Dwa bieguny" sound somewhat different:

> It is just a pity that the author curtails her [the hero's] soul a little by treating her merely as the executor of the will of her brother, an insurgent who died in Siberia (the details about the brother must be read between the lines, just as one must always read there in the land of bondage), as if the female heart were by itself incapable of loving the ideals so strongly that it would sacrifice what in everyday language is called personal happiness to them.[27]

In this critique of Orzeszkowa's hero, Wysłouchowa envisioned a woman sacrificing herself to the overriding ideals of her own convictions rather than a female figure sacrificing her life to her family and children, the *pietà*, the silent suffering.[28] Women were supposed to love their nation on their own without being dependent on male norms or personal, emotional ties. Wysłouchowa called for what feminist research terms an autonomous subject position. Whether she had in mind the independence of women or the sublimity of feeling is not clear from the letter. We can only speculate as to the reasons why Wysłouchowa assessed "Dwa bieguny" and the portrayal of the hero so differently. Perhaps she was less critical in her letter to Bohemia because it was traveling to the outside world. The comments, however, emphasize how important the ideal of a hero was to her as well as how closely female independence and national sacrifice could be intertwined in contemporary views. Sacrifice and emancipation were by no means opposites in Wysłouchowa's eyes.[29]

"Hero" has a double meaning: the character that stands out from ordinary life, and the literary concept of a protagonist, the hero of a story.[30] The former is guided by the idea of becoming immortal with a deed that lives on after death, of giving supra-individual meaning to the life of an individual.[31] Although the ancient hero had to literally sacrifice or at least endanger his life and was male, an act that survives one's death could also be a work created by female heroes. According to Wysłouchowa, the latter hero, the literary one, should not only reflect life, but more importantly present a righteous model.[32] If both quotations, both heroes, are read together, it becomes apparent that Wysłouchowa saw role models in literature as well as in life, that literature and life were interwoven. The mutual penetration of feminist and national discourses was just as much a central thread in Wysłouchowa's life as the romantic connection between life and work. The genre of the letter underlines this combination of the personal, the political, and the literary. By doing so, central aspects of her biography are touched upon: one central pattern for her women's policy was that of the author. The author wrote narratives about political positions and demands. One of the subjects determining this narrative was love, which united the subject and the collective, life and politics.

Political Engagement in Warsaw

Maria Wysłouchowa[33] came from a Polish landowning family with several estates *(ziemiaństwo)* in Polish Livonia which, after the partitions of the Polish–Lithuanian Commonwealth, was incorporated into the Vitebsk governorate, which had existed in the Russian Empire since 1802. The family members had participated in the uprising of 1863/64, whereupon her father was arrested and did not survive captivity. The estates were confiscated in the course of tsarist repression and her mother had to look after the family. She worked as a governess and private teacher in Vitebsk.[34] Participation in the uprising, the early loss of her father and the family estates combined to form an almost archetypal biography of a Polish landowning family characterized by patriotism, oppression, and resistance.[35]

Wysłouchowa's educational development was also quite typical, a combination of institutionalized and self-organized, formal and informal, aimed at one of the few professions recognized for women in the intelligentsia, namely teaching.[36] Wysłouchowa learned Belarusian and apparently also a little Latvian from her nanny,[37] while the language of instruction at school was Russian. She became acquainted with Polish literature and history at home and on illegal private courses. After attending a private boarding school for girls in Vitebsk and a girls' high school in Pskov, from 1878 to 1882, Wysłouchowa enrolled at the Department of History and Literature of the Higher Scholarly Bestužev Courses for Women *(Vysšie ženskie Bestuževskie kursy)* in Saint Petersburg, where she received a state-approved teaching qualification.[38] From 1883, she taught at first in a boarding school for girls in Warsaw, and later in L'viv until she had to retire in 1897 for health reasons.[39]

Through her family and her educational career, Wysłouchowa associated with politically active circles.[40] In Saint Petersburg, she met Polish female students who supported prisoners, exiles, and their families, and strove to educate young people in the "Polish spirit." She was also introduced to the agrarian-socialist ideas of the Narodniks (friends of the people) there.[41] After moving to Warsaw, Wysłouchowa became involved in her first women's circle, the illegal Women's Circle for People's Education *(Kobiece Koło Oświaty Ludowej)*.[42] The Circle considered reading to be the most important means of educating women and therefore published, among other things, women's supplements for various magazines.[43] Gradually, the Women's Circle for People's Education focused its work on rural areas, leaving urban education and enlightenment to other organizations. It began by offering Sunday courses for women and girls who had migrated from the countryside to the city. These courses spawned multipliers of the knowledge taught there, who became the first nursery teachers for village children.[44] Wysłouchowa's activities in Warsaw touched on the various areas that would characterize her political work: patriotism, education, the people, and women. The move from women's education in general to concentrating on rural women was something she would later repeat in her Galician period.

Peasant Politics in L'viv

From 1883, Wysłouchowa was active in the illegal Revolutionary Red Cross (*Rewolucyjny Czerwony Krzyż*), which was also dedicated to supporting exiles and detainees. She visited prisoners as its representative, which was how she first met her later husband, Bolesław Wysłouch, who had been imprisoned on charges of socialist agitation.[45] In 1885, after their wedding, the couple moved to L'viv.[46] Although Galicia was the place of exile for the Wysłouchs where they fled from repression in the Kingdom of Poland,[47] it also offered opportunities for legal political activity which they made use of in many ways. After the association and press laws on freedom of publication, organization and assembly of 1861 and 1867 and the establishment of an elected parliament, a publishing sector, associations and political parties emerged though curia suffrage granted privileges to the elites and censorship and bans on organizations and individuals classified as socialist or antistate continued.[48]

Wysłouchowa worked closely with her husband. Her correspondence testifies to love, longing, and care: "Eat fruit, I beg you, and compote,"[49] she urged him when she herself was already seriously ill with heart disease. The Wysłouchs could be described as a working couple.[50] They were united by their dedication to the peasant population, whom they regarded as the basis of a renewed Polish nation.[51] They encouraged peasants to actively participate in association work and strove for adequate education and local amenities by founding reading rooms in rural areas. Wysłouchowa traveled across the country to give lectures for educational associations and the Adam Mickiewicz Association for Adult Education Center (*Towarzystwo Uniwersytetu ludowego im. Adama Mickiewicza*).[52]

Since women were not allowed to join political associations,[53] Wysłouchowa's organizational scope was limited. Nevertheless, the couple evidently reached an intramarital arrangement between external representation and internal dialogue. Together, they built up the most important publications and organizations of the peasant movement. From 1886 to 1887, they jointly published the newspaper *Przegląd Społeczny* (Social Review), which became a medium for journalists from the Kingdom, but soon had to be discontinued because of countless confiscations.[54] From 1887 to 1919, Wysłouch was co-owner and editor of the *Kurjer Lwowski* (L'viv Courier), whose literary supplement *Tydzień* (The Week) was edited by Wysłouchowa. From 1889, they jointly produced *Przyjaciel Ludu* (The People's Friend), which became the organ of the peasant movement in Galicia.[55] The couple's house was a kind of intellectual and organizational center of the movement.[56] In 1890, they initiated the Association of Friends of Education (*Towarzystwo Przyjaciół Oświaty*) with Wysłouch as its chair. The primary goal of the Association was to establish libraries and reading rooms in rural locations, as well as to start a publishing house for popular, inexpensive literature; this was no different from the various other organizations that came to the villages with the idea of people's education.[57] The Association also prepared the establishment of a peasants' party. It was from among its members that the Peasant Party was founded in 1894, also on the Wysłouchs' initiative.[58]

Simply because of their origin in the Eastern Borderlands and the landed nobility, the Wysłouchs referred to a geographically and socially united Polish nation, which encompassed different partitions and classes.[59] They reached symbolic geographical agreement by means of, for example, the distribution of publications through legal and illegal channels to the Province of Poznań and the Kingdom of Poland as well as to the Eastern Borderlands and the diaspora.[60] In addition, the Wysłouchs participated in the transfer of the mortal remains of Adam Mickiewicz, the foremost romantic poet, from Paris to Kraków in 1890, the centenary of the May Constitution of 1791, and the centenary of the 1794 Kościuszko Uprising, which was celebrated in L'viv with the opening of the Racławice Panorama and the Galician Provincial Exhibition.[61] Wysłouchowa was a speaker at the commemorative ceremonies and organized a visit to the Provincial Exhibition for about 3,000 peasants (whether they included female peasants is not clear), who had been mobilized by *Przyjaciel ludu* and were personally guided through the exhibition by her.[62] There was also a big rally on the exhibition square at which she, her husband, and another activist in the peasant movement, Jan Stapiński, spoke.[63]

Having been diagnosed with heart disease,[64] Wysłouchowa spent every summer from 1895 to 1900 convalescing in the Beskids region of Cieszyn Silesia.[65] There she was in touch with the village's inhabitants, supporting them whenever they were ill or in financial difficulty, and bringing them books and magazines. She participated in summer schools and gave lectures on the history and legends of Poland and Silesia.[66] From her letters, she sounded as if she was working so hard that her mother and husband were worried about her.[67] After spending considerable time in the mountains, she became friends with Jan Wantuła, a Silesian movement journalist of peasant origin, with whom she shared literary publications.[68] Wantuła later thanked her for her dedication in his obituary of her and pointed out that the Silesian peasants had been turned into "real Poles" by the peasant journalism from Galicia.[69]

In several travelogues, Wysłouchowa described customs and traditions, wisdom, legends, history and ethnographical aspects of Silesia.[70] For her, the peasants there represented true Polishness, working rationally and culturally educated, with intact social structures and shared cultural practices. For example, she wrote that there was no begging there because the parishioners took turns caring for the poor.[71] There may have been several reasons why she idealized the peasant population in Cieszyn Silesia, a region dominated by coal mining with a predominantly Polish-speaking population yet with substantial numbers of Czech and German speakers. Psychologically interpreted, a more distant object of longing was easier to idealize than the economic and social problems of Galician peasants closer to home or their lack of interest in education and reform. Politically, this view could be seen as the idea of rescuing a Polishness threatened by "depolonization" in an industrial region with a high level of migration. From a socio-historical point of view, perhaps the unity of the Polish people seemed more likely to her in Silesia, where in many cases, large landowners and the urban population spoke German, where social opponents, unlike Galicia, were also national.[72] Polish Livonia, Wysłouchowa's homeland, was unsuitable as the Polish-speaking population there belonged to the noble and urban elite.

The Wysłouchs' agitational work was aimed not only at the rural population as addressees of socialist politics in the countryside or as the audience of educational initiatives, but also as writers and activists. In her letters, Wysłouchowa enthused about the peasant language: "And our peasants really can write excellently!"[73] She also shared the hope of the intelligentsia active in the peasant movement for renewal through peasant culture: "From the people come the bold campaigners for truth, progress, light!"[74] For her contemporaries, it was no contradiction that the rural population with its customs and traditions, songs, ways of thinking, and legends were invented on the one hand as a genuinely natural basis of Polish culture and nation, while on the other hand, they had to learn the enactment of a political and emotional bond to the nation and thus became objects of far-reaching educational and enlightenment work.[75] Wysłouchowa solved this paradox by means of her idealizing and romanticizing language and by the spatial shift of idealization to Silesia.

Women's Politics in Partitioned Poland

Like her peasantry-focused activities, Wysłouchowa's engagement in support of women also stemmed from initiatives in Warsaw. After moving to L'viv, she became one of the Galician representatives of the Women's Circle for People's Education. She was among its leading authors and persuaded female artists, including the famous Kraków painter Maria Dulębianka, to illustrate publications dedicated to people's education.[76] From 1886 to 1892, Wysłouchowa was a member of the Women's Reading Room in L'viv (*Czytelnia dla Kobiet we Lwowie*), an educational association for women whose main activity comprised organizing lectures on aspects of Polish nationalism as well as popular scientific, cultural, and political topics.[77]

All these associations used personal connections between Warsaw and L'viv in order to build up all-Polish structures and cultivated contacts in the Province of Poznań as well as in the Eastern Borderlands. In 1891, for example, various women's educational associations staged an event for the writer Eliza Orzeszkowa to celebrate her 25 years of work.[78] In 1894, several women's circles organized the II Congress of Polish Women from the Three Partitions in L'viv (*II Zjazd Kobiet Polskich z trzech zaborów we Lwowie*) in connection with the General Provincial Exhibition. The informal, nonpublic assembly (to protect delegates from the Russian partition) took place in Wysłouchowa's house. Among other things, the merger of two organizations dedicated to educational work for rural women was approved.[79] The initial call for this union probably came from Wysłouchowa herself. It urged women to go out to the villages and "take food to hungry hearts and minds."[80] In 1894, after the death of Kasylda Kulikowska, a close friend of Wysłouchowa who was also active in women's education in Warsaw,[81] her legacy was used to set up the K. Kulikowska Foundation (*Fundusz im. K. Kulikowskiej*), which Wysłouchowa controlled, and which was partly used to finance a publishing house for folk literature called Kasylda Kulikowska Publishing House (*Wydawnictwo im. Kasyldy Kulikowskiej*).[82]

In the Women's Savings Association (*Towarzystwo Oszczędności Kobiet*),[83] founded in 1886 in L'viv to support the Real Estate Bank in Poznań (*Bank Ziemski w Poznaniu*), Wysłouchowa served as secretary to the presidium between 1886 and 1892. The purpose of this association was to generate money by means of economical financial management to finance low-interest and even interest-free loans to benefit impoverished landowners.[84] An appeal in 1892 called in very general terms for the improvement of the moral and material situation of the people as well as for sacrifices to achieve nationalist goals.[85] Above all, the association conducted fundraising activities with the aid of bazaars and similar events, which was a common way to raise money for initiatives in the nineteenth century, not just in Galicia.[86] When in 1890 poor harvests in Galicia led to food shortages in the countryside, the Women's Savings Association organized a bazaar, to which Orzeszkowa donated a flower album and two platters decorated with dried flowers, which raised a lot of money when they were sold.[87] In addition, an anthology *Dla głodnych* (For the Starving)[88] was published, for which Wysłouchowa and various other active Polish and also some Ruthenian

44 Finding Roles: The Participants

women, including Natalja Kobryns'ka, wrote contributions. The Women's Savings Association combined the mobilization of the "generality of Polish women,"[89] as Wysłouchowa put it, across national and state borders with mobilization for the needs of the rural population: women's, nationalist and peasant goals.

The feminist and nationalist political associations overlapped in terms of their membership—there was no clear separation between the different movements.[90] Although Wysłouchowa's focus was on people's education and national political representation, she also actively supported the training of women and took part in organizing an exhibition on women's employment.[91] She thus touched on central themes of the feminist movement. It was therefore no coincidence that in 1893, a group of women from Warsaw, including Paulina Kuczalska-Reinschmit, who was often referred to as the female captain (*hetmanka*) of the Polish women's movement,[92] proposed sending Wysłouchowa to Chicago as the representative of Polish women at the congress of the International Council of Women. Wysłouchowa refused, initially with the gesture of female modesty—she could not imagine why she had been chosen (probably because such a journey would have been easier for her owing to the legal situation in Galicia[93]). In the end, however, it seems she did not accept for political reasons, as she explained in a letter to Sokolová-Seidlová:

> In my last letter—did it reach you?—I wrote about the planned trip to America. Since I had somehow succumbed to the will of the women from Warsaw, I collected material for my presentation at the congress and practiced my unsightly English by reading the beautiful poetry of Longfellow, Byron etc. But when I received the detailed congress program together with the list of delegations from European countries from the president in the first days of March, that changed my plans, for the congress will be first and foremost feminist in character, excluding all political and nationalist issues, while the delegation from Russia—very large, twenty-nine people—will not include a single progressive woman known for literature or social work of any kind, whose heart beats for great ideas expressing the great sufferings of humanity. The Tsarina took the lead and various princesses, countesses, wives of generals, etc. rushed in, so there was no room for women who worked, suffered and loved their nation. The Prussian delegation, which gathered under the patronage of Empress Frederick, had an almost identical make-up.[94]

Wysłouchowa distinguished between feminist and political or nationalist issues. She measured the women's delegations from Russia and Prussia—actually from the German Empire—against the policy of the partitioning powers. If it was not condemned, to Wysłouchowa's mind, the women were neither political nor progressive. It is remarkable that she also refused to accept that the women's delegations were involved in social work, of all things one of the essential areas of feminist politics at the time. This was a false accusation to level against Empress Frederick (as Empress Victoria, the wife of Frederick III, was known) since she was one of the leading patrons of social work activities in the German Empire.[95]

The letter reports on Wysłouchowa's path of knowledge—from her decision to undertake the journey, via her interpretation of the list of delegates, to an almost polemical explanation for her change of heart:

> Under these circumstances, it would be a sin for us poor people to waste money and time on a chimera. Because for us, demanding women's suffrage if nobody has it is a chimera; the demand to participate in public life when even men have no right to hold the shabbiest of offices is a chimera; even the right to attend university if one is not even allowed to be a primary school teacher is a chimera! So I abandoned America and returned to my ordinary duties, which had greatly suffered in the time my head was preoccupied with something else.[96]

With the "chimeras" of women's suffrage, participation in public life, and access to university, Wysłouchowa criticized the demands of the feminist movements as unjustified as long as they continued to ignore the policy of Germanization and Russification in the Prussian and Russian partitions. Wysłouchowa used rhetorical elements of a speech. The use of repetition raises the urgency of the passage. In "for us," she appealed to a united (Polish) nation, even though the reasons that made the demands chimeras did not apply at all to Galicia, where men had the vote (albeit in the form of curia suffrage), where they held public office and were allowed to teach at school and university in Polish. Wysłouchowa's yardstick was the conditions in the Kingdom of Poland.[97] The letter is an example of not only her priorities but also of her ability to tell a story. The amusing, self-mocking tale of her planned trip to America begins and ends with her modestly described practicing of her "unsightly English" and "ordinary duties."

In Wysłouchowa's view, there was tension between feminist and nationalist politics, competition for the prerogative of interpretation of goals and demands. She may also have been aware of the problems faced by women's movements not representing nation-states, especially the Habsburg women's movements. Since only national umbrella associations representing states could join, women's movements from for instance the Habsburg Empire were excluded from official participation.[98] Perhaps Wysłouchowa's decision not to travel and her account about the causes were also a response to the ignorance of international women's organizations regarding movements, which were unable to collaborate on an equal footing. Then again, there are no indications of this.

46 Finding Roles: The Participants

Another important element of Wysłouchowa's further work was the decision taken in 1899 to found a magazine for rural women. Back in 1897, the Kraków journalist and feminist Maria Siedlecka[99] had proposed such a publication[100] to the editorial board of *Kurjer Lwowski* in the name of the Women's Reading Room in Kraków (*Czytelnia dla kobiet w Krakowie*), one of the central women's associations in the Polish women's movement. She suggested devoting a monthly supplement to women's areas of work and interests since they had been largely neglected in the newspapers aimed at the rural population:

> The content [of the supplement] must be the rural cottage industry, women's domestic duties, horticulture, beekeeping, hygiene, education, domestic science, fiction, ethics and historical works, and from time to time a section for the little ones. Articles from these fields will be popular, but should be academically formulated such that any woman who has completed elementary school can read them with profit and pleasure.[101]

By covering hygiene, pedagogy, and natural science, the areas of knowledge regarded as new sciences were addressed. And by including fiction, ethics, and history, areas attributed to higher education also featured whose popularization was hotly discussed in political movements and the relevant institutions in the course of a general increase in significance. By linking knowledge transfer to female areas of work, women were to be included in this new canon.

Siedlecka received no reply and so she repeated her request a year later.[102] However, it was only the decision taken by the congress of the Polish women's movement in Zakopane that led to its implementation. At the Summer Congress of the Women's Circle of the Kingdom [of Poland] and Lithuania in 1899 in Zakopane (*Wakacyjny Zjazd Koła Kobiet Korony i Litwy w 1899 r. w Zakopanem*), the chief representatives of the Polish women's movement from all three partitions met to discuss the main issues across Europe at the time, namely marriage, ethics, education, and child protection.[103] Wysłouchowa not only attended but also delivered one of the main lectures: "O doli i niedoli kobiety wiejskiej" (The Woe and Well-Being of Rural Woman), in which she presented rural women as children, young women, wives, mothers, and grandmothers.[104] She derived their different tasks for the Polish nation, yet also the demand for extensive education, from the phases of their lives. Her talk ended with a concrete proposal to create a magazine for rural women.[105] The first issue of the monthly magazine *Przodownica: Pismo dla kobiet wiejskich* (The Female Activist. A magazine for rural women) came out at the end of 1899. It was edited by a committee based in Kraków, which included representatives from all three partitions. Wysłouchowa was a member of the L'viv committee.[106]

In the very first few months, there were disagreements concerning the political orientation of the magazine. Although what exactly happened can only be pieced together one-sidedly from Wysłouchowa's letters, it nevertheless throws light on her view of moods and polarizations. The reason was apparently differences over how to react to the slurs published in the press even before the first issue had appeared that the magazine was socialist and godless,[107] not to mention to an episcopal ban on reading. According to Wysłouchowa, some of the women in Kraków planned to curb the idea of allowing the rural population—especially women—to become involved by no longer publishing letters to the editor. In addition, the editors had apparently suggested that Wysłouchowa should only publish anonymously in order not to provide a target for attacks owing to her personal ties to the peasant movement, which was feared by sections of the public in Galicia as socialist.[108] According to Wysłouchowa, these restrictions could only be attributed to a lack of political stability. In a letter to Sokolová-Seidlová, she maligned Siedlecka as uneducated and influenceable:

> Miss Siedlecka, a person of the greatest intentions and highly respectable, with enormous energy, rich in good ideas, has no comprehensive world view and no literary education. And the worst part is, she is all too easily susceptible to the most contradictory influences. The last one to talk is always right.[109]

These one-sided accusations, as her further account shows, resulted from Wysłouchowa's general claim to leadership: "[E]very day I was tormented by the uncertainty over whether she [Siedlecka] had done what I'd asked her to do, or not done what I considered harmful to the magazine."[110] Thus, it was that the conflict over the leadership of the editorial board ended with the harshest accusation of all, namely supporting conservative-clerical positions: "Under the influence of conservative-clerical magazines, Ms Siedlecka was anxiously prepared to make various concessions."[111]

Whatever Siedlecka did or said, Wysłouchowa's interpretation of the clash reinforced and confirmed the polarization of the political public in Galicia into conservative-clerical and progressive-democratic sides. Different ideas were thus constituted as social opposites of political milieus: the milieu of the conservative nobility in connection with the institution of the church and the democratic milieu of the intelligentsia with the peasant population. To describe Siedlecka as influenceable not only disparaged her personally but also conveyed these political connotations.

Wysłouchowa responded to the suggestion from the editorial board with an ultimatum:

> When I saw that things were going badly, that I might even have lost the confidence of the people, I addressed the members of the

editorial committees in Warsaw, Poznań, L'viv and Kraków and gave them the following ultimatum: either I would relocate the magazine to L'viv or I would resign altogether. All the committees were unanimously in favor of relocation; however, Mrs Siedl. was offended, viewed the ultimatum as a vote of no confidence, and claimed that something decided by a congress could only be changed by a congress. It is not customary for me to snatch anything from anyone. That is not my style.... So I gave her *Przodownica,* which she had wished for so much, and resigned from the editorial board.[112]

Siedlecka was doubtless not entirely wrong to interpret Wysłouchowa's ultimatum as a vote of no confidence. The letters from the Kraków committee also speak a somewhat different language. Although the editorial board did not want to lose Wysłouchowa, they did not see themselves in a position to act against Siedlecka:

Since Mrs Siedlecka does not consider relocating *Przodownica* desirable or useful, and is only giving it up at the request of the majority of all the committee members, the Kraków committee regards the ultimatum as something that can't be helped.[113]

Nevertheless, the Kraków women kept in touch. In May 1900, the Committee for a Women's Rally in Kraków (*Komitet wiecu kobiet w Krakowie*) chaired by Siedlecka requested assistance from Wysłouchowa.[114]

How exactly the conflict between the women arose is difficult to fathom since the correspondence is not complete. Clearly, sensitivities were involved on all sides. At any rate, it is interesting with regard to two aspects: Wysłouchowa's claim to leadership and political polarization. The conflict was a power struggle between two competing leaders with different points of reference: the women of Kraków on the one hand and the peasant movement on the other. By arguing that conservative-clerical circles predominated and influenced Siedlecka, Wysłouchowa employed a central topos in Galician politics to denigrate her rival and cement her claim to hegemony—the polarization between a conservative and a progressive camp. The clashes constructed and confirmed the dichotomy by assigning to the camps the subjects negotiated in each case—in this case, feminist politics against peasantry-based politics. That same year, with the support of Orkan, Wysłouchowa founded *Zorza: Pismo miesięczne z obrazkami* (The Dawn: An illustrated monthly magazine), published from 1900 to 1904 as a supplement to *Przyjaciel Ludu*.[115] This manner of publication was sufficient to confirm its affiliation with the peasant movement. Like *Przodownica*, it was distributed not only in Galicia but also in other partitions in the country and abroad.[116] In 1902, Wysłouchowa had to resign her editorial position following the onset of heart disease.[117]

This describes the aspects of Wysłouchowa's feminist politics: Warsaw connections, patriotism, emphasis on education, focus on rural areas, the all-Polish perspective. She attended various women's meetings, conferences, and associations dedicated to essential topics of the women's movement. Nevertheless, she was not one of their leaders; on the contrary, when feminist faced political, by which she meant dedication to Polish independence, her position was clear, as was her claim to leadership in terms of progressiveness.[118] For Wysłouchowa, both the demands of the women's movement and her commitment to the rural population were part of her work for the nation.[119]

Writing

During the 1890s, Wysłouchowa began to focus more and more on writing and translating,[120] both of which were part of her political practice.[121] In addition to letters and articles for the magazines she coedited, she wrote numerous popular history booklets arguing that existing folk literature was naïve, banal, and conservative.[122] She complained that far from combating social disadvantage, it consolidated it. In her opinion, in order to be enlightening, folk literature needed to be determined by both an excellent knowledge of the people and inspiring love for them. Socio-political ambitions for the rural population were to be accompanied and supported by intellectual and cultural development, which in her opinion were ensured by a romantic, national history, stories of sacrifice and heroism, and of the participation of peasants in the uprisings. She began publishing popular stories to mark commemoration days in order to kindle peasants' understanding for the events and to inscribe the people in the collective memory of the nation. She wrote popular booklets about the Kościuszko Uprising, the May Constitution, several about Adam Mickiewicz, and other romantic poets, yet also about the likes of Emilia Plater and Emilia Sczaniecka.[123] Her style and ductus are apparent from the preface to the booklet on the May Constitution:

> This little book tells you about bright and sad moments in our past, especially the joyful rebirth of the sun, which after a long and dark night rose above our beloved fatherland and spread its rays of light and warmth.... Poland lives and will live!.... Numerous representatives of famous scholars, writers, poets and artists admired throughout Europe bear witness to its life. Millions of the peasantry testify to its life, who now lift their long-lowered heads and feel love for the depths of this precious soil, soaked with their blood and sweat.[124]

The poetic language, the direct, familiar address of the readership, the emotionality explain the May Constitution (the sun) as an achievement of Polish history and combine it with a cry for Poland, the expressions

"Poland lives" and "rebirth" originating from the language of the independence movement. Equating the achievements of the cultural and scientific elite with those of the peasant population constitutes a new, expanded concept of the Polish nation as represented by the peasant movement.[125] In addition, a sense of attachment to one's homeland (love for one's country) is explicitly combined with peasant sweat.

Many of the booklets began with a personal address to the readership;[126] they contained pictures, not only portraits of people but also of houses and villages, small vignettes that made the text more appealing. Wysłouchowa's writing style was very emotional, rich in references and images, poised between literature and history, as some subheadings already indicated.[127] Contemporaries repeatedly described her style as simple, understandable, and heartfelt, emphasizing that she regarded the peasantry as her equals and that she allowed them to participate. They recalled that Wysłouchowa addressed the peasants in a sisterly manner and did not show the arrogance usually displayed by the intelligentsia.[128]

In the commemorative publication dedicated to her, her eloquent use of language was emphasized right at the start:

> Maria Wysłouchowa possessed a tremendous gift and the art of the word. Her style was noble, simple, not tortuous, yet gilded with the glow of the heart, it was a precise expression of her crystalline spirit. And she was a born speaker. She talked the way she wrote.[129]

Her clarity and emotionality came in for special praise; the publication stated that she mastered both orally and in writing.

In her booklets, she built on the historical novel and popularized it as a folk tale.[130] In this respect, it can be classified under the "realistic idealism" of a Henryk Sienkiewicz emerging from the crisis of positivism, which understood history as consolation, as the "strengthening of hearts."[131] Witold Kośny describes neoromanticism as follows: "By combining historical disputes with conflicts in love, every historical event is upgraded to a personal test, and every private enterprise, no matter how personal, is given the appearance of a patriotic act."[132] Although Kośny had the conflicts more in mind, for Wysłouchowa, it was more about harmony, for the combination of history and emotions, the elevation of events through emotional charge applies to her writings. Literary research into Polish romanticism and neoromanticism emphasizes in general that the reference to the people or the peasantry as well as the use of vernacular language is to be understood as dynamic rather than conventional aesthetics: romanticism leads to opposition.[133] Gender studies argue similarly by viewing romanticism as an emotionally, femininely connoted countertradition against the norm of objective male rationality.[134] The parallels between these interpretations lie in the marginal position of gender or nation, from which the thesis of dynamic opposition is derived.

In the course of the scientification of history, the historical novel increasingly became a genre for those who were denied access to academic institutions.[135] However, the division between science and literature in the Prussian and Russian partitions was not as strict as in sovereign states, for the policies of Germanization and Russification prevented the consistent institutionalization of Polish historiography. History belonged to the nonpublic, private canon of education. Polish language, history, and culture were taught in nonpublic, partly illegal organizations, such as the "flying university" (*uniwersytet latający*),[136] with which Wysłouchowa was in touch in Warsaw. In Galicia, on the other hand, with its two Polish-speaking universities in L'viv and Kraków and corresponding history departments, the difference between a popular historical narrative and the scholarly program was more clear-cut. Educational initiatives there served to integrate excluded and disadvantaged people such as women and peasants. They did not constitute a nation against a foreign government, but against an elite regarded as conservative and clerical. It is obvious that Wysłouchowa's booklets could be connoted with the intra-Polish and thus intrasocietal opposition. Nevertheless, the Polish opposition movements in Galicia sought to establish themselves as part of an oppressed nation, as Wysłouchowa's comments on the cancellation of her trip to America made clear. The movements inscribed themselves in an all-Poland context of suffering and struggle.[137]

Wysłouchowa believed in the high value of emotional commitment.[138] She combined the creativity of opposition and marginality by nobilizing her heroic figures.[139] The central importance that the hero had for her writing is underlined by various titles of her works such as "Bohaterka" (The Female Hero)[140] and "Chłopi—Bohaterowie" (Peasants—Heroes).[141] Nature and language were united in the characters of romantic female and male heroes to form the utopia of a patriotic, participatory society.

Networks

The female hero was not just a figure in Wysłouchowa's stories, but also in her life, as her admiration for Orkan's mother, Katarzyna Smaciarz, shows.[142] In a letter to him, she sent her kindest regards:

> I ask you to convey to your mother that I have the warmest feelings for her. When I spoke at the Zakopane Congress about the rural woman as a mother, I had her first and foremost in my head and on my lips; her love and sacrifice were for me the most expressive arguments, because they were vivid and moving down to my blood.[143]

Wysłouchowa equated the ideal of a mother presented in her speech at the Women's Congress in Zakopane with Orkan's own mother. They

52   Finding Roles: The Participants

were both distinguished by what Wysłouchowa saw as the connection between life and work: sacrifice and love.

The emotionality with which she connected life and work is reflected in her letters to Sokolová-Seidlová. She explained her love and admiration to her several times, addressed her with pet names, raved about her blue eyes and her blond hair. "Again, I sincerely and warmly kiss your charming blue eyes."[144] And: "So steadfastly do I believe in the friendship and kindness of the precious, golden, hearty sister Vilma that... I boldly come to her, greet her with joy, and kiss her sweet blue eyes and golden hair."[145] Wysłouchowa visualized her affection for Sokolová-Seidlová; life and literature were fused into a unity—metaphysical connections were physically realized.[146] This romanticism was not unusual for nineteenth-century women's friendships. Wysłouchowa, however, interwove ideal and life in a far-reaching way, similar to how she interpreted the story "Dwa bieguny."[147] In her correspondence, she generally wrote above all about romantic idealizations of work, the village, the nation, and less about difficulties or mutual support in the face of disadvantages, and if she did, then at most about how they had been overcome.[148]

The reference to divergences remains: not all letters were equally romantic, neither were all texts. Wysłouchowa was also a close observer, especially regarding the gender issue. She was, for example, one of the few people to tackle excessive alcohol consumption among not only men but also women.[149] She dealt confrontationally with conflicts and problems relating to the orientation of her policies, such as the cancellation of her trip to America or her resignation from the editorial board of *Przodownica*.

Her activities were enabled by a large number of networks,[150] the threads of which were tied through correspondence[151] and at informal, personal meetings, and arranged while traveling[152] or even in the Wysłouchs' home, such as the above-mentioned all-Polish Women's Congress. Wysłouchowa corresponded with numerous other women, such as feminists and writers.[153] She was friends with Maria Werhyo and Kasylda Kulikowska, active in education, consulted Eliza Orzeszkowa, corresponded with Paulina Kuczalska-Reinschmit and Maria Konopnicka, Czech writers and activists in the women's and national movement in Bohemia, Vilma Sokolová-Seidlová and also Karolína Světlá,[154] as well as writers and journalists of peasant origin, particularly Władysław Orkan and Jan Wantuła. Her journals and editorial work also functioned as centers and nodes, allowing Wysłouchowa to meet activists who came to exchange views, publish, and edit, such as Jan Stapiński at *Przyjaciel Ludu*, and Bolesław Limanowski and Ivan Franko[155] at *Przegląd Społeczny*.[156] All these networks enabled and connected working relationships and friendships. For Wysłouchowa, they connected Warsaw, L'viv, Prague, and Poznań, Silesia, the Province of Poznań, the Kingdom of Poland, Lithuania, Livonia, and Bohemia, education, participation and nation, people and women. These multifaceted ties prompted her to narrate.

Her stories were widely read. The public picked up Wysłouchowa's romantic interpretation of writing, love, and politics. The romantic perception of Wysłouchowa, both as a person and of her works and projects continued.[157] Like her narrative style, the vivid, emotional quality of her language struck home with her audience. According to the description in the commemorative booklet containing contributions from friends and comrades, her funeral was attended by delegations from associations, organizations, and magazines from all over Poland, not only by the intelligentsia but of course also by peasant delegations and the schoolgirls she had taught.[158] They appeared with wreaths, flowers, and slogans and walked to the cemetery in L'viv together in a manner reminiscent of a demonstration, parade, and procession. Wysłouchowa was mourned as a hero of the Polish people, as a brilliant writer and speaker who had personified love of the people, who had spoken to the people as equal to equal, as a tireless worker who had sacrificed herself to the point of heart disease—and as an angel.[159] Orkan wrote in his obituary: "And if Bolesław Wysłouch was (and is) the spirit of the party, she was its heart."[160]

A story that reads as if it had been written by Wysłouchowa herself was told in the commemorative publication under the title "How She Loved the People" by an anonymous author introducing himself as "One of those whom she inspired to work."[161] He had been stirred by Wysłouchowa's booklet about the Kościuszko Uprising. Thereupon, he had wanted to improve his education to become a worker for the good of the fatherland. He had therefore traveled to L'viv, where he had met Wysłouchowa in person, who had even invited him (and his delegation), taken him seriously in their conversation, and treated him as an equal. With her support, he had been able to attend the teacher-training seminar, and had married a teacher.

The entanglement of literary and real heroes, of novel and life, was also adopted by Wysłouchowa's contemporaries. As Orkan wrote: "I would like to note that Orzeszkowa definitely did not pluck the patterns for the female heroes in her novels out of thin air; she must have met them in Lithuania. After all, Marja Wysłouchowa seems to me to be related in the spirit of these female heroes ..."[162] Another voice highlighted how impressive she was, "*[l]'enfant terrible* in the women's sphere of L'viv,"[163] comparing her manner to the explosive power of dynamite: "She travels through the Galician villages with a magic lantern with which she gives lectures on Polish history, illustrated with corresponding portraits and group scenes. In the philistine little women's world of L'viv, her name is synonymous with nitro-glycerine, bombs and dynamite."[164] Wysłouchowa's aim was to persuade the rural population to join political and in particular nationalist activity. Popular historical and patriotic publications were one of her central media. She brought life and writing together: just as she had admired Sokolová-Seidlová in her letters, she told of Mickiewicz or Plater, and reported to her husband and others about the life of the rural population. During her political work, she set various priorities and gradually found her way to her role, that of author.

Wysłouchowa represents the heroic narrative. She interpreted past, present, and future as a history of male and female heroes, as the search for the beautiful, romantic, and expressive. She brought together her contingent experiences—the loss of estates, change of language and place, illness—within a unifying history. The experiences of convergence culminated in narratives about adoration and love. The term "author" refers not just to her writing of numerous articles and popular booklets, not just to the writing of letters, but also to the fact that Wysłouchowa found her calling as an author. She was the author of not only her texts but also her life and politics. "Author" literally means that Wysłouchowa wrote, but also that she conceptualized and represented, interpreted and narrated her life like an author of a performance. The romantic female hero is a powerful plot, a narrative of the political. It can serve as a model for one's own life as well as for a life in letters. Wysłouchowa adopted this romantic mindset—as a narrative perspective, a life plan, and a perception of the world. Yet she also used it to translate and contextualize in order to shape and resolve differences, contradictions, and conflicts, and to set directions.

Dramatic Directing, or: Natalja Kobryns'ka and Books

Natalja Kobryns'ka was born in 1851 or 1855[165] in the village of Beleluja in southeast Galicia. Her family belonged to the Greek Catholic clergy[166] and she herself became an important Ruthenian-language writer who, apart from literary works, also wrote a great deal on feminist topics. In addition, she founded women's associations and was involved in socio-political projects. After the turn of the twentieth century, she increasingly concentrated on her literary ambitions. She died in 1920 in Bolechiv, a small town near Stryj (Figure 1.2).

At the beginning of the 1890s, Kobryns'ka wrote a short autobiography[167] for Omeljan Ohonovs'kyj,[168] a professor of Ruthenian language and literature at Emperor Franz I University in L'viv (*Uniwersytet imienia cesarza Franciszka I we Lwowie*), who published it with a number of revisions in his *Ystorija literaturŷ ruskoy* (History of Ruthenian Literature).[169] Given her consistent first-person perspective, Kobryns'ka's text about her own development steered by personal motives and conflicts can be assigned to the genre of confessional autobiographies.[170]

Kobryns'ka began by introducing herself as a reader who had obtained her knowledge from books. One of the first sentences was: "Even as a little girl, I loved to read it. Whatever book was at home, I read it; I

Figure 1.2 Natalja Kobryns'ka, Gazeta Den', 1900, Wikimedia Commons/ Unknown author/Public domain.

didn't always understand it, but I read it."[171] Her life story continued to be molded by reading experiences which, like awakenings, formed the basis of her socio-political identity. At 12, *Listy z Krakowa* (Letters from Kraków) by Josef Kremer[172] and "national fairy tales"[173] made such a deep impression on her that she stopped reading fashion magazines. The landowner, whose estate included her home village, opened her eyes to the "relations between women and men"[174] with the writings of Klementyna Tańska-Hoffmanowa.[175] Reading various classics categorized as realism "delivered" her from her "religious fanaticism."[176] Henry Thomas Buckle's *History of the Civilization in England*[177] strongly influenced her and was followed by Georg Büchner, Ernest Renan, Ernst Haeckel, and Charles Darwin. Her brothers provided her with Russian, German, and Polish literature, including by much-discussed socialist authors such as Mychajlo Drahomanov,[178] Bolesław Limanowski, Karl Marx, and Ferdinand Lassalle. Her husband brought her books by Ivan Turgenev and Nikolaj Gogol' from Saint Petersburg. Reading Ivan Franko's stories sparked her awareness of "nationalist interests."[179]

Kobryns'ka positioned herself in a broad international reading context; the enumeration sounds like a *Who's Who* of the European educational canon at the end of the nineteenth century. At home, however, she felt lonely with her insights. She found reading as frustrating as the conduct of the socialist circles in Galicia, whose radical criticism of society she rejected. Kobryns'ka emphasized in especially negative terms that the socialists and their environment looked down upon Ruthenian women as "more unenlightened than the peasant masses."[180] Once again, she acquired new awareness from a book, namely John Stuart Mill's *The Subjection of Women*, which at that time was part of the standard reading of European women's movements.[181]

A watershed in Kobryns'ka's life was the death of her husband. This turning point is reflected in her autobiography by a thematic change. She now focused on her own political and literary activities, which were also motivated by a kind of awakening. To overcome her grief, Kobryns'ka was taken to Vienna by her father for a period of time. While she was there, she was encouraged to write literature by Ostap Terlec'kyj, a leading activist in the Ruthenian student organization The Cossack Camp (*Sič*)[182] with socialist leanings. When she asked what she should write about, Terlec'kyj replied: "About what you say and how you say it."[183] With this aesthetic concept enshrined in the directness of speech, Kobryns'ka joined the contemporary literary trend of realism and placed her subjects in the Ruthenian environment in Galicia.[184] Recalling how she began writing literature, she stated that her first story was read out at a meeting of the Cossack Camp and was an immediate success, prompting her to continue writing.

According to her autobiography, Kobryns'ka was motivated to consider the woman question by a rally held in 1883 at which the Cossack Camp publicly demanded equal rights for both sexes and she was personally introduced to Franko, who from then on supported her literary and political ambitions. The meeting induced her to launch the Association of Ruthenian Women in Stanislav (*Tovarystvo ruskich žinok v Stanislavovi*). Since the "old clerical party,"[185] i.e. in Kobryns'ka's view the conservative, authoritarian wing had gradually gained the upper hand (she recalled), she was forced to resign and achieve her publishing ambitions together with the journalist and writer Olena Pčilka,[186] who lived in Kiev.

Finding herself in a transnationally constructed educational world, Kobryns'ka explained her political activities with her educational history: "Through literature I had arrived at an understanding of the position of women in society—therefore I wished to bring others onto this path as well."[187] Reading led not only to knowledge but also to political attitudes, feminist politics, and national consciousness. Reading, including fiction, guided the idea of one's self (by ordering thoughts) and of the world (by ordering impressions and observations). The knowledge acquired through reading resulted in specific interpretations that made it necessary to position oneself and others.

Kobryns'ka regarded transnational education as a strengthening of national orientation, as her characterization of Drahomanov shows: "Drahomanov, a man of European education, writes in Ruthenian, even though he speaks the most widespread Slavic language, and I really began to understand that the masses can only rise to universal culture and civilization on a national foundation."[188] Education was European, and was mobilized by representatives of the intelligentsia, in this case by Drahomanov, for the small disadvantaged nations by using not Russian, the "most widespread Slavic language" and above all the dominant language, but Ukrainian, which suffered discrimination and was banned in the Russian Empire.[189] The rural population, the socially underprivileged, could only become a better society and be brought to true civilization by returning to their own national basis. Civilization, in turn, was universally conceived. This connection between the individual and history constituted by education was reflected in the text.

The conclusiveness, the whole point of Kobryns'ka's autobiography stems from her awakening. The experiences of awakening drive the narrative forward as a creative motif and turn the chronicle of a life into a biography, an intrinsically logical context.[190] Educational aspiration becomes the supporting motif of the narrative and anchors the writer in a canon of knowledge; it proves to be an agent of discourses.[191] This context encounters a hostile world, which motivates political action, such as the founding of an association. Action results from the clash between internal and external logic, the balance of power in the world.[192]

Autobiographies are usually interpreted as being poised between historical and literary narrativity.[193] Written for a specific purpose, the factuality of Kobryns'ka's autobiography does not seem contentious. Her direction of her life was reflected in most biographical texts; her educational history and the stories about how she came to write and take up political engagement are repeatedly encountered.[194] The subject of her autobiography and the author were immediately assumed to be identical; the autobiographical pact between author and reader, as Lejeune calls the writing strategies for the identification of the author with the first-person narrator of an autobiography, was successfully concluded.[195]

Being part of Ohonovs'kyj's literary history, the text is more than just a life story. In it, the author also wrote her way into a literary canon, because a history of literature determines the texts and authors belonging to the canon. At the same time, Ruthenian literary history was a contribution to the establishment and codification of an independent Ruthenian language and nation in Galicia, both of which were highly controversial in the nineteenth century.[196] With the genre of literary history, Ohonovs'kyj adopted the means of representation of established literatures, the criterion required for inclusion in *The World Republic of Letters*.[197] An independent literary canon demonstrates disentanglement from other dominant literatures—in this case, Polish and Russian.

58 Finding Roles: The Participants

Furthermore, history connects literature to nation, not only through the adjective *rus'kyj* (Ruthenian) but also through a narrative that brings works and writers together into a collective.[198]

Kobryns'ka's direction of her life as literary is therefore certainly owed to the addressees and the place of publication. This also applies to the narrative about her adoption of an aesthetic of realism geared toward the vernacular. The motif of a love of books in early childhood also recalls, on the one hand, middle class educational conventions of the genre, while on the other hand, the motif of self-education and the elements of awakening are evocative of tales of escape from the closed Jewish world or writing conventions in workers' autobiographies, which included reading as a central practice of self-empowerment and the development of political engagement from one's reading experiences. They are conventions of social climbers of both genders.[199]

By joining a genre with a male connotation, and with the vision of a life as a profession and a vocation,[200] the autobiography conveys another message, namely resisting the discrimination of women and the discrimination or disregard of Kobryns'ka herself: the lack of institutional education for girls, the oppression of the female sex in Galician society, clerical attitudes to women, the provocative attitude of socialist circles and her surroundings in general. Kobryns'ka focused her perception of herself and the world around her on interpreting and directing. For example, she accused the women in the association of having a clerical mindset, thus placing them in a specific position, assigning them a role—in this case in the play "Publishing a Women's Almanac." The creative potential claimed by the actor in her autobiography resulted from conflicts. Disappointments were inevitable. This touched upon essential aspects of her biography: the pattern that determined Kobryns'ka's life story was that of artistic director, the person who assigned roles and shaped policy. One of Kobryns'ka's central subjects was the loneliness of insight as a plot motif. The loneliness underlined the conflict-ridden interpretations of society and led to positioning in politics.

Paths into Politics

Natalja Kobryns'ka's parents, Ivan Ozarkevyč[201] and Teofilja Okunevs'ka, came from established clerical families, i.e. from the Ruthenian intelligentsia. Kobryns'ka's grandfather founded a popular theatre in 1848 and worked on the first Ruthenian-language newspaper, *Zorja Halyc'ka* (Galician Star), which was also founded that year. In addition to his duties as a priest, her father was a member of the Vienna Imperial Council.[202] The eldest of five children, Natalja had a close bond with her father. Her three brothers went to the German- and Ukrainian-speaking high schools in Chernivtsi and L'viv and subsequently the University of Vienna (*Universität Wien*). By contrast, she (and probably her sister, too) was taught at home, at first by a teacher, then by her father and brothers.[203] A priest's household was an open house to which parishioners came with questions and problems;[204] Ozarkevyč's socially, culturally, and politically engaged household maintained a kind of salon or discussion circle, which was also attended by some of Natalja's brothers' fellow students.[205] The networks of people and thoughts stemming from her father's mandate stretched far beyond the village. As a result, Kobryns'ka had access to international literature and contemporary debates.

In 1871, she married Teofil' Kobryns'kyj, a graduate of a seminary and a musician,[206] whom she had met during meetings in her parents' house and with whom she had intensively discussed social work, women's emancipation, and socialism. They planned several joint projects, including a translation of *The Subjection of Women* into Ruthenian.[207] However, when Kobryns'kyj died in 1882, Kobryns'ka had to return to her parental home, now in Bolechiv, where her father had taken over a new parish. After the death of her husband, she began her literary and organizational feminist politics. She wrote her first two stories in Vienna, "Pani Šumins'ka (Obrazok z žyttja)," what literally means "Lady Shuminska (A Picture from Life)," translated as "The Spirit of the Times," and "Zadlja kusynka chliba," translated as "For a Crust of Bread."[208] Both dealt with the living conditions of women from the Greek Catholic clergy, including the lack of employment and educational opportunities as well as arranged marriages—key topics of the European women's movements, which also determined Kobryns'ka's life and work.

Via her connections to the Cossak Camp, Kobryns'ka had got in touch with the Radicals—a group which had emerged from the Young Ruthenians and Ukrainophiles and was joined by figures such as Ivan Franko, Mychajlo Pavlyk[209], and Ostap Terlec'kyj. They were inspired by Mychajlo Drahomanov's concepts of rural socialism and founded the Ruthenian-Ukrainian Radical Party (*Rus'ko-Ukraïns'ka Radykal'na Partija*) in 1890. The women's politics of the Radicals was to become a point of contact and friction for Kobryns'ka's entire political, journalistic, and literary work.

About a hundred women joined the above-mentioned Association of Ruthenian Women founded by Natalja Kobryns'ka in 1883.[210] In line with her ideas,[211] it was decided to educate women through literature, inform them about their position in society, and also finance a women's publishing house. This work was intended to bring together women from different social backgrounds and be non-partisan.[212] Stanislav was chosen because the Association of Ruthenian Ladies (*Obščestvo ruskych dam*), which carried out educational and socio-political work, had existed in L'viv as early as 1878. Money was raised by means of lotteries, evening entertainment and tea dances to finance the Ruthenian-language girls' lyceum of the Basilian Order in L'viv as well as dormitories for female pupils of municipal schools.[213] With its projects for girls' higher education,

60 *Finding Roles: The Participants*

the association set itself goals that were both supported at that time by female religious communities active in education policy and in particular propagated by women's movements.[214] With her own association, Kobryns'ka sought to counteract the largely Russophile and ecclesiastical orientation of L'viv's women.[215]

After just a short time, there was opposition to her within the Stanislav association for whatever reasons, be it her anticlerical attitude or the dominant manner with which she strove to impose her opinions. Things came to a head when she tried to realize her plans to publish the first women's almanac with Ivan Franko,[216] who had been dogged by a reputation as a dangerous subversive ever since he had been convicted in 1878 in the L'viv socialists' trial together with siblings Mychajlo and Anna Pavlyk[217] as well as Ostap Terlec'kyj.[218] But Kobryns'ka's style of leadership was also problematic, for her letters from Bolechiv were understood by the women as decrees (*ukazy*).[219]

The conflict over the publication escalated, at least in Kobryns'ka's view, when in 1885 a faction in the association campaigned for a school and a dormitory for rural girls instead of the women's publishing house. This position was supported in an article in *Dilo* (The Deed), the Ukrainophiles' organ. Kobryns'ka was so outraged that she wrote to the editors:

> The [school project] really comes at such a time that it could be a fatal blow to the association's original aims because it looks as if our society is demanding nothing more than the lowest basic knowledge for women. The association has great existential fears, that is true, but it has not yet had time to become stronger. What a great achievement it would be for such an important organ as *Dilo* if it were to be involved in its [the association's] downfall.[220]

Her comparison of the weak association with the strong (important) *Dilo* was of course meant ironically. The competition between two educational projects, almanac versus school, forced Kobryns'ka to set out her position: she railed against the school, saying it would teach only the "lowest elementary knowledge," and ennobled her own project as a higher goal. Later on in the letter, she made herself the focus of her argumentation:

> I honestly and openly admit to having founded the association with the intention of arousing the woman question in Galicia, and you yourself know, sir, what elementarily [poorly] educated people I am dealing with. Among my neighbors there is not a single woman who even understands this question. They are trapped in a vicious circle, like sick people who want to live but do not know how to help themselves. Because I myself am unhappy, I wanted to help my sisters, and that is the sin for which I may be stoned! At first I thought I would gather them beneath the banner of literature, because I realized that this might be a way to enable the question to be explained

to them—which is based on the historical fact that in times of political bondage, literature is a refuge of freedom, such as in France in the eighteenth century. I knew that my ideas for my women were unclear, hidden in gloomy mist, but I counted on time, patience and help from well-meaning men.[221]

Kobryns'ka placed herself above the Galician women, whom she regarded as little educated, and on the one hand on the side of *Dilo* and the "well-meaning men" with whom she constituted a knowledge community. On the other hand, she constructed a community of misfortune with the women, "her sisters," to legitimize her ambitions. In addition, by referring to France, she indicated her own education and argumentation skills. She presented her historical knowledge and placed the conditions in Galicia in a European context. What is striking is the egocentricity of this passage, into which the role as artistic director—apart from irony and tragedy—can be read. And at the end, following the appeal to the men, she set out her main request with rhetorical skill:

This is not a quick fix; how can you expect any rapid, visible results from just one person if you don't give her any support at all? I therefore ask you, sir, to hold back the school projects in Stanislav only until I have managed to collect, compile and publish the women's almanac, which was approved by the committee on the second day of the month, meaning I have already begun collecting material. This will not take long, and then come what may. I predict the downfall, I just wanted to remember my dreams close to my heart, which may later find an echo and more approval.[222]

Her ambitions as a writer may well have played a role in the propagation of the almanac, but judging by the letter, she also regretted the lack of like-minded people to help her achieve her goals. Kobryns'ka regarded herself as the artistic director of politics on the road to a better society, to her "dreams close to [her] heart," and had already cast the roles in the play: the women to be enlightened by reading her almanac and the men providing support.

However, her position as artistic director was not secured. The association no longer concerned itself with the almanac, even though it had originally been adopted as one of its objectives. Instead, it used part of the money raised for an offering to the new Greek-Catholic bishop appointed in 1885. Kobryns'ka complained to Franko: "Those Stanislav women are truly unbearable! They plan to buy a silver platter for the bishop."[223] It is impossible to state whether the religious women had prevailed, the gift was supposed to demonstrate their patriotic directing, or was a deliberate blow against Kobryns'ka.[224] However, this rivalry highlights the complexity of political positioning in the context of different discursively formed collectives and rhetorics as well as diverging practices and traditions. Apart from the ecclesiastical orientation, Kobryns'ka may also have been put off by the parish links, which was not her way of organizing things. She sought intellectual women who shared a socially critical attitude freed from social ties, from which a new collective "women" was to emerge, an attempt to create a new female elite.[225] Kobryns'ka was dismissed as chair and resigned from the association. She financed the almanac independently with her coeditor Pčilka, partly by offering subscriptions. Final editing was done by Franko.

Peršyj vinok: Žinočyj al'manach (The First Garland: A Women's Almanac)[226] came out in 1887. It contained texts by women from Galicia and Eastern Ukraine, including Lesja Ukraïnka,[227] Pčilka's daughter, who was destined to become one of the best-known female poets writing in Ukrainian. The almanac featured journalistic and ethnographic texts, novellas, sketches, poems, and stories. The stories dealt with arranged marriages, what it was like for women studying in Zurich, and the multiple burden suffered by female workers. The ethnographic studies addressed the *zadruha* (rural community), a family structure of the Boykos analyzed as patriarchal, and the unhappy situation of rural women. Women's lack of freedom was examined by using wedding rites and songs as examples. Another article described the customs of the Hutzuls as a national culture.[228] Kobryns'ka set aside the most space for her own writing. She included two short stories—"The Spirit of the Times" and "Pan Suddja: Obrazok z žyttja" (The Judge: A Picture from Life), translated as "The Judge"[229]—as well as articles on the women's movement, Ruthenian women in Galicia, married middle-class women, and (in another demonstration of her position) the goals adopted by the Association of Ruthenian Women in Stanislav when it was founded. The analyses of the patriarchal conditions in rural areas did not go down well everywhere as they revealed the critical attitude of the authors. Nevertheless, the almanac was also received positively.[230]

In 1887, Natalja Kobryns'ka accompanied Sofija Okunevs'ka, her younger cousin and friend, who had lived with the Kobryns'kyjs for some time,[231] to Zurich, where she was to study medicine. Okunevs'ka went on to become the first female doctor in Galicia and one of the first women from the Habsburg Empire to obtain a doctorate.[232] In Switzerland, Kobryns'ka contacted activists in women's movements, collected material on the woman question, studied socialist theories, attended lectures on political economics, and was personally introduced to Drahomanov and Limanowski while on a trip to Geneva.

Rivalry

A prominent theme in Kobryns'ka's activities and publications was the rivalry between Polish and Ukrainian women.[233] She was furious about an assembly of Polish, Jewish, and Ruthenian women organized

Finding Roles: The Participants 63

by *Narod* (The Nation), the organ of the Radicals, at the end of 1890 in support of the demand for universal and secret suffrage because it was "an advertisement for the Polonization of society in Galicia."[234] Instead of in Galicia, she therefore made contacts in the wider surroundings, above all in Prague. In spring 1891, she asked the lawyer Mykola Šuchevyč, who was traveling to a meeting of Slavic youth in Prague, to speak about the woman question in his lecture on behalf of Ruthenian women. She backed up her request by explaining that it would be good for a man to take up this cause, adding that she could not expect much from the women, who did not understand her. She sent Šuchevyč a lecture she had written and put pressure on him in several letters to convey her opinion. Simultaneously, she flattered him by appealing to his male authority. She also invited him to Bolechiv since there was no one there who understood her.[235] Kobryns'ka's approach reveals much about her view of herself: her complaints about the lack of support from Ruthenian women, her search for external approval, as well as her manipulative abilities.

That summer, a delegation of about 200 Ruthenian women, including Kobryns'ka, traveled to Bohemia together with a choir named L'viv Fighters (*L'vôvskij Bojan'*). The occasion was the General Provincial Centennial Exhibition in Prague, where the group visited a pavilion designed by the Czech ethnographer František Řehoř featuring Slavic folk art and related artefacts.[236] Afterwards, the choir undertook a concert tour of the country.

According to Kobryns'ka, the tour was a complete success. Ukrainian flags were hoisted at the railway stations, while the women (dressed in traditional costumes) were welcomed with flowers and greetings like a political delegation. This direction as an honorary, almost state reception underlined the Czech and Ruthenian claim to national representation, to recognition as an equal nationality within the multi-ethnic Habsburg Empire, a message addressed to the Germans in Bohemia, the Imperial Council in Vienna, and the Galician *Sejm*. Whether the message actually arrived is another matter; at any rate, further ovations at railway stations were banned.[237] More importantly, this event demonstrated the participation of women in the project of a nation and above all generated its political significance with the symbols of an act of state. Both the Ruthenian and the Czech women viewed their action as just as political as some of the demands issued by male-dominated political parties.[238]

In addition to concerts, the tour program included visits to museums, libraries, and women's projects, including kindergartens and home economics schools as well as the first girls' lyceum founded by the Minerva women's association, to which a high school had been attached that very year.[239] The trip enabled Kobryns'ka to establish networks with feminist and female nationalist activists, and women writers from Bohemia and

64   Finding Roles: The Participants

Bukovina. Among the Czech women were Vilma Sokolová-Seidlová and Eliška Krásnohorská.[240] Collaboration during the tour with Jevhenija Jarošyns'ka, a teacher, writer, and translator from Bukovina, was to last even longer.[241]

Apart from a description of the reception and the visits, the travelogue Kobryns'ka wrote for the Ukrainophile literary magazine *Zorja* (The Star) largely concentrated on how men and women conducted themselves in public spaces. For example, she described how "a Ruthenian woman" (she was probably referring to herself) stood up to a male opponent of women's education in conversations at an evening reception. She reported how Krásnohorská had explained her strategies for dealing with influential men: "And do you have powerful, energetic women among you [Ruthenian women] who can stand up for the cause? ... You're tragic figures... You don't possess the most important weapon, namely laughter."[242] The travelogue can partly be read as stage directions, so to speak, on how women could strategically behave when it came to enforcing their demands as well as for posture and body language in a male-dominated public environment.

In addition, the journey served to direct Slavic and women's friendship. The tension between nation and gender seemed to be eliminated, even if the intra-Galician rivalry between Ruthenians and Poles remained. After her trip to Prague, Kobryns'ka began corresponding with Sokolová-Seidlová, and expressed herself in this vein on several occasions. Shortly after her return, for example, she wrote: "However, I can boldly state that the Czech women did not find such warm acquaintances among the Polish women as they did among the Ruthenian women. The Poles are a terribly jealous people and claim to be the first among the Slaves."[243]

The essentialization of the disputes about institutional dominance and the politics of the Polish elite preserving the status quo as national characteristics tallied with contemporary thinking about the formation of national identities and alterities as well as the intensity and emotionality of their language: "They [the Poles] are striving to become a highly cultural people at all costs, but what results is wild conservatism, terrorism and lies, lies, lies,"[244] was her comment in early 1907 on the intensified nationalist conflicts between Polish and Ruthenian students at L'viv university.[245]

When Kobryns'ka heard of petitions from Czech and German-Austrian women's movements calling for the right to attend regular university studies, she herself organized her own. Called "Petition by Ruthenian women from Galicia and Bukovina for women to be admitted to regular university studies and for the creation of at least one high school for girls in Galicia," (*Petition der ruthenischen Frauen aus Galizien und Bukowina um Zulassung der Frauen zu den Universitätsstudien und Creirung wenigstens eines weiblichen Gymnasiums in Galizien*) she gathered 226 signatures from her immediate and wider environment, and it was submitted to the Imperial Council in 1890 by her father, Ivan Ozarkevyč.[246] For Ozarkevyč, campaigning for higher education for women probably served to demonstrate the Ruthenians' opposition and their readiness for action. Given the increasing severity of nationalist disputes over electoral groups, votes, schools, and language policies, an attempt was made in 1890 to reach a Ruthenian-Polish agreement that would hopefully put an end to the practice of hampering each other when it came to the organization of educational institutions, electoral organizations, and economic development.[247] This agreement was initiated by Galician governor Kazimierz Feliks Graf Badeni and the spokesman of the Ukrainian Club (*Ukraiński Klub*) in the *Sejm*, Juljan Romančuk. However, it finally lost its authority following the attempted assassination of Badeni's successor, Andrzej Graf Potocki.[248] Ozarkevyč rejected the agreement from the outset as in his view it represented an expansion of Polish hegemony. In Kobryns'ka's view, the petition was also a sign of Ruthenian readiness to act. She stressed several times that Polish women had not yet organized a petition for women's higher education.

Kobryns'ka brought back from Prague a proposal for a new type of women's assembly, which took place on September 1, 1891 in Stryj. It was attended by 40 women, including Jarošyns'ka. One of the items on the agenda was a revision of the petition, reformulating it as an appeal to all women regardless of nationality and faith,[249] while Kobryns'ka first tabled the idea of kindergartens and communal kitchens. By doing so, she expanded her spectrum of feminist engagement to embrace social work which, in the context of professionalization efforts, was also one of the central pillars of European women's movements.[250] Kobryns'ka gave lectures and produced several publications about these institutions, which she expected would reduce the burden on rural women and free up time for education and (political) activity.[251]

On April 10, 1892, another gathering took place in L'viv, this time with Polish and Jewish women. Kobryns'ka reported on educational efforts and the woman question in general and in the world, raised the need for a joint petition for university access, and proposed an association to run a girls' high school modelled on the Czech Minerva. Although all her motions were accepted and a committee was elected, which included Kobryns'ka, the projects never came to fruition.[252] Only her speech about kindergartens was published as a separate booklet that same year.[253] According to Bohachevsky-Chomiak, women's cooperation did not work because Kobryns'ka fought against Polish hegemony while Polish women feared being accused of a lack of patriotism from the Polish community.[254] Nevertheless, the Polish-dominated Galician suffrage committee that was named Equality for Women Committee (*Komitet Równouprawnienia Kobiet*), which was accepted into the International Woman Suffrage Alliance in 1913, also included Ruthenian women's organizations.[255] The rivalry between the national organizations was

66 *Finding Roles: The Participants*

probably not the only reason why the petition failed, especially since collaboration with Polish women was only sporadic; Kobryns'ka's arguments with the Radicals are likely to have been another contributory factor.

Conflicts

Kobryns'ka's most protracted conflicts were with the Radicals. Her disputes with them over her most important concern—a place of publication by and for women—were just as intense and polemical as her comments on Polish women. The dispute concerned on the one hand the type of publication—another almanac based on *Peršyj vinok* model or a periodical—and on the other hand the role of the Radicals, including the women in their close environment. The Radicals argued for a periodical to assert their influence and perhaps also their leadership.

Pavlyk tried to establish a regular column in the Ukrainophile magazine *Bat'kôvščyna* (Fatherland)[256] entitled "From the Life and Work of our Women,"[257] albeit edited by Jarošyns'ka rather than Kobryns'ka. However, he failed to overcome the resistance of the editorial board and a lack of interest in the topos. At the rally in 1891, Kobryns'ka successfully proposed founding a women's publishing house and another almanac. Fundraising activities were approved and a committee appointed. But although the almanac had been agreed, it failed to come about because of the Radicals who—especially Pavlyk—promoted the idea of a periodical instead under the leadership of the party entitled *Rivnist'* (Equality). The title was evocative of social democratic women's publications, such as *Równość* by female socialists in Kraków[258] and *Die Gleichheit* published by German female social democrats, both titles also translating as equality. Franko, too, spoke out in *Narod* in favor of a party-led magazine, euphemistically referring to it as "a little help from men": a periodical would bring more profit, it could be partly written by other women (i.e. not just those who had been intellectually educated), and it would unite the participants. He tried to persuade Pčilka to support such a project behind Kobryns'ka's back. Since the latter did not want and would not be able to edit a magazine from Bolechiv, the opportunity for a showdown had arrived. The Radicals demonstrated that they could also play a role in women's politics without Kobryns'ka.[259] In the end, however, they failed to receive the final backing of some of the women involved, who considered a project without or even in defiance of the most important person in Ruthenian feminist politics to be out of place and unenforceable. In the end, therefore, *Rivnist'* was not published. This was a mark of Kobryns'ka's importance. But the *Rivnist'* affair also showed that, although an autonomous women's policy did not prevail, it was nevertheless a factor that self-styled progressive groups could not ignore.[260]

The disputes took place on various levels. First of all, pragmatic positions were adopted: Kobryns'ka countered Franko's arguments regarding profit and the participation of poorly educated women by stating that she could not edit a periodical from Bolechiv. Both thus implicitly insisted on intellectual and organizational leadership among women. Then the level changed to the national stage: Kobryns'ka criticized the Radicals for working with the Polish socialists. Pavlyk held up the activities of Polish women as a model for female Ruthenians and appealed to them to work with Jewish and Polish women.[261] Finally, more fundamental arguments were leveled: Kobryns'ka accused *Narod* of disregarding women's activities and reporting on them far too late (or not at all), while Pavlyk slated *Peršyj vinok* and in particular her articles. When Jarošyns'ka complained about a lack of support from the Ruthenian press in the early 1890s, he became confrontational again, claiming that *Narod* published everything it received—but that Kobryns'ka hadn't delivered anything.

The fact that women striving for access to male-dominated areas was perceived as (and in part actually denoted) rivalry meant that the situation in Galicia was no different from the debates and conflicts involving other socialist and social-democratic movements.[262] The Radicals as well as the women around Kobryns'ka (and Kobryns'ka herself in particular) believed themselves to be representatives of the most progressive section of society, the political avant-garde. The movements argued about "first place," about the how and where of society, about the power of interpretation over "modernity," "progress," and "civilization." What both sides had in common was intellectual leadership and the high importance they attached to education, despite Kobryns'ka's own views about its forms, as her stance against the school project of the Association of Ruthenian Women had shown. True, the Radicals demanded active and passive suffrage for women and men as well as equal access to education, academia, and university. But Kobryns'ka's ideas of the autonomy of feminist politics and the priority of gender antagonism met with resistance, as reflected in the publishing question as well as what educational institutions should take priority.

Another element the Radicals and Kobryns'ka had in common was economic interpretation: the latter considered the material independence of women to be the paramount goal in all classes.[263] She thus assumed a fundamental gender antagonism, whereas the socialist-oriented Radicals assumed class antagonism. This resulted in different demands: economic independence for women coupled with access to academic education and to all fields of employment as far as Kobryns'ka was concerned, and emphasis on workers' protection and the demand for equal pay for equal work among the Radicals. Their mental and performative ideas therefore differed in some centrally constructed points—and this was the arena of feminist politics. In this context, the direction of Ruthenian-Polish rivalry also had the function for Kobryns'ka of opposing the intellectual circles around the Radicals that still advocated cooperation and internationalism in the early 1890s.

Politicizing the Private Sphere

The fierce conflicts with the Radicals were preceded by Kobryns'ka's rejection of Pavlyk's unexpected proposal of marriage in December 1888. After all, Pavlyk was one of the critics of marriage as a middle-class convention and coercion. Kobryns'ka also greatly admired his story "Rebenščukova Tetjana," in which he expressed his criticism of marriage.[264] From his correspondence with Drahomanov's wife, it appears that Pavlyk had hoped that marrying Kobryns'ka would intensify their collaboration. He courted Kobryns'ka by proposing moving to L'viv, where the libraries would have been open to her and they would both have benefited from working together. He had apparently not even entertained the idea that she might turn him down and accused her of fearing being associated with an "antichrist" condemned as a socialist.[265] The marriage proposal drove a wedge between Pavlyk and Kobryns'ka.[266] From then on, he withdrew his previous support for her projects and literary works not only in private letters but also in public. Whether this was a case of affronted male vanity or peasant honor hurt by rejection by a socially superior woman is a moot question.[267] Kobryns'ka spared neither her accusations regarding his conduct in her letters nor her criticism of the Radicals in her journalism.

Some years earlier, Franko had already attempted to trial new forms of relationships between the sexes.[268] In 1880, he planned to set up a commune in the countryside. The members included Ol'ha Roškevyč, his lover at the time, whose parents would never have allowed her to marry Franko because he was a socialist, and Volodymyr Ozarkevyč, a brother of Natalja Kobryns'ka. Against the background of his own unhappy love, Ozarkevyč agreed to formally marry Roškevyč so that she could leave her parents. A house in the countryside had already been found, but the project failed when Franko was sent to prison again.[269] Pavlyk's ideas of marriage could be interpreted as an attempt to transfer the industrial or peasant working couple[270] to the intelligentsia. Franko's project, by contrast, idealized the compatibility of (male) genius with (female) love and all it entailed.

Kobryns'ka shared the contemporary criticism of marriage as a material arrangement or forced wedlock and, to back up this view, cited the dichotomous separation of work and family life and their assignment to the male and female spheres. She condemned the enlightenment model of middle-class sexual stereotypes[271] as an ideological pattern that was conservative and hostile to women. She criticized the lack of communication between spouses living in separate spheres and the choice of partners of Ruthenian men, claiming they married either intellectual Poles or women who were beneath them solely as providers of physical satisfaction and housework.[272] Given the ill-fated affair between Franko and Roškevyč and the resulting commune experiment, she therefore initially applauded Pavlyk's criticism of the conventions of marriage.

Later on, after the relationship with Pavlyk had soured, Kobryns'ka criticized the Radicals as advocates of free love (*volna ljubova*), referring again to his above-mentioned story. She claimed that for the Radicals, free love was the first and possibly only goal of women's emancipation. As long as they remained dependent on the opposite sex, this would mean women "being humiliated even more and turned into a toy for men."[273] Kobryns'ka declared that, by contrast, she was fighting for women's economic independence from men. She was not alone in this criticism. She shared the position adopted in the course of debates in the women's movements about a new morality between the sexes that free love served above all male desire and left women unprotected.[274]

To illustrate Kobryns'ka's disagreements with the Radicals, in his biography Ohonovs'kyj published excerpts from letters in which she criticized their views on relations between the sexes. Pavlyk was incensed again by the publication of the letters and tried to refute the accusation of propagating free love. Even in 1905, the matter was still so important to him that in the preface to his edition of some letters from Drahomanov to Kobryns'ka, he asserted that neither he nor the Radicals had regarded free love as the central goal of women's emancipation. He continued that the Radicals had never understood free love to mean "uncontrolled aberrations—an ancient human sin," but instead interpreted it as love free of constraints. He even pointed out that he himself had not had "a single woman on his conscience" for ten years.[275] By choosing the preface to Drahomanov's letters to Kobryns'ka, Pavlyk crossed the line between private and public. He switched from his editorial role to that of himself and slipped into the style of a letter. True, Pavlyk stood alongside Franko at the focus of public polemics against the Radicals, who had been criminalized and despised as socialists. "Immoral lifestyle" was a common insinuation or accusation used to disavow them. Even so, this "stylistic incongruity" went beyond self-defense. He drew attention to the meanings and (utopian) hopes associated with this theme as well as to differences, discussions, practices, and misunderstandings.

Kobryns'ka idealized the spiritual harmony of the couple, two personalities facing each other as subjects. In her autobiography, she described her relationship with her husband as very exclusive:

> I didn't even share my thoughts at all ... with other people. My books set me apart from them a little; I noticed that they were starting to find me strange. I fell silent and slowly came to the conclusion that I almost lived in two different worlds: in one I lived with the

people, and the other I had for myself and my husband, a patient listener for my fantasies and a source of loving comfort after bad experiences.[276]

She used the image of two worlds, placing herself and her husband on one and her surroundings on the other. She made her reading experience, which no one but her husband shared with her, a criterion for distinction. She did not feel she belonged to other intellectual groups, the socialist circles, either, although or because what she criticized about them—their exclusive identity—was something she evidently shared. In 1898, she took stock in a way in a letter to Osyp Makovej, the editor of *Literaturno-naukovyj vistnyk* (Literary Studies Courier): "There was only one person who knew how to curb me, and that was my husband."[277]

Franko sought muses, Kobryns'ka a mentor.[278] She never remarried after the death of her husband. Her correspondence with Franko clearly shows the difficulties of keeping a balance between a mentor and preserving independence. In 1885, during the preparations for the women's almanac, she complained that he did not reply:

> I write you a letter, ask something or other, and wait impatiently for an answer. And as soon as I start waiting, I wait and I wait until I can't wait any more. And finally the answer arrives, I open it, and realize that you have not answered everything, only a few points. I already feel that I am beginning to have the same respect for you as I have for most men. That is why I have not written to you what I should have written to you a long time ago.[279]

Kobryns'ka perceived Franko's silence as an imbalance between them, which she expressed quite clearly. She, for her part, ironically threatened to conceal important matters and to demote Franko from the high position he had held in her eyes. She wasn't looking for guidance; she was looking for support.[280]

The simultaneity of personal and political aspects of the disputes about gender relations culminated in Pavlyk's and Kobryns'ka's polemics about free love. Kobryns'ka's denunciations of material dependence and social inequality banished free love to a utopia, a place represented as male that did not or could not exist.[281] There was no place for women there as long as they remained economically dependent.[282] Kobryns'ka's utopia, on the other hand, was the harmonious relationship of couples who were in tune with each other. The criticism of middle-class marriage and the options of free love or partnership were metonyms for social utopias and political goals, controversial precisely because they started from similar assumptions. But of course, expectations of leadership and subjugation also resonated—on both sides.

Writing

In 1892, Kobryns'ka took up the publishing question again. Following the resolution adopted by the rally, she arranged collections of money in all parts of Galicia and Bukovina. However, after the disagreements over the ill-fated *Rivnist'*, she did not work with Pčilka again. Instead, this project strengthened contacts with Ol'ha Kobyljans'ka,[283] a modern Ukrainian-language writer from Bukovina who is still important today, with whom Natalja Kobryns'ka had become friends.[284] The first product of the publishing house she managed known as Women's Library (*Žinočna Biblioteka*), the three-volume *Naša dolja. Zbirnyk prac' riznych avtoriv* (Our Fate. A collection of works by various authors), was published in late 1893 in Stryj, and in 1895 and 1896 in L'viv. The volumes were financed by subscriptions and donations.[285]

Kobryns'ka recruited new authors for *Naša dolja;* only Hanna Barvinok[286] had already been involved in *Peršyj vinok*.[287] The proportion of literary texts had also grown, and a new column—reviews of foreign publications—was introduced. Rural women wrote in all three volumes, which included poems translated from Yiddish. Under the title "News from Home and Abroad,"[288] Kobryns'ka and Kobyljans'ka reported on women's movements in European countries and America. Dedicated women and their literary successes, their ethnographic collections and their activities, as well as the Ruthenian women's associations founded in Galicia from the 1880s onwards were described in detail.[289] Long articles were devoted to the political context of the woman question and its proponents and opponents in the Habsburg Empire.

Of course, Pavlyk also railed against *Naša dolja*. He wrote that in literary and political terms, it was weaker than *Peršyj vinok*, something which in his opinion came as no surprise considering that Galician women were still particularly uneducated. In this context, he reproached Kobryns'ka for her criticism of the Radicals and sarcastically presented her as unreasonably hostile to men: "[A]nd here, Mrs Kobryns'ka has lost all this [an objective view] due to her hatred of men who interfere in a matter in which she considers herself a specialist... But it is necessary [for Kobryns'ka to pull herself together] if she does not want to gamble away her divine gift."[290] Although the impact of Pavlyk's public polemics can barely be assessed, Kobryns'ka's influence on the circles of young Ruthenians definitely waned. In the 1890s, she was still a well-known figure among Ruthenian speakers in Galicia. She spoke at various anniversaries, for example to celebrate Drahomanov's 30 years of writing in 1894 and Franko's 25years of work in 1898.[291] But *Naša dolja* sold badly. Above all, the Ruthenian women proved to be independent; the associations founded around 1900 managed without Kobryns'ka. In 1893, when the Club of Ruthenian Women in L'viv (*Klub Rusynok u L'vovi*) was founded, she had been asked to open it. But 15 years later, her importance had declined. For example, she was not involved in the first Ruthenian-language women's magazine *Meta* (The Goal), launched in 1908. This decline in importance can be interpreted as a conflict between generations—or as the assertion of socialist feminist policy influenced by party politics, as Bohachevsky-Chomiak believes. Both aspects were closely related.[292]

Kobryns'ka took care of her parents until they died in 1903 and 1904. She then moved to L'viv to press ahead with new publications and the establishment of a federation of Ruthenian women's associations, but soon returned to Bolechiv.[293] Biographical literature speculates about the reasons for her rapid return. On the one hand, it is attributed to her resolute, uncompromising conduct; on the other hand, it is claimed that she was far too ahead of her time (and even more so her place, i.e. Galicia). She herself described the events in a letter to Sokolová-Seidlová thus:

> The statutes [of the association] had already been ratified when something happened that convinced me that nothing could come of it. That completely devastated me, because it seemed to me that the last thread that connected me to Ukrainian womanhood had been torn. Everything became repugnant to me and my soul was so hurt that I do not even want to touch it and now can only write about it with difficulty, out of gratitude for your kindness to me.[294]

Once again, Kobryns'ka described a conflict as a dramatic attack on her person; this time, not even the cause could be identified.

In Bolechiv, she dedicated herself to local projects, including a kindergarten and a reading room.[295] In particular, she now concentrated on writing. Under the influence of Wacław Moraczewski,[296] the husband of Sofija Okunevs'ka, who was in touch with *Młoda Polska* (Young Poland), a group of artists in Kraków, she began to search for new avenues in literature.[297] She turned to symbolism, wrote stories about supernatural phenomena, popular beliefs, providence, the unconscious.[298] Like other Ukrainian-language authors, such as Kobyljans'ka, she thus sought a connection to the European trends of literary creation at the turn of the century, to classical modernism.[299] Kobryns'ka's adoption of symbolism was accompanied by her estrangement from the Radicals and, in literary terms, from Franko who, as one of the most successful writers and a leading figure in Galician literature, sharply criticized the aesthetic orientation of *Moloda Ukraïna* (Young Ukraine).[300]

In 1912, Kobryns'ka began publishing a new series on women's literature with a focus on translations, again under the title Women's Library. Works by for instance Czech writer Karolína Světlá and the 1911 winner of the Nobel Prize for Literature, Maurice Maeterlinck, were published.[301] During the First World War, Kobryns'ka's writing became more realistic again, and her output included a cycle of war novels.[302] She now worked together with the much younger Ol'ha Dučymins'ka, with whom she was also friends, on translations for the Women's Library and published other stories as well as literary studies and reviews.

Networks and Friendships

Despite repeatedly complaining about too few visitors and too much work,[303] Kobryns'ka was very well connected and had a large library. She cultivated relations through correspondence and maintained an open house in Bolechiv, where she received members of the intelligentsia from L'viv and Vienna. She also had many contacts in Eastern Ukraine and Bukovina, partly because of her publishing work. She was close friends with Kobyljans'ka, Okunevs'ka, and Jarošyns'ka as well as with Hanna Barvinok and her husband Pantelejmon Kuliš.[304.] She corresponded with the Drahomanovs, Sokolová-Seidlová, and other Czechs active in the national and feminist movement, literature, and journalism.[305] She, like Wysłouchowa, was immediately charmed by Sokolová-Seidlová. This was her conclusion in her report on the Prague trip: "Nevertheless, two women, Vilma Sokolová and a Ruthenian woman, who had devoted herself with all her soul to the understanding heart and soul of her new friend during this short time, bade farewell the most cordially."[306] By addressing in the published report the friendship that had developed on the trip and stylizing it as its end point, political cooperation became a "spiritual" connection between women. Although even Wysłouchowa and Kobryns'ka knew each other, they are unlikely to have been in close contact.[307] Whether they knew that they both corresponded with Sokolová-Seidlová is unknown.

Many of Kobryns'ka's ties were severed not because of the lack of contact, but following disagreements, for example with Pčilka, Pavlyk, and the women in the Association of Ruthenian Women. In 1900, she wrote to the Eastern Ukrainian writer Ivan Nečuj-Levyc'kyj:[308] "With the feminist cause, I have angered so many people and endured so much untruth because of them that despite all my willpower, I feel I am beginning to lose faith in myself."[309] At home, Kobryns'ka was dependent on postal communication, which explains the urgency with which she demanded replies from Franko, for instance.[310] Like Wysłouchowa, she also organized publications and text editing by letter, and described travel experiences and political events. Furthermore, her letters served the purpose of communication and discussion about her interpretations of the world. She sought support for her views and approaches, and complained about confrontations and conflicting assessments and opinions.

Kobryns'ka's letters reflect the artistic director from a subjective perspective, as shown in particular by the correspondence with Franko over the years. While at first responding to him with gratitude for his interest and encouragement, in later letters, a sense of rivalry with other female writers emerges: "I am really surprised by your severe assessment of me as well as the merciful indulgence with which you assess other women."[311] The letters to Franko deal with suffering: suffering over writing, life in the provinces, rejection, and the lack of attention. Despite political and literary differences, she kept in touch personally and in correspondence with him and his wife for years, and also became the godmother of their children: political and private matters did not always go hand in hand. It could be claimed that Kobryns'ka's letters represent comments or footnotes to her published texts—footnotes in the sense of her own commenting genre.[312] In other words, her letters and journalistic texts communicated with each other, and although they did not mirror each other, occasionally their style and content overlapped. The letters were part of Kobryns'ka's self-presentation as artistic director, part of the direction of the power of interpretation and self-determination, such as her literary and journalistic texts as well as her organizational activities.[313]

Kobryns'ka's political engagement was aimed at a Ruthenian feminist movement in line with her ideas, but she also worked closely with the socialist-oriented Radicals, which repeatedly led to disagreement. She set out her views, analyses, and aims in the almanac *Peršyj vinok* and in the three-volume *Naša dolja*, in several articles and a series of literary stories. In Malančuk-Rybak's view, Kobryns'ka was a representative of liberal feminism with social demands and an eye for sociopsychological change in gender relations.[314] She therefore emphasizes Kobryns'ka's critical attitude toward socialists and considers her classification to them in the historiography unfounded. In fact, Kobryns'ka was in direct conflict with the Radicals precisely because she expected their support seeing as she shared a number of their views. Kobryns'ka had discussions with the Ruthenian intellectual milieu about the fundamental autonomy of feminist politics as well as about relations between the sexes. She commented on the life plans discussed there and defended her own ideas of love and marriage. However, her political goals also contradict Bohachevsky-Chomiak's thesis of a feminism anchored in the community in Galicia.[315] Kobryns'ka did not succeed particularly well in rooting herself in the community; instead, she was on the lookout for intellectual, independent, and radical women.[316]

Kobryns'ka took up the plot of "Women's Emancipation," which was circulating throughout Europe and, inspired by a broad spectrum of ideas on feminist politics, successfully directed her own interpretations and readings. However, casting the roles proved tricky. The actors involved brought stubbornness, different interpretations, and often their own audience with them. The themes or subjects of direction—association or publications, community work or ideological enlightenment—turned into contested, symbolic places of political positioning in Galician society. Kobryns'ka was convinced of her own power: "I developed my ideas myself without any help from men, through my own life and originally through my own experiences."[317] Dučymins'ka attributed this power to her in her memoirs. Bringing progressiveness to Galicia is a difficult task, because "[n]ot only men, but also many women are on the side of tradition and custom."[318]

Above all, however, Kobryns'ka was the artistic director whose politics shaped visions for society: "Alongside Drahomanov, who brings the social question to us, and Franko, who modernizes our literature, Kobryns'ka provides the modern, necessary slogan of women's emancipation."[319] An artistic director deserves recognition, acceptance, and subordination. Kobryns'ka fought, but alliances and compromises were not one of her strengths. The design of her political vision was complex, set by possibilities and limits, resistances and conflicts. The complexity reflected in the connections between life and work, the oscillation between public and private. What is meant by this is not a realistic aesthetic or socio-historical interpretation in the sense of shaping literary and political work according to the experiences of life, but conversely the relationship between life and work.

Kobryns'ka suffered, she suffered from her creative abilities, from her insights, from her narrow-minded environment: "This constant reading of books led me into different phases of spiritual development, sometimes bringing joy, but mostly restlessness and pain. I know I suffered a lot when I began to become acquainted with the school of Positivists."[320] Throughout her life, she did not feel sufficiently supported, not even or especially not by women, and therefore insisted that she not be honored after her death.[321]

Theatrical Enacting, or: Rosa Pomeranz and Charisma

Rosa Pomeranz was born in 1873[322] in Tarnopol in Eastern Galicia. She died in 1934 as Róża Melcerowa in L'viv, where she had moved with her husband, Isaak Melzer, in 1908 (Figure 1.3).

From the 1890s, Rosa Pomeranz worked for the Zionist movement in Galicia, founded Zionist women's associations, and was a delegate to the Zionist World Congress in Basel. From the beginning of the twentieth century, she centralized Zionist women's associations and was active in educational and social work projects. Following the introduction of women's suffrage after the First World War, she was elected to the *Sejm* of the Second Polish Republic as a deputy representing the Zionist movement and remained active in social policy. She wrote a series of stories for Zionist magazines and programmatic articles on women's policy. In the 1920s and 1930s, her publications were primarily feminist.

76 Finding Roles: The Participants

Figure 1.3 Rosa Pomeranz. 1936. In Pamięci Róży Melzerowej, [edited by Sabina Feuersteinowa, Berta Jegerowa, and Henryka Schreiberowa], n.p. L'viv: printed by Koło Kobiet Żydowskich, by kind permission of the National Library of Israel.

After her death, the Jewish Women's Circle in L'viv (*Koło Kobiet Żydowskich we Lwowie*), which she herself had founded in 1908, brought out a commemorative volume containing memorabilia and obituaries by friends and companions. Emil Sommerstein, a deputy at the *Sejm*, presented his recollection of her as a series of images:

> I see her in different stages of her activities. ... I see her with a special glow in her eyes when she set off for Western Europe to organize

Finding Roles: The Participants 77

relief for war orphans ... I see her, a quiet, modest persevering worker when the gate of the Polish parliament opened in front of her as the only Jewish woman ... I see her when, despite the serious illness of her irreplaceable husband and her own illness, despite many personal worries, she had lost none of her mental vivacity, of her high, true, universal human culture.[323]

Sommerstein visualized Pomeranz in various activities. "I see" creates a vivid impression of physicality, characteristics, and activities; his use of repetition elevates his individual recollections into (political) signifiers. Her social work projects, her activities as a deputy and wife are outlined. Sommerstein connected the political movement, the institution, and her private circumstances. Yet the phrase "I see" also activates the role of the audience. The sequence of images turns the snapshots into a performance, into interaction between actor and audience. A comrade from the Jewish Women's Circle also emphasized the interaction: "I precisely remember the level and mood of our meetings; a productive spirit always prevailed... After all, each of our actions was guided by Róża Melzer's strong, formative will, determined by awareness of the goal."[324] By sketching a scene, the author emphasized Pomeranz's leadership role. Meanwhile, another female voice summed up her memories as follows: "A person with a lively spirit and unusual initiative, Róża Melzerowa was a born fighter."[325]

For posterity, Pomeranz was a tireless politician, a charismatic initiator and leader, a faithful companion and wife, a born fighter—a female hero. Being a role model entails corresponding character traits, which were then also listed by her friends and companions: perseverance, friendship, wisdom. All these memories served to highlight the person and her actions, to emphasize a life of self-sacrifice dedicated to war orphans, politics, her husband, and "Jewish youth, especially Jewish girls."[326]

The commemorative volume lays a "documentary trail"[327] about Pomeranz in the context of the history of the Zionist movement. In it, her parental home is characterized as a "Zionist house," the center of an "old-new nationalist ideal."[328] Her parents, her brother, her sister, in fact the whole environment was permeated by the spirit of Zionism. The publication also creates a role model and constructs a narrative in which the female hero was active: that of the Zionist movement in Galicia and the Second Polish Republic.

The importance of memories for national movements has frequently been stressed.[329] Accordingly, the commemorative volume can be interpreted as a memorial for Zionism in Poland[330] or as an attempt (one of many) to contribute to the restoration of the group memory of Jews, which has been perceived as eroded since the Enlightenment.[331] It represents the creation of a tradition, which connected the period before, during, and after the First World War—the partition era and the reestablishment of Poland—and constituted a Zionist continuity in the new state.[332] In this narrative, Pomeranz became a central figure of Zionism from the end of the nineteenth century until the 1930s.

But the hero of the commemorative volume is a female hero. With Pomeranz, the publication constructed a traditional story of emancipation inasmuch as it recalled her political activities, her assertiveness, and her creative powers, culminating in her election as a deputy to the *Sejm*. The precondition for this narrative was the notion that a movement like Zionism had granted women new opportunities, giving them access to areas from which they had traditionally been excluded. The Zionist World Congress had indeed met the demands of campaigning women and at its second assembly in 1898 granted them active and passive suffrage, a political gesture that was not entirely meaningless since at that time this was a right, which existed in hardly any countries.[333] One of the leading representatives of the movement, Rozia Ellmann from Romania, stressed: "The Jewish woman has been given a seat and a voice in the council of men. This *right* granted to her also imposes on her the *duty* to use all her strength to support this great work."[334] The combination of rights and duties was a widespread rhetoric in not just national but also feminist movements to legitimize claims to equality and political activity. By citing this combination, movements implied or promised a change to society as a whole, not just the enforcement of particular demands.[335]

However, the commemorative volume also testifies to the connection between femininity and domesticity when the home is emphasized as a shelter for Zionism and a field of female activity, and the sacrificial attitude of the wife is stressed. Conceptions of femininity in national movements have often been analyzed as ambivalent, oscillating between mothers and fighters, between the nationalist upbringing of new generations and a committed, journalistic, social, political, and (less often) armed public deployment.[336] However, the divergent narratives are not just explained by the fact that Pomeranz was an exception, one of the few women to be remembered. They also reflect the complex meanings of gender in national movements in general and Zionist movements in particular, including their complicated debates about equality and difference, modernity, and tradition.

Various strands of debate intersect in the recollections: women's equality, their place in Zionism, the place of Jewish history in the memory and the family. They open up a perspective on the complexity of a life for Zionism, which included organization and mobilization as well as social work projects and the goals of the women's movements, and also affected private life, friendship, and marriage. Given the social engagement of the first female deputy and this self-sacrificing wife, all these strands came together in Rosa Pomeranz. Her variety of roles highlights the performative aspect of making politics. The memories represent discursive intersections and also the deeds of a female hero; here, the emphasis is on the deeds. The female hero as a narrative figure and an extraordinary character points to *agency*,[337] to the performative and the ritualized, to the roles and the spectacular dimension of political engagement, yet also to the participation of the audience. The biography of Pomeranz shaped the pattern of the performer, who was aware of the performance of political discourses and practices as well as the significance of charisma.

First Enactments in Zionism

The Pomeranz family belonged to the middle classes; Rosa's father was a bank clerk.[338] In addition to eight years of school, Pomeranz took private music lessons and was introduced to the German language and literature by her father. She then went to Leipzig, where she received private piano lessons for a year[339] before enrolling at the Royal Conservatory of Music (*Königliches Konservatorium der Musik zu Leipzig*).[340] There are partly conflicting details about her higher education in contemporary literature. Under her matriculation number, we learn that she spent a year at the conservatory studying the piano, music, and composition theory, and Italian, and also attending lectures on the history and aesthetics of music. The commemorative volume, on the other hand, mentions that she spent three years studying, taking not only music and drama but also several foreign languages.[341] It is possible that in her first years in Leipzig, she received private acting and language lessons alongside private piano tuition. At any rate, she was destined to prove her acting abilities in her political activities.

In 1906, Rosa Pomeranz married Izaak Melzer, an official in the railway administration who, like her, was active in the Zionist movement and, like Teofil' Kobryns'kyj and Bolesław Wysłouch, was described as a loving, faithful partner who was full of understanding for her aspirations and work.[342] In 1908, the couple moved to L'viv where, like Pomeranz's parents, they ran a Zionist house where like-minded people enjoyed social gatherings.[343] The only time that Pomeranz went to Palestine was to attend the opening of the Hebrew University in Jerusalem (*ha'universita ha'ivrit biruschalayim*) in 1925. There are no indications of immigration plans; solely Thamar Buchstab Awi-Jonah recalled letters in which Pomeranz allegedly declared that she had once wanted to emigrate, but her plan had been thwarted by material difficulties.[344] In the final years of her life, Pomeranz cared for her seriously ill husband. He died in 1933 and a year later she, too, passed away.[345]

Pomeranz's rise to become a charismatic politician can be traced through the regular columns containing brief news on associations and events in the organs of the Zionist movement, in *Die Welt,* and in the

Galician magazines *Przyszłość* and *Wschód*, in which she was mentioned from the 1890s onward. She began her career with musical performances at various public festivities to mark Jewish holidays, in particular the Maccabee festival so important for the Zionist movement.[346] In 1895, she played the piano in L'viv[347] and in 1899, it was said of a celebration in Stanislav: "Miss Pomeranz" deserves "special merits" for the musical part of the celebration.[348] For the first performance by the Harp (*Kinor*) academic choir in 1901, she composed and accompanied a song performed by Wilhelm Flama-Płomienski, a future professor of singing.[349]

In 1895, Rosa Pomeranz organized a Maccabee celebration in Tarnopol, where she also declaimed a poem in German and performed a sonata by Ludwig van Beethoven. At that time, her name was already well known: there was talk of a committee headed by "the famous artist Miss Pomeranz." Her appearance was described as follows:

> Miss Pomeranz, accompanied by Mr. C. Wolfsthal, had barely stepped out when a torrent of applause broke out, although that was nothing compared to what followed her masterful performance of Beethoven's brilliant sonata! There was no end to the applause and shouts from the audience, but the most beautiful prize for the artist was two magnificent bouquets of real flowers. She deserved this prize not just for her artistic playing, but also for the zeal with which she supported the Zionist movement and with which she used her efforts to organize this recital.[350]

In addition to the praise, it is remarkable in this report that music by Beethoven was played and flowers were presented to the artist—a perfect, secular, and edifying evening of music for the middle classes. The Zionist context in which the evening was to be perceived was determined by the appearance of the report in the section headed "Maccabee celebrations." The description was typical. It was reported that classical, occasionally folkloric music, recitations of poems and a "tendency speech" were performed, amounting to aesthetic enjoyment with a Jewish and Zionist touch.

Shortly afterward, Pomeranz appeared as a passionate speaker. According to the description of a Hanukkah celebration in Kołomyja in 1899, she combined physical presence with rhetorical talent:

> After the introduction by Dr Rosenheck, Miss Rosa Pomeranz, invited from Tarnopol, arrived at the podium. Delicate and of noble facial features, with a calm but extremely pleasant voice, extremely vivacious, she made the very best impression on the audience. She stepped onto the podium, and within a few sentences she had pierced everyone present with her enthusiasm. She spoke about the needs of the Jews, about the aims of Zionism, about our few enemies and not

least about the position of women in our movement. The speaker presented to us an excellent picture of all the sufferings and thorns of life, especially of Jewish life, not arguments drawn from random works, not stereotypical phrases, but reality, our terrible reality, declaimed so vividly, so perfectly, so rationally and so confidently that it seemed as if this truth described in such colorful, vibrant words was palpable. Other participants of the evening also tried to measure up to the standard of Miss Pomeranz's excellent, carefully composed speech.[351]

Her speech was made powerful and vivid merely by virtue of her appearance and her voice, which conveyed emotion. However, the speech itself is reproduced in a stereotyped manner of the type in which it was allegedly not given. Readers were left in the dark as to exactly what the "suffering and thorns" and the "terrible reality" referred to. According to the report, the effectiveness of the presentation consisted precisely in the obviousness of its content.[352] The report published in *Die Welt* about the same celebration sounds similar:

> She [Pomeranz] began with a complaint about the suffering of the Jews, continued with a strong accusation, and concluded with an unsurpassed, unprecedented, convincing and penetrating portrayal of Zionism. The women's movement played an outstanding part in the speech; she described so gracefully, so powerfully and in a manner which touched the heart the need for women to enter the movement that no one could escape the forcefulness of her speech. Her speech was followed by stormy applause which did not want to end.[353]

Once again, Pomeranz's rhetorical brilliance is emphasized; once again, the readers learn nothing about the content of her speech. Instead, the focus is on its effect. The ambiguity of the terms "women's movement" and "movement" referring not to an autonomous feminist movement but to working for Zionism underlines the emotional perception. The Zionist aspect and the importance of the event were assured not by the reproduction of the content, but by the applause of the audience and above all by the place of publication, the organ of the movement.

In 1903, Pomeranz gave the official speech at a popular celebration in Bielsko organized by the women's and girls' section of The Dawn (*Haschachar*) Academic Association, as always with great success: "Jubilant applause followed her words and numerous applications for membership corroborated the impact of this speech." The celebration ended with dancing, which kicked off with a "waltz composed in honor of Miss Pomeranz."[354] Elsewhere, her rhetoric is described as "perfect in form and yet folksy"[355] and, similar to Wysłouchowa, her closeness to the audience is emphasized. Pomeranz clearly understood how politicking worked: the interweaving of knowledge and pleasure, of compassion and indoctrination. The emotionally moved audience and its applause turned voice, character, and speech into a Zionist performance. The content of the speeches and their main arguments hardly ever played a part.

In the late-1890s onward, Pomeranz began using her appearances at festivities to encourage the founding of Zionist women's associations and circles, another focus of her political work. Mind you, she was not the only one to do so, and not even the first. As early as 1888 and 1893, agitation evenings for ladies took place at the L'viv Zion Association (*Stowarzyszenie Syjon*).[356] On March 1, 1899, about 200 women gathered in Kołomyja to hear Pomeranz speak "about the need for a women's organization with convincing, fiery words."[357] For her "great merits," she was made an honorary member by the club of Jewish students in Kołomyja, a fact which *Die Welt* considered worth reporting. The Rachel (*Rachela*) association for women and girls was not founded until 1901. Once again, 200 women attended and Pomeranz gave another "uplifting speech."[358]

She founded the Judith (*Iudyta*) women's association in Tarnopol, her hometown, surprisingly only in 1903, but then shouldered its management. According to the report in *Die Welt*, its original membership was 190 women. The inaugural evening began with an "excellent welcoming speech" by Pomeranz and ended with dancing. It had close ties to the local student association known as Bar Kokhba[359] and regarded itself, at least according to a report in *Wschód,* as Jewish rather than Zionist, despite or precisely because it was chaired by Pomeranz, a well-known Zionist. Its aim was to guide members toward Zionism by a combination of enlightenment and raising awareness so that at some point the association would declare itself Zionist. Moreover, after a devastating fire in a small neighboring town, it was one of the first associations to organize a Jewish evening and donate the proceeds to the victims. This marked the start of another aspect of Pomeranz's dedication: organizing relief campaigns after severe emergencies, from which she later developed social work and educational projects.

Travel and agitation were part of the practice of Zionist politics. In some cases, deputies traveled from one place to the next on a daily basis to give lectures, motivate the associations, integrate them into the organizational structures, and register their money collections.[360] Between 1898 and 1900, Pomeranz visited almost all of Galicia's important towns to encourage the establishment of women's associations.[361] Traveling as well as the subsequent media coverage connected small associations in small towns with large associations in large towns. As a result, discursive and concrete networks emerged. However, the activities also made individuals such as Pomeranz well known and turned them into mediators who not only explained convictions, demands, and goals but also represented personal nodes and couriers in the networks. These networks conveyed the political aspects of individual events and a tangible collectivity: a movement.

Pomeranz was an acting talent. Her enactments were successful, her name the program, summoning up as it did the image of a tireless, successful, convincing female politician. Hardly any reports failed to make mention of her organizational, artistic, and rhetorical talents.[362] The events themselves and their coverage in the corresponding organs created a sense of belonging and thus clearly defined the community that was presented. Her posture, character, and voice generated the significant aspects of the event. The reports also refer to another aspect of performativity: just as what a registrar has to say is performative only in a registry office, the Zionist aspect of an event only occurs at an event held by a Zionist association. The reports in the Zionist organs were performative insofar as they made the festivities into a Zionist contribution by means of the place of publication.

The Expansion of Organization

Although the association reports about Pomeranz give the impression that her activities were limited to traveling and "tendency speeches," she also campaigned for social work initiatives, for a league of women's associations, and their positioning in the movement as a whole. The projects she initiated and carried out in the first few decades of the twentieth century mainly involved nationalist education and vocational training. In 1908, after moving to L'viv, Pomeranz founded the Jewish Women's Circle, which she chaired until 1926.[363] The association operated various educational institutions. Its activities focused on girls and women, although it taught Hebrew and Jewish history to both sexes. Another main goal was the organization of a nationwide league of Zionist women's associations, and a corresponding attempt was first undertaken with the participation of Pomeranz in 1903.[364] She was involved for two years, during which time 12 more local women's associations were founded by the Women's Circle.[365] In 1910, it initiated a conference at which the National Jewish Women's League of Galicia and Bukovina (*Narodowo-Żydowski Związek Kobiet z Galicji i Bukowiny*)[366] based in L'viv was established with Pomeranz as its chair. The umbrella organization united a considerable number of Zionist and national Jewish women's associations and groups.[367]

The disagreements at the founding assembly of the National Jewish Women's League resulted from two hotly debated topoi: the demand for the autonomy of women's political organizations and the orientation of Zionist work in Galicia.[368] It was not just in the Women's League that the adoption of the Basel program was a bone of contention. At the First Zionist World Congress in 1897, the program was adopted, which laid down the aims of the movement—the "creation of a national home in

84 Finding Roles: The Participants

Palestine" and the means for its implementation—ranging from diplomatic efforts to establish its own territory (the term "state" was avoided) to the strengthening of Jewish nationality in the diaspora as a prerequisite for a "national home." Although the program was a compromise between *Gegenwartsarbeit* (contemporary work) i.e. local politics in Galicia, colonization in Palestine and political Zionism, i.e. the diplomatic efforts of Theodor Herzl and others, and endeavored to integrate the various currents, the disputes over the fundamental orientation of Zionist politics remained. By signing up to the Basel program, the Zionist organizations decided against an autonomous policy, joined the movement, and subordinated themselves to the central organizations.[369]

At the founding assembly of the National Jewish Women's League, the extent of integration was debated on the basis of whether participation in the shekel collection for the National Fund should be a prerequisite for membership.[370] A strong minority vehemently demanded that joining the Zionist World Congress be linked to an autonomous federation of women's associations. In the end, the assembly decided to join immediately with the compromise of wanting to promote a federal and autonomous consciousness, and agreeing to carry out shekel collections to prove members' Zionist sentiments. The League thus acquiesced to the policy of the World Congress, something which is also supported by the fact that Pomeranz sent the minutes of the meeting to *Die Welt*.

The debates over autonomy versus integration are reminiscent of Kobryns'ka's arguments with the Radicals. In addition, they also reflect discussions about women's strategies and goals in the Zionist movement after they had been granted suffrage in 1898. For example, that same year, a women's assembly was held in Drohobycz with several male speakers discussing the role of women in the movement.[371] "Female Zionists from Stanislav" wrote in an "Appeal to Jewish Women" (*Odezwa do kobiet żydowskich*) that they should not cease women's struggle as happens in "happier nations" because although they might win as women, they would lose as Jews.[372] The goal was not the emancipation of women, but a Zionist policy. A response from "L'viv Zionist" immediately appeared in the next issue:

> Is emancipation only an expression of the happy and contented?... It is a fact that when we stand in the ranks of the Zionists in the defense of the nationalist cause, we emancipate ourselves because, as Professor Schapira rightly stated at this year's Basel Congress, "While we strive for Zionism, we are also striving for women's emancipation."[373]

The rivalry between feminist and Zionist concepts—or the rivalry between the collective of women and the collective of Jews—was decisive for the activities of female Zionists.[374]

Pomeranz's activities in founding associations and leagues and their integration into the Zionist World Organization testify to her orientation toward the structures of the movement and her talent for organization and implementation. By founding a women's league, she succeeded in activating Zionist women in Galicia and giving them a voice, a presence in the movement, as well as integrating women's demands, while conversely persuading women to adopt the Basel program and preventing autonomous organizations.

After the merger of the Zionist associations in Cisleithania in 1901, Pomeranz joined the regional executive committee of the Tarnopol district in Galicia.[375] She participated in the debate about means of successful agitation, spoke about national education, and represented women at various banquets.[376] In 1911, she was elected as one of the few female delegates for the district of Eastern Galicia to the X World Congress.[377] At a women's assembly during the Congress, she gave an overview of the goals of an organization of Zionist women and called for the merger of the existing women's associations, which was recommended in a resolution adopted by a large majority to the plenum.[378] Her eloquence and rhetorical abilities apparently also went down well with an international audience, judging by the coverage, which spoke of an "extremely interesting, theoretically and practically fundamental lecture" followed by a "very lively debate."[379] However, it would be a few years yet before a worldwide women's league was founded; the Women's International Zionist Organization was established in London in 1920.[380] In 1926, Pomeranz was one of the co-organizers of L'viv branch.[381] She stood as a candidate again for the XI Basel Congress in 1913 but was no longer elected.[382]

Social Work Projects

In the First World War, Pomeranz increasingly turned to social work policies. She was prompted to campaign for children's homes, care and education, training centers, and employment opportunities for girls by the hardship suffered by refugees. As early as 1903, she had campaigned for the victims of the Kishinev pogrom, then in the Russian Empire. Upon the outbreak of war, the National Jewish Women's League and thus also Pomeranz became active in the ad hoc rescue committee founded in L'viv, including building a soup kitchen[383] and workshops for girls.[384] After emigrating to Vienna due to the war, Pomeranz began supporting Jewish refugee children from Poland.[385] She soon returned to L'viv to set up a soup kitchen with a laundry and a disinfection facility, an outpatient clinic for children and a kindergarten.[386] When the Zionist organizations resumed their work in 1916, she was elected to the L'viv local committee.[387]

In 1919, she traveled with Flora Rothfeld to Switzerland, France, Great Britain, and the Netherlands in order to establish contacts in Jewish

86   Finding Roles: The Participants

philanthropic circles and raise money for war orphans and pogrom victims. Rothfeld described the trip as quite adventurous since they set off without any money or accommodation, had to obtain travel documents en route, and also had to deal with antipathy toward East European Jews. They financed the trip with donations and by selling their jewelry, and obtained recommendations from one organization to the next. Furthermore, Pomeranz gave lectures and published articles.[388] Rothfeld particularly emphasized her talent for performing:

> Her outward appearance, perhaps too elegant for our proletarian-gypsy circumstances, found recognition and resonance in the sphere to which we were to appeal... Melzerowa's lecture in the large Paris synagogue gathered the Jewish elite of Paris and was a great success for her.[389]

Not only her performance in Paris but also the trip as a whole raised a great deal of money, enabling a building for the Jewish Women's Circle[390] as well as an agricultural training enterprise for Jewish girls in Stanislav to be financed and workshops in L'viv to be supported.[391] The building became a center of Zionist social and educational work and political agitation.[392]

In 1922, Pomeranz was nominated for the constituency of Stanislav as a candidate of the Zionist Organization in Poland (*Histradut ha-Tsyonit be Poloniah/Organizacja Syjonistyczna w Polsce*)[393] and elected as one of the first female deputies and the only Jewish woman in the *Sejm* in the interwar period.[394] She represented the Jewish Circle (*Koło Żydowskie*), the association of Jewish *Sejm* deputies, at conferences of national minorities as well as the Jewish women of Poland at various international congresses.[395] She ran again for the *Sejm* in 1928 and 1930 but lost.[396]

Also as a deputy, she was particularly involved in social work, including in the Commission for Work and Social Welfare (*Komisja Pracy i Opieki Społecznej*).[397] She was vice-president of the Central Land Committee for War Orphan Care (*Centralny Krajowy Komitet Opieki nad Sierotami Wojennymi*)[398] and was engaged in child and youth welfare under the auspices of the Jewish World Aid Conference (*Jüdische Welthilfskonferenz*).[399] Furthermore, she was the founder and curator of a Jewish orphanage in L'viv, a member of a Jewish primary schools association and of an association that ran training workshops.[400] In a Women's Association (*Zrzeszenie Pań*) of the Leopolis humanitarian association (B'nai B'rith), Pomeranz drafted the statutes and also initiated lectures and evening events. In 1925, she established the first home for Jewish children with multiple disabilities in Poland in Bojanowo in the Poznań voivodeship on the border with the German Empire. Vocational training was offered there—housework, sewing and handicrafts for girls, printing, bookbinding and shoemaking for boys—while Braille, reading, writing, arithmetic, and drawing were also taught. In addition, importance was attached to teaching religion, although the educational and medical care of the children took center stage.[401] The home in Bojanowo had to close again after a short period of time due to financial problems when a fundraising trip to the United States of America undertaken by Pomeranz was not as successful as her previous trip through Europe.[402] But after she had managed to find donors in Warsaw, the home was relocated there in 1934 and named after her.

Considering her organizational work as a whole, it is striking that since the turn of the century and increasingly after 1918, her activities shifted from founding Zionist women's associations with cultural activities and prestigious educational programs to social work projects in children's welfare (especially for girls) with training programs. The projects were supported by associations and included health, education, and family support for youngsters of all ages, i.e. a traditional area of social work activities which in the 1920s and 1930s was developed into community and state welfare in Poland and many other European countries.[403]

Before the First World War, Pomeranz repeatedly advocated emigration to Palestine as the only promising solution to the social and economic problems of Judaism; she thus strengthened practical Zionism, i.e. support for settlement projects. As her activities and initiatives show, another focus of her work was the creation of training opportunities for girls and young women from the lower and lower middle classes in the diaspora. After the war, she participated in a variety of social work projects at various levels. Her experience of the misery suffered by refugees in Vienna and L'viv may have been a contributory factor, although the main reason was the power to act she had as a politician and a deputy.[404] She apparently used her opportunities of established, legitimized politics. The newly founded state also opened up opportunities for development and organization, hopes for the achievement of a better future, which were only disappointed as time went on by growing anti-Semitism and the increasing exclusion of non-Polish minorities.[405] Pomeranz had professionalized her enactments from a piano player starting out in the movement's cultural program to a politician.

Writing

Another important focus of Rosa Pomeranz's politics was publications. She wrote in German and Polish and produced several propaganda texts, numerous stories, plays, including *Matka* (The Mother), which premiered in L'viv, and two novels, *Im Lande der Noth* (In the Land of Need) and *Król Chazarów* (The King of Chazars). She wrote for various Zionist magazines, especially *Die Welt, Przyszłość, Wschód*,[406] and *Ewa: Tygodnik* (Eve: A weekly), a women's magazine published in Poland between 1928 and 1933.

In small episodes, her short stories tell of the suffering of the Jewish people in the diaspora; they are didactic pieces or parables that ultimately always lead to Zionism.[407] Her combination of history and story was praised in the commemorative volume: "In images with bright colors and deeply pulsating emotions, she drew the tragic story of a diaspora nation embodied in the twists of an individual or a family."[408] Her poetry developed in the realization of the plight of the Jewish population in Galicia and their struggle, just as a large part of her political engagement had been directed at tackling hardship and crises. In contrast, her most important goal, the recruitment of women, remained conspicuously unspecific in her fictional literature. Generally speaking, there are relatively few female heroes in Pomeranz's stories, and in contrast to her journalism and organizational projects, women's issues are hardly addressed except in her novel.

Mark H. Gelber classifies Pomeranz under German-speaking cultural Zionism, which he places in Berlin and Vienna, the Zionist centers of the German and the Habsburg Empire, citing her stories in *Die Welt* and the novel *Im Lande der Noth,* which was first published in German.[409] According to Gelber, cultural Zionist writing contains a double message. Beneath the manifest and programmatic message about pride and Jewish identity, a latent message about suffering in a hostile environment is also contained. This contradiction (Gelber continues) will only be resolved once a nationally aware Jewish life has been established, a good example of which is provided by *Im Lande der Noth*. However, given her many Polish-language texts, exclusive attribution to German-language cultural Zionism is not convincing. Moreover, the suffering in Pomeranz's literature is not latent, but manifest. There are therefore some arguments in favor of multiple connections, for example alongside cultural Zionism also to Polish-speaking non-Jewish neoromanticism.[410] In addition, her short stories with their parable-like teachings clearly draw on the Hasidic narrative tradition.[411]

In terms of style and subject matter, as in her speeches, Pomeranz used the genre of folk tales to evoke Zionist feelings (not just attitudes). The stories are set in the Jewish context, which is produced through the use of Bible quotations, Yiddishisms and Hebraisms. They contain aspects of "ghetto literature"—stories addressing the modernizations of the nineteenth century as a way out of the Jewish community.[412] It is presented both as a self-contained idyll and as an inclusive constraint, both topoi being directly related to Zionist views, to the dignity of the Jewish people and the history of their martyrdom.[413] In addition, Pomeranz's work is reminiscent of contemporary Galicia literature.[414] Often, the perspective of a distant province is used, for which the outside world is unimaginable.[415] Provinciality can be read as both an aesthetic and a social phenomenon; aesthetic insofar as it makes foreignness a narrative principle, and social in that it denounces historical marginalization, namely that of the Jews as a nation.

In her journalistic texts, Pomeranz often dealt with women, above all the fundamental question of their significance for Zionism, and conversely with the significance of Zionism for Jewish women. She thus took up the *Querelles des Femmes*[416] conducted everywhere in such lively fashion at the end of the nineteenth century. One of her first journalistic texts, "Die Frauen und der Zionismus" (Women and Zionism) was published in *Die Welt* in 1897.[417] In this and other articles, she established the importance of Jewish women from biblical history. She emphasized the historical achievements of female figures from the biblical period and used them to conclude national duties of women. Conversely, in contrast to socialist and feminist concepts, she stated that only Zionism could and would lead to the true emancipation of Jewish women.[418] Occasionally, however, she also interfered in debates to demand or support the professionalization of female occupations, not so much with the middle classes in mind as the lower classes, such as Jewish maids, for whom she suggested setting up vocational schools.[419] Before the First World War, she still exclusively addressed Jewish women and avoided the language of women's movements widespread throughout Europe.

In contrast, during the Second Republic, Pomeranz wrote not only about feminist topics, including marriage, abortion, sex education, and "conscious motherhood,"[420] but also about other women's movements, especially for *Ewa*, a magazine with an "intellectual, emancipatory and nationalist Jewish profile."[421] *Ewa* associated women's politics with Zionist goals and emphasized that progress was inconceivable without modern feminist positions. It devoted itself to women's matters such as fashion, housekeeping, cosmetics, and recipes, as well as to cultural, feminist, and nationalist issues, aspects of health, and legal and political matters in both Poland and Palestine, as long as they concerned women.[422] *Ewa* was aimed at secularized Polish-speaking Jewish women and promoted feminist awareness.[423]

With its articles on birth control and abortion, the journal positioned itself as decidedly modern and rational, against religious traditions and values, and aimed at a readership who distanced themselves from both Orthodox Jewish and strictly Catholic women.[424] Birth control was seen not only as a means of strengthening the population, of combating poverty, but also as a right for unmarried women with an unplanned pregnancy, especially in view of the prevailing double standards. Against accusations that such a policy would destroy the family and permit immorality, *Ewa* emphasized the importance of "conscious motherhood" for the preservation of the family, and advocated social support facilities for Jewish mothers and children in order to prevent targets for anti-Semitic propaganda.[425] The oscillation between gender justice and the perfection of mankind, feminism and eugenics, was not an exclusively Jewish or Polish phenomenon. The promise of perfect humanity drove utopian visions and ideals into a eugenic argumentation that was widespread in the interwar period.[426] Such engagement was rooted precisely in the connection between collective utopia and notions of feasibility.

In some ways, *Ewa* continued the course that Pomeranz had already established in Galicia before the First World War. Being guardians of tradition, culture, and nation, women were particularly important for Zionism; the "enemies" of the movement were above all the "indifferent women" who had turned their backs on Judaism. While Pomeranz saw potential in Orthodox Jewish women for "true, namely Zionist Jewish women,"[427] *Ewa* was more critical of them for being unenlightened. Moreover, in contrast to Pomeranz's earlier writings, references to the language of feminism, to the construction of a collective of women extending beyond ethnic, national and religious differences was more pronounced in the magazine. This is surprising because *Ewa* was skeptical about cooperation on an equal footing with the Polish women's movement.[428] All in all, *Ewa* and the articles published in it by Pomeranz are examples of the search for discourses and topoi on modernity, which included gender equality scientifically based demographic and socio-political issues, as well as the connection between family and nation. Despite the high importance of Palestine as an ideal, practical point of reference for Zionist policy, the demands and proposals, the ideas and initiatives of *Ewa* and also those of Pomeranz (who now repeatedly used the phrase "our state") referred to Poland.[429]

In the final years of her life, Pomeranz supported the creation of Advice Centers for Conscious Motherhood (*Poradni dla świadomego macierzyństwa*) staffed by female doctors: "[T]his matter [birth control] will be sanctioned by the governments of the most progressive states, which our state will eventually join."[430] In 1933, the women's association under the aegis of the Health Protection Association (*Towarzystwo Ochrony Zdrowia*) opened a Family Counselling Center (*Poradnia dla rodzin*).[431] Pomeranz's work for the controversial issue of birth control, which was mainly criticized by religious groups disqualified as backward, shows her to be an adherent of contemporary ideas of modernity. The feasibility of a utopia is demonstrated by the arguments of demographic studies and the legal power of the state, the addressee of demands in the context of eugenic ideas.[432]

Pomeranz insisted on the viability of utopias. This is apparent from her article "Kobieta przyszłości" (The woman of the future), a response to an anthology presented in *Ewa* under the same title with writings by various well-known male authors (Pomeranz commented smugly on the absence of female writers) such as Stefan Zweig. While some contributors deplored the loss of eroticism in a modern partnership, while others emphasized professional activities or independence, Pomeranz saw the future in a harmonious combination of love and independence: "The positive main types will dominate women's world in the future—on the basis of lively vitality and love."[433] The hope for the realization of her ideals is even clearer in an article on the contemporary significance of feminism, which concludes with the statement: "From this house [a house in a common, free and beautiful world], she [the woman]—as educator and citizen—*together with the man*—will rule the world."[434] Pomeranz was no different from Kobryns'ka in her vision of a collaborative partnership. But more than Kobryns'ka, Pomeranz was guided by the optimistic attitude that the right path would lead to a better future. Her views on freedom and independence were marked by positive ideals: true love is never forced, and an equal sexuality is a right of nature, a right for the health of mind and soul.[435] The female educator, who governs the world in partnership with the man (and does not only bring up children), also envisions a specific implementation of the politicized motherliness of feminist and national movements around 1900.

At first glance, Pomeranz's engagement seems contradictory as it changed the focus of its activities. While in her initial journalistic texts, she emphasized above all the ideological significance of women for Zionism and revealed few references to the goals of the women's movement, her organizational dedication was based on political participation as well as educational and employment initiatives for women and girls, i.e. on its traditional themes. In her socio-political activities, she took up new projects of the social work movement, which among other things strengthened the professionalization of women. Before the war, Pomeranz emphasized emigration as the main solution to social problems; after the war, she oriented her projects toward the new state and eugenically underpinned social work. While before the war, recruiting women for Zionism prevailed, after the war she concentrated on support for feminist goals, symbolizing the modernity of Zionist women's policy. Above all, her relationship ideals based on partnership can be understood as metonymies for the connection of her Zionism with contemporary notions of modernity.

A comparison of Pomeranz's journalistic texts before and after the First World War therefore suggests a shift from radicalization to feminist positions with reference to other women's movements in which nationalist arguments and issues were addressed. The publications, themes, and style evidently represented the fundamental changes that took place after the First World War: suffrage and equal legal status for women, opening up the possibilities of political activity in government institutions, social welfare and educational practice, feminist-Jewish politics, and publication in a Polish state for Pomeranz. Nevertheless, in the basic tenor of her publications and activities, she always represented the "other" side: feminist demands for education before the war, and an identity-forming Zionist cultural policy after the war. Her women's policy before the First World War, too, is characterized by an idealistic perspective. For her, ideal values automatically resulted in equality between the sexes, so to speak.[436]

Some remembered Pomeranz as one of the foremost Jewish social work activists: "The historian of Jewish social work lists many names, but in one of the top places is the late Róża Melzerowa."[437] This meant above all her political engagement in the midst of Jewish women, i.e. her activities from the First World War onward. Others, however, in addition to her social and cultural work, stressed her dedication to "emancipation and equal rights of women," her sharp criticism of "conservative inertia, of the limited worldview of men, of the lack of ideology among young people."[438] Kobryns'ka's and Wysłouchowa's perceptions of Galicia are discernible here. For yet others, what stood out above all else was Pomeranz's Zionist policy and her charisma in the cause.[439]

Pomeranz pursued the goal of recruiting women for Zionism by trying to persuade them in speeches and publications and to create a close bond between them and the associations. The organizational, educational, and socio-political aspects grew stronger over time, and Zionist feminist texts took up much of her writing and publishing after the First World War. But the objective remained identical. The spectra of her engagement reflected the different stages of her life. In their narrative unambiguity, the contributions from the commemorative volume quoted above turn the stages into roles played by Pomeranz. The roles point to the active significance of the audience—to the active function of reception in politics. Their diversity indicates the plurality (and rivalry) of political narratives and the creative role of the audience in the construction of clarity. Nevertheless, we should not be tempted to believe we know all about Pomeranz's thoughts and deeds from the author's selection of individual aspects from the various recollections.

Although Pomeranz spent most of her life in Galicia, she imagined—doubtless due to her education, but also due to Zionism—a virtual stage and a broad audience. In her enactments and publications, she juggled with the multiple meanings of fighter, activist, and faithful wife in debates about progress and regression, feminism and Zionism, gender and nation, domesticity, social work, and political institutions. She stands for performance, not only because she studied music in Leipzig and learned stagecraft, and not only because she was repeatedly said to possess charisma, but also because she appeared and performed in her politicking. She campaigned against Jewish hardship, as a delegate, as a deputy, and as a founder of social work institutions after pogroms and after the First World War:

> She died on October 19, 1934, mourned not only by the Zionist organization, on whose spiritual front the death of the noble activist and faithful comrade leaves a painful gap, but also by the broad Jewish masses to whom she sacrificed her entire life with the most strenuous efforts.[440]

***

Finding Roles: The Participants 93

The three women operated in the arenas of political movements: peasant, feminist, and Zionist. In them, they talked of oppression and discrimination, directed these narratives at various levels, and performed them. All three women were educated, albeit in different ways; all of them had acquired specific skills. Three patterns emerge from their biographies: narrating, directing, and enacting. Although one pattern is especially pronounced in each biography, the politics of the women cannot be reduced to a single pattern. All three women were involved in narrating, directing, and enacting. All three of them ran an open house, hosted gatherings, and traveled. They cultivated contacts, were organized in various ways, and went out into the world. For all three women, life and politics were closely intertwined, public and private levels merged. Networks were a central structural principle of their ways of making politics; letters and meetings were essential media. The letter differs from a conversation in that it is set out in writing and characterized by a phase delay—which offered Wysłouchowa, for example, the possibility to narrate, to produce monologues.

With her performances, Pomeranz compiled a personally strengthened organizational network in Galicia, spinning the threads all the way to the centers, to Basel and the *Sejm*. Kobryns'ka's correspondence linked Galicia to Eastern Ukraine, Wysłouchowa's connected town and country. The correspondence confirms the thesis that among Polish women, relations between Lithuania, Warsaw, L'viv, and Kraków were relatively close, while women in the Prussian partition were less involved in the networks.[441] The contacts of Kobryns'ka and Wysłouchowa with Bohemia bear witness to transnational networking—and to the difficulties of networking in Galicia itself. While political commonalities arose with Czech women, who also combined nationalist and feminist politics, it was precisely this similarity of politics, the connection of nationalist and gender policy goals, which led to competition in Galicia and prevented the long-lasting union. The common ground which led to ties with Bohemia was precisely what led to division in Galicia.

The roles implied the historical possibilities of making politics. The women were not narrators, artistic directors, or actresses because they were Polish, Ukrainian, or Jewish. On reading their biographies together, they complement each other, despite their different origins, educational careers, and lives in terms of political engagement, for all three women were active in political arenas and were among the leading minds of contemporary political movements. Their biographies represent different nodes of discourse, abrupt "fixations" in permanent processes of differentiation and ritualization. Central to this connection seems to have been the idea of and the claim to a vision of the future, of the formability of a better society and historically essentialized collectives.

One pattern of their life plans was the claim to the prerogative of interpretation, decision-making, and performance competence. Who had the right and the competence to talk about women's matters and gender relations? Criticism of marriage as an unequal, unfree relationship stood metonymically for criticism of the lack of freedom and inequality of society. Above all, however, it fronted the orientation of the respective women's policies, as the sharp disagreements between Kobryns'ka and the Radicals showed. A recurring theme was the autonomy of the initiators. This was how Wysłouchowa interpreted the conflicts over the *Przodownica;* there was also rivalry between socialist and feminist or Zionist projects, for example over the publication organ for women, which the Radicals wanted to subordinate to party politics, as well as over the question of how closely the Zionist Women's League should be connected to the Zionist movement. In 1912, the representative of the women's organizations at the Galician Provincial Conference demanded "a stronger appreciation of the party work done by Zionist women."[442]

Identification with the political collective was a subject of controversy everywhere. Demands for autonomy were repeatedly interpreted as a sign of weakness (if not disloyalty)—not only by men in the movement but also by women. For example, a Galician Zionist butted in as follows: "But what would the relations of Jewish women be like with women from other nations with whom they had fought side-by-side and been victorious? Probably just like those which have prevailed hitherto between Jews and other nations—in other words, relations with unfulfilled demands on both sides: equality on the one hand and exclusion on the other."[443] The author concluded that Jewish women ought to devote themselves to bringing up children at home for Zionism. Nevertheless, "emancipation" was evidently such a widespread slogan that no movement could ignore it if it wanted to be perceived as progressive and to secure female grassroots.

Another pattern that made this interdependence possible and describable was the ideal of marriage based on partnership, which for the identity of politically active women took on a significance that was not to be underestimated.[444] Talk of harmonious marriage fitted into the narrative of all three women. It strengthened their respective (self-)image: romantic harmony, political independence, charismatic practice. The ideal was intertextual, a topos employed in different text combinations—by the Wysłouchs in their correspondence, by Kobryns'ka in her autobiography, by the authors of the commemorative volume about Pomeranz. The supportive husband represented symbolic capital demonstrating possibilities for action, resources, and commitment for the respective movements. In doing so, he opened up the scope for women to think and act. Being a rhetorical figure, he assured the readers of successful engagement and highlighted the feasibility of a better future.[445] The marriage ideal referred to the independence of the "new woman"[446] at the turn of the century and in the interwar period, and simultaneously represented a countermodel to free love, which is what Kobryns'ka was alluding to with her remark on the unique significance of her husband.

The search for a new, modern society took place not only as a criticism of marriage, in debates about gender roles or literary narratives about marriages of love and reason, but also as an emotional structuring of friendly, marital, and political relationships.[447] The husband was often the women's muse and mentor in one. The women also found a mentor or a muse in friendships. Franko, for example, sometimes fulfilled the role of mentor for Kobryns'ka, while Sokolová-Seidlová was apparently a muse at times for Wysłouchowa. Although the idea of the unity of life and work, the total claim of romanticism,[448] often meant the female muse and the male artist, this model was flexible and transferable.

The debate about free love was a complex play with various possible interpretations. It amounted to competition between all kinds of models of gender relations, and also to masculinity and femininity.[449] In this way, Pavlyk's remarks about the free choice of partners could be understood as a norm violation, yet also as a code for a radical revolutionary attitude. They were confessions of radical internationality or expressions of sympathy with the radical milieu of Eastern Ukraine and thus a symbolic union.[450] Similarly, in *Ewa,* Pomeranz confirmed the modernity of her Zionism with debates about contraception, the protection of women, and demographic arguments. The direction of debates about modernity—apparent from discussions about love, marriage, and sexuality—conveyed a message about traditionality. It was directed at the public in Galicia, who were pressurized to decide; those who wanted to be modern had to position themselves accordingly. Modernity, marriage, friendship, and nation constituted each other. They were discursive fields with diverse nodes that could expand endlessly, open concepts, open to different ideas of society, order, change, and meaning.

What the three women also had in common was their "love of the people." Nevertheless, there were differences. Wysłouchowa represented the romanticism of ideals, love as a narrative overcoming opposites, Kobryns'ka the conflicts, love as a practice to be formed, while Pomeranz represented charisma, the admiration flowing between performer and audience. Unlike Wysłouchowa, Kobryns'ka's politics were not directed at the village but women and the intelligentsia or the Radicals. Pomeranz's addressees were less clear-cut; on the one hand, they were Jewish women, on the other hand, Jews as a collective. The differences between the women include multiple localizations, strategies and discourses, and the intersectionality of politicized "fixations" such as nation, class and gender, the simultaneity of competition, and the entanglement of identity politics at the end of the nineteenth century.[451]

What the women had in common was writing, organizing, and positioning in polyphonic movements. They dealt with the central aspects of political engagement, the plot, stage, and enacting, or literary and

96 Finding Roles: The Participants

journalistic texts, spaces, intertextual combinations, and networks. In the following chapters, the common and structural aspects, or the performative of politics will be selected from the visions and life plans of Wysłouchowa, Kobryns'ka, and Pomeranz and analyzed in a contemporary context. The aim is to establish the links between different life plans, individuals, and contexts. Just as the letter conveys a transition between oral and written culture, between conversation and short story, and between private and public,[452] politics is also a mixture of oral and written culture, a formation and dissemination of emotions and arguments, narratives and collectives. As will be demonstrated below, this transition is not chronological, but ritualized.

Notes

1 See for example Bödeker, "Biographie."
2 See Bernhold and Gehmacher, *Auto/Biographie*, 63; Gehmacher, Heinrich, and Oesch, *Käthe Schirmacher*, especially 13–21.
3 Harriet Anderson, "Feminismus."
4 Regarding the gesture of modesty among women, see Holdenried, *Autobiographie*, 66–68; among authors with elementary school education, see Warneken, "Schichtspezifik," 142–46.
5 Shepherd, *Price*, 17. This sweeping statement is untenable since a great deal has of course been written about the history of Jewish women. Instead, it is a writing gesture. See for example Kaplan, *Movement*; Heinsohn and Schüler-Springorum, *Geschichte*; Rose, *Women*; Glenn, *Daughters*; Rüthers, *Töchter*.
6 See for example Bernhold and Gehmacher, *Auto/Biographie*, 20; Schaser, *Helene Lange*, 20.
7 In her study of the various biographies of Bertha Pappenheim, Elizabeth Loentz shows that they often say more about their authors than their historical subjects. Pappenheim is particularly illustrative because she went down in the history of psychoanalysis as Sigmund Freud's Anna O. and in the history of the Jewish women's movement in the German Empire as Bertha Pappenheim. This is why her "case" is frequently re-examined. Loentz, *Truth*, 195–238; see also Gehmacher, Heinrich, and Oesch, *Käthe Schirmacher*, 513–28, who emphasize "self-biographizing" as a central part of biographical writing.
8 Bernhold and Gehmacher, *Auto/Biographie*, 18–21, 63.
9 Brinker-Gabler, "Metamorphosen."
10 Stegmann, *Töchter*, 112–33; see also Freidenreich, *Lifes*, 23–25.
11 Bohachevsky-Chomiak, "Natalia Kobryns'ka," 197.
12 See also Sarasin, "Geschichtswissenschaft," 21.
13 Davidoff, "'Adam.'"
14 See also Bernhold and Gehmacher, *Auto/Biographie*, 7–8; Loentz, *Truth*, 196.
15 Loentz, *Truth*, 199–200; Gehmacher, Heinrich, and Oesch, *Käthe Schirmacher*, 13–36.
16 Bryll, *Maria Wysłouchowa*, 32. Sokolová-Seidlová wrote in Polish; Wysłouchowa claimed that she could not write in Czech. Bryll, *Maria Wysłouchowa*, 146, footnote 40.
17 Dużyk, "Orkan." Władysław Orkan was originally called Franciszek Xawery Smaciarz. In 1898, he changed his surname to Smreczyński, a modified form of Smreczak, his mother's maiden name.

Finding Roles: The Participants 97

18 Regarding the ambiguity of the term *lud* (people), in the sense of "nation" (*naród*) and "working classes" (*warstwy pracujące*), see also Molenda, *Chłopi*, 41–47; Struve, *Bauern*, 29; Chapter 3, Designing society.
19 PNP, f. 33/44.
20 See BJ, 10465/III, folios 199–200; BJ, 10471/III, vol. 1, folios 42–44; BJ, 10472, vol. 2, folios 54–95, 101–03, 106–08, 110–15, 119–23, 126–28, 131–32, 171–74; BJ, 10473, vol. 3, folios 185–86; BO, 12295/III, folios 129–31; Brodacki, "Listy."
21 Regarding the relationship between politics and friendship, see also Bosch, *Politics*.
22 Jansen, "Briefe," 199.
23 Wysłouchowa to Sokolová-Seidlová, June 5/15, 1894, PNP, f. 33/44. "Dwa bieguny" first appeared in 1893 in *Kraj* (The Country) and *Nowa Reforma* (The New Reform) as well as that same year in Saint Petersburg as a separate novel. The hero, a young landowner, saw in farm work and village education the fulfilment of her brother's will and, despite her feelings, turned down a Warsaw suitor skeptical about the ideals of the rebellion and rural life since she thought it would be impossible to reconcile her attitudes to life, choosing instead to sacrifice her personal happiness to the memory of the rebellion. Romankówna, "Dwa bieguny."
24 Regarding tsarist land policy after the uprising, see Chwalba, *Historia*, 400–05.
25 For a contemporary understanding of art as a reflection and problematization or idealization of "real life," see Balzer, *Einführung*, especially 42–44. For more on Orzeszkowa and her importance for Polish feminist politics, see Chapter 4, Dialogues; regarding positivism, see Górnicka-Boratyńska, "Idea." Regarding the perspective of the actors, the intelligentsia, see also Micińska, *Inteligencja*.
26 The term "organic work" was used to describe grassroots political work intended to organically unite society as a whole. The concept originated in the 1840s in the Grand Duchy of Poznań as an alternative to insurrection and became a political benchmark in the Kingdom of Poland after the failed uprising of 1863/64. In Galicia, against the background of autonomy, this policy had a somewhat different character. It was directed against conservative, traditional preservation policies and also established links to the other partitions. See Serrier, *Provinz*, 44–45; Kozłowska-Sabatowska, *Ideologia*; Caumanns, "Arbeit."
27 Wyłouchowa to Orkan, January 27, 1900, BJ, 10472, folios 54–55, here: 54.
28 Davis, "Heroes," 325. Regina Schulte, "Opfer," also discusses the maternal victim.
29 The victim myth, a topos handed down since Polish romanticism, played a central role in the social discourses of the nineteenth century. Far from unique, it was characteristic of national movements as a whole. Maria Janion, however, sees something uniquely Polish in its dual role of a colonizing and a colonized country. Janion, *Polen*, 35–54; Janion, Vorwort to *Romantik*. See also Gall et al., Einleitung to *Romantik*; Malečková, "Women," 297.
30 Davis, "Heroes," 324.
31 Martinsen, *Wille*, 9; Liebhart and Rásky, "Helden," 239; see also Stegmann, "Kampf."
32 See Filipowicz, "Daughters," 35.
33 For the main biographical data, see "Wysłouchowa"; Wawrzykowska-Wierciochowa, "Maria Wysłouchowa"; Brock, "Maria Wysłouchowa—wielka nauczycielka"; Brock, "Maria Wysłouchowa (1858–1905)."

98 Finding Roles: The Participants

34 Wawrzykowska-Wierciochowa, *Wysłouchowa*, 126.
35 The family became politically engaged again later. In 1886, Maria's mother was arrested on the Russo–Austrian border with a suitcase containing illegal writings, imprisoned in Warsaw, and banished to Siberia in September 1887. Wawrzykowska-Wierciochowa, *Wysłouchowa*, 129–30; Wawrzykowska-Wierciochowa, "Maria Wysłouchowa," 405.
36 Being a private tutor or governess as well as a teacher at a girls' school or lyceum were among the few socially acceptable occupations for middle and upper class women. Other possibilities were literature and journalism as well as medical professions such as midwives. Freidenreich, *Lifes*, 12. Regarding the Russian Empire, see Pietrow-Ennker, "'Menschen,'" 257–311.
37 Bryll, *Maria Wysłouchowa*, 20.
38 According to Pietrow-Ennker, the Bestužev Courses were started in 1878. They were preceded in the Russian Empire by debates over the formal opening of universities to women in the 1850s and early 1860s—which continued until women were explicitly barred from higher education in 1864 during the repressive policy following uprisings and university riots in the early 1860s. In the 1870s, training occupations for women were formalized and institutionalized in a number of academies and institutes. See Pietrow-Ennker, "'Menschen,'" 130–39, 157–87, 325–26; Kobchenko, "Geschichten." However, according to Yvonne Piesker, the Bestužev courses did not begin until 1894. In this case, Wysłouchowa must have attended other higher education courses for women, perhaps the Alarčin or Vladimir courses. See Piesker, "Frauenbildung," 304. Regarding the discursive references of the debates over academic education and employment opportunities for women in the nineteenth century, see also Hüchtker, "'Mädchenbildung'"; moreover, see Piesker, *Diskurse*, especially 157–201.
39 Wawrzykowska-Wierciochowa, *Wysłouchowa*, 305.
40 In the Russian Empire, political organizations and associations were subject to massive police controls, socialist activities were forbidden, and Polish organizations were forbidden in the wake of post-insurrectional repressive policies. Therefore, most active groups were illegal and informal. Many groups called themselves "circles." Veidlinger, *Culture*, 37.
41 Bryll, *Maria Wysłouchowa*, 21. In the Russian Empire from the late 1860s onward, followers of agrarian socialism were referred to as Narodniks. By "going to the people," they sought to enlighten and empower the rural population to help themselves. Initially, organizational support was provided by Saint Petersburg intelligentsia circles. See L[öwe], "Narodniki"; Venturi, *Roots*.
42 Nietyksza, "Kobiety."
43 Wawrzykowska-Wierciochowa, "Koło," 51.
44 Wawrzykowska-Wierciochowa, "Koło," 54.
45 Wawrzykowska-Wierciochowa, "Maria Wysłouchowa," 402. Wysłouchowa was also active in the Association of Women of the Kingdom of Poland and Lithuania (*Zrzeszenie Kobiet Korony i Litwy*), which similarly looked after prisoners and Siberian exiles and their families. Bryll, *Maria Wysłouchowa*, 21.
46 Bryll, *Maria Wysłouchowa*, 22. The year 1884 is occasionally cited.
47 Wysłouch also spent at least a few months in prison in Galicia. See "Wysłouch"; Kisielewski, *Heroizm*, 31–30.
48 However, the implementation laws were restrictive. The notorious newspaper stamp, a printing license for each issue that had to be purchased, and which meant that controls and confiscations were still possible, was not abolished until January 1, 1900. The emergence of a public sphere in civil

society remained uncertain—although this situation was no different from, say, the German Empire. Rumpler, "'Öffentlichkeit,'" 11–12.
49 Wysłouchowa to Wysłouch, August 7, 1901, BO, 7185/II, folio 501.
50 Heide Wunder described the *Arbeitspaar* (working couple) for the early modern era, but the concept aptly describes the Wysłouchs, too. Wunder, *Sun*, 63–71.
51 In 1884, Wysłouchowa wrote enthusiastically in a letter to her husband: "The brightest point where the tired thought enjoys relaxing is the local people, who are very poor, but still very righteous and honest. I can study the various aspects of their character to my heart's content, because the great love and sense of fraternal communion with the younger brothers here filled the abyss normally separating the village from the manor house." Wysłouchowa to Wysłouch, November 13, 1884, BO, 7185/II, folios 461–62.
52 For instance in L'viv, in the surroundings of the town, and in Cieszyn Silesia. Bryll, *Maria Wysłouchowa*, 25.
53 Kisielewski, *Heroizm*, 142, also explains the Wysłouchs' division of labor with Habsburg legislation, which prohibited women from joining associations. Regarding the exclusion of women from associations and the press after the suppression of the 1848 Revolution using the example of the German states, see Gerhard, "Grenzziehungen," 524–34; for Galicia, Najdus, "O prawa."
54 Dunin-Wąsowicz, *Czasopiśmiennictwo*, 70; Jarowiecki, "Prasa," 413–14.
55 Jarowiecki, "Prasa," 414. According to Bryll, *Przyjaciel Ludu* became Wysłouchowa's most important place of publication alongside *Tydzień*. Bryll, *Maria Wysłouchowa*, 26.
56 This is mentioned for example in Dunin-Wąsowicz, "Bewegungen," 55–57; Dunin-Wąsowicz, *Czasopiśmiennictwo*, 88; Myśliński, "Wysłouchowie," 145.
57 Dunin-Wąsowicz, *Czasopiśmiennictwo*, 103–04.
58 Struve, *Bauern*, 164, footnote 136; Terlecki, *Oświata*, 128–29. The association backed cooperation with the Ruthenians. In 1891, disagreements arose between the peasantry-oriented and the more national-democratic members of the association, which led to its activities petering out.
59 Wysłouch's concept of the nation was ethnically based. It is repeatedly emphasized in the literature that he strove for the equitable coexistence of ethnic groups. Terlecki, *Oświata*, 77.
60 "Wysłouchowa"; Stauter-Halsted, "Celebrations."
61 The panorama depicts the victory of Polish insurgent troops led by Tadeusz Kościuszko at Racławice.
62 In its obituary, *Przyjaciel Ludu* described the day as follows: "Thousands of participants in the peasants' rally in L'viv in 1894 recall how on the exhibition square the late Lady Maria [Wysłouchowa] initially tried to serve everyone their daily bread, and then strengthened the ideas of the peasant question in the Racławice Panorama with an inspiring account of the Battle of Racławice." Redakcja Przyjaciela Ludu, "Marja Wysłouchowa."
63 Dunin-Wąsowicz, *Czasopiśmiennictwo*, 111–13. There is some research on the General Provincial Exhibition, but hardly any information about Wysłouchowa's address. For an overview, see Stauter-Halsted, "Celebrations"; Hofmann, "Utopien"; Wendland, "Bilder"; Kozińska-Witt, "Selbstpräsentation"; Siadkowski, "Exhibition."
64 Wysłouchowa to Orzeszkowa, no year (probably 1898), PAN, Warsaw, 800.
65 In the second half of the nineteenth century, Cieszyn Silesia belonged to the industrialized regions of Bohemia and was a destination for labor migrants

100 Finding Roles: The Participants

from Galicia. Socialist, national, and feminist Polish organizations were active there. Regarding the region, see Chwalba, *Historia*, 553–60; Kotowski, "Deutsche."

66 For example, the local agricultural circle contacted Wysłouchowa several times, see BO, 7188/II, folios 139–54; Bryll, "Śląskie kontakty," 56; Bryll, "Listy ze Śląska."
67 Zofia Bouffałowa to Wysłouchowa, July 26, no year (after 1898), BO, 7187/II, folios 263, 265; Wysłouch to Wysłouchowa, September 7, 1898, BO, 7190/II, folios 501–02.
68 BN, 7601; Bryll, "Listy Marii Wysłouchowej."
69 W[antuła], "[Obituary]," *Przegląd Polityczny*, April 1, 1905. Reprinted in [Dalecka et al.], *Marja Wysłouchowa*, 112–13, here: 112.
70 Wysłouchowa, "Ze śląskiej ziemi," *Tydzień*, 1896/97; Wysłouchowa, "Z Wisły"; Wysłouchowa, "Z ziemi śląskiej," *Zorza*, 1901; Wysłouchowa, "Z pobratymczej ziemi." Wysłouchowa went to Istebna on several occasions and also recommended it to Orkan as a place to stay. Wysłouchowa to Orkan, March 5, 1900, BJ, 10472, folios 65–67, here: 65–66. According to Wysłouchowa, although the official name of the place was Izdebna, the local population referred to Izdebno or Istebno; Istebna is presumably meant. Wysłouchowa, "Z Wisły," 384, footnote 4.
71 Bryll, "Śląskie kontakty," 66.
72 Regarding the constituent meaning of a nationalized and nationalizing contrast to the rulers, see also Serrier, *Provinz*, 277.
73 Wysłouchowa to Orzeszkowa, October 27, 1890, PAN, Warsaw, 800.
74 Wysłouchowa to Sokolová-Seidlová, March 21, 1900, PNP, 33/44.
75 Kizwalter, "Nationalismustheorie."
76 Wawrzykowska-Wierciochowa, "Koło," 57, 61–62. Regarding Dulębianka, see Jaworska, "Dulębianka."
77 "Wysłouchowa"; Wawrzykowska-Wierciochowa, *Wysłouchowa*, 136, 139. The term Women's Scholarly Reading Room (*Czytelnia naukowa kobiet*) is also to be found in the secondary literature; "scholarly" is missing in both reports: [Wechslerowa and Czemeryńska], *Historyja; Sprawozdanie z czynności wydziału czytelni dla kobiet*. Since Stefania Wechslerowa is cited as the chair of both institutions and there are no other indications of two reading rooms, I assume they are one and the same. See Chapter 3, Ritualizing education.
78 Wawrzykowska-Wierciochowa, *Wysłouchowa*, 175–76; see also Stegmann, *Töchter*, 171; Dadej, "Damen."
79 Two circles founded in the Kingdom and active in Galicia merged: the Women's Circle for People's Education and the Women's Circle of the Kingdom and Lithuania (*Koło Kobiet Korony i Litwy*). Wawrzykowska-Wierciochowa, "Koło," 64.
80 Głos kobiet z Korony i Litwy, październik 1894 r., Archiwum Akt Nowych, Odział VI, 305/305/III/45, Liga Polska, Liga Narodowa, quoted after Wolsza, "Organisatorki," 87.
81 Wawrzykowska-Wierciochowa, "Maria Wysłouchowa," 401; Wawrzykowska-Wierciochowa, "Kulikowska."
82 Wawrzykowska-Wierciochowa, *Wysłouchowa*, 252.
83 Najdus, "O prawa," 106.
84 *Statut Towarzystwa Oszczędności*. The main aim of the association was to support Polish landowning farmers in the Province of Poznań. Regarding the struggle for land ownership against the background of Prussian Germanization policy, see Chwalba, *Historia*, 461–65; Serrier, *Provinz*, 46–52; Sabine Grabowski, *Nationalismus*, 185.

Finding Roles: The Participants 101

85 [Zarząd Towarzystwa oszczędności kobiet], "Do kobiet."
86 Nitsch, "Sozialreform."
87 Orzeszkowa, *Listy*, 639, footnote 1.
88 Towarzystwo Oszczędności Kobiet, *Dla głodnych*. Kobryns'ka wrote in Ruthenian—but the Cyrillic letters of her first name were apparently mistaken as Latin because she is listed in the contents as "Kobryńska Amelia." See Kobryns'ka, "Na przebój."
89 Wysłouchowa to Orzeszkowa, March 25, 1890, April 6 and April 24, 1890, PAN, Warsaw, 800.
90 Regarding the close overlaps for Galicia, see Homola-Skąpska, "Galicia," 87; Lorence-Kot and Winiarz, "Movement."
91 Wawrzykowska-Wierciochowa, "Koło," 62. The initiative stemmed from the Warsaw section of the Women's Circle of the Kingdom and Lithuania, which in 1893 had founded a Committee for a Women's Work Section (*Komitet Działu Pracy Kobiet*) together with the Women's Circle for People's Education and the Women's Reading Room in L'viv. The exhibitions mostly presented an ethnographic view of textile works by women. Some villages managed to commercialize these works as folklore. At the General Provincial Exhibition in 1894 in L'viv, a pavilion was set up to display textile and other works as well as literature and art by women. Wawrzykowska-Wierciochowa, *Wysłouchowa*, 203–04. Regarding the presentation of women's gainful occupations in an ethnographic context, see also Kobryns'ka's activities in Chapter 1, Dramatic directing.
92 Krzywiec, "Kuczalska-Reinschmit"; Hulewicz, "Kuczalska-Reinschmit."
93 Wysłouchowa to Sokolová-Seidlová, February 1, 1893, PNP, 33/44.
94 Wysłouchowa to Sokolová-Seidlová, April 6, 1893, PNP, 33/44.
95 See Nitsch, *Wohltätigkeitsvereine*, 366–73. Although Bianka Pietrow-Ennker refers to an interest in reform among noblewomen in the Russian Empire, she mainly mentions initiatives from the intelligentsia, a new "social middle," rather than from courtly circles. Pietrow-Ennker, *Menschen*, 361–62.
96 Wysysłouchowa to Sokolová-Seidlová, April 6, 1893, PNP, 33/44.
97 See Chapter 4, Recitations.
98 The two central associations were the International Council of Women founded in 1888 and the International Woman Suffrage Alliance set up in 1904. Between 1911 and 1913, the Galician Equality for Women Committee, to which various organizations belonged, including Ruthenian ones, was accepted into the latter association. See Zimmermann, "Reich"; Zimmermann, "Challenge."
99 Bujak, "Siedlecka."
100 Regarding the orientation and activities of the association, see Chapter 3, Ritualizing education; Dadej, "Czytelnia."
101 The Women's Reading Room in Kraków to the editorial board of *Kurjer Lwowski*, December 2/7, 1897, BO, 7191/II, folios 139–41, here: 140–41. The letter is signed by Siedlecka.
102 The Women's Reading Room in Kraków to the editorial board of *Kurjer Lwowski*, n.d., BO, 7191/II, folios 143–46. The letter is signed by Siedlecka. See also Dormus, *Problematyka*, 79.
103 Sikorska-Kulesza, "Trójzaborowe zjazdy." The third all-Poland Congress in Zakopane, like the two previous ones, was not held in public. The first public conference in Warsaw in 1905 was often counted as the first by contemporaries and researchers, sometimes causing confusion. Wawrzykowska-Wierciochowa, *Wysłouchowa*, 326–27.
104 Wawrzykowska-Wierciochowa, *Wysłouchowa*, 329.

102 Finding Roles: The Participants

105 Wawrzykowska-Wierciochowa, *Z dziejów*, 123–24; see also P. de C. "Zjazd"; "Zakopane"; M., "Pierwszy zjazd."
106 Dormus, *Problematyka*, 80. Regarding the foundation of *Przodownica*, see Sokół, "'Przodownica.'" *Przodownica* was published from 1899 to 1912 and financed by subscriptions and the K. Kulikowska Foundation. See also Dunin-Wąsowicz, *Czasopiśmiennictwo*, 255–56; Zaleska, *Czasopisma*, 99–101.
107 Regarding the polemical use of terms such as "socialist," "revolutionary" and "nihilistic" in journalism, see also Franke, *Polska prasa*, 289.
108 While Zaleska, *Czasopisma*, 101, claims that the reasons for the disagreements are unknown, Bryll, *Maria Wysłouchowa*, 95, argues that *Przodownica* had clerical leanings.
109 Wysłouchowa to Sokolová-Seidlová, March 21, 1900, PNP, 33/44.
110 Wysłouchowa to Sokolová-Seidlová, March 21, 1900, PNP, 33/44.
111 Wysłouchowa to Sokolová-Seidlová, March 21, 1900, PNP, 33/44.
112 Wysłouchowa to Sokolová-Seidlová, March 21, 1900, PNP, 33/44. There is a letter from Wysłouchowa to Orkan dated February 5, 1900 in which she expressed the idea of setting up her own magazine, to be published in L'viv, in order to be able to pursue her "peasantry-oriented and radical" (*chłopski i radikalny*) approach. Wysłouchowa to Orkan, February 5, 1900, BJ, 10472, folio 56. She also advised him of her final decision including her outrage over the events. Wysysłouchowa to Orkan, February 27, 1900, BJ, 10472, folio 64. See also Sokół, "'Zorza,'" 57–58; Dormus, *Problematyka*, 80–81.
113 Editorial committee of *Przodownica* to Wysłouchowa, February 8, 1900 and February 24, 1900, BO, 7188/II, folios 119–23, here: 121. The letters were signed by Gabriela Balicka-[illegible], Marya Siedlecka and M. T. Błotnicka.
114 Committee for a Women's Rally to Wysłouchowa, May 15, 1900, BO, 7188/II, folios 125–26. Wysłouchowa continued to write occasionally for *Przodownica*, which paid tribute to her when she died in 1905. See "Ś. p. Mariya Wysłouchowa."
115 Orkan bolstered her ambitions to found her own magazine in L'viv. Orkan to Wysłouchowa, February 7, 1900, reprinted in Brodacki, "Listy," 95: "These 'committees'—such a horror!" He also commented on the naming and organization. Orkan to Wysłouchowa, March 4, 1900 and April 20, 1900, reprinted in Brodacki, "Listy," 98–99.
116 Bryll, *Maria Wysłouchowa*, 96; Sokół, "'Zorza,'" 64.
117 Although Wysłouchowa retired from her political and editorial work in 1902 due to ill-health, *Zorza* continued to be published until 1904. See Zaleska, *Czasopisma*, 101.
118 She wrote to Sokolová-Seidlová that she had too little time to deal with the woman question in detail. Wysłouchowa to Sokolová-Seidlová, November 20, 1896, PNP, 33/44.
119 See her observations on the women's movement, Wysłouchowa, "Ruch," and Chapter 4, Recitations.
120 She translated from Czech, Russian, Bulgarian, Serbian, and Slovenian. Wysłouchowa to Sokolová-Seidlová, October 28, 1898, PNP, 33/44. See also Wawrzykowska-Wierciochowa, "Maria Wysłouchowa," 414.
121 Bryll, *Maria Wysłouchowa*, 19.
122 Bryll, *Maria Wysłouchowa*, 23; Wysłouchowa to Sokolová-Seidlová, October 24, 1899, PNP, 33/44.
123 Wysłouchowa, *O Kościuszkowskiem powstaniu*; Wysłouchowa, *O Konstytucyi*; Wysłouchowa, "Emilja Platerówna"; Wysłouchowa, "O przeznacej Polce." Wysłouchowa wrote about Mickiewicz when his

remains were transferred from Paris to Kraków in 1890 and to mark his centenary in 1898. Wysłouchowa, *O życiu;* Wysłouchowa, *Adam Mickiewicz.* She probably contributed substantially to the cult of Mickiewicz in Galicia. Wawrzykowska-Wierciochowa, *Wysłouchowa,* 309. Regarding her bibliography, see Bryll, *Maria Wysłouchowa,* 160–69.
124 Wysłouchowa, *O Konstytucyi,* 3.
125 Regarding the change from a noble to an ethnic nation, see Kizwalter, "Demos."
126 For example Wysłouchowa, *O Kościuszkowskiem powstaniu,* 4: "Let's hurry up." Wysłouchowa, *O życiu,* 3: "To our readers."
127 See for example Wysłouchowa, *Za wolność.*
128 Wanda Dalecka. 1905. "Ze wspomnień pośmiertnych." *Tydzień,* 34–35, reprinted in [Dalecka et al.] *Marja Wysłouchowa,* 54–69, here: 62–63; "[Obituary]." 1905. *Słowo Polskie,* L'viv, March 21, 1905, reprinted in [Dalecka et al.], *Marja Wysłouchowa,* 83–86, here: 84.
129 Orkan, "[Obituary]," 10.
130 Bryll, *Maria Wysłouchowa,* 36–37.
131 Kośny, "Positivismus," 381. Henryk Sienkiewicz switched from the crisis of positivism around 1880 and the simultaneous reception of naturalism in France to the path of "realistic idealism." Regarding the neoromantic 1890s, see also Porter, *Nationalism,* 98–99.
132 Kośny, "Positivismus," 382. Much has been thought and written about the terminology for literature at the turn of the century. Neoromanticism for the period after 1890 is also in dispute. Instead of a correct classification, however, the questions dealt with here require the analysis of strategies, descriptions, and conflicts that can be interpreted not only as national literary histories or canons but also as a contemporary phenomenon of a transnationally networked intelligentsia. See Makowiecki, *Polska,* 5–12 regarding the classification; regarding criticism of a generational sequence of literary directions, see Pavlychko, "Modernism"; Gloger, "Modernizowanie"; Możejko, "Modernizm"; for a more general overview, see Casanova, *World,* 1–7.
133 Tatarowski, *Ludowość,* 373; see also Janion, *Polen.*
134 For example, the debate analyzes Favret, *Correspondence,* 10.
135 Regarding the connection between gender and institutionalization, see Kraft, "Historiography"; see also Epple, *Geschichtsschreibung;* Smith, *Gender.*
136 "Flying university" was the name given to the illegal courses at university level organized and mainly attended by women in Warsaw from 1882 onwards, which were intended to counteract the Russification of universities in the Kingdom of Poland. Well-known and trained women and men were hired as lecturers. See Stegmann, *Töchter,* 72–77.
137 Konstantinović and Rinner, *Literaturgeschichte,* 228–29, 248; see also Hüchtker, "Blick."
138 Bryll, *Maria Wysłouchowa,* 31.
139 Gall et al., Einleitung to *Romantik,* 12–13. Żmigrodzka, "Probleme."
140 W[ysłouchowa], "Bohaterka." The author used this short article to introduce to readers the poem *Śmierć pułkownika* (The Colonel's Death) by Adam Mickiewicz, which was written in honor of Emilia Plater.
141 Wysłouchowa, "Chłopi."
142 Dużyk, "Orkan," 189.
143 Wysłouchowa to Orkan, November 16, 1899, BJ, 10471/III, folios 43–44, here: 44.
144 Wysłouchowa to Sokolová-Seidlová, December 21, 1903, PNP, 33/44.
145 Wysłouchowa to Sokolová-Seidlová, January 15, 1899, PNP, 33/44.

104 Finding Roles: The Participants

146 Bagłajewski, "Krasiński."
147 French, *Women*, 13–28; Labouvie, "Einstimmung"; Eickenrodt and Rapisarda, "Freundschaften"; Dadej, "Przyjaźnie."
148 This is in contrast to Kobryns'ka, see Chapter 1, Dramatic directing.
149 Wysłouchowa to Wysłouch, July 16, no year, BO, 7185/II, folios 491–94, here: 493; Bryll, "Śląskie kontakty," 61, footnote 47, thinks the letter was written in 1896, although I believe it may also have been written later.
150 Sdvižkov, *Zeitalter*, 132, states "a social fabric of the intelligentsia in the three partitions and even in 'distant' foreign countries in west and east." Regarding the term, see also Saurer, "Frauenbewegung."
151 See notes on bypassing the censor in: Wysłouchowa to Orzeszkowa, June 24, 1890, PAN, Warsaw, 800; also Schlientz, "Botschaften."
152 Regarding the lengthy meetings between Wysłouchowa and Orzeszkowa, see PAN, Warsaw, 800; PAN, Kraków, 4527; PAN, Kraków, 5591.
153 Listed in Bryll, *Maria Wysłouchowa*, 19–20.
154 Chitnis, "Světlá."
155 Ivan Jankovyč Franko, who was born in 1856 in the village of Nahujevyči near Drohobyč in Galicia and died in 1916 in L'viv, was one of the foremost writers and journalists of his time. He wrote in Ruthenian, German, and Polish for numerous magazines, edited Ruthenian-language magazines such as *Zorja* (The Star) and *Dilo* (The Deed), and was involved in the radical wing of the Ukrainophile movement. *Dilo* was its organ while *Zorja*, a literary journal, was also aligned with it. In 1890, Franko cofounded the Ruthenian-Ukrainian Radical Party (*Rus'ko-Ukraïns'ka Radykal'na Partija*). He was in close contact with Kobryns'ka. See Chapter 1, Dramatic directing. Hrytsak, *Ivan Franko*; Hrytsak, "Answer"; Binder, "Das ruthenische Pressewesen," 2106–07; Humenjuk, Peredmova to " *Zorja*."
156 Myśliński, "Wysłouchowie."
157 Bryll, "Śląskie kontakty," 75–76.
158 [Dalecka et al.], *Marja Wysłouchowa*.
159 See the description of the funeral in the commemorative publication. "Pogrzeb," 23.
160 Orkan, "[Obituary]," 8.
161 Jeden z tych, których Ona do pracy wskrzesiła. 1905. "Jak kochała lud," *Przyjaciel Ludu*, May 14, 1905, reprinted in [Dalecka et al.], *Marja Wysłouchowa*, 109–11, here: 109–10.
162 Orkan, "[Obituary]," 6.
163 Chołoniewski, *Nieśmiertelni*, 81–82. Emphasis in the original.
164 Chołoniewski, *Nieśmiertelni*, 81–82. Maria Wysłouchowa was not the only one to be attacked in the press. Natalja Kobryns'ka and another Ruthenian-language writer, Uljana Kravčenko, came in for similar treatment. See Knyš, *Smoloskyp*, 52.
165 Regarding discrepancies about the year of her birth, see Bohachevsky-Chomiak, "Natalia Kobryns'ka," 197, footnote 2. Knyš, *Smoloskyp*, 10, claims that 1851 is correct, and that 1855 is a widespread error attributable to her autobiography.
166 In Galicia, the Ruthenian-speaking population mainly comprised rural inhabitants in Eastern Galicia and the Greek Catholic clergy. Around the mid-nineteenth century, some 90% of the Ruthenian-speaking population worked in agriculture. Over time, the nobility had largely assimilated to the Polish elite (or the Russian elite in Eastern Ukraine). In the nineteenth century, a Ruthenian-speaking secular intelligentsia emerged. This was partly due to the Habsburg policy of promoting the educational level of the Greek Catholic clergy and positioning it against the ruling elite in Galicia,

Finding Roles: The Participants   105

the Roman Catholic Polish nobility. See Pacholkiv, *Emanzipation*, 7–24, 36–42; Jobst, "Nationalbewegung."
167 Kobryns'ka, "Avtobiohrafija." Regarding its publication history, see 403. The original is to be found in the manuscript department of BS, f. NTŠ, 475/III.
168 Regarding the biography, see Bilec'kyj, *Omeljan Ohonovs'kyj*, 9–19; Kozik, "Ohonovs'kyj."
169 Ohonovskij, "Natalja Kobryn'ska," *Zorja* (1893); Ohonovskij, "Natalja Kobryns'ka," In *Istorija*. Regarding the history of literature, see Bilec'kyj, *Omeljan Ohonovs'kyj*, 53–68.
170 Lehmann, *Bekennen*, 59–60.
171 Kobryns'ka, "Avtobiohrafija," 373.
172 Kremer, *Listy*.
173 Kobryns'ka, "Avtobiohrafija," 373.
174 Kobryns'ka, "Avtobiohrafija," 374.
175 Klementyna Tańska-Hoffmanowa wrote novels and published articles on the woman question and patriotic education. She was also involved in founding an institute for women's higher education. See Pietrow-Ennker, "Women," 18–19; Borkowska, Czermińska, and Phillips, *Pisarki*, 42–45.
176 Kobryns'ka, "Avtobiohrafija," 374–75.
177 Buckle, *History*.
178 Drahomanov taught at the Saint Vladimir Royal University (*Imperators'kyj Universytet SvjatohoVolodymyra*) in Kiev. He spent some time working in the illegal Ukrainian organization The Old Community (*Stara Hromada*) before being forced into exile. A political theorist and philosopher, he developed concepts for rural socialism which he believed hinged on developing a national consciousness. He became an important theorist for the Radicals in Galicia. Although he normally spelled his name "Drahomanov," occasionally the Ukrainian spelling "Drahomaniv" is found. Kobryns'ka corresponded with him and got to know him personally in Geneva. See below for more information. Regarding Drahomanov, see Subtelny, *Ukraine*, 284–86; Rudnytsky, "Drahomanov."
179 Kobryns'ka, "Avtobiohrafija," 377. She explicitly mentioned Ivan Franko's stories about Boryslav, "Boa Constrictor" (1878) and "Boryslav smijet'sja" (Boryslav Laughs, 1882). See Ivan Franko, *Boa Constrictor*. This is interesting because the narratives take a socialist rather than a nationalist perspective. One criticizes the capitalist mode of production in the Boryslav oil industry; the other describes a labor struggle fought in an atmosphere of solidarity. Moreover, they are visions for a possible labor movement, not realistic analyses. But precisely this—the anchoring of theoretical concepts in regional contexts and a blueprint for a possible future—may have impressed Kobryns'ka. Regarding the embedding of the narratives in Franko's political positions as well as the model character, see Hrytsak, "Cycle," Hrytsak, *Ivan Franko*, 240–64.
180 Kobryns'ka, "Avtobiohrafija," 377.
181 Kobryns'ka, "Avtobiohrafija," 377; Mill, *Subjection*. The book was translated into Polish as early as 1870. It should be noted that Wysłouchowa, too, had read both Buckle and Mill and used them for an analysis of the women's movement. See Suchmiel, "Books," 545; Wysłouchowa, "Ruch," 25; Chapter 4, Recitations.
182 *Sič* denoted the area of the strengthening Cossacks in the sixteenth century, whose collective coexistence as a protective alliance in the less fortified southeast border regions of the Russian Empire came to symbolize Ukrainian identity, especially in Eastern Ukraine. Subtelny, *Ukraine*,

106 Finding Roles: The Participants

108–12. The fact that the Ruthenian (i.e., mainly Galician) students in Vienna came together under this name is probably due to Drahomanov's influence on the socialist-nationalist ideas of the circles around Terlec'kyj and others. The name reinforced the Ukrainophiles' cross-border ideas of nationhood. Subtelny, *Ukraine*, 322.

183 Kobryns'ka, "Avtobiohrafija," 378.
184 Regarding Ukrainian realism, see Čyževs'kyj, *History*, 588–618. He describes realism as a "metonymic style" since the subjects dealt with represent society, contexts, and surroundings that are as important as the subject itself.
185 Kobryns'ka, "Avtobiohrafija," 379.
186 Monakhva, "Pchilka"; Onyškevyč, "Biohrafični informaciï," 477. Olena Pčilka was actually Ol'ha Drahomaniv-Kosač and was Mychajlo Drahomanov's sister as well as the mother of Lesja Ukraïnka, nowadays the most famous Ukrainian poet and playwright, who wrote her first poems for Kobryns'ka and Pčilka, *Peršyj vinok*. See Ukraïnka, "Pole"; Ukraïnka, "Rusalka"; Ukraïnka, "Ljubka"; Ukraïnka, "Na zelenomu horbočku."
187 Kobryns'ka, "Avtobiohrafija," 379.
188 Kobryns'ka, "Avtobiohrafija," 377.
189 In the Russian Empire, although the use of Ukrainian was restricted from the mid-nineteenth century and completely banned from the 1876 Ems Ukaz, its discrimination dates back to the Polish–Lithuanian period. A brief overview of its development and ban is provided by Moser, "Entwicklung," 491–92.
190 Stierle, "Geschichte."
191 Gilmore, "Mark."
192 Harriet Anderson, "Feminismus," 71.
193 Holdenried, *Autobiographie*, 24.
194 See for example the main biographical works on Kobryns'ka: Bohachevsky-Chomiak, *Feminists*, 71–86; Bohachevsky-Chomiak, "Natalia Kobryns'ka"; Knyš, *Smoloskyp*. The biography by a colleague and friend of Kobryns'ka is best described as a memoire: Dučymins'ka, *Natalija Kobryns'ka*.
195 Lejeune, "Pakt."
196 Himka, "Construction."
197 Casanova, *World*, 12.
198 Regarding the role of literature in the process of constructing national collectives, see for example Benedict Anderson, *Communities*, 67–82; regarding the invention of "small and large" literatures, see Casanova, *World*, 175–204; Prunitsch, *Konzeptionalisierung*.
199 Lyons, "Leser," 489; Lyons, *Culture*, 111–38.
200 Lionnet, *Voices*, XI–XIV; Mason, "Voice"; Neuman, "Autobiography."
201 Kozik, "Ozarkevyč."
202 Knyš, *Smoloskyp*, 9–14.
203 Bohachevsky-Chomiak, *Feminists*, 72.
204 Examples in Gleixner, *Pietismus*, 76–90. For a reference to the important part played by the pastor's wife, albeit primarily economic rather than cultural or social, see Mark, *Galizien*, 32–33.
205 Bohachevsky-Chomiak, "Natalia Kobryns'ka," 198–99.
206 Labins'ka, "Kobryns'ka," 120.
207 Bohachevsky-Chomiak, *Feminists*, 73.
208 Kobryns'ka, "Pani Šumins'ka"; Kobrynska, "Spirit"; Kobryns'ka, "Zadlja kusynka," 1958; Kobrynska, "Crust."
209 Senkus, "Pavlyk"; regarding his work see also Kačkan, "'Ja vid vas nikoly nikudy ne išov...'"

Finding Roles: The Participants 107

210 Bohachevsky-Chomiak, *Feminists*, 75.
211 Kobryns'ka to Franko, August 28, 1883, IlŠ, f. 3, 1618.
212 Kobryns'ka, "Pro pervisnu cil," 458–59; see also Malančuk-Rybak, *Ideolohija*, 401.
213 Bohachevsky-Chomiak, *Feminists*, 55–56.
214 See for example regarding the German Empire Jacobi, "'Entzauberung.'"
215 Bohachevsky-Chomiak, *Feminists*, 56.
216 See for example Kobryns'ka to Franko, July 23, 1884, September 5, 1885 and September 17, 1885, IlŠ, f. 3, 1603, reprinted in Kobryns'ka, *Vybrani tvory*, 1980, 390–93.
217 Onyškevyč, "Biohrafični informaciï," 475. The Pavlyk siblings came from the Galician countryside and were politically active in the socialist field.
218 Regarding the socialists' trial, see Jobst, *Nationalismus*, 33.
219 According to Knyš, *Smoloskyp*, 81–82; Voznjak, *Jak dijšlo do peršoho žinočoho al'manacha*, 44.
220 Kobryns'ka to the editors of *Dilo*, September 11, 1885, IlŠ, f. 100, 1801.
221 Kobryns'ka to the editors of *Dilo*, September 11, 1885, IlŠ, f. 100, 1801.
222 Kobryns'ka to the editors of *Dilo*, September 11, 1885, IlŠ, f. 100, 1801; see also Knyš, *Smoloskyp*, 79–80; Bohachevsky-Chomiak, *Feminists*, 78.
223 Kobryns'ka to Franko, December 16, 1885 and December 21, 1885, IlŠ, f. 3, 1603; Knyš, *Smoloskyp*, 81; Bohachevsky-Chomiak, "Natalia Kobryns'ka," 209.
224 For example the presentation at Dučymins'ka, *Kobryns'ka*, 21.
225 Bohachevsky-Chomiak, *Feminists*, 76.
226 Kobryns'ka and Pčilka, *Peršyj vinok*.
227 Monakhova, "Ukrainka"; Onyškevyč, "Biohrafični informaciï," 480. Her official name was Larysa Kosač-Kvitka.
228 The term *zadruga* (*zadruha* in Ukrainian) is used to describe a mainly south Slavic rural community or clan under the leadership of a patriarch and with common land, money and livestock. The Boykos and Hutzuls belong to the highlanders living in the western part of Ukraine and southeast Poland to this day.
229 Kobryns'ka, "Pan Suddja"; Kobrynska, "Judge".
230 Knyš, *Smoloskyp*, 116–17. Bohachevsky-Chomiak emphasizes the positive reception of the almanac. Bohachevsky-Chomiak, *Feminists*, 78.
231 Knyš, *Smoloskyp*, 17, 118–21; Onyškevyč, "Biohrafični informaciï," 474.
232 Pacholkiv, *Emanzipation*, 278.
233 Bohachevsky-Chomiak, "Nationalism," 148–49.
234 Kobryns'ka, "Žinoča sprava," 12.
235 Kobryns'ka to Šuchevyč, March 13, 1891, April 9, 1891 and April 23, 1891, BS, f. NTŠ, 824.
236 Bohachevsky-Chomiak, *Feminists*, 89. Regarding the General Provincial Centennial Exhibition in Prague, see Hofmann, "Utopien," 9–15.
237 Knyš, *Smoloskyp*, 163–64; K[obryns'ka], "Spomyny," 478.
238 See the extensive research on gender and nation, for example Pierson, "Nations"; Marakowitz, "Gender"; Ryan, "Question."
239 See *Dvě populární přednášky*.
240 Heczková, "Krásnohorská."
241 Knyš, *Smoloskyp*, 166. See also her correspondence in IlŠ, f. 101. The letters deal mainly with current feminist matters: petitions, appeals to women's assemblies, draft statutes for a kindergarten, etc.
242 K[obryns'ka], "Spomyny," 478.
243 Kobryns'ka to Sokolová-Seidlová, September 26, 1891, PNP, f. 33/40.
244 Kobryns'ka to Sokolová-Seidlová, February 21, 1907, PNP, f. 33/40.

108 Finding Roles: The Participants

245 Subtelny, *Ukraine*, 332; Pacholkiv, *Emanzipation*, 173; Gehmacher, "Nation."
246 [Kobryns'ka] "Petition." Regarding the number of signatures, see Knyš, *Smoloskyp*, 146.
247 The surveys of vernacular (*Umgangssprache*) by the Habsburg Empire formed an essential basis for the nationality conflicts, the struggle for "national possessions." Vernacular referred to everyday language, not necessarily the same as one's mother tongue. The languages to be employed in regional administrations and local schools were concluded from the distribution of different vernaculars, which was therefore fiercely contested. Vernaculars were demanded and used, and election campaigns were conducted with them. See Brix, *Umgangssprachen*, 353–89.
248 Partacz, *Od Badeniego*, 48–60; Buszko, "Consequences."
249 Knyš, *Smoloskyp*, 183 Against the background of the politics of the New Era, however, the Ruthenian deputies were no longer prepared to submit the petition, allegedly because it emphasized the pioneering role of Ruthenian women over Polish women. Instead, the petition was presented by a Czech deputy. Wysłouchowa was apparently also involved in the appeal to all women. In a letter to Solová-Seidlová, she mentioned the Bohemian initiative but disregarded the Ruthenian initiative. Wysłouchowa to Sokolová-Seidlová, December 7, 1891, PNP, 33/44.
250 The rally received little press coverage. See Bohachevsky-Chomiak, *Feminists*, 89–90. In addition, an appeal to finance the second women's almanac was adopted and signed by Kobryns'ka and Jarošynska. CDIA, f. 381, 1, 3, folio 48.
251 See Chapter 3, Rehearsing nation.
252 Malančuk-Rybak, *Ideolohija*, 222–26. In 1893, the joint petition organized by Teofil' Okunevs'kyj, a relative of Natalja Kobryns'ka, was presented in the Galician *Sejm*. On Okunevs'kyj see Wytrzens, "Okunevs'kyj." Support lists arrived from all parts of Galicia. Knyš, *Smoloskyp*, 88. The petition was printed in *Przedświt* (Dawn), which inaccurately claimed that the petition had been organized at the initiative of the Women's Reading Room in L'viv, Female Teachers' Association (*Stowarzyszenie Nauczycielek*), Women's Savings Association, and an Association of Girlfriends (*Związek koleżeński*). In 1894, on the initiative of Kazimiera Bujwidowa, one of the most active feminists in Galicia, 54 women applied to enroll at the Jagiellonian University (*Uniwersytet Jagielloński*) in Kraków. In addition, another petition was submitted to the Imperial Council, this time by a raft of Polish women's associations from L'viv and Kraków. In 1897, the first women were admitted to regular studies at the philosophical and medical faculties of the universities of Kraków and L'viv. See "Petycja"; Hulewicz, *Walka*, 52–53; Hulewicz, *Sprawa*, 247–48. Polish studies make no mention of the previous petitions.
253 [Kobryns'ka], *Promova*.
254 Bohachevsky-Chomiak, "Nationalism," 151.
255 Zimmermann, "Reich," 121; Leszczawski-Schwerk, *Tore*, 265–80.
256 Binder, "Das ruthenische Pressewesen."
257 Knyš, *Smoloskyp*, 150.
258 Dormus, "Galicyjskie stowarzyszenia," 343.
259 "A little help from men, even if only in the field of newspaper technology, would probably be necessary in the end, but this should not discourage our progressive women." Ivan Franko, "Almanac čy hazeta?," *Narod*, November 7, 1891, quoted by Knyš, *Smoloskyp*, 175–76, here: 176. The appropriation of women by the possessive determiner "our" and the latent threat

Finding Roles: The Participants 109

that working for the almanac would not be regarded as progressive are apparent.
260 Knyš, *Smoloskyp*, 175–80.
261 Regarding cooperation between the Ukrainian Radicals and the Polish peasant movement, see Hornowa, *Ukraiński obóz*, 114. Franko, for example, was the treasurer of the Association of Friends of Education. With regard to the social democrats and the Radicals, see Jobst, *Nationalismus*, 52–72, who stresses that the escalation of conflicts from 1895 onward was due not only to the dominance policy of Polish social democracy but also to the Radicals' efforts to set themselves apart.
262 See for example Evans, *Comrades*; Boxer, "Socialism."
263 See also [Kobryns'ka], "Petition"; Bohachevsky-Chomiak, *Feminists*, 88.
264 Kobryns'ka, "Avtobiohrafija," 379. Dučymins'ka, *Kobryns'ka*, 25. The coercion of marital conventions was a frequently discussed topic in nineteenth-century literature, for example in *Anna Karenina* and *The Kreutzer Sonata* by Lev Tolstoy, *Madame Bovary* by Gustave Flaubert, Henrik Ibsen's *A Doll's House*, and *Effi Briest* by Theodor Fontane. See Pavlyk, "Rebenščukova." Regarding the story's publication history, Kačkan, "Komentari," 147. It was first published in 1879 in *Hromads'kyj druh* (Friend of the Community), a magazine aimed at the sphere of the Radicals and the village. Binder, "Das ruthenische Pressewesen," 2117.
265 Bohachevsky-Chomiak, *Feminists*, 79–80; Bohachevsky-Chomiak, "Natalia Kobryns'ka," 211–12; Knyš, *Smoloskyp*, 131–35, here: 132–33.
266 The letters preceding the proposal bear witness to the fact that Kobryns'ka had hitherto expressed her deep respect to him and happily discussed literary and feminist political developments with him. See Kobryns'ka to Pavlyk, November 28, 1888, CDIA, f. 663, reprinted in Kobryns'ka, *Vybrany tvory*, 1980, 402.
267 See for example Bohachevsky-Chomiak, *Feminists*, 80.
268 New forms of relationships were much discussed and occasionally practiced in radical circles. See Alpern Engel, "Separatism"; Brower, *Nihilists*, 25–26, 219–25.
269 Hrytsak, *Ivan Franko*, 280–82. See also Knyš, *Smoloskyp*, 31–36. Kobryns'ka's brother consented because he himself could not marry his true love for family reasons, a state of affairs which inspired Kobryns'ka to write the story "For a Crust of Bread," according to Bohachevsky-Chomiak, *Feminists*, 377–78, footnote 11. See Chapter 2, Composing experience.
270 Wunder, *Sun*, 65–67.
271 Hausen, "Family."
272 See also Chapter 4, Monologues.
273 Kobryns'ka to Ohonovs'kyj, November 14, 1892, quoted after Ohonovs'kyj, "Natalja Kobryns'ka." In *Istorija*, 1270; Kobryns'ka, "Slivce," 105. This was preceded by experiments and debates among the radical Narodniks from the Russian Empire as well as the influences of romantic ideals of love and ideas about relationships from the early-nineteenth century, especially from France. Hrytsak, *Ivan Franko*, 277–86; Spurlock, "Love," 765; regarding the gender proposals of Charles Fourier, Henri de Saint-Simon and Robert Owen, see Kleinau, *Frau*; for an overview, see Kuhn and Kohser-Spohn, "Liebe," 489–96; Arni, "Seelengesetze"; see also Bohachevsky-Chomiak, *Feminists*, 109; regarding the Polish context, see Lorence-Kot and Winiarz, "Movement," 208–09; Stegmann, *Töchter*, 37–38.
274 Moszczeńska, "Mężczyzna"; Meyer-Renschhausen, *Kultur*, 271–372.
275 Pavlyk, "Peredne slovo," 9. The sideswipes against Kobryns'ka regarding, say, poor translations should be noted to underline the persistent

hostility on both sides. Pavlyk, "Peredne slovo," 12. In a letter to Franko, Kobryns'ka claimed that Pavlyk had stolen her letters from Drahomanov. Regardless of what had happened, the letter also testifies to the continuing resentment between the two. Kobryns'ka to Franko, August 1, 1906, IlŠ, f. 3, 1631.
276 Kobryns'ka, "Avtobiohrafija," 376.
277 Kobryns'ka to Makovej, September 10, 1898, quoted after Knyš, *Smoloskyp*, 264.
278 Knyš, *Žinka*, 62–69, especially 63–64. Regarding the exaggeration of the beloved and male self-direction, see also Bagłajewski, "Krasiński," 349.
279 Kobryns'ka to Franko, October 5, 1885, IlŠ, f. 3, 1603.
280 This interpretation is directed against the account frequently encountered that Franko had guided Kobryns'ka. For example, Onyškevyč, "Jak sleteno vinok," IX–XI. For a more complex description, see Hrytsak, *Ivan Franko*, 290, which highlights Franko's ambivalent role regarding mutual support for feminist activities.
281 Greenway, "Place," 201. See also Alpern Engel, "Separatism," 71, concerning the ascetic attitude of many radical women who rejected both physical and emotional desire as a codification of traditional femininity like marriage and bringing up children.
282 See also Ritz, "Polska," 111.
283 Polowy, "Kobylianska"; Hundorova, *Melancolica*.
284 Bohachevsky-Chomiak, *Feminists*, 106. See also the correspondence in IlŠ, f. 14.
285 [Kobryns'ka], *Naša dolja*. See also the appeal for donations in which Kobryns'ka and Jarošyns'ka addressed the dispute over a newspaper or an almanac and pointed out that no periodical had yet appeared, which is why they felt obliged, given the assembly's decision, to now tackle the publication of another almanac. Kobryns'ka and Jarošyns'ka, "Zinocyj al'manach."
286 "Barvinok"; see also Onyškevyč, "Biohrafični informaciï," 467. Hanna Barvinok was her stage name; her real name was Oleksandra Bilozers'ka-Kuliš and she was married to Pantelejmon Kuliš.
287 Men also wrote sporadically. For example, Kobryns'ka had asked Drahomanov who, however, refused. See Drahomanov to Kobryns'ka, May 14, 1893, reprinted in Pavlyk, *Perepyska*, 14.
288 Kobyljans'ka and K[obryns'ka], "Zvistky."
289 Leszczawski-Schwerk, "Frauenbewegungen," 68–76. See also the activities of Wysłouchowa and her women's circles regarding the bringing together of ethnographic studies as a basis for national interpretations and the presentation of employment for women, Chapter 1, Heroic narrating.
290 Mychajlo Pavlyk, "[No title]," *Narod*, January 9, 1894, quoted after Knyš, *Smoloskyp*, 217, 219.
291 Knyš, *Smoloskyp*, 226, 258.
292 Bohachevsky-Chomiak, *Feminists*, 83, 92–95.
293 Knyš, *Smoloskyp*, 272–73; Bohachevsky-Chomiak, *Feminists*, 95.
294 Kobryns'ka to Sokolová-Seidlová, February 21, 1907, PNP, f. 33/40; see also Knyš, *Smoloskyp*, 271–73.
295 Dučymins'ka, *Kobryns'ka*, 26.
296 Brzozowski, "Moraczewski," especially 691. Moraczewski came from Warsaw, studied chemistry and medicine in Zurich, and after various positions as a doctor and chemist, he was appointed professor at the Academy of Veterinary Medicine (*Akademia Medycyny Weterynaryjnej*) in L'viv in 1921. He was a patron of the fine arts and a connoisseur of Ukrainian culture. Interestingly, the author does not know his wife's maiden name.

Finding Roles: The Participants   111

297 On the ambivalence between social problems and the primacy of aesthetics in modern Ukrainian works, see also Simonek, "Literatur."
298 For the phases of Kobryns'ka's literary work, see Hundorova, "Kobryns'ka"; Moroz, "Natalja Kobryns'ka," 23–25. For general information on modernism in Central Europe, see Konstantinović and Rinner, Literaturgeschichte, 247–57.
299 Luckyj, "Overview," 687; see also Casanova, World, 303–23 for the example of Ireland.
300 Luckyj, "Overview," 690; Moroz, "Natalja Kobryns'ka," 20. Pavlychko, "Modernism," 83, speaks of a deep conflict between diverging artistic convictions.
301 These works were in print when the war broke out. Dučymins'ka, Kobryns'ka, 29.
302 Moroz, "Natalja Kobryns'ka," 25. Dučymins'ka, Kobryns'ka, III.
303 See for example the letters to Franko (1886–87), IlŠ, f. 3, 1608.
304 See the correspondence IlŠ, f. 13, f. 19; Kobryns'ka, "Zhadka."
305 PNP, f. 33/40. Kobryns'ka wrote about national events and considerations, reported on women's political goals and rallies, also personal matters, and expressed the hope that she would be visited in Bolechiv. For example, Kobryns'ka to Sokolová-Seidlová, May 25, 1892, PNP, f. 33/40.
306 K[obryns'ka], "Spomyny," 478.
307 At least there is a letter from Kobryns'ka to Wysłouchowa in which she admired her style and belittled her own work in comparison to Franko's. She was hopeful of collaboration, but probably nothing came of it—possibly because Wysłouchowa was already too ill. Kobryns'ka to Wysłouchowa, May 30, 1901, BO, 7188/II.
308 Kravtsiv and Horbach, "Nechui-Levytsky."
309 Kobryns'ka to Nečuj-Levyc'kyj, October 10, 1900, IlŠ, f. 1, 27895, reprinted in Kobryns'ka, Vybrani tvory, 1980, 415.
310 She was no exception. Life in the provinces was also the reason for the urgency of correspondence elsewhere. See Baasner, "Briefkultur," 16–17; Herres and Neuhaus, Vorwort to Netzwerke.
311 Kobryns'ka to Franko, January 16, 1899, IlŠ, f. 3, 1631.
312 Concerning the footnote as subtext and debate, see Gierl, "Polemik"; Lüdtke, "Alltagsgeschichte: Aneigung," 89.
313 Regarding the different aspects of letters, see also French, Women, 75–111.
314 Malančuk-Rybak, Ideolohija, 208–09; see also Bohachevsky-Chomiak, Feminists, 86–102.
315 Bohachevsky-Chomiak, "Nationalism," 145; Zhurzhenko, "Women," 263–65.
316 Malančuk-Rybak, Ideolohija, 205–06, footnote 117.
317 Kobryns'ka to Pavlyk, November 28, 1888, CDIA, f. 663, reprinted in Kobryns'ka, Vybrani tvory, 1980, 402.
318 Dučymins'ka, Kobryns'ka, 18.
319 Dučymins'ka, Kobryns'ka, 18.
320 Kobryns'ka, "Avtobiohrafija," 375.
321 Bohachevsky-Chomiak, "Natalia Kobryns'ka," 219.
322 According to the information on her diploma from AHMT, A, I. 2, 5586. Both 1872 and 1880 are also quoted as the year of her birth, e.g. B[rzoza], "Pomeranc-Melcerowa"; Brzoza, Żydowska mozaika, 207; Rudnicki, Żydzi, 416.
323 Sommerstein, "Krzewicielka," 31–33.
324 Buchstab Awi-Jonah, "Pamięc," 18–19.
325 Reichensteinowa, "Pozgonne dla Róży Melzerowej," 49.

112   Finding Roles: The Participants

326 Schaff, "Wspomnienie," 56.
327 Ricœr, *Rätsel*, 119.
328 Schreiber, "Wspomnienia," 12–13. Whether M. Pomeranz from Tarnopol, who was elected a representative of the executive committee of the Zionist World Organization in 1894, was a relative of Pomeranz is unknown. Landau, *Geschichte*, 56.
329 See for example Gillis, "Memory"; Sellin, "Nationalbewußtsein"; regarding Poland, Kobylińska, "Gedächtnis."
330 Regarding the concept of memorials, see the remarks in Assmann, "Gedächtnis."
331 Concerning the deterioration of Jewish group memory in modern times, see Yerushalmi, *Geschichte*; regarding the outstanding role of history in the Polish-Jewish press, see Steffen, *Polonität*, 92.
332 Regarding competing remembrance policies, see Hüchtker, "Blick."
333 Or, *Vorkämpferinnen*, 23–24; regarding the history of women's suffrage in the Habsburg Empire, see Bader-Zaar, "Bürgerrechte"; Bock, *Women*, 145–56.
334 *Stenographisches Protokoll der Verhandlungen des II. Zionisten-Congresses*, 239–40, here: 239. Emphasis in the original.
335 Regarding the national movements, see Planert, "Vater," 25–34; Berkowitz, "'Tzimmes'"; concerning feminist movements, see Bock, *Women*, 156–68.
336 Research on Zionism emphasizes the movement's patriarchal nature. See Prestel, "Frauen"; Montel, "Women"; Rose, "'Familie.'"
337 Gilmore, "Mark."
338 AHMT, A, I. 2, 5586.
339 AHMT, A, I. 2, 5586.
340 AHMT, A, I. 1, 5586. Regarding the admission of girls and women to conservatories, see Whistling, *Statistik*. From the 1850s onward, piano and harmony classes for girls were introduced at Vienna Conservatory (*Konservatorium Wien*), serving middle-class education. Although the Leipzig Conservatory was regarded as traditionalist from the 1870s, its international appeal was high, possibly due to the low importance of the entrance examination. Wasserloos, *Konservatorium*, 63. Reference is also made to art academies and conservatories in Freidenreich, *Lifes*, 21.
341 AHMT, A, I. 3, 5586. Concerning her education there, it is occasionally claimed that she studied in Vienna and Paris, for example Rudnicki, *Żydzi*, 416. The details contained on her diploma supplemented by the commemorative volume seem to me to be the most likely. "Jej życiorys," 3.
342 "Jej życiorys," 5.
343 According to Schreiber, "Wspomnienia," 13, they moved in 1909.
344 Buchstab Awi-Jonah, "Pamięci," 17–18.
345 B[rzoza], "Pomeranc-Melcerowa."
346 Maccabee celebrations were organized by the various local Zionist associations. The Maccabees' revolt in 168 BCE was celebrated as an example of national strength and (male) heroism. François Guesnet pointed out that these celebrations served the secularization of Zionist practice and made them part of the middle classes. Guesnet, "Chanukah," 244; for an overview, see Stanislawski, *Zionism*, XXI. In Galicia, too, advancement was more widespread (above all in towns aspiring to middle-class values, especially education) than might be assumed judging by the research literature, which tends to emphasize the poverty of the crownland and in particular its Jewish (and peasant) population. Thus, as Freidenreich, *Lifes*, 33, points out, there was a high proportion of female Jews from Galicia among Swiss

students. School education up to university entrance level and studying abroad required considerable financial means, even if students lived on a shoestring.
347 Obchody Machabeuszowskie: Korespondencya: Lwów. 1895. *Przyszłość* III (6): 43.
348 Makkabäer-Feiern: Stanislau. 1899. *Die Welt* III (51): 12.
349 "Jej życiorys," 4.
350 Obchody Machabeuszowskie: [Israeil Halevi], Tarnopol. 1895. *Przyszłość* III (6): 44–45.
351 Ruch syoński: Kołomyja. 1899. *Przyszłość* VII (10): 82–83.
352 See Chapter 4, Dialogues.
353 Vereinsnachrichten: Kolomea. 1899. *Die Welt* III (10): 14.
354 Aus der Bewegung: Berichte: Bielitz. 1903. *Die Welt* VII (14): 11. See also "Ms Pomeranz set out the motives and aims of the Zionists in a long, fiery speech and earned resounding applause." Aus der Bewegung. Berichte: Podwoloczyska, *Die Welt* VI (1902) 41, 13. The occasion was a "declamatory musical evening" in Podwołoczyska. At the Zion association's Maccabee celebration in Brody, Pomeranz gave a "perfect speech." Aus der Bewegung: Makkabäerfeiern: Brody. 1904. *Die Welt* VIII (53): 12; also at the Maccabee celebration in Grzymałów: Wieczorki Machabeuszowskie: Grzymałów. 1898. *Przyszłość* VII (5): 39. Pomeranz gave the main speech at the Maccabee celebration in Tarnopol. "The speech made a powerful impression." Wieczorki Machabeuszowskie: Tarnopol. 1901. *Wschód* I (17): 7.
355 Berichte: Kolomea. 1900. *Die Welt* IV (16): 12.
356 N. M. Gelber, *Toldot*, 804–10.
357 Die zionistische Bewegung: Kolomea. 1899. *Die Welt* III (10): 12–13.
358 Berichte: Kolomea. 1901. *Die Welt* V (16): 12. The association still existed in 1907. Gaisbauer, *Davidstern*, 243. The close connection between academic and women's associations and their distribution in Galicia points to the main grass roots of the movement: students, young women, and educated people.
359 Aus der Bewegung: Tarnopol. 1903. *Die Welt* VII (12): 13 and (17): 11. This association is not mentioned in Gaisbauer's list for 1907 and was a section of Bar Kokhba. Gaisbauer, *Davidstern*, 241.
360 See for example Max Geyer to the Zionist Central Bureau, Kraków, May 8, 1913; Rzeszów, May 13, 1913: Gorlice, May 22, 1913; Sanok, May 25, 1913, CZA, Z3/813. Geyer reported on disputes, including physical ones, with the local rabbis and the synagogue visitors, about the conditions in the associations, about the success of speeches, and the proceeds of the shekel collections as well as the itinerary.
361 N. M. Gelber, *Toldot*, 809. Pomeranz apparently also reminded the nationwide Zionist associations not to neglect agitation among women. A women's group was founded in Stryj as a result of her visit there in 1898. N. M. Gelber, "Stryj"; Mark H. Gelber, *Pride*, 179.
362 See the other references in *Die Welt*: "Miss Rosa Pomeranz [spoke] with persuasive, fiery words." Die zionistische Bewegung: Kolomea. 1899. *Die Welt* III (10): 12–13, here: 13. "Accomplishedly and using persuasive dialectics, the speaker demonstrated the need for Zionism." The report mentions her "proven leadership" of a boarding school for Jewish girls. A "particularly interesting speech" is mentioned in the report on the first women's conference. See [Von unserem Berichterstatter], "Die I. Konferenz."
363 B[rzoza], "Pomeranc-Melcerowa." The Jewish Women's Circle served as a model for other similar initiatives, for instance in Rzeszów. N. M. Gelber,

"History." Contrary to Gelber's account, it was not the first women's association there. Shulamit, a Zionist association for women and girls, is recorded in Rzeszów for 1907 and its foundation may date back to the 1890s. Gaisbauer, *Davidstern*, 240.

364 At the Second World Congress, the women already set up "a provisional committee for the creation of a world association of Jewish women." The above-mentioned appeal by Rozia Ellmann was read out and then disseminated in *Die Welt*. See Die zionistische Bewegung: Wien. 1898. *Die Welt* II (46): 12; Bovermann, "Gegenwartsarbeit," 51–58.

365 N. M. Gelber, *Toldot*, 810.

366 Brzoza, *Żydowska mozaika*, 207. After the First World War, the association was renamed Association of Jewish Women of Eastern Lesser Poland (*Związek Kobiet Żydowskich Małopolski Wschodniej*).

367 Gaisbauer, *Davidstern*, 271, names 14 from all four Galician districts.

368 By the time of the First Zionist World Congress in 1897, the Galician Zionist movement was well organized. A considerable number of Zionist associations and different currents already existed. Nationalist cultural work and colonization policy in Palestine often contrasted with political Zionism of the type represented by Theodor Herzl and others. Gaisbauer, *Davidstern*, 194–244.

369 Gaisbauer, *Davidstern*, 88–89, 96; Haumann, "Zionismus," 36–37.

370 The shekel collections and contributions to the National Fund were intended to finance colonization projects in Palestine. There were collecting tins for donations everywhere in the associations. The amounts collected were reported. Contributions were regularly broken down by region, and large donations were listed with the name of the source in *Die Welt*. The collections represented a specific form of networking of the transnational movement.

371 Ruch syoński: Drohobycz. 1898. *Przyszłość* VII (3): 23.

372 [Syonistki stanisławowskie], "Odezwa."

373 [Syonistka lwowska], "Słów kilka."

374 See also Chapter 4, Dialogues.

375 Gaisbauer, *Davidstern*, 207; "Landesconferenz," 5; "Krajowa konferencya," 8. This conference dealt with the integration of the Galician Zionist associations into a Cisleithanian organization. "Krajowa konferencya," 4; see also Gaisbauer, *Davidstern*, 206–07.

376 "Krajowa konferencya," 7. In 1910, she expressed her views on nationalist education at the Provincial Conference of Galician Zionists and toasted David Wolffsohn, President of the Zionist World Organization, who was staying in L'viv, at the banquet of honor. "Die IX. Landeskonferenz," 312, 314.

377 "Der X. Zionisten-Kongress," 800. She had run for several electoral groups in different districts. The sum of the election results was used to decide the delegates. In the Husiatyn electoral group, Tarnopol district, she was made an alternate delegate; the same thing also happened in the constituency of Złoczów-Jezierna-Zborów. In Drohobycz VI she came third, but first in Tarnopol I–III. Two hundred shekel-counters from Drohobycz VIII formed a special electoral group who likewise chose Pomeranz. CZA, Z2/191; see also "Der X. Kongreß."

378 Pomeranz delivered her speech at the women's assembly on August 11, 1911. See "Versammlung." Mirjam Schach, a Zionist from Paris, presented the resolution to the entire congress. At the same time, she criticized the Zionist movement as being dominated by men. *Stenographisches Protokoll der Verhandlungen des X. Zionisten-Kongresses*, 219–32. The Congress decided almost unanimously to found a league of women's organizations.

Finding Roles: The Participants 115

Stenographisches Protokoll der Verhandlungen des X. Zionisten-Kongresses, 233. Regarding Schach, see also Vilmain, "Woman."
379 "Versammlung."
380 At the beginning of 1910, a Central Office for Women's Zionist Work (*Zentralstelle für die Zionistische Frauenarbeit*) was set up in the Central Office of the World Zionist Organization (*Zentralbüro der Zionistischen Weltorganisation*) in Cologne. However, the resolution adopted by the X Congress remained controversial and was repeated under an amended title at the XI Congress. See Or, *Vorkämpferinnen*, 143–55, 180–87; Bovermann, "Gegenwartsarbeit," 174–84.
381 Schorrowa, "Plon," 34.
382 "Delegiertenmandate." 1913. *Die Welt* XVII (23): 734 and (25): 802.
383 Jewish soup kitchens had existed before. Kronika: B., Stanisławów w grudniu 1902. 1902. *Wschód* III (114): 11.
384 Such a society was founded in 1916, also under the management of Pomeranz. *Z działalności tow. warsztatów rękodzielniczych dla dziewcząt żydowskich. Sprawozdanie z lata 1915–1932*, L'viv 1932, 8–19, quoted after N. M. Gelber, *Toldot*, 812.
385 After the invasion of Galicia by Russian troops in 1914, part of the Jewish population fled. One of the first destinations within reach was Vienna. By 1915, the number of refugees had already decreased again significantly. Klaus Hödl states 125,000 for 1914, compared to just 77,000 in 1915. Hödl, *Bettler*, 280.
386 Schorrowa, "Plon," 35.
387 N. M. Gelber, *Toldot*, 812–36.
388 Rothfeld, "Wspomnienia," 23.
389 Rothfeld, "Wspomnienia," 25–26.
390 According to N. M. Gelber, *Toldot*, 812, the association had already acquired the building shortly before the outbreak of war.
391 The promotion of agricultural education for girls (as well as for boys) was part of the Zionist program and targeted settlement projects in Palestine. Agricultural work promised not only employment opportunities but also the strengthening of the body, according to Zionist ideas. See Prestel, "Frauen," 58–59.
392 See Chapter 3, Designing society.
393 The Zionist Organization in Eastern Lesser Poland (*Organizacja Syjonistyczna w Małoposlce Wschodniej*) is also mentioned occasionally. Brzoza, *Żydowska mozaika*, 91, 128, 207; Jaworski, *Struktura*, 33; Rudnicki, *Żydzi*, 416. For the 1922 *Sejm* election, the Zionist organization joined the list of the United League of Zionist Parties (*Farajnigter Farband fun di Cionistisze Organizacje in Pojlen/Komitet Zjednoczonych Stronnictw Narodowo-Żydowskich*). The development of independent Zionist organizations in southeast Poland had been favored by the fact that until 1923, due to postwar border conflicts, the region was only administered by the state and not considered part of the national territory. Rudnicki, *Żydzi*, 25–26; see also Borodziej, *Geschichte*, 97–124.
394 Halpern, "Polityka." Davies, *Playground*, 408, erroneously claims 1919.
395 Brzoza, *Żydowska mozaika*, 91, 128, 207; "Jej życiorys," 7. A reference to a trip to Berlin and participation in a public women's meeting where among other things the subject of abortion was discussed can be found in Melcerowa, "Jeszcze o kontroli." In what capacity Pomeranz attended is unfortunately not stated in the article, and neither is the nature of the assembly.
396 B[rzoza], "Pomeranc-Melcerowa"; Brzoza, *Żydowska mozaika*, 207.
397 Schreiber, "Wspomnienia," 14. Regarding welfare state policy in the partition areas and the Second Republic of Poland, see the brief summary by Dagmar Schulte, "History," 112–17.

116 Finding Roles: The Participants

398 B[rzoza], "Pomeranc-Melcerowa."
399 Hecht, *Feminismus*, 244. The Jewish World Aid Conference was an international association of delegates from Jewish social organizations. It met in 1920 and again in 1924.
400 Jewish People's School Society (*Żydowskie Towarzystwo Szkoły Ludowej*), Skilled Trades Association (*Towarzystwo Warsztatów Rękodzielniczych*). Brzoza, *Żydowska mozaika*, 207.
401 Schaff, "Wspomnienia," 55.
402 See Melzerowa to an unnamed woman from Warsaw, May 14, 1925, reprinted in [Feuersteinowa, Jegerowa, and Schreiberowa], *Pamięci*, 43–45, here: 44. She went to the USA in 1923/24.
403 Kondracka, "Aktywność"; Sachße and Tennstedt, *Geschichte*, 66–67; Bock, "Poverty," 422–28.
404 See Chapter 4, Monologues.
405 Steffen, *Polonität*, 31.
406 "Jej życiorys," 6; Brzoza, *Żydowska mozaika*, 207.
407 Shmuel Feiner arrives at a similar conclusion regarding the literature of the *Haskala*, the Jewish Enlightenment. See Feiner, "Pseudo-Enlightenment," 63.
408 "Jej życiorys," 4.
409 Pomeranz, *Im Lande*. In *Die Welt*, the novel was announced prior to publication with reference to the author known for her "excellent articles." See Zeitschriften- und Bücher-Rundschau. 1900. *Die Welt* IV (49): 10; regarding the novel, see also Chapter 2, Enacting history.
410 See for example Tatarowski, *Ludowość*, 372–77 concerning the connection between the ethnographic and romantic interpretation of peasant life in literature; see also Grözinger, "Volkserzählungen."
411 Bechtel, *Renaissance*, 123–39. For more on cultural Zionism with its literary ambitions briefly referred to as the Young Jewish Movement, see Mark H. Gelber, *Pride*, 17–54. However, I doubt that the term "Young Jewish" is owed to the youth cult of the Zionist movement as Gelber believes. A reference to contemporary concepts such as "Young Poland" or "Young Ruthenians," i.e., to a change of generation and position, appears more likely.
412 Von Glasenopp, *Judengasse*; Schiffmann, "Ghettogeschichte"; Häusler, "'Ghetto.'"
413 See Mark H. Gelber, *Pride*, 190–93; in general, see Heyde, *Ghetto*.
414 Kaszynski, "Anteil"; Konstantinović and Rinner, *Literaturgeschichte*, 369–74.
415 See for example Franzos, *Halb-Asien*; Franzos, *Don*; for a more complex approach Wittlin, *Salt*.
416 Bock and Zimmermann, "Querelle."
417 Pomeranz, "Die Frauen und der Zionismus."
418 See Chapter 4, Dialogues.
419 Pomeranz, "Dienstboten."
420 Melcerowa, "Dlaczego milczą kobiety?"; Melcerowa, "Jeszcze o kontroli"; Melcerowa "Uświadomieni."
421 Steffen, *Polonität*, 210.
422 Steffen, "'Mutterschaft,'" 106. *Ewa* appeared once a week and is thought to have had a circulation of 2,000.
423 Plach, "Feminism," 243.
424 Plach, "Feminism," 252. Regarding Zionist women's policy in the interwar period, see also Mickutė, "Woman."
425 Plach, "Feminism," 259–60.

Finding Roles: The Participants 117

426 Stegmann, "Paradygmaty"; Arni, "Seelengesetze," especially 203–06; Turda, *Modernism*, 13–39 regarding the pathos of the sciences at the turn of the twentieth century; for an overview of social policy, see Hering and Waaldijk, *Guardians*.
427 Pomeranz, *An die jüdischen Frauen*, 8–9. Regarding the appeal, see also Chapter 4, Dialogues.
428 Plach, "Feminism," 249.
429 For instance Melcerowa, "Dlaczego milczą kobiety?"
430 Melcerowa, "Jak to zrobić?"; see also Reichensteinowa, "Pozgonne dla Róży Melzerowej," 50. The debates in European women's movements were already taking place before the First World War; the term comes from the Polish women's movement. Stegmann, *Töchter*, 121, 196.
431 Reichensteinowa, "Pozgonne dla Róży Melzerowej," 50–51. In her curriculum vitae, this is called Eugenic Counselling Center (Poradnia eugeniczna). "Jej życiorys," 8. Eugenic and social-Darwinian concepts were widespread in German-speaking Judaism, especially in the Zionist sphere. See for example Stanislawski, *Zionism*, 246–48; Rose, "'Familie,'" 192. Gilman, "Body," shows the connection between anti-Semitism and contemporary debates about the body, the nation, pathologization and degeneration, yet also points to their adoption in Jewish contexts. Even Pomeranz spoke occasionally of the *Rassejüdin* (pure-bred Jewess). See for instance Pomeranz, "Bedeutung," 330.
432 Regarding the different effects of topoi, norms and debates in different contexts using the example of Jewish body politics in the Weimar Republic, see Gillerman, "Körperpolitik," 213.
433 Melcerowa, "Kobieta."
434 Melcerowa, "Niezgoda." Emphasis in the original.
435 Melcerowa, "Miłość," 6.
436 Shilo, "Image," also emphasizes the complexity of the femininity model in Zionism and the rhetoric of equality with its simultaneous non-observance—albeit for early Zionism in Palestine.
437 Schaff, "Wspomnienie," 52.
438 Reichensteinowa, "Pozgonne dla Róży Melzerowej," 49.
439 See above all "Jej życiorys."
440 "Jej życiorys," 9; see also the obituary by Ochs, "Rosa Pomeranz-Melzer."
441 See Stegmann, *Töchter*, 55–57.
442 "X. Landeskonferenz," 11. See also Gmür, "'Women,'" 295–96.
443 Wurzel, "Kobieta," 21.
444 For an overview of research on the topos of love, see Bauer, Hämmerle, and Hauch, "Liebe"; see also Sieder, Editorial to *Österreichische Zeitschrift*.
445 For further information, see Stegmann, *Töchter*, 119. Concerning the complications of such partnerships in an academic environment, starting with the name, see Hahn, *Namen*, 109–39.
446 The "new woman" (Polish: "nowa kobieta," Ukrainian "dívčaty, dívčyny" [girls], English "flapper," French "garçonne"; the terms also have a sexual connotation), a catchword especially in the interwar period, represented a lifestyle considered modern and emancipated: social and sexual independence, employment in the new postal and administrative occupations, short hair and simple clothing. For an overview, see Cott, "Woman"; Sohn, "Wars," 93–94; for the Jewish and Zionist context, see also Shilo, "Image"; Freidenreich, "'Frau.'"
447 See also the relationship between Lesja Ukraïnka and Ol'ha Kobyljans'ka. Pavlychko, "Modernism," 86–90.
448 Lawaty, "Konzeption."

118 Finding Roles: The Participants

449 Regarding Great Britain, see for example Taylor, *Eve*, 183–216; for the Jewish context, Biale, "Eros"; Seidman, "Erotics."
450 Regarding the different concepts of modernism in Europe, see Hutnikiewicz, *Polska*, 54–60. His thesis is that at the turn of the century, modernism no longer meant a norm violation like romanticism, but the search for the true, higher order of life or pure aesthetics against the background of an uncertain existence, the reality of the bohemian, the artist proletariat. In his view, "Young Poland" was by no means as radical and eccentric as the bohemians in Great Britain or Paris, for example. Concerning the various social and political options for radicalizing women's lives, see also Stites, *Movement*, 64–232. Eastern Ukrainian and Russian female students represented the contemporary cliché of female radicalism: short hairstyles, unaccompanied in public, and smoking. See Freidenreich, *Lifes*, 10; Knyš, *Smoloskyp*, 74–75; Pietrow-Ennker, *Menschen*, 157–88.
451 Strasser and Schein, "Intersexions."
452 Chartier and Hébrard, "Entre public et privé."

2 Propagating The Plays

As well as making political demands, the three protagonists wrote literary and historical stories. In Kobryns'ka's view, literature was especially suitable for reaching out to different types of women and attracting them to a common political platform:

> Women who are excluded from general and public affairs, who occupy no position in society where they can exert influence, who have no opportunity to express their *common needs in life* should spend even more time reading literature, where they will find insights into these needs and demands.[1]

Kobryns'ka saw a logical relationship between political insignificance and the study of literature. In her view, since women were excluded from public affairs, they needed other sources of knowledge, which were to be found in belles-lettres: "For if literature in general represents the ideal history of society as a whole, belles-lettres can boldly be called the history of women."[2] In Kobryns'ka's view, belles-lettres helped women learn about their needs as a collective and about their common history. Kobryns'ka's argument was historical, not essentialist. It wasn't woman per se she saw reflected in novels, but rather women's history—their history of exclusion.

Wysłouchowa justified her publishing activity somewhat differently. Regarding the magazine *Zorza*, she wrote:

> My passionate, heartfelt dream is for this little magazine to fill a gap that we in particular experience, where the cultural education of the people does not go hand in hand with political enlightenment. This is why I will above all endeavor to initially familiarize readers with literature from our homeland in essays discussing works by famous writers in order to start providing them with small gems.[3]

Wysłouchowa construed the need to publish from the lack of cultural education, a situation she believed could be remedied by specific literary forms. Both she and Kobryns'ka believed that literature was extraordinarily relevant to politics owing to the need to counteract discrimination, the exclusion of the female sex, and the neglect of general education.

In the course of research into the invention of tradition and the construction of the nation, attention has repeatedly been drawn to the importance of literature and language. Folk literature—songs, poems, proverbs, yet also popular stories—represented the commonalities and inter-temporal connections of the imagined collective, with the relevance of cultural identity formations as a substitute for political institutions being especially emphasized for marginal, colonized, and stateless nations.[4] Seen thus, "minor literatures"—literatures of marginalized nations in the global canon—have a political function. It is assumed that whereas "major literatures" obey aesthetic criteria, in minor literatures aesthetic aspects are frequently sacrificed for political purposes.

By contrast, Pascale Casanova regards the independence of aesthetic criteria to be just such a strategy in the competitive arena of literary significance like the close association between political authority and literary practices of minor literatures.[5] She examines world literature as a literary space, invented as universal and autonomous, into which authors have to write their way. Their strategies are intended to achieve visibility and significance in this space; they may differ, fluctuate between assimilation and dissemination, between individual and collective, world and national literature. She analyzes the criteria of this space—visibility, language, audience—as historical and relational. She understands the idea that the definition of world literature obeys purely aesthetic, politically neutral criteria to be part of a game whose rules are accepted by all the participants. Nevertheless, according to Casanova, backstage there is a struggle for recognition and significance.[6]

Casanova's observations do more than encourage understanding the writing of fictional and historical stories as strategies in the struggle between competing national literatures and between competing political movements. They also enable Kobryns'ka's aesthetic and political intentions to be analyzed as related rather than contrasting goals. The political significance of stories stems from their content and their aesthetic conception. In addition, Kobryns'ka and Wysłouchowa responded with their stories to the establishment of reading as a pastime. The reading practice gradually changed as libraries and reading rooms multiplied thanks to educational efforts by the state and mass movements. And as the proportion of fictional literature in reading matter increased, it became a means to reach the population.[7]

Below, the written output of Kobryns'ka and Wysłouchowa is examined. I will analyze how stories contributed to constituting women's politics[8]—for if political projects are to be examined as performances, the question of the "play" arises. The arena of women's politics required not just rules, such as the language of reasoning, but also a play that shaped the campaigners' enactments. I will explore the workings of the discursive, performative ritualizations and differentiation in the publications of the three women. First, I will show using the example of *Przodownica* and *Zorza* how writing for a collective, in this case for rural women, was shaped by Wysłouchowa. Second, I will analyze stories by Pomeranz and Kobryns'ka, namely "Oci—agitatorami syonizmu" (The Others—Agitators of Zionism)[9] and "Eine offene Frage" (An Open Question)[10] by Pomeranz as well as Kobryns'ka's "The Spirit of Times," "For a Crust of Bread" and "Jadzja i Katruzja," translated as "Yadzya and Katrusya."[11] The first two in particular were considered initiation signals for a Ruthenian women's movement.[12] The strategic use of experience in the narrative to create common ground is examined. In the third step, the perpetuation of commonalities is shown using the example of Pomeranz's novel *Im Lande der Noth*. It is assumed that presenting experience as a story was able to legitimize the desire for change.

The aesthetic value of the texts is only discussed with regard to political strategies. However, it would be interesting to analyze their aesthetics in terms of universality and autonomy, both because the aesthetic significance of Kobryns'ka's writing was important to her[13] and to examine the historicity of aesthetic values. However, the interpretation proposed here focuses on a historical question, that of the importance of stories for political movements around 1900. The starting point is the proposition that a political movement construes a collective based on experiences legitimized by referring to history. The interplay of experience and collectivity turned the story into history and at the same time pointed to changeability and the possibility of a better future. The past was considered a collectively shared experience from which obvious, logical future visions were derived. As a result, despite the differences between political movements, there were similarities in their declared aims regarding the creation of a collective, the construction of experiences, and the historical legitimation of a future vision.

How the meta-narrative functioned can be revealed if we distinguish between the level of the story and that of discourse, i.e. the "how" of narration.[14] The configuration becomes politically legible from the place of publication, for example if the work was published in a movement's organ. Stories were capable of conveying a kind of meta-narrative about the context of collectives, experience, and history going beyond the specific subject matter, the plays called "Discrimination Against Peasants, Women or Jews." Therefore, the decisive element is not the extent to which the stories are to be understood as milieu depictions or constructions of reality or under what literary genres—realism, neoromanticism, or ghetto literature—they can be classified, but how the writing strategies functioned in the contested field introduced by Casanova.

Writing Collectives into Existence

The two magazines *Przodownica* and *Zorza*, founded in 1899 and 1900, were very similar with respect to their layout, language, and structure, as can be seen from the vignettes on the first pages. The lettering "Przodownica" can be seen floating above a cornfield against the rising sun. In the front on the left is a young female harvest worker creating a sheaf with a wooden fork (Figure 2.1).

The lettering "Zorza" also hovers in the treetops above the vastness of a landscape with the rising sun on the horizon. The young female villager is sitting in the foreground on the left with a newspaper on her lap (Figure 2.2).

The drawings and mastheads are very similar, in both cases implying that the magazines are aimed at women, deliver enlightenment to the countryside, and convey the authority of knowledge. Moreover, the mastheads and pictures romanticize rural life, which radiates brightness and naturalness. This blend of romance and reform politics, of image and text, is the starting point for the following observations on the conception and practice of Wysłouchowa's publishing strategies. They refer to her time as an editor, i.e. for *Przodownica* from 1899 to 1900, and for *Zorza* until 1902.[15]

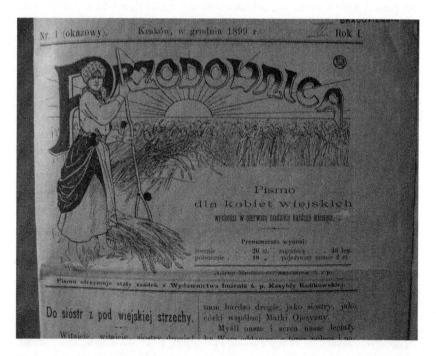

Figure 2.1 Przodownica, detail of the front page, Podkarpacie Biblioteka Cyfrowa, public domain.

Figure 2.2 Zorza, detail of the front page, Polona, public domain.

The aim of both magazines was to address rural women and report on all aspects of life.[16] They pursued both women's aims and national objectives, assuming the former are the empowerment of women[17] and the latter comprise strengthening the Polish independence movement. They were supposed to be comprehensible to the rural population, especially females, to educate readers and familiarize them with modern knowledge. Each issue contained 16 pages and often began with a poem. This was followed by a main article and two or three other items on Polish history (e.g. about famous historical figures and the origins of public holidays) or stories by well-known Polish writers. Both magazines were also the first to publish a new generation of authors and a handful of female writers from the countryside. Other articles dealt with parenting or suggestions on how to improve the efficiency of household management or agriculture. There followed short texts (usually with no byline) addressing aspects of homemaking and farming as well as hygiene and medicine. Several articles and news items dealt with conflicts over Polish religious and historical education in the Province of Poznań and the active role of women in these conflicts.[18] The comparatively extensive coverage underlines the importance attached to strengthening the nation in all three partitions. In addition, the news items can be interpreted as an attempt to integrate women from the Prussian partition more closely into an all-Polish women's politics.

The section "Miscellaneous" (*Rozmaitości*) contained all sorts of announcements, advice, items, and news about political events (e.g. rallies) in women's and national movements. However, little space was devoted to Galician political news;[19] nor were there any reports about political meetings of the peasant movement or party politics. Judging by the advice given, the magazines were aimed at the married female peasant as the head of her farmstead. There was no mention of any problems suffered by unmarried women, farm girls, or the landless rural poor.[20] As in her travelogue on Silesia, Wysłouchowa romanticized conditions in the countryside.

The first issue of *Przodownica* began with "Greetings, greetings, dear sisters."[21] *Zorza* headed its editorial introduction with "A Word to Readers Male and Female!" but then went on to use the phrase "dear sisters" in the text itself.[22] "Sisters" was a salutation widely used in nationalist circles; although intended to convey common ground and overcome social differences, it was not necessarily confined to women's movements.[23] The greeting opened up a direct, personal level of communication. This salutation, also repeated in various articles, created the illusion of a conversation in a number of ways.[24] It was intended to make it easier for female (and also male) peasants to overcome the unfamiliarity of the magazine as a medium. As the introductory article in *Przodownica* continued: "At first you will doubtless not find it easy to read the magazine, it will not be easy to understand everything it says."[25]

In addition, communication was a central rhetorical stylistic device of the magazines. This included printing letters to the editor, which played a prominent role.[26] The letters were selected and edited, some were rewritten to put their point across more clearly, and some may well have been written by the staff themselves. The element of communication was reinforced by another section containing responses to unprinted letters to the editor. The fact that the answers are often difficult to grasp because the original question is unknown heightens the impression of an authentic conversation.[27] Readers responded well to this encouragement to communicate with the magazine, as shown by a raft of letters to Wysłouchowa and the editors of *Zorza* in the Wysłouchs' estate. They were written by priests, students, yet also politically active ironworkers, technicians, and sometimes peasants (both female and male). Occasionally, men wrote on behalf of their female family members, for example to order a subscription.[28] A high school student from L'viv sent in poems he had written for publication.[29] Other letters praised the magazine or reported delivery problems. Rather than the average readership, the letters mainly represented activists (mostly male), many of whom were educated and social climbers. By the way, the magazine was read by men as well as women.[30]

There are several references to reading aloud to others, a widespread custom due to the significant number of inexperienced readers. Researchers largely agree that illiteracy was extremely high in Galicia and the development of the elementary school system poor, despite the reform programs and compulsory education introduced under Joseph II.[31] Recent research paints a more nuanced picture of literacy. It regards reading and writing as contextually bound resources, not as indicators of a general level of development, and emphasizes that an inability to write is not the same as being unable to read, pointing out for example that the Catholic Church encouraged the reading of the catechism.[32] The practice of reading aloud should therefore not solely be interpreted as a consequence of illiteracy, but also seen in the context of (rural) everyday practices. The possibilities of reading aloud paved the way for the new medium (and new knowledge) to become part of everyday life. The communicative language employed corresponded to the suggestions concerning the use of the medium. *Zorza* directed and represented audience participation the most strongly.[33] Its more consistent involvement of the rural population—especially against the background of conflicts between Siedlecka and Wysłouchowa—was the biggest difference between the two magazines so similar in terms of style and presentation.

In addition to participatory and communicative aspects, the involvement of the audience through the use of direct address emphasized the commonality of the collective "women." For example, an article on Polish national heritage in Switzerland begins with the sentence: "We women, and especially peasant women, rarely travel the world."[34] The pronoun "we" refers to all women. The article goes on to say: "Domestic duties and never-ending work keep us at home. Nevertheless, even when sitting down at home, one can also know what is most worthy of attention out in the wide world and find out what is going on."[35] "We" constitutes a commonality of women rooted in their gender, namely being tied to the hearth. But this also leads to the possibility of finding a common way out. The message is that women who are able to read can overcome domestic restrictions. This was worth highlighting since it evoked associations with contemporary discourse on women's emancipation. The construction of a domesticity trapping all women and of escape enabled by education was one of the common narratives of women's movements.

The form of address "dear sisters" harbors another aspect apart from the communicative. "Sisters" creates a common level between writer and reader. The commonality results from both gender and a common family, i.e. origin. But whereas in a family, elder and younger sisters have different, unchanging positions, the use of "female friends" (an equally conceivable form of address) does not specify a hierarchy. Similarly, the character of the relationship was defined: "We ourselves will learn, read, conduct research because we have more time to do so and because it is easier in the cities [to acquire] education, and then with joyful hearts we will share everything we have learned with you."[36] In contrast to "we women," this "we" means the magazine's producers. Although all "sisters" learn, the relationship between them is fixed, for only some of them teach and write. The knowledge to be taught is acquired in cities. The word "city" implies a knowledge created in institutions and written down in books, a knowledge the editors bring with them. This knowledge has not been handed down and does not result from experience in the countryside. The readers are solely passive in this construction. They are objects of the political work of the writer and have no control over what they are taught. This unequally distributed access to knowledge creates a hierarchy among women.

The magazines' message was reinforced by illustrations. In one of the first issues of *Zorza,* the section devoted to homemaking tips begins with an explanation of a reproduced drawing. A woman, identifiable by her attire as Silesian, is reading out from a newspaper while the second woman listens to her without putting her tools down. The explanation reads: "Work bears the best fruit when it is illuminated by the light of knowledge."[37] The written explanation of this fairly clear imagery is performative: it academizes the image through writing, creating a hierarchical relationship between academic and experiential knowledge. The implicitly delivered appeal to women to read out to others refers once again to the direction of communication from those who are able to read to those who are illiterate, thereby formulating the aim to restructure social conditions in rural areas. Incidentally, the Silesian peasant women are presented as role models again.[38]

A letter written to the editor by a female villager also indicates this change in rural hierarchies. She complained that women's access to information was prevented even more than for men by the arduous nature of agricultural toil. As a result, women gossiped and spread superstitious ideas about bewitched food. Only *Zorza* brought a few "bright moments into our sad lives."[39] This letter not only supports the cliché of women being particularly backward but also emphasizes *Zorza's* role in transforming the prerogative of interpretation: denigrating village knowledge as superstition raises those with access to modern knowledge above those without.[40]

What kind of knowledge was conveyed? The magazines claimed to introduce institutional knowledge into villages and integrated rural knowledge into a national canon. Their goal was to amass knowledge that would constitute a united Poland with an outstanding place for women. In particular, the editor herself reported on famous men and women from Polish history, for instance Queen Jadwiga and the establishment of the Polish–Lithuanian Commonwealth through her marriage to Jogaila, Grand Duke of Lithuania, in 1386. Wysłouchowa also wrote about anniversaries and special days, such as the anniversary of the Battle of Racławice in 1794[41] and the celebrations marking a quarter-century of the works of Henryk Sienkiewicz.[42] In addition to imparting historical knowledge, the written language itself and the rural way of life belonged to the canon of a Polish nation. Wysłouchowa urged Orkan to rewrite dialect expressions in his story intended for the first issue of *Przodownica* so that they would be equally intelligible in the Kingdom of Poland, Greater Poland, Galicia, and Silesia: "For our *Przodownica* will operate in the fields throughout Poland."[43] In the section containing homemaking advice, Wysłouchowa suggested sharing recipes and tips. *Zorza*, "which knows where and what women do best,"[44] functioned as a collection and dissemination center. Collection transformed regional characteristics into a system of all-Polish rural production. For example, a Silesian peasant woman wrote about a special method of salting bacon apparently unknown to women in Galicia. Quite in Wysłouchowa's sentimental style, she wrote: "I am delighted to answer this question because I want to serve the dear readers of *Zorza* magazine with all my heart and soul."[45] Wysłouchowa vouched for the quality of the recipe, stating that she had tried it herself. In addition, she pointed out that there were books and newspapers in Silesian farmsteads, describing them as even better than the best breakfast. Apart from this somewhat crude educational tack, female peasants and their knowledge were included in a participatory model, even though selection and mediation lay in Wysłouchowa's hands.[46] As well as incorporating experiential knowledge into the journal with this direct form of communication, she directed herself as an evaluating, mediating authority. She was the one who brought female peasants and readers, villages and regions together to form the Polish nation. The dissemination of recipes was intended to integrate the country into an all-Polish nation and familiarize it with new knowledge.

The "Polonization" of history, language, and modes of production served to construct a cultural memory and overcome local and regional perspectives in order to geographically, historically, socially, and mentally create a nation under the conditions of partition and foreign domination, despite not being represented by a state. The nation united not only the three partitions but also the people and the elite, represented in the magazines by female peasants and the intelligentsia.[47] One of the distinctive stylistic devices for the construction of a participatory community—a collective—was the connection of emotion and rationality, i.e. of descriptions of the countryside with information and expertise. *Zorza* explained how feeling and knowledge belonged together: "Because you can only love what you know."[48]

Another means of constructing an imagined community was tales of heroes. As in her correspondence commenting on Orzeszkowa's novel, Wysłouchowa parallelized life and literature. With her popularization of historical material and her emotive declarations about patriotism and freedom, she drew on both concepts of popular enlightenment and the romantic tradition in Polish literature.[49] Her story "O przezacnej Polce Emilii Sczanieckiej" (The Respectable Pole Emilia Sczaniecka) about a woman from Greater Poland who took part in the 1830/31 November

Uprising was published in *Przodownica* in 1899. It starts with an appeal to honor Emilia Sczaniecka[50] and to take her as a role model. "It is therefore beholden on us to know the beauty of Emilia Sczaniecka's life in order to gratefully pay homage to her blessed memory, but even more so to imitate her deeds as much as possible and thus learn from her self-sacrifice, her faith, and her love."[51] Once again, the author involves her readers by using the word "us." Further on in the text, she addresses them directly as "sisters" and "daughters of the fatherland." The story culminates in the exclamation: "Oh, rural and urban dwellers remember these holy battles and need not be reminded of them."[52] Sczaniecka is presented as a folk hero, as someone preserved in the memory. Wysłouchowa's neoromantic language transports an unbroken nationalism that not only heroizes the countryside, but in addition rails against intellectual doubts and self-criticism. But the discourse also implies that the addressees should *become* like Sczaniecka, i.e. that they were by no means *already* like her.

Wysłouchowa gave an account of a woman who embodied all the main values of a patriotic Polish life: enthusiasm for education, charitable activities in rural areas, participation in the uprising, and dedication to Polish school education. General explanations are contained in the biographical passages about Sczaniecka. After a historical overview of the three partitions, Wysłouchowa described the activities of women during the 1830/31 uprising: some donated jewelry and gold, others cared for the sick and wounded, or fought side by side with their husbands and brothers, sacrificing themselves like them. Of course, Sczaniecka, who treated the wounded in the Warsaw hospital and elsewhere and assisted doctors during the most painful operations, received special emphasis. She then worked in an area hit by cholera, encouraged Polish commercial enterprise in an effort to resist Prussian and Russian occupation, and founded village schools to teach the Polish language and history on the estate inherited from her parents which she managed by herself. Village schools run by noblewomen on their estates had symbolic value, a motif adopted by Orzsezskowa in her story "Dwa bieguny." The schools represented "organic work," the nobility's duty of care, also new forms of knowledge and the resulting emancipation; they signaled the overcoming of feudal differences, thus uniting common people and the nobility within the nation.[53] Women, too, become part of the nation through their hard work and dedication; they demonstrate caring skills and are also mediators of emancipation—for themselves and for others.

The different levels of the story reflect the magazine's approach of combining edification with science, education with emotion. Wysłouchowa alternated between an emotive language of sacrifice and a positivistic language of achievements and presented Sczaniecka as a daughter of the fatherland by describing her devotion as a nurse and simultaneously as the mother of the Polish people by recalling village schools and the performance by rural children at her funeral. She combined a historical with an identificatory narrative style pointing to the present, uniting all women across the ages and all Polish women across the three partitions. The combination of a specific biography with general historical accounts of national movements assured the reader that this was a story about history that contained true facts, and was thus connected to present-day reality. Nevertheless, the romance of the language used created the vision of a (better) future. Whereas in literary narratives, the tension between the "critical-realist portrayal of reality and a poetic 'transfiguration' of reality" points to the historical function of fiction,[54] this structure is reversed in Wysłouchowa's historical narrative. The romanticization of the female hero as a timeless role model functions like a literary story, the author using the emotionality of a fictional narrative to politicize the present and transfigure the future.[55]

Wysłouchowa explicitly equated women with men in terms of zeal and courage. Sczaniecka was an example of this: "And when the fatherland needed greater devotion, heavier sacrifices, she served it like a faithful daughter willing to sacrifice her life for her mother."[56] Like the ancient hero, the Polish hero surrendered her life for higher values. The female hero became a timeless figure of identification. The legend of Zofja Chrzanowska,[57] who excelled in the war between the Polish–Lithuanian Commonwealth and the Ottoman Empire (1672–76), tells of the ideal of a fighting woman. During the Siege of Trembowla in 1675, Chrzanowska, the wife of the commander-in-chief, plunged heroically into the thick of the battle to warn her husband of a plot to betray him.[58] Having become a warrior at her husband's side, she then started wearing a knife on her belt and sneaked into the enemy camp at night: Chrzanowska adopted male traits. The structure of the story is similar to that of Sczaniecka, framed by a direct address to the readers and updated in its importance by reference to the memory kept alive by the town's inhabitants. The legend can be read as a parable on Wysłouchowa's blueprint for society directed against the conservative Galician ruling elite: the female hero seizes a leading position in the fighting while the noblemen appear weak and cowardly. The forms of address "we" and "sisters" transcend the boundaries of time.

Halina Filipowicz showed what the ascent into the pantheon of national heroes (female and male) could look like with the example of the story of the commemoration of Emilia Plater, who armed herself and fought against Russian rule in the 1830/31 uprising.[59] Plater was remembered as a virgin Lithuanian noblewoman and was therefore far more of a symbol for the unity of the Polish–Lithuanian Commonwealth than for the national identity of Poland. Her virgin body is compared to the body of the union injured by partition. She thus sacralized both the commonwealth and the struggle. Wysłouchowa was one of those writers who made Plater's virginity a symbol in order to elevate her to the pantheon. She concluded her biographical story with the words that "the only love of her [Plater's] youth was a powerful, independent Poland."[60]

Wysłouchowa similarly defined the heroic in her article "Chłopi—bohaterowie" about the peasants involved in the 1863/64 uprising: "The insurrectionists... did not think of themselves, only of the fatherland."[61] The heroes were also warriors who sacrificed themselves to the fatherland. In this regard, they were no different from Sczaniecka, Plater, or Chrzanowska—yet they were not noble, but of peasant stock. Wysłouchowa's hero ideal referred to an enlarged Polish nation by including the peasantry. She placed equally active, idealistic, and combative female heroes at the side of the peasant hero, a similarly participatory model. Women were not merely integrated into the nation, but were also placed on an equal footing with men in terms of action and their readiness to make sacrifices, and were even superior to them in, for example, Chrzanowska's rescue mission. However, these women were nobles, not peasants. The social hierarchy remained intact: the female hero is noble—an unattainable role model for the peasant women—and remains the charitable mistress.

Wysłouchowa used female and male heroes to construct a relationship between folk culture and elite culture. Romanticism ennobled the folk style and gave it a place in modern Polish culture.[62] In their sacrifice, peasants and women attained subjectivity and became independent actors in history. We recall Wysłouchowa's criticism that Orzeszkowa conceived her female hero as if a woman was unable to sacrifice her personal happiness for the sake of her independent love of the nation.[63] Gender equality in participation in the nation was enshrined in the ideal of willingness to make sacrifices. Wysłouchowa conceived this equality in devotion to the fatherland and for a better society. Both the peasant hero and the female hero loved the fatherland more than others, they rearranged reality, and thus set an example for the future instead of reflecting the present.

Peasant women were also idealized, albeit not as warriors, but as suffering, passive victims. The addressee of the magazine, the female peasant, was on the one hand the object of teachings about Polish history and culture as well as about rational (i.e. modern) ways of life, and on the other hand raised to a pedestal of suffering. The magazine's message was that the hardship of her life made her strong: "But the woman from the village and from the small town does not shy away from hard work, for her whole life consists of hard work."[64] Nevertheless, the possibilities offered for greater opportunities remain closed to her. She does not gain a position of power, does not fight with male characteristics, and does not even sacrifice her personal happiness. She does not stand for the integrity of the Commonwealth and does not represent any external virtues extending beyond herself.

The peasant woman symbolizes the limits of the participatory model. She assures intellectuals that their power and influence will be maintained. The expansion of opportunities for women and peasants stands for a participatory society, the presentation of peasant women as passive victims and objects of reforms points to the new hierarchies established at the same time. One exception was Orkan's mother: Wysłouchowa wrote down the stories she told her and published them in *Zorza*.[65] This enabled Katarzyna Smaciarz, who published or was published under her maiden name Smreczyńska, to participate in the new medium and in the canonization of new knowledge. The contrast between the image of the peasant population as backward and culturally uneducated on the one hand and embodying the hope of a national awakening on the other was thus resolved in the figure of the peasant woman. While the male peasant actively sacrificed himself, the peasant woman represented passivity and was therefore suitable as a good object of instruction. It is no coincidence that so many of the modernization interventions were directed at the family and thus at the wife and mother (in this case the peasant woman), for example instructions on how to maintain hygiene, caring for infants, and rearing children in accordance with educational principles. Various studies have shown that this applied to all nineteenth-century social work movements: by being aimed at mothers of lower class families, they established professionalism and the ability to intervene.[66]

Wysłouchowa created a new genre: a magazine for the rural population and explicitly for women. Both the magazines she edited are described by researchers as popular and successful.[67] They were both (especially *Zorza*) aimed at rural women wealthy and poor as well as men. But considering the articles and especially the tips they contained, they were all geared to the ideal of a married, well-off peasant couple. Although the magazines were widely read in all the partitions, they did not represent all political and social differences.[68] They united town and country, elite and intelligentsia, region and nation, emotionality and rationality. Visions for the future society and a model of communication complemented each other. A model of hierarchical communication was developed, which enacted the simultaneity of participation and subordination in terms of language, content, and form. The gender-political component of the model substantiated the participatory model of the nation called for without abandoning its hierarchical, exclusive implications. It included women and peasants and at the same time envisioned a hierarchical society that promoted the supremacy of intellectual power resources such as institutionally acquired, professionally disseminated knowledge, and integrated and subordinated other possible forms of knowledge such as agricultural and domestic traditions. The magazines claimed authority in the medialization of institutionalized knowledge from the town and experiential knowledge from the countryside. Accordingly, elements of oral and written culture were incorporated into the magazines, which thus mediated between local and national culture in a regulated, i.e. hierarchized form. They translated the concept of a new, participatory nation with the countryside as its cultural, political, and social basis into language, images, communication, and action.

The linguistic concept, the "we" repeatedly recreated on different levels—women, editorial staff, Poles, peasant women—ritualized the unity of society and of Poland. In addition, journalistic and historical themes were transferred into a popularized literary form: simple genres such as short stories were used, and a colorful language influenced by Polish romanticism was employed.[69] This united feelings and information, romanticism and rationality, tradition, and modernity. The style in particular was perceived and remembered as unusual, comprehensible, and inclusive for readers.[70] By including letters to the editor, the magazine opened up a place for voices from the villages, even if these statements were guided and commented on by the editorial staff and Wysłouchowa herself. The forms of communication in the magazines contained elements of instruction and discussion in the sense of autocratic, democratic knowledge transfer. Sczaniecka can, if you will, be interpreted as an ideal image of Wysłouchowa herself projected into the history of the insurrection: the renewal of the Polish nation will take place under her leadership. In this respect, Wysłouchowa herself was part of the discourse, not just its producer.

Just as the peasants have been analyzed as a trope of future visions,[71] this applies equally to female peasants. They legitimized the claim of female intellectuals to participate in a new vision of society whose objects were peasant women. Even if everyone was able and supposed to work together toward the renewal of the nation, not everyone enjoyed the same access to the resources of power which became increasingly important in the second half of the nineteenth century: professionalism and science. The peasant woman symbolized inequality in the concepts of equality while the noble female hero, the embodiment of integrity, purity, and virtue, symbolized the claim to leadership abilities and a role in the new elite. However, the fact that Wysłouchowa published stories by Katarzyna Smreczyńska, an illiterate peasant, highlights the fragility of these constructions of collective identities, the competition between "peasants" and "women" and the intersection of "peasants" and "women." The texts by Smreczyńska meant the excluded were entitled to participate in the new media.

In this sense, the magazines can be interpreted as an act of writing, as a ritual of a we-construction. Readers were repeatedly addressed in editorial texts, articles, and answers to letters to the editor. The "we" connected writers and readers; it constituted a collective between writers and readers—but of what kind? The ritual was unresolved; it fluctuated between "we" as a nation and "we" as women, between sisters, female heroes, and victims. In order to "identify" this "we" and make it a political movement, something else was needed—and experience and history were other central elements of the rhetoric of political movements.

Composing Experience

Pomeranz's stories start with tales of misery and deprivation, before countering them with a Zionist perspective of a better future. One of her first stories, "*Oci,*" published in 1897, addresses the failure of assimilation and the path to Zionism by means of a generational tale set in a small Galician town.[72] A young man, who has been introduced to Zionism while studying in the capital, returns home, where he starts campaigning among the youth and developing an organization. His father who, despite his religious upbringing and Hebrew and German language classes, has become increasingly assimilated into the Polish language and the elite of the small town, changing from "reb Jankele" to "pan Jakób," tries to dissuade his son from this path. He receives threats from the Polish elite that if his first son does not give up his political activities, his second son will not be granted a permanent post in the town's administration. But before the young graduate can decide, there is a scandal. The younger son is unfairly dismissed and his father realizes that his elder son with his Zionist ideas has been right all along: assimilation is doomed to failure because "the others" are fundamentally negative toward the Jews; assimilation is a chimera, an illusion, and the others are involuntary campaigners for Zionism. As also propagated by Wysłouchowa in *Zorza* and *Przodownica*, the protagonist of this story discovers how to escape the lack of recognition while studying in the capital, too. Education, progress, and politics are inextricably linked. They lend expression to the experience of deprivation and open up fresh prospects. The place of publication, *Przyszłość,* reinforces and confirms interaction between education and a Zionist stance as the only possible way to oppose oppression and discrimination.

By being portrayed in a generational relationship, the positions of father and son, assimilation or Zionism, are not simply opposed to each other, but build up to a dramatic or narrative climax or conflict leading to fundamental change. As a conflict between generations, they are simultaneously arranged on a timeline and placed in an interdependent sequence. This logical chronology represents Judaism's historical path to modernity. The options have also been frequently described as such in the historiography. Assimilation thwarted by continuing, intensifying anti-Semitism is followed by the adoption of Zionism, the teleological final stage of development.[73] The historical account functions like the story or, to take an opposite view, the story transforms historical logics into a plot.

The dramatization of experience is explored below. Dramatization refers to the writing of roles and associating them with overarching significance as well as their arrangement on a line of development. It involves not just the narrative strategies of a fictional text but also its potential for the policymaking ambitions of political movements. Stories by Pomeranz and Kobryns'ka are analyzed. Not representative of their writings or of Zionist or feminist texts, they are atypical in their explicit thematization of experience, which makes them all the more interesting for the question of the discursive, i.e. reality-constituting elements of political rhetoric.[74] They make suitable examples for analysis owing to their atypical reference to experience as an impetus to take action and bring about change and also as propaganda for a political movement because they shed light on how it works.

"Eine offene Frage," another story by Pomeranz, was published in 1990 in *Die Welt*.[75] It begins in an undetermined manner in the middle of a conversation in an inn. A Jewish guest, a representative of a lending bank, is talking to the innkeeper and estate manager Moses Gartenblum. The guest replies to the innkeeper that he doubts the "assertion of Zionism" that the Jews are a nation.[76] When Gartenblum asks what he is, he replies: "I'm a Pole!" When asked the same question, the innkeeper replies hesitantly: "Well ... a Pole, too ... after all, we're all Poles ... Poles of the Jewish confession."[77] The landlord then takes three school reports out of a drawer, one German, one Polish, one Ruthenian, and tells his personal story, the painful times with his sons. Depending on their father's place of work—Bukovina, a village near Kraków, East Galicia— they went to different schools, the first one to a German-speaking school, the second to a Polish school, the third to a Ruthenian one, and being immersed in the local culture became in their own way a German, a Pole, and a Ruthenian. Furthermore, these differences destroyed their brotherly feelings, continues Gartenblum. "When my children come home, they form three hostile camps that seek to fight and conquer each other." He describes the attitudes of his children as "borrowed nationality." His guest remains silent, prompting Gartenblum to comment that "there is just one single answer, but you and your fellow believers don't want to give it..."[78] The end of the story remains unresolved.

The background story is a conversation in an inn, the unspoken answer to the controversial opening and core sentence "The Jews are a nation" is given in the form of a parable, a father's story about his experience, about the suffering inherent in assimilation. Gartenblum does not use arguments to justify his Zionist position; he uses his experience. The central message of the text is: "'I can testify best of all to what is true with my own experience,' he [Gartenblum] is accustomed to saying."[79] Experience is presented as truth. The use of "is accustomed" emphasizes the universality of this view: the protagonist's message is reinforced by that of the narrator. Thus, suffering becomes a collectively shared history, Zionism a logical (true) consequence. However, the story does not provide rational justifications for the statement that Judaism is a nation: for example, there are no references to a common tradition or history. Instead, it refers to the family as a place where feelings are generated. As a result, knowledge about politics and the future becomes experience. Seen as a story, the narrative is a political debate about Zionism. Since, like in "Oci" the history of Judaism is told with exclusively male protagonists (the father and his sons, the guest), a close connection emerges between masculinity and nation. The male succession embodies a Jewish nation and hence makes up the dominance of this gender. However, the significance of this only becomes apparent against the background of the maternal succession applied in Judaism, i.e. anyone with a Jewish mother belongs to the Jewish people.

Both stories thus constitute a new succession or a new concept of the formation of the collective. With regard to the sons rebuffing Judaism, however, the new succession at the level of the story reveals inconsistencies in the concept of the nation. The discourse questions the idea of a naturally given nation. On the one hand, the sons remain Jews despite turning their backs on Judaism—the nation continues to exist regardless of the behavior of individuals. On the other hand, the concept of nation is new and must be distinguished from the tradition of maternal succession. It becomes a question of political decision, not descent. The story can be interpreted in the context of the disputes over the nation and Zionism. Although the story works toward the inevitability of the concept of nation, the discourse makes it clear that knowledge is not self-evident but uncertain, something that must first be recognized (or invented). The three sons' assimilation stories convey insecurity inherent in the concept of nation. The nation was something which, despite the affirmation of its enshrinement in the depths of tradition, language, and history, could apparently be simply lost, which in turn was something that had to be learned. The fact that the simultaneity of historicization and emotionalization of the nation, the relevance of tradition, family, and testimony of truth were not intrinsically Zionist, but applied to more or less all national movements in the nineteenth century, does not contradict this thesis.[80] On the contrary, it confirms the adoption of similar ideas in the various political movements regarding the context of practices to shape change and visions of a new future. The conflict between assimilation and Zionism served to clearly define a connection between experience and knowledge characteristic of movement rhetoric, which in this case should be interpreted as Zionist. Yet only the place of publication, *Die Welt*, confirms its consumption as a specifically politically didactic text.

In her first short stories, "The Spirit of Times" and "For a Crust of Bread," Kobryns'ka (like Pomeranz) used the narrative means of a background story. Lady Shuminska, an elderly woman and the wife of a priest, sits at the window and recapitulates her life beginning with her wedding day:

> Lady Shuminska's thoughts flew into the distant past, somewhere to the moments of her youngest childhood years... And truly, she was reliving the most important moment in a woman's life—the moment she stands beneath the bridal wreath.[81]

As the story unfolds, Lady Shuminska recalls how concepts of ideals, values, and goals have changed over generations. She describes the conflicts resulting from this change: one daughter chose an inappropriate husband, namely a peasant, out of love, one son chose a secular education over the family tradition of priestly ordination, and her granddaughter even wants to become a teacher. Children and grandchildren reject the values of the Greek Catholic clergy such as priestly ordination and endogamous marriage. The goals of Lady Shuminska's offspring are alien to her. Their life plans represent new generations.

The background story connects the characters with their different options within a family and a generational sequence. The starting point of the narrative—the "bridal wreath" as the "most important moment of a woman," i.e. every woman—signifies that Lady Shuminska's life is by no means unusual and in fact represents general female experiences. The life plans of her offspring can therefore be read as representative of the new options of the time. As in Pomeranz's stories, the narrative links experience to the past and the future. The characters' decisions refer to the possibilities of political and simultaneously historic (i.e. irreversible) change. As in Pomeranz's parables, the life plans of the new generations stand for contemporary debates about avenues into the modern age: being able to freely choose one's spouse, educational ambitions, and the demand for gainful employment originating in the women's movement. "The Spirit of Times" was first published in the almanac *Peršyj vinok,* supporting a feminist interpretation. Kobryns'ka's feminist politics which she would pursue in the years to come were presented in this story centered around women. However, the vision for society integrated not just multiple generations of women but both sexes thanks to the inclusion of the son. The character of the son spotlights the complexity of women's politics between difference and equality, the simultaneity of demands for one gender and the resulting vision for the improvement of society as a whole.

Kobryns'ka's second story "For a Crust of Bread" was printed by Franko in *Zorja,* a Ruthenian-language literary magazine.[82] This place of publication indicates the literary ambitions of those writing for it and which Kobryns'ka certainly shared when she agreed to have her story printed. Nevertheless, she did not welcome Franko's proposal at first, only agreeing when he became coeditor of the magazine.[83] On joining the magazine, he had attempted to make it an organ of the socialist movement and to promote female writers.[84] Kobryns'ka evidently hoped for a place of publication sympathetic to her views, namely support for feminist positions and female writers. Although Franko's political ambitions did not prevail in the magazine, Kobryns'ka continued to have her work occasionally published in *Zorja.* "For a Crust of Bread" is considered to be an adapted account of Ol'ha Roškevyč's unrequited love for Franko.[85] It was and still is concluded from this personal experience that the reason for the story's popularity was that it was a true story.[86] It was an initiation; the story was read in Galicia as a revelation, as women's claim to live life as they chose, according to Olena Kysilevs'ka, a member of the Association of Ruthenian Women, in her recollections of Kobryns'ka.[87]

The story begins with a flashback about the fate of a widow who is impoverished for, having been financially dependent on her husband, she is denied all support and has not found a way to earn a living for herself. As a result, some of her children die of poverty and hunger. The actual plot then deals with the fate of her daughter Halya who, after much toing and froing, decides to marry for material reasons instead of for love. Like the adultery novels of the era, the story criticizes arranged marriages and implies the need for independent ways of life for women, especially employment.[88] The message is that financial independence is pivotal for true love.

Flashbacks are a common narrative strategy with which stories can be told as experiences and through which the eye can be directed toward change. In "The Spirit of Times" as well as in the story "Eine offene Frage," the narrators—who turn stories into experiences and make them comprehensible through their narrative position—are identified with by the readers. Whereas the figure of identification and the message in Pomeranz's story coincide, the narrative strategies in "The Spirit of Times" are more complex. The focus is on a woman skeptical of change. The story contrasts the perspectives of tradition and modernity without debasing either of them, yet also without resolving the tension between them. "The Spirit of Times" bridges a cultural gap between conservative life and political radicalism. It shows that mediating between these two poles is possible. Overcoming opposites seems conceivable. All the stories dramatize political demands as experiences of life through variations in the narrated time. They thus establish a logical relationship between experience and expectation as well as between past and future. Moreover, a relational connection between personal experience and collectivized or generalized history holds out the promise of a direct reference to reality, i.e. that the stories address real problems. The narrative strategies themselves create this connection between experience and history, not the coincidence with political debates or the life stories of their authors. They assign roles and are plays for testing a reality.

The third example to be presented here is the story "Yadzya and Katrusya," first published in 1893 in the magazine *Zorja*, too.[89] It juxtaposes the life stories of two women from diametrically opposed backgrounds: estate ownership and rural poverty. For one thing, Kobryns'ka presented two irreconcilable worlds: the life of villagers and that of an impoverished manor. The two women, despite having played together when they were girls, have nothing in common, not even empathy for each other based on their childhood friendship. This alienation becomes particularly apparent when, although the daughter of the manor visits the sick Katrusya, now a single mother, with charitable intent, there is no lasting support or compassion. On the other hand, the author describes the similarities between the two women. They are both dependent on rural morals. In order to have a fulfilled life and an adequate livelihood, they are reliant on marriage, i.e. a suitable husband. However, the daughter of the manor lacks an appropriate dowry for a marriage befitting her station, and over the years she becomes increasingly dissatisfied until she finds a purpose in life in charity. In the end, she finally meets a suitable, albeit impoverished noble husband. Meanwhile, Katrusya, the elder daughter of Yadzya's wet nurse, and one of the poor villagers, fights her way through life with her assertiveness, flirting with various men but not submitting to them. Men are fascinated by her strength and charisma, but in their eyes she is not necessarily a possible wife; only Maksym is so taken by her that he courts her despite her aloof behavior. After his death, despite her attractiveness as a widow and a homeowner, she decides to bring up her children by herself. Katrusya's life plan for a propertied widow collapses when the harvest is destroyed by a storm. She has to give away her two eldest children and return to the tobacco harvest, the seasonal work of the rural poor.

Kobryns'ka combined social and gender differences in her story. The women's dependencies were exacerbated by social problems: belonging to the rural poor and a lack of wealth. In this respect, Kobryns'ka's plot reflected her political views, especially her economic interpretation of gender relations. Nonetheless, unlike "Eine offene Frage" or "Oci," the text does not contain an obvious political message. On the contrary, the end prophesies that women's lives are a never-ending female destiny:

> But when they [the villagers] were told that she [Katrusya] had carried on there in the same way [at the tobacco harvest] as she had behaved when she was still a girl, they realized that her nature had not changed.[90]

Although not further explained in the narrative, the girls' first names Yadzya (Jadzja, from Jadwiga) and Katrusya represent the Polish-speaking gentry and the Ruthenian-speaking peasantry, something which was plain to contemporary readers. The decisive factor for the story, however, is the contrast between peasantry and gentry rather than a national contrast. Even so, Kobryns'ka drew on gender-political implications in her creation of the women's roles.[91] Yadzya is passive and "waits" until she gives up and gets involved in charity, but is disappointed by the villagers' skepticism, which she perceives as ingratitude. Katrusya, on the other hand, is assertive, acts according to her heart, and refuses to be rebuffed by either men or people of superior status: she is "active, independent, strict and creative."[92] She represents a new, employment-focused type of woman.[93] As well as comparing two contemporary concepts of femininity, this passive–active contrast also creates gender difference as a fundamental contradiction of society. In addition, the association of an outdated, conservative Polishness and an active, emerging Ruthenianism resonates. The discourse polarizes tradition and modernity as Polish–Ruthenian opposites.[94]

Although the story could be read as an expression of pessimism and there are romantic traits of tragedy ushered in by the descriptions of nature in the beginning,[95] right at the start, a small word introduces one interpretation of the story as a politicizable view of society, as a metonymy for experience: "Who does not know our delightful province of Pokuttya [Galicia] at the foot of the Carpathian Mountains?"[96] This "our" directly addresses the readers and unites them with the narrator, who only appears in the first person in this "we." "Who does not know" also reinforces the "we" through shared knowledge. This is the pact: we read the following story as common knowledge of experience, just as we share our common knowledge about the beauty of the landscape. The story thus deals with personal experiences as an engine of social change, Yadzya's fate symbolizing the decline of a feudal world view. Apart from the mortgaged estate, the senselessness and lack of prospects of waiting for marriage opportunities was another topos of contemporary social criticism. "With every passing day—or rather, with every evening, and with every ball—Yadzya's admirers increased in number, but not one of them made any definite overtures."[97] This becomes even clearer in her organization of a whimsical charity that disregarded its addressees, colliding with Katrusya's pride.

The women's life plans stand for tradition and progress, autonomy and dependence. They symbolize inevitability and the possibility of change, and thus the break-up of the realm of experience and the horizon of expectations. While the story depicts the entanglements of power relations, the discourse conveys the common ground of experience and the hope inherent in action. The divergent messages of story and discourse underline the difficulty of mediating between tradition and modernity as well as between social strata. On the one hand, the "we" at the beginning unites the readers with the narrator. But on the other hand, Katrusya ends up alone; there is no unification of the Ruthenian-speaking villagers and no reconciliation between town and country or nature and society.[98] The similarity between the two female figures lies in their separate suffering amid the traditional way of life. Beyond this manifest connection, the parallel construction of the women's fates, the discourse, can also be read metaphorically or symbolically: as long as there is no eye for community and social differences are not overcome, the future is uncertain.

Contrary to the messages in the story about the incompatibility of class and gender differences, the discourse refers to the commonality of experience. Just as the hero Plater champions an intact Polish–Lithuanian Commonwealth, Katrusya represents the power of the village, a romantic utopia.[99] This interpretation is reinforced by the place of publication. When Kobryns'ka published the story, *Zorja* was moving in a national direction. For her, too, the importance of the nation had grown.[100] In the context of the place of publication, the political pact consists in reading the story in such a way that changes are linked to the transformation of gender relations; a socialist or national future option by itself is not enough. Contemporary reviewers criticized the composition of the narrative, the weak connection between the parallel stories, but positively emphasized the descriptions of the customs and traditions.[101] This supported both a realistic interpretation and an ethnographic reconstruction of the village as both the core of national renewal and a place of social and national oppression. Although not an explicitly political place of publication, *Zorja* contributed to the political interpretation in the manner formulated by Kobryns'ka: in literature, social problems and political demands become readable and understandable as collective experiences.

Considering Kobryns'ka's three stories together, it is immediately striking that they take up debates of the women's movement: the necessity of employment for women and the tension between arranged and love marriages. With her female protagonists, daughters, and wives of the Greek Catholic clergy, rural poverty, and impoverished nobility, she transferred the themes of the European feminist movements to the social conditions in Galicia. Her stories can therefore be understood as a cultural translation[102] of transnational elements to the circumstances of Galicia and the Ruthenian population. The gender visions symbolize a moral breakthrough into a modern society, a view served by Kobryns'ka with Katrusya.

The stories were enthusiastically received as they reflected female experiences and, like Kobryns'ka's first literary period, were classified as realism.[103] They were regarded by contemporary critics as realistic, ethnographically informed, socially critical, and politically speaking geared to women's rights. Occasionally, the authenticity of their writing was backed up by reference to Kobryns'ka's own origins in the Greek Catholic clergy.[104] The narrative with which she introduced the creation of "The Spirit of Times" in her autobiography—the oral presentation at a meeting of the Cossack Camp—strengthened the identificational interpretation. There was therefore a close connection between literary and socio-critical themes. As stated above, however, this link was the result of the narrative strategies rather than their precondition. Recent research does not regard realism as a "factual" representation of social conditions, but instead as a necessity to relate political goals and their justifications. "[C]onceived as the ultimate point of coincidence between fiction and reality, realism, more than any other doctrine, lends itself to political interests and purposes."[105] Realism replaced the metaphorical style of romanticism with a metonymic one. It no longer described its subjects by comparison, but historically, through a development including origin and context.[106] The coincidences between fiction and politics therefore consisted of the development of a vision for the future.

The interesting thing about the examples presented here is not that they are classed as realism or that this classification is often interpreted as reality, accounting for their significance for political rhetoric. Instead, what makes the stories and their reception so interesting is that they combine experience and expectation, including by means of flashbacks. The way in which experience becomes the driver of the narrative reflects the significance attributed to experience in political movements, where political demands were legitimized by collectively shared experience. Experience emerged in the context of expectation and fantasy. Without historical actors having desired a better future, such conceptualization was inconceivable.

Expectation and experience became interrelated. However, experiences were not just a source of legitimation, for they also turned expectations into conclusions which seemed to be a natural law. By linking back to experience, expectations appeared self-evident and inevitable. By simply transferring individual experiences to collective expectations, the future became a logical development from the past. The close connection thus created specific paradigms and excluded others. The specific achievement of experience consisted of this inclusion and exclusion. This was not an essence prior to writing, but neither was it a construct in the sense that it could be thought of detached from subjects.[107] It was a writing action, i.e. a practice of communication about ideas, decisions, and actions. But this means the examples also show how important context, tradition, and history were for the conceptualization of political ideas. What was necessary for political interpretations was mediating between past, present, and future—and thus historicization. This is addressed in more detail below.

Enacting History

The year 1901 saw the publication of the novel *Im Lande der Noth*,[108] in which Pomeranz addressed central elements of her political worldview: the Jewish collective, the contrast between east and west, the goal of a nationally conscious, modern Jewish future, and her attitude to the women's movement. She promoted national Judaism as an alternative both to Jewish misery in the east and to assimilation (the loss of Jewishness) in the west. The very title is revealing, referring as it does to Galicia as the poorest Habsburg province scarred by misery and deprivation. Pomeranz began with stereotypes typical of literature about Galicia: "On the dusty country road… a large cart pulled by farm horses moves slowly and sluggishly. The passengers [are] Polish Jews and Jewesses... At the front is the coachman, a Ruthenian peasant, who stops at every tavern without fail to take a substantial swig of brandy."[109] The dust of the roads, the alcoholism of the peasants, and the polyethnicity of the region are all proverbial. Written amid the first enlightened descriptions of the province around the turn of the nineteenth century, the images set the scene for the province. And to this day, they are fixed topoi of the vast majority of stories and reminiscences about Galicia.[110]

As the novel continues, it deals with the passengers' journeys through life: their path out of Hasidic traditionality, isolation, and self-restraint; education and marriage; adaptation to the Polish elite in Galicia; emigration to Germany and absorption into German culture accompanied by the loss of Jewishness; emigration to Palestine, where productive work, especially in agriculture, seemed possible; and finally an enlightened, dedicated view of themselves as the prerequisite for a modern Jewish nation. Like several of her short stories, Pomeranz's novel reads like propaganda setting out the options for a modern Jewish world and its political differentiation. The starting point is poor, backward, traditional Judaism. The main part of the story concerns an assimilated German Jew confronting the experiences of a national Jewish family in Galicia. Etterberg, the protagonist, learns from the family what true Jewishness means, and in the end he turns out to be a relative whose ancestors had emigrated west. This union between East and West European Judaism is personalized in an implied love story between him and Mirjam, the daughter of the Thalberg family. In the end, the Galician Thalbergs stand for a nationally oriented, modern, educated, prosperous Judaism interested in its own destiny.

As an authorial narrator, Pomeranz wove the social upheavals of the nineteenth century into a logical explanatory context. A fundamental structural principle used is the contrast between tradition and modernity. Tradition is associated with misery, provinciality and narrow-mindedness, modernity with prosperity, enlightenment, and openness. The path to modernity is constituted by experience, which sets the course of the story. Central to its constitutive role is the life story of the head of the Thalberg family, the old Reb Hirsch, once again presented in a flashback. Reb Hirsch's report is told as an autobiographical historiography of Polish Jewry in the nineteenth century: from humiliation in the shtetl to assimilation and from there to national consciousness. It begins: "[T]herefore, hear the story of my life, it is the story of Polish Jewry in the last century."[111] When he was a young boy, Reb Hirsch saw his elder brother murdered by drunken Polish nobles, while his second brother emigrated and his mother died of grief.[112] Even as an adult, he and his family are still humiliated by members of the Polish nobility, reinforcing the image of arbitrary aristocratic rule and a dependent Jewish population. The desire for revenge prompts Reb Hirsch to have his son trained as a lawyer in order to get even for the contempt suffered using the means of Christian society. The son, however, distances himself from Judaism and becomes a Polish patriot. Accused of treachery by his fellow combatants during the 1863/64 uprising, he commits suicide to protect his honor. In his suicide note, he expresses the realization that he was a "guinea pig" for his father in the search for the correct path to a better life and that he deserted his people.[113] The experience of suffering and decisions repeatedly proving to be wrong have shown Reb Hirsch that the only possibility is self-assured Judaism.

Portrayed on an individual level, this experience becomes a collectively shared pattern and therefore enables identification with the "imagined community."[114] The familiar narrative elements of literature set in Galicia—misery, Hasidism, arranged marriages, and the widespread motif of a love story as a medium of modernization—constitute its communicative moments: on the one hand, their intertextuality, their references among the various texts on Galicia and on the other hand, their recognizable topoi. Even the cart refers to the reading public's ideas of Galicia. At the same time, the story within a story turns the past into experience and connects it to an attainable future. Experience is historicized into the history of a collective, the nation. The conception of the life story as the history of Judaism places the various options in a logical, chronological order. And its construction in the form of experience makes it natural and authentic.

Inserted into the main narrative are short episodes of Hasidic families. A father tries to prevent his son's escape from the seclusion of the Jewish community to the city by an arranged marriage. In another episode, a young woman successfully asserts her rejection of marriage candidates of Hasidic origin and marries a modern Jew (as indicated by his clothing and hairstyle). Pomeranz thus addressed a topos that had already been debated since the *Haskalah* (the Jewish enlightenment), for marriage practice as well as the youthful age of the bride and groom were regarded as backward and inhuman.[115] The countermodel to these episodes is Mirjam and Etterberg, a happily united, self-determined couple, who hold out the prospect of a harmonious future, not to mention respectability and normality. They represent a new model as an established norm.[116]

The story also deals with the question of women's emancipation, which was relevant to women's politics in Zionism because it was debated at the time. However, the question was presented not as history via experience, but as reflection by means of difference: as a conversation about women's gainful employment. As far as the vocabulary is concerned, the conversation clearly refers to the contemporary demands of women's movements. The Thalberg family is explicitly against employment for women, for although the Zionist woman does her bit for modern Judaism, she does so within the confines of the home. The women of the family also express their feelings: "It is self-evident that we are absolutely opposed to earning! We are in favor of work, but out of love and fidelity for love and fidelity within the confines of domesticity."[117] The somewhat cryptic formulation "In our families there is rarely disagreement... so I am also against emancipation"[118] sets priorities. The family stands above individual aspirations; women's emancipation takes place within the limits set by the family and thus by the people or the nation. On the other hand, the reason given for wanting to avoid debates indicates that possibilities for individual emancipation are conceivable. The nature of the justification breaks with the previously expressed notion of natural gender roles as it is based on a different level, that of family peace. Just as assimilation in "Eine offene Frage" questions the nation as a natural phenomenon, the change of level conveys that gender models, too, were controversial and not taken for granted.

The rebuttal of women's employment refers to the complementary life plans of "sexual stereotypes,"[119] but regards them as a difference between Jews and Christians, and claims gender conflicts to be "unnatural" in Judaism. This confirms the rejection of assimilation efforts. Nevertheless, the ideal of female work in the home should be understood not only in the context of antifeminist ideologies but also as a counterpart to the vision of a new Jewish modernity combining masculinity with gainful employment.[120] The positions in the novel resulted from a gender model opposing the contemporary mainstream. The Jewish Enlightenment claimed that in Orthodoxy (and especially in Hasidism), men's religious "unproductiveness" was a virtue, while gainful employment was profane and degrading, and therefore a women's affair. This division of labor was denigrated as unnatural and traditional, and countered with the model from the non-Jewish Enlightenment: that of the active, working man and the passive, domestic woman. What the Jewish and non-Jewish Enlightenment had in common was the assumption of a dichotomous gender order. At the end of the nineteenth century, women's movements criticized the Enlightenment as traditional and patriarchal, and proposed female employment and gender equality as new, modern models. In the Zionist movement, views oscillated between the concept of the modernity of the Jewish Enlightenment and that prevailing the turn of the twentieth century, which included the discourse on women's emancipation.[121] Like other national movements, however, the Zionist movement barely questioned the dichotomous juxtaposition of femininity and masculinity.

When Pomeranz had Etterberg claim that Jewish women were not gainfully employed in the east, this was on the one hand an idealization of East European Judaism.[122] In true Judaism, according to the message, women did not seek employment. As in the Jewish Enlightenment, female employment was seen as a sign of depravation. On the other hand, it was an emancipatory act of writing. Pomeranz considered the national family task to be a parallel to male religiosity.[123] Given the responsibility of presiding over a national family, she gave women access to the spiritual work they were deprived of—and thereby collided with the women's movement's demand for gainful employment.[124] By taking up the nationalization of domesticity, education and women, she positioned Zionist women's politics in the context of nation and gender. This role allocation tied in with gender stereotyping. The nation was structured in complementary gender images in which women represented tradition and men modernity: mothers passed on their love for the land of their fathers, while men and sons worked for the renewal of the "whole people."[125] Like the succession of generations in "Eine offene Frage," the story of the Jews as told by Reb Hirsch has a male structure. Female experience, by contrast, is limited to short episodes, denials, or escapes. This is reflected by the change in narrative style. Whereas Reb Hirsch tells a life story, the utterances on gainful employment are summed up as statements. This inconsistency in style points to the strong competition between what women's movements had to offer and that of Zionist women's politics.[126] The model of Jewish femininity presented by Pomeranz cannot be integrated into historical experience. What remains is a discussion of positions, a cultural critique of western emancipation concepts.

The novel can be classified under the "ghetto literature," which was widespread in the second half of the nineteenth century and dealt with historical change, the "escape from the ghetto." As was so often the case in this literature, in *Im Lande der Noth*, the different attitudes toward marriage signify the possibilities and failure of escape. Various stories about gender relations are told: forced marriage, romantic love, and the camaraderie of equals, with a couple sharing equal rights being presented at the end. A happy couple promises a hopeful, nationally united Jewish future. The love story in the novel combines tradition and modernity in a vision of the future.[127] The experiences of the sexes represent different Jewish positions in the spectrum between traditionality and modernity: orthodoxy, assimilation, and national consciousness.

Through east–west dichotomization and by equating individual experience with collective history, a homogeneous historiography of Judaism arises, which appears to be based on reality and therefore seems to have no alternative and to be inevitable. Like the gender models, the vision is a hybridization of dominant and marginal discourses. Differences in Judaism are ordered on a linear (and teleological) axis of history. This view adopts and supports the historically reinforced model of progress of the era. At the end is the unification of West and East European Judaism, albeit with the dominant direction of non-Zionist progressive thinking being reversed: "The east will embrace the west… It sounds like a prophecy to those gathered, and wordless praise of this higher unity speaks from their eyes when Mirjam almost unconsciously places her hand in that of her German cousin."[128] The connection between Mirjam and Etterberg is presented as a model for the future: modern and with equal rights for men and women. The community of Judaism presented as a nation is brought about in the blood relationship of East and West European Judaism. The image of a large family denotes not just reconciliation but also the togetherness of the Jewish collective, of the people scattered in the diaspora, using modern symbolism widespread in contemporary national movements. Furthermore, the love story as a catharsis of the problems, the unification of east and west Judaism, the Zionist visions of a future in a separate Jewish state combine Jewish tradition with a modern equal vision of a couple, even though—or precisely because—the family speaks out against the western women's movement and its central demand for employment opportunities for middle-class women.

The reviewers (all male) interpreted the novel as a *Tendenzschrift* (tendential writing), a plea for sympathy and interest in the suffering of Polish Jews. This view was put forward in for instance the review carried in *Israelitische Rundschau* (Israelite Review), the organ of the Zionist movement in the German Empire. However, the reviewer was seemingly unconvinced by the story in literary terms, seeing in it "lamenting and angry outpourings."[129] The review in *Die Welt,* on the other hand, rejected the description of the book as a novel, instead of categorizing it as "a series of cultural novellas skillfully woven into a whole by the destiny of the same person." It paid tribute to the author for her "loving and precise" description of Jewish life-worlds and described the work as an argument for women's emancipation because it refuted previous bad experience of reading women's novels.[130] By contrast, the review in *Das litterarische Echo* (The Literary Echo), a German literary magazine, was devastating. It claimed that while attempting to portray the life of the Jews in Galicia, the author had written too woodenly and emotionally, employing a style that was too "feminine" and oscillating between orthodox Jewish and modern Jewish ideas. Neither a work of art nor a *Tendenzschrift,* the book was too unfinished (the review continued). "A book which is intended to help a cause compromises it if it is as dilettantish and bad as Rosa Pomeranz's."[131] The review in the magazine *Ost und West* (East and West), the organ of Alliance Israélite Universelle, was no more positive regarding the novel's artistic dimension. Even so, the reviewer stressed that he was touched by the author's sympathetic, proud stance. Such an attitude, no matter how awkwardly it may be presented, was preferable to him to an accurate yet distanced, ironic use of language.[132] In *Wschód*, J. Tisch psychologically analyzed the emphatic reading experience as the "instinct of a persecuted being" to seek refuge in heroism and martyrdom. The reviewer saw in the description of Judaism an idealization whose objective—to move and interest "indifferent, western Judaism"—was doomed to failure for precisely this reason.[133] Despite their different views, the reviewers were in agreement about the book's emotional impact. They equated the ductus with the author—it was the author (not the narrator) who confronted them in the text, something which most of the reviewers criticized as poor or immature use of aesthetics and composition. The fact that some reviews praised the ethnographic depiction of the milieu refers to the distinction analyzed by Casanova between strategies for the establishment of a universal, purely aesthetic world literature and for the political-nationalist interpretation of small literatures.[134]

Some reviews took the debate in the novel seriously by laboriously seeking a feminist reading and writing about the book's significance for female authors. In addition, all the reviewers clearly distanced themselves from Galician Judaism, which they described as foreign, different, an object. Political disputes about Zionism in both literary and journalistic works were structured by the dichotomous distinction between an assimilated, rich Judaism in the west and an impoverished, orthodox (or Hasidic) Judaism in the east. This was the subject of a lengthy debate in *Die Welt*[135] and led to friction between Pomeranz and the Jewish feminist Bertha Pappenheim two years after the publication of the novel.[136] This dichotomy has already been analyzed many times as a political, literary, and socio-psychological phenomenon, above all as a projection of western or assimilated Judaism.[137] Yet as the novel and reviews show, it also structured the debate with experiences of change.

Unlike contemporary critics, Judaist Mark H. Gelber declares *Im Lande der Noth* to be an ambitious Zionist-feminist work of early cultural Zionism.[138] He sees in it delicate irony as well as a mild criticism of the views and ways of life of religious Jews in Galicia. The young Jew in the novel has to revise his prejudices about the filth and neglect of Polish Jews, who now appear more human, wiser, and better able to cope with life than the artificial world of assimilation. This was a motif found in various stories about Galicia, which emphasized characteristics such as the humanity of the periphery, of the people and of the oppressed as well as the naturalness of the country. Gelber sees the statement on women's employment as a rhetorical exercise that concealed the true attitudes of women.[139] Certainly, the shift in style from story to statement in the passage on employment for women is an indication of the need for a movement like Zionism intending to present itself as progressive to engage with contemporary positions of the women's movement. However, in my opinion, the feminist aspect of the novel lies, if at all, in the vision of a couple living on equal terms as well as in the strong Mirjam, who successfully persuades the young assimilated Jew to adopt Zionism.

***

In a political context, stories only make sense if they present their problems as temporal and thus changeable rather than general and timeless.

By combining places of publication and narrative styles, readers are offered a pact to accept stories as political concepts, as a cultural interpretation promising a better future. The stories link the assurance of talking about historical experiences with the creation of a collective and conclude focused, formable possibilities for change.

The narrative styles of the three women were different, as were their political objectives. What the styles had in common was the construction of a collective, of experience and of history. Political activity meant not only writing collectives into existence but also composing experiences and enacting history. Experiences were understood as something "made," something conceived beforehand, and as far as the future was concerned, as something aspired to, something formulated as new in the movements of the nineteenth century, according to Scott and Koselleck. Constructed as adapted experiences, they were also communicable, i.e. collectivizable and thus politicizable. Referring to experience enabled the simultaneity of politicization and essentialization.[140] In the stories presented here, literary narratives were historicized. Experience thus became a collectivizable story. Wysłouchowa's popular historical and biographical stories, on the other hand, literarized history so that it could be experienced. Using the example of her magazines, it has been shown how a collective "we" was created—yet also that the roles in this collective were differently cast, and that the view of historical figures varied and became politically readable.

The work of the three women appeared mainly in magazines, mostly movement organs in the broadest sense. The places of publication differed depending on their orientation to women's politics. Although aimed at different addressees, above all they were communicative media within the movements. *Peršyj vinok* was directed at women who were not yet involved and were to be persuaded to join, yet it was a source of information for women participating in political work. In addition, the almanac also sent a message to interested males, and especially to the literary public in which Kobryns'ka was keen to position herself. *Przodownica* and *Zorza* were journals of the peasant movement aimed at women in the countryside. *Die Welt,* the organ of the Zionist movement operating worldwide, had to mediate between different contexts and circumstances and imagine unity. *Zorja,* by contrast, represented the constitution of a (national) literary canon. The publication of *Im Lande der Noth* by Breslau publishing house Schottländer, which specialized in novels, may have targeted a broad reading public.

How was the new form of historical knowledge incorporated into more or less fictional stories? How was a relationship established between historical and literary narratives? First, fictional stories did not address social problems; instead, the problems themselves are to be understood as specific contemporary interpretations of meaning. In this respect, stories are not just literary or linguistic forms used to transform events or phenomena into facts but are also a mode of self-knowledge and world knowledge.[141] Second, it has been shown how fictional and historical adaptions of narratives could be read politically, i.e. with an eye on the future. True, the political pact referred to a preceding context, yet it also created essentialized collectives and the option of formable change. The assurance of authenticity, i.e. reference to a presupposed reality, was based on collectivized experiences.

What all the stories have in common is that they deal with both the experience of time and future visions. The narrative structure of cultural interpretations was particularly well implemented in stories since they allowed for a combination of different, sometimes opposing narrative styles. The interpretation of the texts that emerges in the act of reading refers to a future world, to new experiences of time. As the stories about Wysłouchowa's female heroes have shown, fictionalization may even be advantageous in this process. Although the places of publication politicized the texts in different ways, they referred to the aim of political practice, namely writing, dramatizing, and performing politics. The following chapter examines the practices of political activity by studying the three women's organizations. The example of reading rooms is used to illustrate the ritualization of education, kindergartens are used to show the rehearsal of the nation, while a design of society is drawn by using the example of the centers of movements.

Notes

1 Kobryns'ka, "Pro pervisnu cil," 461. Emphasis in the original.
2 Prohrama tovarystva, IlŠ, f. 3, 3366. See also Ohonovs'kyj, "Natalja Kobryns'ka," in *Istorija*, 1273.
3 Wysłouchowa to Orzeszkowa, December 17, 1900, PAN, Warsaw, 800.
4 Hroch, *Nations*, 163–228.
5 Casanova refers to functioning aesthetics. Casanova, *World*, 199–200.
6 Casanova, *World*, especially 4, 12; see also Roberts, *Disruptive Acts*, 7.
7 Veidlinger, *Culture*, 89.
8 Concerning the connection between literature and ideology, see also Hrytsak, "Cycle," 183–88.
9 P[omeranz], "'Oci.'"
10 Pomeranz, "Frage."
11 Kobryns'ka, "Jadzja," in *Vybrani tvory*, 1958; Kobrynska, "Yadzya."
12 Knyš, *Smoloskyp*, 35.
13 See Chapter 1, Dramatic directing.
14 Nünning and Nünning, "Analysekategorien," 34.
15 Information on the magazines' print runs varies. In 1900, *Przodownica* had a circulation of slightly over 2,000. See Wysłouchowa to Eliasz, February 3, 1900, BO, 12009/II. Wysłouchowa wrote that *Zorza* had a print run of 3,000. See Wysłouchowa to Sokolová-Seidlová, July 6, no year (presumably 1901), PNP, 33/44. *Przyjaciel Ludu* achieved a circulation of 8,000 in Galicia, but *Zorza* had to be subscribed to separately. *Gazeta Polska* (The Polish Newspaper) allegedly ordered 4,000 copies before the first issue appeared, a figure which seems rather high to me. Bryll, *Maria Wysłouchowa*, 15.

150   Propagating: The Plays

Sokół quotes orders for about 10,000 copies as supplements to various newspapers, even for the Polish community in Brazil and Berlin. She assumes a total circulation of 20,000. Sokół, "'Zorza,'" 63–64. Dormus, *Problematyka*, 83, footnote 107, considers this estimate to be too high.

16 Bryll, *Maria Wysłouchowa*, 99; more generally, see also Hüchtker, "Bäuerin."
17 For instance Offen, *Feminisms*, XV.
18 The Polish population responded to the policy of Germanization and Russification in the Prussian partition and in the Kingdom of Poland by demanding Polish-language religious and history lessons in elementary schools. The resistance became radicalized particularly in 1901 and 1906/07 (in Prussia) and during the 1905 revolution in the Kingdom of Poland, adopting school strikes, i.e. a refusal to send children to school. Chwalba, *Historia*, 459–60; Hüchtker, "Politics," 90–92. See for example "Wiec." Conflicts between the tsarist army and workers on May 1, 1900 in Warsaw were mentioned in the section "Chronicle." Kronika. 1900. *Zorza* I (2): 30. Short reports on school strikes in the Province of Poznań and the Kingdom of Poland are to be found in "Bohaterskie dzieci"; "Dzieci polskie"; "O mowę." *Przodownica* devoted a whole issue to the strikes in 1901. Zaleska, *Czasopisma*, 100.
19 This political restraint may have had something to do with the press censorship remaining in force, albeit not as strictly as in the 1850s; after all, Wysłouchowa had witnessed the confiscations and the failure of *Przegląd Społeczny* (Social Review). However, the infamous newspaper stamp, which had had to be purchased from the administration before distribution and allowed content to be monitored, was rescinded shortly beforehand on January 1, 1900. Olechowski, "Preßrecht," 1515.
20 For more about the manifest interests and intravillage social differences that led to the split of the Peasant Party in 1913, see Dunin-Wąsowicz, "Bewegungen," 65.
21 Komitet redakcyjny, "Do sióstr," 1.
22 Redakcja *Zorzy*, "Słówko."
23 Bohachevsky-Chomiak, *Feminists*, 93.
24 See for example the direct address to the "young shepherds," who were asked not to destroy birds' nests. Rozmaitości: "Nie wyrządzajcie krzywdy ptakom." 1900. *Zorza* I:14; or the address in the report Rozmaitości: "Tytułowy obrazek naszej gazetki." 1900. *Zorza* I:14.
25 Komitet redakcyjny, "Do sióstr," 2.
26 Franke, *Polska prasa*, 264–65; Myśliński, "Wysłouchowie," 151–52.
27 Regarding the contemporary rhetoric of authenticity, see Salomon, "'Simulacrum.'"
28 Bryll, "Listy ze Śląska," 62–70; Broda to the editor of *Zorza*, December 4, 1901, BO, 7193/II, 257. Broda was ordering a subscription on behalf of his sister.
29 Boner to the editor of *Zorza*, undated, BO, 7193/II, 253–56; see also Baron to the editor of *Zorza*, February 10, 1902, BO, 7193/II, 247, 249–51.
30 See also the examples in Dunin-Wąsowicz, *Czasopiśmiennictwo*, 257.
31 Some figures are to be found in Potoczny, *Rozwój*, 75–87; Stopińska-Pająk, "Polska oświata." The illiteracy rate was said to be between 76% and 80%, although it is unknown how these figures were calculated. The high rate of illiteracy cannot be denied when compared to literacy rates of 88% in the German Empire and 90% in France around 1880. Regardless of exactly what reading and writing skills were understood to mean or how they were measured, the figures in Galicia were clearly much lower. Then again,

Propagating: The Plays 151

Galicia is a province and should be compared to regions like Bavaria or Brittany. Adina Lieske, on the other hand, points out that the high literacy rate in Bohemia may have contained a high share of functional illiteracy. Lieske, *Arbeiterkultur*, 183–84.
32 In many European countries, the illiteracy rate was also significantly higher in rural areas than in towns and cities until the end of the nineteenth century. Literacy increased when it proved to be a valuable resource—for social advancement, say, or for the preservation of elite positions and influence. This suggests closer consideration of the historical importance and practices of reading and writing. Lyons, "Leser," 457, 493.
33 See Chapter 4, Monologues.
34 W[ysłouchowa], "Z wędrówek." See also Wysłouchowa, "Dni."
35 W[ysłouchowa], "Z wędrówek."
36 Komitet redakcyjny, "Do sióstr," 1.
37 Rozmaitości: "Tytułowy obrazek naszej gazetki." 1900. *Zorza* I:14.
38 See Chapter 1, Dramatic directing.
39 Listy do "Zorzy": [Józefa Jarorzówna]. 1900. *Zorza* I (4): 62–63.
40 See also Stauter-Halsted, *Nation*, 142–84; Molenda, *Chłopi*, 78–94. Both assume a development toward nationalization and modernization. Stauter-Halsted summarizes the process as "from serfdom to citizenship" (Stauter-Halsted, *Nation*, 3), despite criticizing the concept of an inevitable development toward nationality. Nevertheless, an irreversible and thus ultimately teleological process is implied. If, on the other hand, we assume the existence of arenas where conflicts over hierarchies and social significance were enacted, a teleological view can be rejected.
41 Wysłouchowa, "Racławicka bitwa."
42 "Jubileusz." The importance of such celebrations as a didactic tool of the Polish national movement was mentioned in Chapter 1, Heroic narrating. They demonstrated the nation both internally and externally. See Stauter-Halsted, "Celebrations."
43 Wysłouchowa to Orkan, November 16, 1899, BJ, 10471/III, 43.
44 M., "Rady."
45 M., "Rady."
46 See as an example of the contributions made by female peasants the instructions from Silesia for baking bread: Maryna Glajcarowa to Wysłouchowa, April 24, 1900, BO, 7187/II, quoted after Bryll, "Listy ze Śląska," 69–70. The letter was printed with a few editorial corrections in the section "Homemaking Tips." Rady gospodarskie: [Maryna Glajcarowa], "Sposób wypiekania smacznego chleba." 1900. *Zorza* I (2): 31–32.
47 Kizwalter, "Demos,"
48 W[ysłouchowa], "Nasze obrazki," 12.
49 Bryll, *Maria Wysłouchowa*, 37, 101.
50 Rezler, "Sczaniecka."
51 Wysłouchowa, "O przezacnej Polce," 4.
52 Wysłouchowa, "O przezacnej Polce," 5.
53 See Chapter 1, Heroic narrating.
54 Jürgen Hein, "Berthold Auerbach," 173.
55 See also the reference to the mixture of styles: journalistic, reportage-like, yet also narrative and fictional. Bryll, *Maria Wysłouchowa*, 99.
56 Wysłouchowa, "O przezacnej Polce," 5. The Polish word *ojczyzna* (fatherland) is grammatically feminine, giving "mother" a double, partly metaphorical meaning.
57 Piwarski, "Chrzanowska." For unknown reasons, her first name changed to Zofja. Wysłouchowa, "Zofja Chrzanowska."

152   Propagating: The Plays

58 In another version, she criticizes the cowardice of her husband and her fellow combatants.
59 Filipowicz, "Daughters."
60 Wysłouchowa, "Emilja Platerówna."
61 Wysłouchowa, "Chłopi," 2.
62 Tatarowski, *Ludowość*, 373–74.
63 See Chapter 1, Heroic narrating.
64 Komitet redakcyjny, "Do sióstr," 2; Redakcja "Zorzy," "Słówko."
65 See for instance Smerzyńska, "Pierwsze kroki." Katarzyna Smaciarz was not used to writing, but she was accustomed to telling stories. Józef Dużyk describes her as semi-illiterate—today one might say structurally illiterate. Dużyk, "Orkan," 189.
66 Sachße, *Mütterlichkeit*, 55–79; Weißbrod, "'Control.'"
67 For example Dormus, *Problematyka*, 84.
68 See also Dunin-Wąsowicz, *Czasopiśmiennictwo*, 269.
69 See Bryll, *Maria Wysłouchowa*, 17, 31.
70 For example Orkan, "[Obituary]," 10; Sokół, "'Zorza,'"54; Bryll, *Maria Wysłouchowa*, 99.
71 Hüchtker, "Bäuerin"; Stauter-Halsted, *Nation*, 98.
72 P[omeranz], "'Oci.'"
73 Alfred Nossig is regarded as an important example of one such historical journey through life. Ezra Mendelsohn, contrary to a view often encountered in research, emphasizes that personal disappointments were the driver behind Jews turning to Zionism, that they were concerned with structural possibilities, the strengthening of nationalism in general, and the search for new prospects to be found in the formation of collectives and collective commonalities. Mendelsohn, "Assimilation"; see also Shimoni, *Ideology*, 3–51; Hroch, "Zionism."
74 See Landwehr, "Diskurs."
75 Pomeranz,"Frage."
76 Pomeranz, "Frage," 12.
77 Pomeranz, "Frage," 12.
78 Pomeranz, "Frage," 13.
79 Pomeranz, "Frage," 13.
80 Regarding the significance of emotionalization for the national, see Gehmacher, "Nation."
81 Kobrynska, "Spirit," 238–39. A revised version of the story was published separately under the title *Duch času* (*The Spirit of the Times*): Kobryns'ka, *Duch*, 1899. For the publication history, see Kobryns'ka, *Duch*, 1990, 339; Kobryns'ka, "Duch," in *Vybrani tvory*, 1958, 393.
82 Kobrynska, "Crust"; initially Kobryns'ka, "Zadlja kusynka," *Zorja* (1884); see also Kobryns'ka, "Zadlja kusynka", *Vybrani tvory*, 1958; for the publication history Kobrynska, "Crust", 393; Kobryns'ka, *Duch*, 1990, 339. Regarding the magazine, see Humenjuk, Peredmova to "*Zorja*," 4–5.
83 Kobryns'ka to Franko, August 31, 1884 and October 16, 1884, IlŠ, f. 3, 1603.
84 See Hrytsak, *Ivan Franko*, 330.
85 Bohachevsky-Chomiak, "Natalia Kobryns'ka," 202; see also Chapter 1, Dramatic directing.
86 See Chapter 4, Recitations.
87 Olena Kysilevs'ka. 1930. "Spohad pro Natalju Kobryns'ku," *Žinoča dolja*, 4, quoted after Knyš, *Smoloskyp*, 35.
88 Regarding the demand for modernization, see also Bohachevsky-Chomiak, "Natalia Kobryns'ka," 207.

Propagating: The Plays   153

89 Kobrynska, "Yadzya"; initially Kobryns'ka, "Jadzja," *Zorja* XIV (1893); see also Kobryns'ka, "Jadzja." In *Vybrani tvory*, 1958. The story was reprinted several times. Regarding its publication history, see Kobryns'ka, *Vybrani tvory*, 1980, 418.
90 Kobrynska, "Yadzya," 381.
91 Regarding the connotation of progressiveness with girls (or young women)— *divčaty*, *divčyny*—in Galicia at the turn of the century, see also the founding of the Circle of Ukrainian Girls (*Kružka ukraïns'kych divčat*) in L'viv. Bohachevsky-Chomiak, *Feminists*, 92.
92 Knyš, *Smoloskyp*, 195.
93 Regarding the "new woman," see also the references in Chapter 1, Theatrical enacting.
94 Regarding Kobryns'ka's corresponding interpretations of the world, see also Chapter 3, Rehearsing nation, and Chapter 4, Monologues.
95 Hutnikiewicz, *Polska*, 8.
96 Kobrynska, "Yadzya," 310.
97 Kobryns'ka, "Yadzya," 319.
98 Regarding the ambivalence of rural stories, see Jürgen Hein, "Berthold Auerbach," 183–84.
99 Regarding the act of identification with fictitious persons as well as models of femininity in nineteenth-century literature, see also Harmak, "Prototypy."
100 Humenjuk, Peredmova to *"Zorja,"* 5.
101 Ohonovskyj, "Natalja Kobryns'ka," in *Istorija*, 1284–85.
102 Bachmann-Medick, "Einleitung"; Bachmann-Medick, "Übersetzung in der Weltgesellschaft"; Bachmann-Medick, "Übersetzung im Spannungsfeld."
103 Korenec', "Natalija Kobryns'ka." Regarding Ukrainian Realism, see Čyževs'kyj, *History*, 603.
104 Moroz, "Natalja Kobryns'ka," 14–15.
105 Casanova, *World*, 197.
106 Čyževs'kyj, *History*, 589–90.
107 Regarding the discussion of experience as a historical category, see Scott, "'Experience'"; Scott, "Phantasie"; Canning, "History"; Canning, "Dichotomien."
108 Pomeranz, *Im Lande*.
109 Pomeranz, *Im Lande*, 5.
110 Schieb, *Reise*; see also Hüchtker, "'Mythos'"; Wiegandt, *Austria*.
111 Pomeranz, *Im Lande*, 203.
112 The motif of the complete loss of contact between parents and emigrated children recurs frequently in literature. Depicted as an escape, emigration and turning to the Gentile world were equated with the loss of religion and origin. See the examples in Kłańska, *Schtetl*, 241–68.
113 Pomeranz, *Im Lande*, 252.
114 Benedict Anderson, *Communities*.
115 Biale, "Eros"; Glenn, *Daughters*, 34–35.
116 See Mosse, *Nationalism*, 1–22, especially 18–19.
117 Pomeranz, *Im Lande*, 196.
118 Pomeranz, *Im Lande*, 196.
119 Hausen, "Family."
120 Regarding the strong Zionist see Berkowitz, "'Tzimmes.'"
121 Seidman, "Erotics"; see also Stampfer, *Families*, especially 121–41.
122 Regarding literature, see also Ruth Berger, "Frauen."
123 See also Pomeranz, "Die Frauen und der Zionismus." In the article, she emphasizes the "high importance" of women in the history and religion of Judaism.

154 *Propagating: The Plays*

124 Pomeranz was not alone in rejecting the demands of the women's movement. Regarding the disputes, see for instance Or, *Vorkämpferinnen*, 45–50.
125 See for example Wenk, "Representations"; McClintock, "'Heaven.'"
126 See Chapter 4, Dialogues.
127 Regarding love stories as metonymies for change, see Hüchtker, "'Mythos,'" 96–97; Mark H. Gelber, *Pride*, 201–02.
128 Pomeranz, *Im Lande*, 306.
129 Litterarisches. 1901. *Israelitische Rundschau*. According to Mark H. Gelber, *Pride*, 194, footnote 66, this was a reprint from *Vossische Zeitung* (Voss's Newspaper).
130 Emes, "Romane."
131 [Hoffmann], "Im Lande."
132 [Zlocisti], "Rosa Pomeranz."
133 Tisch, "'Im Lande.'"
134 Casanova, *World*, 175–204.
135 Shedletzky, "Ost."; Estermann, "Ost"; Nordau, "Gegensatz"; Nacht, "Ost- und Westzionismus."
136 See Chapter 4, Dialogues.
137 Gilman, "Rediscovery"; Bechtel, "Transfers"; Bechtel, *Renaissance*, 176–99; Steffen, "Connotations."
138 Mark H. Gelber, *Pride*, 194.
139 Mark H. Gelber, *Pride*, 200.
140 Regarding the relevance of narrative literature in this process of popularization, see Dohrn, "'Zionsliebe,'" 117–19.
141 Nünning and Nünning, "Analysekategorien," 24.

3 Organizing
The Stages

The plays—written to form collectives as well as to construct experience and legitimize it as politically relevant by means of history—were enacted. This required spaces, filling the roles, an interpretation of each play, and a corresponding production design, i.e., a stage, an ensemble and scenery. The three women used their political activities to not only open up a temporal perspective by linking past, present, and future, but also to create and mold spaces in a concrete and metaphorical sense: geographical spaces and action spaces. In order to carry out their projects, they acted in associations—concrete places where new social relationships were tested and rehearsed, where different initiatives came together in the same place, allowing a new, better, "modern" society to be planned.[1] Below, the organizational activities of the three women are analyzed with regard to the construction of places. I will explore how the women created concrete spaces, how they acted in them, and how the creation of political concepts functioned there. I start with the observation that a diverse landscape of associations and societies emerged in Galicia around the turn of the twentieth century. They ran reading rooms, libraries, holiday camps for poor children, kindergartens, day nurseries, hygiene courses, and training programs as well as education and reform centers such as Toynbee Halls and people's houses.[2] These initiatives addressed central strands of the social work debate: education, integration, and participation as well as family and gender policy. The reform initiatives studied by researchers usually associated with industrialization, civil society, and often with cities were also set up in rural regions, which were regarded as socially and economically backward.

Of the many places where the three women worked, I have selected three examples for analysis: reading rooms, kindergartens, and reform centers. They represent different priorities set by the women in their respective activities and are of key importance for their political goals and reform proposals. The women made use of sociopolitical programs and projects that were current at the time depending on their needs and convictions. Although hardly any concrete links between them are known, fundamental parallels nevertheless existed, which are attributable to similarities in the different contexts. One aim is therefore to demonstrate the transnationality of political practices and their translation into local conditions. The respective priorities did not result from basic political or even national differences. They were not prerequisites; they were part of the play.

As already shown, Wysłouchowa's political activity for rural areas and women began with education. As well as writing folk literature, she undertook lecture tours and was involved in educational institutions, including reading rooms. Reading rooms—both networks of local facilities and integrated into larger educational institutions—were operated by most political movements at the turn of the twentieth century. For her part, Kobryns'ka strove to improve the living conditions of women and therefore propagated the establishment of kindergartens. These, too, were one of the main projects of social work policy. They served to demonstrate and rehearse a model of cooperation among women from different social strata, the need for the professionalization of women's occupations, and a pedagogically guided, nationally supported system of intervention in early childcare. And Pomeranz, in turn, campaigned for the integration of women into nationalist politics. She organized centers for women's social and educational projects. These centers drew attention to the general need for reform in society, represented the wide range of activities of the movements, and opened up possibilities for change.

According to the thesis, the projects were designed as places of presentation and vision. They were a stage in two ways: a play was performed within them, while their specifics allowed for different roles to be rehearsed.[3] The reading rooms provided a stage on which the importance of education for society was demonstrated. People could enter reading rooms to watch or join in the demonstration. By regarding the performances in reading rooms as rituals, it can be shown how hierarchy and participation were transformed by specific forms of distribution of education. Kindergartens also required places where children could be looked after and socialized by (exclusively female) volunteers or professional nursery teachers. The kindergarten can be seen as a stage on which the roles in the family and society were assigned. A female-connoted sphere brought women from different social backgrounds and education together while early childcare was allotted central importance in shaping society. The reform centers combined rituals and rehearsals. Moreover, they reflected the oscillation of movements between the desire to have their own spaces and the claim to participation. With their extensive educational, cultural, and support offerings, they also provided solid evidence of the possibility of social work. They outlined a new society with regard to education, the family, and professionalism, and also the identification of the participants with this space. These spatial designs are analyzed on the basis of association reports and contemporary descriptions of the projects. These interpretations are an attempt to pinpoint specific aspects and should not be understood as exclusive interpretations. Rehearsals also took place in reading rooms, while in connection with the operation of kindergartens, rituals were also established and a modern society outlined.

Ritualizing Education

Wysłouchowa explained the importance of reading rooms for her political work in a letter to Orzeszkowa. She described to her the tasks and working methods of the Association of Friends of Education, which she had set up with her husband:

> [The Association of Friends of Education] differs from other [associations] related to it in that its members are almost all peasants. In return for an annual subscription of two guilders, the members receive a magazine (*Przyjaciel Ludu*), all the publications of the association, and become members of the reading rooms founded by it. Moreover, we have set up eight such reading rooms in the province, published a book (about Mickiewicz, distributed in 12,000 copies), while a second—the abridged and popularized *The Misery of Galicia in Figures* by Szczepanowski—is in press. Next month, we'll open a reading room here in L'viv which is free for members and will cost ten cents a month for non-members.[4]

By noting that the Association of Friends of Education, unlike similar associations, included a significant number of peasants,[5] Wysłouchowa underlined her and her husband's policy geared to participation. The association provided members with internally produced publications, including its own organ, *Przyjaciel Ludu*. The book about Adam Mickiewicz was probably the booklet written by Wysłouchowa that same year.[6] Although the sociopolitical and economic publication *Nędza Galicyi w cyfrach i program energicznego rozwoju gospodarstwa krajowego* (The Misery of Galicia in Figures and a Program for the Vigorous Development of the Country's Economy) by the liberal oil entrepreneur Stanisław Szczepanowski had not originally been published by the peasant movement, the abridged version was. *Nędza Galicyi* was much read and discussed then (as it is today).[7] The Association of Friends of Education was keen to influence its members, as Wysłouchowa's notes reveal. With its eight reading rooms in the province and one in L'viv, the association managed to establish a rural network and presence. Its members were linked in virtual terms by the free distribution of the peasant movement's publications. By reading the same material, the peasants shared views, analyses, and knowledge. Mind you, this free or inexpensive distribution of information was not unique to the Association of Friends of Education, for other organizations did the same, and the membership fee of two guilders was not particularly low.[8] Furthermore,

158 *Organizing: The Stages*

the Association of Friends of Education was not as democratic as Wysłouchowa suggested. After all, despite claiming to favor participation, she planned members' access to books in a paternalistic way. As she continued about the Association of Friends of Education:

> I will lend books there [in the L'viv reading room] twice a week, drawing up a selection corresponding to the borrower's intelligence and adding explanatory remarks with the spoken word to the printed letters, etc., etc.[9]

Wysłouchowa's claim to the intellectual leadership of the rural population is clearly apparent from this project. The distribution of roles shows that books, in particular, functioned as a means of hierarchization. Interestingly, Wysłouchowa and her husband evidently expected much from the educational associations' repertoire of symbolic and concrete instruments for the foundation of the Peasant Party (for which above all the Association of Friends of Education paved the way), particularly when it came to establishing leadership and the prerogative of interpretation in rural areas.

From 1867, when the red tape surrounding the foundation of associations was simplified, a number of adult education initiatives arose in Galicia.[10] They were mainly supported by the reform-oriented political movements, i.e., the socialist, peasant, women's, and national movements, which established associations concerned with education and enlightenment. Both the Polish peasant movement and the Ruthenian Radicals regarded the village to be the main terrain of political struggle and enlightenment to be the key to the village. The Jewish reform movements and the women's movements also promoted education. Among the foremost institutions of adult education in Galicia were the Association of People's Enlightenment (*Towarzystwo Oświaty Ludowej*), the Association of People's School (*Towarzystwo Szkoły Ludowej*), the Ruthenian associations Enlightenment (*Prosvita*) and Mychajlo Kačkovs'kyj Association (*Obščestvo ymeny Mychayla Kačkovskoho*), the Adam Mickiewicz Association for Adult Education Center, the association Zion (*Syon*), the Jewish Association for People's Education (*Żydowskie Towarzystwo Oświaty Ludowej*), and others popularizing education and culture in various ways. Developing methods to attract the grassroots—the people, peasants, women—was a key aspect of their activity.[11] The associations founded publishing houses, magazines, libraries, adult education centers, and lending libraries, and organized series of lectures on a wide variety of topics.[12] Thanks to local networking through the establishment of a large number of reading rooms, the Association of Friends of Education drew on the organizational structures of older educational associations, above all the Association of People's Enlightenment and the Association of

People's School, although they already covered a much larger area at that time.[13]

Lectures, lending libraries, and reading rooms were not of course invented by Galician associations. The use of such resources as a means of socialization in the world of education was a widespread, international phenomenon. Adult education centers, workers' training institutes, and various forms of libraries were all part of the activities employed to shape society at the time.[14] Reading rooms were a fundamental strand of these educational facilities. Newspapers and books could be read there (including aloud), while popular booklets were sold or even distributed free of charge. The associations organized the publication of books and founded their own publishing houses, as Wysłouchowa's publishing activities show.[15] They also organized the practices of the procurement and lending of books, and above all lectures held in reading rooms. Lectures on various economic, domestic, social, hygiene, religious, historical, and political themes were seen as the main way of imparting education. The reading rooms thus became mediators of new forms of knowledge and new interpretation of the world; they were concrete places where campaign literature, political ideas, and arguments could be disseminated and where interested people came together.[16]

In research, the Galician reading rooms have so far been addressed in the context of adult education, i.e., with a view to imparting knowledge, and in the context of political movements as places for the propagation of corresponding political ideology, be it socialist, national, or feminist. This was evidently also Wysłouchowa's view, who primarily regarded the mission of the Association of Friends of Education to be the dissemination of literature close to the movement. In other words, analysis has hitherto mainly focused on the content and political leanings of educational projects. However, there were certainly other aspects of reading rooms. They constituted a new habitus and new hierarchies, the special importance of knowledge. "Knowledge popularization" meant defining what was considered meaningful, rational knowledge as well as who was able to disseminate it. Places were created where this knowledge could be acquired. Moreover, it was in such places that education and participation became inextricably linked. The importance of this link for political understanding in the era had already been expressed by Wysłouchowa with her emphasis on peasant parliamentarians' literacy abilities.

The educational initiatives succeeded in establishing new resources in rural power structures. Thanks to progress being equated with patriotism and considered part of academic knowledge, literacy gained relevance in rural areas and for the position of villagers in society as a whole. A form of cultural capital was offered that could and was intended to be acquired through learning rather than experience.[17] The acquisition of knowledge held out the prospect of participating in the improvement of their own living conditions and hence of society, too. Education thus became a means and a prerequisite for social advancement. Printed publications caught on as symbols of this new importance. In *Zorza*, for instance, Wysłouchowa had shown books on the tables of Silesian peasant cottages as an example to follow.[18] Similar theses have been formulated for Jewish girls' education. Secular school education, little appreciated in the male-dominated community context, prompted girls and women, in particular, to read secular literature, making them catalysts of social change.[19] Education became an essential resource for performance on the various stages of the debates over advancement, participation, and interpretive competence.

A letter written by Kazimiera Bujwidowa,[20] one of the leaders of the Polish women's movement who devoted herself to the struggle for academic education and was active in adult education, shows what the new habitus could look like and how it ought to be implemented. Being on the Adam Mickiewicz Association for Adult Education Center committee, she was keen to persuade Wysłouchowa to commit to a lecture tour of villages. According to Bujwidowa, the Association needed an introductory talk before proceeding with "something scholarly," the actual program. The introduction was to contain four points:

1 [One should] address the village citizen with the question of whether he knows *who* he is (Pole, a small part of the Polish nation, relations with the three partitioning powers).
2 Were things always as they are today (the partitions and national uprisings)?
3 Where he lives (the geographical location of Poland, the three occupied territories, and the neighboring states).
4 Whether the cultural level of today's villagers leaves something to be desired? (Incentive to enlightenment.)[21]

Bujwidowa explained that the rural population was still rather ignorant about such matters, which was why an introductory talk was so important. In addition, she wanted it to have an animated, emotional style as even "the most beautiful lecture may be completely worthless if delivered in the wrong way."[22] In her eyes, Wysłouchowa was the only suitable candidate:

> And your address to the villagers during the L'viv Exhibition made such an indelible impression on me that I would consider it a matter of extraordinary importance to engage you as a lecturer for the Adult Education Center.[23]

The letter confirms that the "how" of a speech was considered to be at least as important as the content. Furthermore, it shows that thought had been given to the didactics of imparting a new form of knowledge.

The listeners had to be prepared for a scientific lecture by reflecting on their identity as well as by a direct approach rather than via basic knowledge of the field concerned. The questions were intended to encourage the peasant audience to view themselves as citizens of a divided state and members of the Polish nation as well as to simultaneously make them aware of their social discrimination. It was with this basic attitude and this view of themselves in mind that the scientific talk afterward was to be listened to. Putting the audience in the right frame of mind conveyed an emotionally based nationalist identity, and moreover emphasized that the talk they were about to hear was a new, special form of knowledge, which only attained its educational significance by means of a specific—in this case nationalist—sense of identity.[24] All in all, in the letter, Wysłouchowa was treated as a specialist in the matter of "people," something which was reinforced in the subsequent letter thanking her for agreeing to the request. In this letter, she was asked whether it would be a good idea to organize lectures in April, bearing in mind that this was the start of the working year for the peasantry.[25] The lecture desired by Bujwidowa functioned as a ritual intended to shape the transition from a rural population to educated listeners aware of their nation and their history. The last question on satisfaction also drew attention to the discrimination which—as implied by the sociopolitically active context of the Association—was to be overcome. This question transformed the audience into politically active citizens. Just as in a transfer or translation process, the ritual constituted not only the new but also the old: the rural population as apolitical and unenlightened.

Contemporary reports about Pomeranz's appearance at official functions and rallies underlined the importance of emotionalization as lecture rituals played out:

> In her convincing and penetrating talk, she [Pomeranz] explained the tasks of the Jewish woman in the present day and described the necessity for Jewish women to join our movement so gracefully and enthusiastically that no one could escape the impression of her speech.[26]

The conclusion of the ritual consisted in the audience's reactions as the reports about Zionist rallies show, for the speech only gained its significance from the description of the applause:

> After the introductory address by Mr. Löbel Taubes, the speaker Miss Rosa Pomeranz took the floor and in a speech lasting over half an hour she appealed to the feelings of the assembled women. The speaker's moving words acted like the sun on ice, and so the women present rewarded the speaker for her words with a storm of unending applause.[27]

Not only the success of the speech but also its interpretation depended on the participation of the audience. It was only the applause, which really brought out the emotionality—and thus a decisive part of the message. The report assigned the roles such that the speaker and the audience confirmed each other. What ultimately embedded the speech and the audience in a Zionist context was the locations, i.e., not just the association hall but also the magazine in which the report was published. They made the singular event of "emotive words" part of a political movement. The place of the performance and the place of publication belonged together.

According to the many accounts, the lectures followed a series of rules. After a welcome extended by association officials such as Löbel Taubes, the speaker, endowed with the authority of the respective movement, appeared. Male speakers often had a doctorate; women were naturally less likely to have one. The lecture emotionalized or conveyed new knowledge. The performance ended with applause. Subsequent reports in the corresponding movement magazines highlighted (interested) questions from the audience or lively discussion, some referred to the resolutions passed, many to lively applause, while the participation of the audience was also mentioned briefly. Lectures can therefore be understood as a ritual with the traditional three phases of entrance, the liminal phase of transition, and exit.[28] The participants entered the ritual via the introduction, the welcoming address, and perhaps an additional warm-up talk, as suggested by Bujwidowa. This first phase separated the participants from their current situation. This was followed by the actual ritual, the speech, which was intended to ensure transition to the respective political convictions. The ritual authority of the speakers required a rousing manner of presentation. Rhetorical skills and charisma were part of direction. This was followed by communication between the speaker and the audience, the exit. Whether it succeeded or not was an open question. The process of transition was ended by the report, which interpreted and confirmed the event as political. Accordingly, the ritualization of the imparting of knowledge included a speaker, an appealing, stirring style, and an audience who not only measured success through its reactions but also created the character of a "tendency speech," to borrow a term from the Zionist movement.

The transition from one social state to another supported by the ritual was in this case the meeting between dedicated members of the intelligentsia and the enlightened grassroots—peasants, women, youth, the Jewish nation, or the lower classes. The ritual made the transition repeatable and transferable. It constructed a new relationship between the participants: the mediators armed with the power of knowledge, and the audience as yet without it. This new hierarchy was explicitly and also socially enshrined as far as the village and the urban lower classes were concerned—an audience that rarely had direct access to the institutions of knowledge, neither to secondary schools and higher education nor to research and writing. Knowledge became something which was acquired from books, which (academically) educated people, men and women, passed on orally. The listeners and readers had to absorb the knowledge as something to be cognitively processed. The ritual therefore contained a dual message—emotionality and knowledge—which in Bujwidowa's adult education didactics was covered by two speeches.

As well as being part of adult education, educational institutions and lecture programs also had a role to play in political mobilization, as both the founding of the Association of Friends of Education by the Wysłouchs and the educational and cultural program of Zionist associations have shown. The dissemination of education was a central concern of movement politics and encompassed adult education and self-study. Not only those who were not in touch with the corresponding institutions were educated, but also the collective of the respective movement. Similarly, knowledge transfer structured a group not constituted by social distance. For example, the Polish women's movement founded several associations known as reading rooms.[29] During the establishment phase of the Women's Reading Room in Kraków, Maria Wysłouchowa received a request for support from the chair, Maria Siedlecka:

> We therefore very much hope that all outstanding Polish women will support our work, whether by words or by deeds. We hope that all those who join our association will form its moral strength, and will provide advice, encouragement or guidance if necessary.[30]

The Women's Reading Room in Kraków was regarded as a project intended to serve the welfare of all women. The desired support by "all outstanding Polish women" was seen as a way of gaining authority by achieving an important position in society. Of course, Siedlecka was flattering Wysłouchowa, but her ability to do so stemmed from the fact that fame represented symbolic capital. Wysłouchowa and Siedlecka shared their dedication to reading rooms and worked together until their dispute over the *Przodownica*. They were both active in the Kraków Women's Reading Room and in various adult education institutions.[31] Wysłouchowa was also, as already mentioned, a member of the Women's Reading Room in L'viv.

What the women's associations understood by a reading room can be deduced from their activity reports. The aims of the Kraków association were to campaign for better employment conditions for women and to nurture artistic, social, and philanthropic activities.[32] In its view, the starting point for these reforms was intellectual education, the aim of which was to benefit the "welfare of all women." In 1905, the Kraków association was divided into different departments or sections: lectures (*sekcya odczytowa*), support for youth from the Kingdom (*sekcya pomocy dla młodzieży z Królestwa*), education (*sekcya pedagogiczna*), the protection of neglected children[33] (*sekcya opieki nad*

164 *Organizing: The Stages*

zaniedbaną dziatwą), the library (*sekcya biblioteczna*), book-lending (*sekcya wypożyczalniana*), and the organization of social events (*sekcya dla organizowania zebrań towarzystkich*).[34] These sections indicate a large, active association as well as the subdivision of its work into various strands focusing on specific areas.

Like other reading room associations, the Women's Reading Room in Kraków maintained a library, lent books, and organized lectures. Leading lights of the Polish women's movement in Galicia and the Kingdom of Poland were invited, such as Kazimiera Bujwidowa, Paulina Kuczalska-Reinschmit, and Iza Moszczeńska, a journalist who also lived in Warsaw and was active in the feminist and national movement.[35] Some male public figures from Galicia were invited, too, such as the journalist and literary critic Wilhelm Feldman.[36] The titles of the lectures included "Women and the Reform of Civil Law in Austria," "The Education of Young People on Gender Issues," "The Need to Unite Women on the Basis of a Common Program," "The Importance of Political Rights for Women," "Child Protection," "The Protection of Motherhood," and on Otto Weininger's book *Sex and Character*.[37] Other talks were planned on topics such as the economic liberation of women, the reform of home economics and domestic service, and moral reform. In addition, there were lectures on Greenland, talks about history and nation, literature, eye diseases—a wide variety of topical themes, as was customary in other reading rooms. Various aspects of women's politics were addressed, such as the reform of civil law, morality, ethics, and sexuality, and organizational amalgamation. The association's interest in scientific and medical subjects signaled its modern, progressive outlook, something which was backed up by its slogan: "We are an organization of progressive women!"[38]

The educational section founded in 1905 pursued the goal of advancing the professionalization of adult training. By working in three areas—"self-study, popularization and agitation"—it aimed to reach both mothers and nursery teachers. Its aims were the "rational reform of education" and the dissemination of corresponding new knowledge.[39] Lectures, talks, and discussions were also planned for this section, including in conjunction with other associations, along with a magazine entitled *Szkoła Polska* (Polish School). The main objective, however, was to institutionalize the teaching of knowledge in the form of regular courses. The women's movement insisted on professional training. As far as it was concerned, the "tasks of women in society" did not simply result from the character of the female gender, as often claimed in secondary literature. Instead, the "female vocation" had to be acquired, which required institutional instruction. Education became a professional task for women which they shouldered on behalf of society by creating new spaces[40]—and the educational section contributed to this with its program.

The Women's Reading Room in Kraków was not limited to education, enlightenment, and professional matters. It also acted politically in the narrower sense, i.e., it frequently took a stand on various issues. For example, it passed a resolution condemning attacks by the conservative daily newspaper *Czas* (Die Zeit) on a middle school for girls. As early as 1894, it participated in the petition to the Imperial Council campaigning for women's equality in university education, and in 1903 in the Section for the Defense of Women's Rights (*Sekcja dla Obrony Praw Kobiet*) calling for resistance to violence, and demanding equal moral and political rights for men and women.[41] In 1905, the Women's Reading Room signed a petition for equal, secret, universal, and direct suffrage for men and women at the local level. In response to the 1905 Revolution in the Russian Empire and the Kingdom of Poland, several public meetings were held under the title of "The Role of Women in the Present Situation" (phrased in this way to avoid the prying eyes of the police) where political events in the Kingdom were discussed and a resolution adopted.[42] The latter honored the "heroes fighting for freedom" and prevailed upon women to support their fighting husbands, sons, and brothers. By referring to freedom and a battle order divided by gender, the association emphasized the national policy aspects of the Revolution. The formulations referred to the militarily led uprisings and the struggle for nationalist goals rather than the labor struggles, which also constituted the Revolution.[43] The second meeting addressed the school strikes held to make Polish the language of instruction. Against the background of revolutionary developments, the association set up a section to deal with the youth in the Kingdom as a way of perpetuating solidarity with the struggles.

The Kraków Women's Reading Room adopted a stance in nationalist and feminist politics. It made extensive demands for democratization and participation in all the partitions, was involved in nationalist politics in support of the Revolution in the Kingdom, and became publicly involved in all the issues dealt with by the women's movements, from educational matters to the moral debate. Over time, the development of educational concepts became increasingly important to the association. In the end, a separate section was established reflecting the professionalization of educational work, even though no institutionalized, formalized training was set up.[44] For the Women's Reading Room, the lecture ritual was the pivotal form of knowledge transfer: in addition to academic knowledge, feminist matters, and aspects of general politics such as the professionalization of "female" activities and the "scientification" of education were explained to women in this way and established in a continuous lecture program. As well as traditional lectures ending with questions from the audience, audiences were sometimes called upon at the end to make a statement, pass a resolution, or adopt a petition. The ritual of the lecture constituted a relationship between expert and lay people similar to that developed in *Zorza* by Wysłouchowa.[45] It also implied a relationship between leadership and grassroots. In this sense, the Women's Reading Room in Kraków can be seen as the ritualized institutionalization of a movement and its central demands for gainful employment, education, and gender equality.

The Women's Reading Room in L'viv founded in 1884/85[46] or 1886[47] (there are discrepancies among contemporary reports) concentrated on activities related to nationalist policy. Both internal descriptions known of the association refer to attending commemorations, sending wreaths, and paying respects to deceased figures. Detailed mention is made of speeches dealing with suffering and misery, struggle and oppression in Polish history held to mark national holidays (e.g., the return of Mickiewicz's remains to Kraków and the anniversary of the Kościuszko Uprising). Just as with the Zionist associations, reporting devoted much attention to the festive framework provided on such occasions involving speeches, music, declamations, and singing. The 1892/93 annual report also mentioned the association's library and book-lending facilities as well as the organization of series of lectures. However, the Committee for a Women's Work Section (*Komitet Działu Pracy Kobiet*) founded with the Women's Circle for People's Education in 1893 was not mentioned in either report.[48] The lectures dealt with Polish, French and Hungarian art and literature as well as natural history and laws of nature, such as gravity. The fact that there was only one lecture on a nationalist topic (the importance of anniversaries) is astonishing given the emphasis on nationalist involvement. Interestingly, *Historya rozwoju i działalności czytelni dla kobiet we Lwowie* (The History of the Development and Activities of the Women's Reading Room in L'viv) published in 1894 makes no mention of the library or the series of lectures, and only refers to involvement in a petition to the *Sejm* for the establishment of a high school for girls. The self-defined goal is mentioned as "joint work on the nationalist spirit and on the awakening of an intellectual movement."[49] In this way, the L'viv Women's Reading Room strengthened a concept of the nation that integrated females.[50] It focused on directing general education. The corresponding lectures were framed by festive acts related to nationalist policy, the education program being associated with political statements, as was the case at the Kraków association. On the other hand, according to the reports, the feminist component in the Women's Reading Room in L'viv was restricted to the petition for a girls' high school. The two reading rooms in Kraków and L'viv were organized centrally rather than locally like the educational associations presented above. They combined different strands of their activities in the same place, albeit in multiple sections.

Educational events, social work projects, and nationalist and women's political demands were also part of the program of the women's associations in Ruthenian and Jewish political movements. While the two Polish associations known as women's reading rooms emphasized a specific institution (yet in practice encompassed far wider activities), the names of Ruthenian women's associations and groups were more general, examples including the Club of Ruthenian Women in L'viv and the Ruthenian Women's Circle in Kolomyja (*Ru'skyj žinočej kružok v Kolomyï*). These associations also maintained libraries with a wide range of newspapers and magazines (including women's magazines in Czech and German), and organized book-lending, dances, amateur dramatics, and concerts. They supported social work and cooperative projects, such as a school for home economics as well as the Labor (*Trud*) initiative that began in 1902 and offered training courses for girls.[51] The organization of lectures dealing with women's politics as well as literature, history (both Ruthenian and Ukrainian), and geology was also important in these associations and societies.[52] Like the women's reading rooms, the associations combined aspects of women's policy with general education and scientific themes indicating progressiveness, participation, and positioning. In 1899, a Jewish nationalist Reading Room for Young Women "Ruth" (*Narodowo-żydowska Czytelnia młodzieży żeńskiej "Ruth"*) was established in Kraków.[53] The Thamar Association for National Jewish Young Women (*Stowarzyszenie panien narodowo-żydowskich "Thamar"*) founded in 1903 in Jarosław aimed to provide "mutual education in a nationalist-Jewish sense."[54] Although there is relatively little information about what these associations considered important, there are occasional references to social work projects, such as collections for poor schoolchildren,[55] the organization of kindergartens and Hebrew-speaking schools,[56] evening classes for Jewish women and girls,[57] and of course festivities.

Above all, lectures are reported, frequently including the title and speaker. The overwhelming majority of them dealt with topics from Jewish history, literature, and culture, while about half of them referred to women in the title. The 1903 annual report of the Jewish nationalist Women's Association "Ruth" in Kraków also lists a broad range of general educational, academic, philosophical, and scientific topics, at least judging by the titles: "Darwinism," "The Individual and Society," "The Factor of Interest," "The Influence of Women as Nursery Teachers," "Kant's Critique," "The Ideals of Women," "The Genius" and "The Third Gender."[58] Even more revealing is the detailed description of programs accompanying such lectures: performances of classical music and Zionist folk songs as well as Hebrew and Yiddish poems and stories. The names of the performers are also listed. While the basic structure of the lecture ritual did not differ from that of other reading rooms—spectators and listeners encountered speakers and performers—great importance was attached to the accompanying program in Zionist women's associations and circles as well as in the L'viv Women's Reading Room. The mission of these associations was not just to provide education by imparting knowledge from books, but also to form a national culture, its elements stemming from the repertoire generally regarded as high culture.[59] The accompanying program represented a ritual of unification (into a national collective), which also included the ritual of social hierarchization. Nation and education were closely interwoven. The conclusion of the liminal phase was formed during a lecture by the audience's reaction and the report in the movement organ.

Women were largely or exclusively organized in the associations described here; occasionally, men participated in their foundation or were honorary members. However, males almost always appeared alongside females as speakers. This does not come as a surprise concerning the Zionist movement, for women's societies were usually a subgroup of the local Zionist organization. The participation of male speakers demonstrated the unity of the movement.[60] The situation was different at women's reading rooms, which saw themselves as part of an autonomously organized feminist movement. The Women's Reading Room in L'viv reported having only female members in 1892/93, while in Kraków, there were two male honorary members. In both reading rooms men gave lectures.[61] The presence of male speakers on an education program in an association of the women's movement demonstrated that women were capable of participating in the canon of academic knowledge—the doctorate therefore had symbolic meaning. The fundamental exclusion of men (as applied by the Congress organized as an exclusive event in Zakopane in 1899) was not widespread.[62]

Just like reading rooms in general, women's reading rooms cultivated the ritual of the lecture. This ritual was also applied to educating members of their own group rather than outsiders, a situation in which there were no social differences between speaker and audience. For example, if middle-class women delivered lectures to other such women in order to persuade them to join political campaigns, the lecture ritualized the knowing speaker and the unknowing audience being enlightened about gender inequality to enable them to act politically. As the example of the Women's Reading Room in Kraków showed, lectures symbolized a virtual network of solidarity that was intended to overcome the borders of the partitions or differences among women. The directing of petitions created a common ground of interpretation and action. Knowledge and politics were closely interrelated. Politicking was not just a question of indignation or experience but also one of knowledge—knowledge about inequality, yet also history, nature, and literature. Knowledge contributed the interpretation that turned events into experience.[63]

All these associations used similar practices to popularize knowledge, reading, and listening. What these different aspects of the ritualization of spaces had in common was education. Lectures, book procurement, and lending facilities were therefore essential aspects of their work, and knowledge transfer was at the core of their politics. The reading rooms were part of an extensive reform program in the various movements, and the adult education initiatives were structured as follows, depending on their context. The reading rooms in the peasant movement mainly combined education and participation in rural areas, whereas the reading rooms with nationalist priorities such as the Women's Reading Room in L'viv and the Zionist reading rooms combined education, gender, and nation. The L'viv Women's Reading Room was quite similar to the Zionist women's associations in their emphasis on nationalist positions. The feminist Women's Reading Room in Kraków combined education and gender with women's various demands ranging from gainful employment for middle-class women to participation in the nation and society. Despite the differences in their orientation, both women's associations were part of the Polish women's movement.[64] All the associations connected education to political positioning—they produced a link between educational culture, progress, and collective action. Being a decentralized network, reading rooms represented the local presence of associations. In contrast, women's reading rooms were examples of the concentration of reform projects in the same place. Both organizational forms had multiple functions: they provided magazines and books, hosted lectures, and occasionally served as meeting rooms. In addition, the Kraków Women's Reading Room supported social work projects, adopted political positions, and above all promoted the professionalization of educational work, i.e., women's occupations. I will return to the centralization aspect later on.

The provision of education required not only popularized knowledge but also places, time, membership, payment, and practices of reading (aloud) as well as lecturing and listening. Reading rooms were specific spaces for such practices of transition rituals. The transition from an unenlightened, oppressed society to an educated, participatory one was directed. The borrowing and reading (including reading aloud) of books constituted participation in this form of knowledge dissemination; apart from knowledge, the lecture ritualized a hierarchical relationship between the actors, i.e., teachers and learners. Yet a large gathering could also be transformed into a ritual of political statement: speakers and audience shared emotions with each other or for example banded together in joint petitions. The ritual of reading and above all the ritual of the lecture can therefore be seen as ordinary people (workers, the poor, and peasants) and the intelligentsia coming together, which at the same time constituted unity, participation, and hierarchy. People gathered in the same place, consumed the same knowledge and the same culture delivered by specialists, regardless of whether they were professionally or politically informed. The lecture implied different positions, those of the teachers and those of the learners. Embedded in the ritual of the lecture, politics became a question of knowledge: whoever is enlightened about social and political conditions is involved in the respective movement, according to the performative direction. Hierarchy was constituted by the different access to socially recognized knowledge promising access to the elite. This was gained through academic training and translated into popular forms. Political positions were also communicated in this way—with lectures, festivities, and resolutions. But this also meant that the ritual of the lecture, the provision of education remained liminal. As well as serving the distribution of knowledge, it also conveyed the message of involvement. It fluctuated between the promise of integration into a collective and the call to protest. It suggested the universality of education as well as equality in participation, and at the same time directed new elite positions. This liminality required additional practices. One way in which relations between society and activists were structured is shown below using the example of kindergarten initiatives.

Rehearsing Nation

Another area of focus of the movements was the establishment and support of social work associations, which organized kindergartens, day nurseries, holiday camps for poor children, school meals, canteens, and other projects. To varying degrees, the associations fulfilled the criteria of social work and welfare policy, replacing and supplementing previous support for the poor and charity with the aim of prevention. Central aspects of this reform policy were professionalization, educationalization, and intervention in the family.[65] The practice of such projects was quickly adopted by churches and local councils, which enhanced them with their own ideological concepts and objectives, and incorporated them into their own charitable activities in order to modernize them.[66] Kindergartens were paradigmatic for the ideas of social work. With their educational concepts, they were considered extremely progressive and combined professionalism with the shaping of family, nation and society. Kobryns'ka gave a speech in 1891 at a women's rally in Stryj, which she had called after her trip to Prague, on the need to set up kindergartens for the Ruthenian-speaking rural population. In 1893, she returned to this subject, drafting a statute for a kindergarten association which appeared in the first volume of *Naša dolja*.[67] In the 1895 volume, she published an article on kindergartens by Maryja Nahirna, and also addressed this topic in a longer article on women's associations.[68] In the third volume (1896), the editorial board appealed to Ruthenian women to found associations to run kindergartens in villages.[69] In 1901, the speech given by Kobryns'ka at the opening of the first kindergarten was printed as a separate booklet.[70] She made the ideal of rural childcare the theme of her story "Perša včytelka" (The First Teacher), in which village life, nature and childhood happiness are interwoven.[71] Kobryns'ka spent ten years endeavoring to establish kindergartens among the rural Ruthenian-speaking population.

Early childcare and education had become a hotly debated topos during the Enlightenment, and in the first half of the nineteenth century, the working conditions of lower class mothers came under fire. According to the contemporary diagnosis, mothers were less likely to work in workshops near their homes, at home in a putting-out system, or in their own horticulture and agriculture, which is why children were often unattended during the day. Against the background of this combination of educational attention for infants and the perception of social and economic changes, institutions for the supervision of infants were established. Known in German-speaking areas as *Kleinkinderbewahranstalten* (infant care institutions) or *Warteschulen,* and usually referred to in Polish as *ochronka,* these institutions were supported by church and parish organizations.[72] Children were supervised and taught by means of songs, prayers, and moral stories. Ideas for systematic, scientifically based, professional early childhood education spread from the 1840s onward. Assuming that parents were not up to this task, Friedrich Fröbel developed an institutional concept through which children were to be appropriately nurtured, a system of early childhood education from birth to the age of six. The key principles were that these institutions were to have their own premises with an adjoining garden as well as trained nurses.[73] Fundamental criticism of the previous childcare system and thus also competition with existing infant care institutions was implied.[74] Fröbel's students first spread his ideas in Great Britain and the USA, although initially the overall number of followers remained low.[75]

The institutional care initiatives for young children thus came from two contexts: one aimed at lower class families and the other focused on the professionalism of education. This dual origin and interpretation of kindergarten projects are reflected in the terminology. Kobryns'ka and Nahirna used *ochoronka* (day nursery or infant care institution). In Polish, the terms employed were *ochronka* (day nursery or infant care institution), *ogród dzieciowy* (kindergarten), *ogród freblowski* (Fröbel garden), *szkoła freblowska* (Fröbel school) and *wychowanie przedszkole* (preschool education), while in the Jewish context, *Kindergarten* or *ochronka* were used.[76] These terms set different priorities: explicit reference to Fröbel, emphasis on childcare, upbringing, or preschool teaching. They cannot be unambiguously classified as educational or political.

There was considerable resistance from various quarters to (professional) intervention in the area of the family. Bringing up children was regarded as a natural female calling within an emotional charging of the dichotomous gender model, which is why care outside the family had negative connotations and was often regarded as an emergency solution. In Prussia, the kindergarten was associated with nationalist and revolutionary activities and was banned until the 1860s. For a long time, the Catholic Church also considered kindergartens dangerous, associating them with secularization and the destruction of the family. Nevertheless, it maintained its own facilities which could be classified as infant care institutions of poor relief and Christian charity. In liberal circles, although the kindergarten was controversial on the one hand because private life was supposed to be free of public intervention, on the other hand it was promoted as a progressive, scientifically rational achievement. Socialist movements also shared the connotation of kindergartens as progressive, although occasionally this kind of intervention (like social work projects as a whole) was criticized not only as the colonization of worker culture but also as a pacification strategy or a bourgeois problem thwarting the labor struggle. It was assumed that living conditions could only be fundamentally improved by revolutionizing production conditions. Similarly, despite the establishment of kindergartens as spaces of nationalist education, the Zionist movement (including Pomeranz) repeatedly polemicized against social work initiatives. It was claimed that they were pointless, a drop in the ocean, and that the only way to end misery and persecution was by emigrating to Palestine.[77] In the closing decades of the nineteenth century, however, the Fröbel kindergarten spread around the world astonishingly rapidly despite all the criticism.[78] Roberta Wollons highlights its global reach and local implementation.[79]

The history of childcare in Galicia reflects contemporary ambivalence from a transnational viewpoint and was simultaneously integrated into local conditions. From the mid-nineteenth century onward, more and more church and municipal institutions were founded for children in need: orphanages, infant care institutions, schools, and vocational training centers.[80] They were set up in Polish, Jewish, and Ruthenian contexts. In L'viv, there is evidence of a Polish infant care institution from 1840, and a Jewish one from 1843.[81] Corresponding facilities in rural areas existed from the 1860s at the latest, primarily maintained by convents.[82] The Fröbel movement also began to catch on at this time. In the early 1870s, the liberal democrat faction decided the policy of the Provincial Education Board (*Rada Szkolna Krajowa*), focusing on professionalization and obliging seminaries for teachers to adopt Fröbel's educational principles. The first three Fröbel kindergartens, founded in 1874 in L'viv, Kraków, and Przemyśl, had educational concepts and required nursery teachers (*nauczyczelki*) to have taken a one-year training course.[83] After the conservatives had come to power, the Provincial Education Board lost interest in Fröbel kindergartens. Instead, the administration now promoted facilities run by religious and philanthropic associations that were more in keeping with the concept of the infant care institution. They were founded on noble estates and run by convents. According to contemporary polemics, they raised the children "into diligent future workers" in unpaid 12-hour supervision including a meal, catechism lessons, and needlework.[84] Since the schemes applying Fröbel's principles now lacked municipal and regional financial support, their success was generally limited everywhere. Training course graduates founded private kindergartens, which only the middle classes could afford to use, and their popularity was low. However, the first three private kindergartens survived along with two public ones, which followed Fröbel's system (at least to some extent). Because all these ambitious kindergartens charged fees, they were mainly attended by children from the scientifically and pedagogically interested middle classes. The support for institutionalized early childcare is revealing to the extent that it had apparently become so widespread that it was unavoidable, while Fröbel's ideas connoted as progressive were so well established that an alternative program was deemed necessary.

Against the background of growing criticism of the Galician government's schools and education policy, educational reform projects including kindergartens and the training of nursery teachers were increasingly discussed in the 1890s. The supporters of kindergartens polemically defamed the childcare facilities promoted by the nobility and the church as infant care institutions characterized by coercion and indifference, and tried to quash the reputation of their own institutions as being geared towards atheism, socialism, and the destruction of the family. The interest in modern educational methods was not just pedagogically motivated, but also a result of competition with the kindergartens of religious communities and the provincial administration. In practice, the distinction between a kindergarten and an infant care institution was blurred. Although the educationalization of kindergarten care rose in importance and the training of nursery teachers caught on, both kindergartens and infant care institutions were considered establishments for poor and abandoned children. In 1906/07, there were 18 Fröbel kindergartens and 65 other kindergartens in the diocese of L'viv, including 10 at provincial level and 8 opened by elementary schools and funded by the municipal budget.[85]

Bringing up children had become a field of professional and scientific activity.[86] Just how far the principles of professional education had become established is apparent from the view of early childcare held by kindergarten advocate, pedagogue, and author Maria Weryho:

> Many intelligent mothers have familiarized themselves with the system of preschool education by reading corresponding works and attending lectures, and are introducing it into early childcare.[87]

For Weryho, education was based on the acquisition of systematic knowledge as represented by the Fröbel concept; the kindergarten was brought into the family, so to speak. This example shows that it was not so much a question of providing institutional care everywhere for all children—small children being looked after by the family remained the norm[88]—but rather of kindergartens representing a new, systematic form of education. They were part of the professionalization and scientification of housework and upbringing, which also included the dissemination of hygiene rules and the popularization of nutrition science, yet also the introduction of home economics as a school subject and the establishment of home economics schools.[89] With her columns in *Zorza,* Wysłouchowa was in tune with the zeitgeist.

Kindergartens were understood as instances of nonfamily socialization that offered ways of shaping society.[90] They were fixed premises, ideally with a garden, which offered a stage on which to signal modernity: education in childcare, professionalism, and intervention. The roles of nursery teachers, the active members of the association, and the educated children were practiced on the stage and could be transferred to other places, as propagated by Weryho regarding upbringing in the family by mothers. In addition, the concept defined neglect and thus legitimized intervention in families, especially in the lower classes.[91] Kindergarten associations were closely linked to women's movements, for the desire for professional childcare underpinned the demand for training and appropriate employment for middle-class women: the establishment of trained nursery teachers, housekeepers, nutritionists, and so on. The kindergarten supported the general increase in importance of childcare and domestic work. It thus referred to two strands of social debate: educational and vocational policy on the one hand, and social work on the other.

From the turn of the century, the Zionist movement also began establishing places of professional nursery education.[92] However, the differences between privately run schools, day nurseries, and kindergartens became blurred. All these facilities served the teaching of Hebrew and, depending on the age of the children, Jewish history, celebrations, customs, and traditions. Supervising unattended children from poor families also played a role. A Jewish kindergarten was founded in Drohobycz in 1903 by the Moriah women's association. Meanwhile, the Rachela women's association ran a day nursery in Stanislav for "poor girls who attend school but are not looked after at home"[93] and also opened a kindergarten in 1904.[94] In Kraków, on the other hand, the failure to apply Fröbel's principles was lamented. In 1914, it was even the subject of negotiations by the delegates from all Zionist associations in the district committee.[95] The Provincial Zionist Conference adopted a motion to establish Hebrew kindergartens throughout Galicia, forming the basis for the creation of Hebrew elementary schools:

> In the field of Jewish education, the association for Hebrew schools has established Hebrew schools. The provincial and state school is alien, there is nothing Jewish about it. The Hebrew school intends to teach children at least the Hebrew language and Jewish history. However, this is still far from educating full Jews under galuth conditions. For this, the time must be used before the alien school takes hold of the child.[96]

The application referred to the assumption on which the kindergartens were based that early childcare (i.e., the deliberate molding of children) was necessary. From a Zionist viewpoint, the function of kindergartens was to provide an exclusively Jewish space. This space was created by the Hebrew language, which was to lay the foundations for Jewish education. This separate Jewish space also constituted the other space as non-Jewish and "alien." Hebrew-speaking kindergartens were therefore an element in an exclusive nation concept based on the separation and hierarchization of spaces and languages.

At the end of the nineteenth century, several kindergartens also existed in the Ruthenian context, for instance in Horodenka, Husiatyn, and L'viv, run by Greek Catholic communities.[97] The Association of Ruthenian Women in Stanislav established a girls' school in order to educate pupils "in the national Ruthenian spirit" and was comparable to Zionist projects in this respect.[98] Given these diverse contexts, what did Kobryns'ka associate with her kindergarten project? It did not tie in with the existing municipal associations or with the initiative of the Ruthenian Women's Association—presumably because of the existing differences. She had in mind kindergartens run by an association and financed and supported by a dedicated public, founded in various towns and above all in villages.[99] Upon request, the association would provide financial assistance toward the construction of the building, initially help to find suitable premises with a garden, and pay the nursery teachers.[100] The kindergarten was to be financed in the long term by membership fees, savings deposits, financial, and material donations, and income from lectures, amateur enactments, and entertainment evenings. The kindergarten board was to accept children and hire nursery teachers.[101]

Kobryns'ka initially justified the need for kindergartens with the poverty of mothers resulting from advancing industrialization and the resulting decline of home-based businesses. She emphasized the aspect of supervision and legitimized kindergartens as a way of combating misery and neglect. The argument that female peasants and workers neglected the upbringing and hygiene of their children, and above all the explanation that this resulted from the changes in employment structures making it impossible for women to take their children to work with them, echoed the justification for infant care institutions. In addition, Kobryns'ka pursued early childcare concepts with her project. The example statutes published for an association named "Ochoronka" formulated the goal of having preschool children looked after full-time by female supervisors in order to "promote their development and occupy them according to their age."[102] The references to nurturing development and age-appropriate activities contain a nod to Fröbel's principles. Kobryns'ka described the supervisors' tasks as follows:

> [A]nd it is sufficient if the children are under the care of older, respectable peasant women, who have already raised children themselves,

and under the supervision of some women from the intelligentsia, who treat the children more gently and politely than is the case in peasant families. In the end, practice will show the way; the most important thing now is the goodwill and willingness of the women.[103]

By citing the experience and respectability of female peasants, she was referring to traditional rural values. The female intelligentsia, who were also to be involved, were responsible for good manners. Kobryns'ka derived expertise in early childcare from experience and respectability as well as from education and status. She implied that people in the countryside were uncouth and that education meant implementing the habitus of the educated class. The reference to the goodwill and willingness of women is also telling. For Kobryns'ka, the kindergarten was a matter of dedication and devotion rather than training.

She also associated the establishment of kindergartens everywhere with another task that she felt was urgent. One of her central arguments for rural kindergartens was the preservation of the mother tongue, enabling children to be withdrawn from "denationalization" (*vynarodovlenja*):

> It is less a matter of [the child] learning the Lord's Prayer at all than of this being done in Ruthenian and children being spoken to in their mother tongue and not in Polish, as is the case in the kindergartens founded, despite the presence of philanthropic Polish women there.[104]

Kobryns'ka called for "own" kindergartens in contrast to Polish-speaking institutions—and was not alone in her views. This argument was also strongly made by Nahirna in her presentation of kindergartens. Both women argued that the influence of Polish kindergarten teachers on Ruthenian children should be reduced.[105] Like Kobryns'ka, Nahirna proposed having children supervised by "ladies" from the intelligentsia or older women from the village who no longer had to support their own family. She justified this model by saying that such a concept was only the first step. The implementation of Fröbel's ideas was too expensive for the villages, and given their simple organization and support, no professionally trained personnel would be necessary at first. Later on, they could resort to their "own" trained nursery teachers and introduce their own courses.[106] Like Kobryns'ka, Nahirna relied on the experience of rural women, but did not fundamentally reject the idea of professional early childcare and education.

All in all, in fact, Kobryns'ka and Nahirna seemed to argue in many respects for infant care institutions. Their references to professional early childcare and education, however, show that educationalization had prevailed in Ruthenian just as it had in Polish and Jewish reform-oriented circles, building on its connotations as a progressive project. Both women implicitly measured kindergarten projects against the Fröbel concept. They considered it necessary to explain why they did not choose to adopt his principles, at least not in their entirety, the main reason being because they regarded their program as progressive. But Kobryns'ka changed the connotations associated with "modern" versus "traditional." She claimed that a professionally run but Polish-speaking kindergarten was a field for the "retrograde efforts" of the Poles instead of for the "civilization" of the Ruthenian nation.[107] In contrast to the professionalization of education emphasized by the Polish projects, Kobryns'ka stressed dedication to a Ruthenian women's movement and a Ruthenian nation. It wasn't professionalism that was connoted with progress, but dedication—an argument shared by the Zionist movement. This view drew on the common contemporary analyses of social structures in Galicia—conservatism and tradition in institutions on the one hand, progress and civilization in political activity on the other. This dichotomous view of Galician society was shared by many movements, but differently characterized. Wysłouchowa, for example, equated conservatism and tradition with the church and nobility, but would doubtless not have included Polish-speaking kindergartens.[108]

Above all, Kobryns'ka saw kindergartens as a way to build society, something she expressed in all her appeals: "However our women are, founding and supporting kindergartens would really mean the fulfilment of *a great cultural mission*."[109] The "cultural mission" was to build a Ruthenian society, but also to mobilize women. The appeal published in *Naša dolja* set out the future vision associated with the kindergarten as follows:

> Such an association must include every female Ruthenian, the wife of the priest, of the civil servant, of the craftsman, and the female villager, as well as the men, for institutions such as kindergartens are not just beneficial for one class or one gender, but an approach for the organization of future society.[110]

The task of the association was to address both women of all social classes and occupational groups as well as men. Men's role, however, was to be rather subordinate, marking the reversal of the usual occupational and class assignment. In male-dominated contexts, men were socially differentiated, whereas women were appended as a collective noun. Uniting women from different social classes was the main directional aim of the project. This also explains the two different education concepts of the experienced female peasant and the educated woman from the intelligentsia, whom Kobryns'ka intended to bring together. She expressed this message central to her dedication to women's politics on multiple occasions, sometimes in passing:

> The actual goal of the association is set out in the statutes; it must perhaps be added that the association's endeavors will be to encourage as many women as possible to try to found kindergartens everywhere by themselves or with men's assistance, and with this aim to organize female villagers and women from other classes.[111]

This time, men's role was visible: their job was to lend assistance rather than to lead.

The organization of a kindergarten fronted the concept of a collective of women pursuing the same interests. The kindergarten acted as a concrete, practical project for the achievement of this goal. In 1896, Kobryns'ka again stressed in *Naša dolja* the high importance of the kindergarten project by emphasizing its transnationality and topicality. She pointed out that kindergartens had been discussed in Stryj four years before the 1896 International Congress of Women's Activities and Women's Aims (*Internationaler Kongress für Frauenwerke und Frauenbestrebungen*) in Berlin.[112] She hence spotlighted the pioneering role of the Galician debate and incorporated the kindergarten into the context of international women's movements. She defended it as a popular institution against the criticism often leveled by socialist parties—including the Radicals—that it only met the interests of middle class women.[113] However, she also complained that, unlike other nationalities, Ruthenian women were not very nationally focused, that they were conservative in their religious views and somewhat lethargic, and that they were only gradually turning to politics and the needs of the people. And she cited the instructive example of Jewish kindergartens, which in her view were successful.[114]

Kobryns'ka's concept was aimed not just at childcare, but also—even mainly, perhaps—at women, at her goal of building up a Ruthenian women's movement. Kindergarten projects were used in other women's movements to underpin demands for the professionalization and legitimization of female employment. Kobryns'ka linked the kindergarten to the construction of a collective of Ruthenian women. Despite or perhaps precisely because of her reluctance to embrace Fröbel kindergartens, she also regarded her project as a reform from which a new society could emerge: a modern, gender-equitable Ruthenian society. Considering kindergartens of all things as a precondition for this goal set Kobryns'ka apart from other Ruthenian lobby groups and political parties which, as Svjatoslav Pacholkiv pointed out, primarily campaigned for Ukrainian higher education.[115] She also criticized *Narod* for demanding provincial high school education for girls instead of kindergartens.[116] In 1899, the Ruthenian Kindergarten Association (*Tovarystvo Rus'ka zachoronka*) was founded, albeit not in a rural location, but in a city, namely L'viv. The kindergarten was probably opened in 1901 and Kobryns'ka gave the inaugural speech.[117] She was also involved in a kindergarten in Bolechiv, which she remembered in her will.[118]

Kobryns'ka addressed various themes ranging from women's participation and social work efforts for deprived children to the nationalization of early childcare and education. She rehearsed with the kindergarten the play "Progressive Society by Educating the Nation," which was widespread by the end of the nineteenth century. Kindergartens, in her view, represented a nucleus of a social structure encompassing the Ruthenian population. As far as the Polish peasant and women's movement was concerned, it was instead the Fröbel kindergarten which, through professionalism, became part of the play "Modernity"—a synonym for a better and thus also nationalist society. In its program, the Peasant Party called for kindergartens based on Fröbel's principles.[119] Meanwhile, the Jewish kindergartens had a slightly different focus. They were a moment in the direction of the "Jewish people," they were repeatedly mentioned, but only rarely discussed in terms of content or conceptual aspects. The Zionist movement rarely reported in detail on its sociopolitical activities. As already mentioned, reporting focused on Jewish festivities and highlighting educational events on Jewish topics. Kindergartens were intended to teach Hebrew and were thus a prerequisite for directing a Zionist culture: scenery rather than a stage.[120]

The kindergarten can be interpreted as a directed production, as a metonymy for a modern society. The roles of women (and children) were united in *the same* play. It had different scenes, commitment to progress, the shaping of relations between women, family, gainful employment, and nation. It was for this purpose that a stage was built, a room hired, and roles defined: a new importance in the part of women for society and for the nation, the integration of men as supporters of the project, experienced and educated nursery teachers for the children. The play "Early Childcare and Education" stood for progressive gender relations and a nation capable of action. Kindergartens were transnational and transpolitical, they were used by different tendencies. A policy or movement geared towards nationalist politics like Zionism integrated the kindergarten into the nation. The women's movement associated with it a project that professionalized and put into practice both women's employment (trained nursery teachers) and early childcare and education. Kindergartens were therefore a directed production of political demands and social ideas which could be used in various ways. They represented a miniature utopia of a new society, models for a social order.[121] Nevertheless, these plays had a common plot: they illustrated the assumption underlying social work that the relations between family and employment could be modernized without fundamentally questioning the gender order. Kindergartens defined the relationships between family and knowledge as well as between femininity and knowledge. Women as professional nursery teachers and schoolteachers represented the link between family, employment, and nation, while women from different strata rehearsed the commonality of a nation.

In many respects, the kindergarten corresponded with the reading room: the creation of concrete spaces and the aim of forming a new society. However, Kobryns'ka translated the teaching of knowledge or early childhood education on a professional, academic basis into outlining a connection between the women's movement and nation. She transferred the connection between the women's movement and professionalization to that between the women's movement and nationalization. While the lectures represented a ritual in which the transition to new hierarchies and the power of book knowledge was practiced, the kindergartens rehearsed the roles in women's politics—the collective of women, the mothers and nursery teachers dedicated to the nation. How these aspects of political activity were incorporated into an outline of the possibilities of a new society is discussed below using the example of reform centers.

Designing Society

As well as standing for the ritualization of education and the practice of professional early childcare and education across different social strata, reading rooms and kindergartens were also part of women's politics focusing on educational policy and social work. In order to develop a blueprint for a new society from the ritual of the lecture or public early childcare, it was necessary to have spaces where projects and demands came together and where ideas of the Zionists, feminists, or peasant movement could be represented. Such spaces were stages for movements with concrete addresses: houses, libraries, halls for reading and studying, seats on various association boards, meeting rooms, and kindergartens. The Women's Reading Room in Kraków was one such address.

The associations founded by Pomeranz—the Jewish Women's Circle in L'viv in 1908 and the National Jewish Women's League of Galicia and Bukovina in 1910—were also women's centers for Zionist social and educational work. Association and League combined educational, vocational policy, and social work initiatives and organizations. The League's aims were the "close interaction of all means and forces" and "ideal ... practical successes".[122] In 1910, the work program included the founding of a boarding school for initially fifteen girls who were to be educated in a "national sense" and receive a good secondary school education, the financing of another secondary school for Jewish girls, the popularization of the Hebrew language and Jewish history, and promoting a Zionist youth magazine. Support was to be given to a school's association planning to establish a system of Hebrew education ranging from a Hebrew-speaking kindergarten to studying Jewish history in Hebrew.[123] In addition, Pomeranz proposed setting up a labor exchange for Jewish women and girls as well as vocational schools for female Jewish workers, especially seamstresses, embroiderers, and milliners. Apart from vocational training, these schools were also to teach reading, writing, and arithmetic. In 1914, Pomeranz supplemented her proposals with a Jewish educational institute for boys, a Jewish parents' association, and another Jewish secondary school for girls. By this time, the Jewish Women's Circle boarding school was already up and running while the youth magazine had launched a Hebrew supplement.[124]

Organizing: The Stages 181

The building of the Jewish Women's Circle, which Pomeranz had bought with the money raised on her tour of Europe after the First World War, served as a materialized place for the centralization of Zionist women's politics. The building was the seat of the National Jewish Women's League, housed various educational, vocational, and social work initiatives, and became a center of Zionist agitation as well as social and educational work. The vocational school proposed in 1914 was opened there,[125] a department for war orphans was set up, which operated a kindergarten and a day nursery, and meetings and conferences were held there. Later, a boarding school for *chalucoth* (settlers), Hebrew courses for teachers, a kindergarten for working class children, and a club for working women were added. Seamstress and home economics courses were also offered for orphans, for every child was to receive vocational training.[126] Pomeranz and her organizations pursued the establishment of Zionist centers that focused on women's politics, addressed women both as actors and as clients, and above all tackled social work projects for children and young people. Although these centers offered the usual Zionist education program, Hebrew courses, and lectures, it is striking that the emphasis was on vocational training. Courses were offered for youngsters and young women. The centers thus expanded the usual educational and cultural program of Zionist associations. It has already been shown that Pomeranz campaigned more for social work projects from the turn of the century and above all from the First World War and her time as a parliamentary deputy.[127]

Since Pomeranz did not express herself in detail regarding her intent or conceptualization,[128] the following section examines the frames of reference which existed in Galicia for these types of reform centers as well as how they were discussed and set up. By focusing on a policy of social work, Pomeranz built on projects of the women's, labor and settlement movements. The centers of the women's movement, such as the Women's Reading Room in Kraków, hosted a combined education and training program, often augmented by social work initiatives, especially for youngsters. Pestalozzi-Fröbel-Haus in Berlin, for example, a training center concentrating kindergartens and day nurseries, training courses for nursery teachers as well as series of lecture in the same place, had a similar set-up. Pestalozzi-Fröbel-Haus thus linked the demand of the women's movement's for adequate gainful employment to the professionalization of education and training opportunities for girls from the lower and lower middle classes.[129] Other varieties of these centers include the people's houses of the labor movement and the institutions in the settlement movement. People's houses referred to projects which, like Pomeranz's Jewish Women's Circle, combined educational and social projects in the same place:

> The need for people's houses comes from two sources. The first and more important one is *the need to satisfy the desire of the broadest*

> sections of the population for culture and education through libraries, reading rooms, lectures, theatrical performances, etc. The second task of the people's houses, which is related to the first one, is *to provide suitable premises for various social institutions*.[130]

The labor movements and Zionism combined self-help in their centers with assistance for those who lacked access to necessary resources. The main target group were the "others" in their own collective.

Settlement houses were centers with educational and social work programs in poor neighborhoods, in ideal cases with socially committed members of the middle classes living in them, too, at least for a while. In these projects, the social work aspect—helping the "others," the lower classes, migrants, and the socially disadvantaged—predominated.[131] One of the most prominent projects of the settlement movement was Hull House in Chicago, which Pomeranz did not visit until 1923/24 during her trip to the USA, but which she was probably aware of earlier.[132] Hull House was founded in 1894 in Chicago's immigration district and initially run by twenty women headed by the American feminist and social work activist Jane Addams. The building served as a meeting place and offered educational programs as well as a number of social work initiatives: English lessons, vocational training courses, lectures on hygiene and cooking, music, literature and art events, evening classes, a kindergarten, activities for schoolchildren, a library, and many more.[133] The program was aimed at immigrants, especially women. Addams had been inspired by the first Toynbee Hall established in 1884 by Samuel and Henrietta Barnett in the slums of Whitechapel in London's East End. It had been named after Arnold Toynbee, a British philanthropist and economist. The idea was to let students live there for part of their studies so that rich and poor could meet and benefit from each other, simultaneously learning and teaching. Toynbee Hall offered courses in business administration, accounting, arithmetic, English, French, German, and history, as well as excursions, trips to concerts, singing groups, art and literature societies, first aid and home hygiene courses, chess clubs, and legal aid.[134] This institution was the first so-called "settlement house," the name catching on and becoming a generic term.[135]

Pomeranz was not the only one setting up such reform centers, for they were important for the policy of the Zionist movement as a whole. The movement took up the idea of Toynbee Halls from the turn of the century and spread its interpretation of them in Galicia.[136] They were based on the Toynbee Hall founded in Vienna in 1901 by the high school teacher and Zionist Leon Kellner.[137] It was presented as

> an adult education center under the business name "Toynbee Hall" [based on the] model of the institution in London... Toynbee Hall is a temple of knowledge for the grey masses. This is created there

through popular adaptations, including lectures, music products, singing, declamations, and similar pleasures that ennoble the mind. Prof. Kellner has copied this monument of English culture and founded an oasis for Jewish peddlers, rag-and-bone men, and skilled craft workers on the now bitter Viennese soil.[138]

Interestingly, the educational aspect predominated; despite the reference to the London model, social work and training projects were few and far between. Nevertheless, "people" in the semantic field of "people's libraries," the masses, rag-and-bone men, and skilled craft workers tended to connote the lower and middle classes rather than the entirety of the (Jewish) people or nation. This, in turn, was a parallel with the London institution. A link to settlement houses was established by the term "oasis," which implied a surrounding (educational) desert.

Toynbee Halls following the Viennese example were built in L'viv, Drohobycz, Kołomyja, Brody and other towns.[139] In 1904, four Toynbee Halls in the district of L'viv as well as another one in the district of West Galicia were mentioned at the Zionist Provincial Conference.[140] Their orientation differed. In some founding and annual reports in *Die Welt*, *Przyszłość* and *Wschód,* there is talk of proletarians and the masses. Regarding the Toynbee Hall in L'viv:

> They flocked there in large numbers, the doubly miserable, the Jewish proletarians, men and women, to spiritually disperse themselves on Saturday and Sunday evenings (the only free ones in the week).[141]

The visitors are characterized by several attributes as from the lower classes: as the "doubly miserable," exploited and oppressed as Jews and wage laborers, as well as by "the only free evenings," alluding to the long working hours criticized by labor movements.

In other reports, Toynbee Halls are regarded more as an institution for all Jews. Concerning the foundation of a Toynbee Hall in Kołomyja, it was stated that "different spheres of the Jewish population" had attended the opening event of this institution "for the Jewish people."[142] In some accounts, self-help and reciprocity were emphasized, appealing to the commonality of a national collective: "And instead of the educated teaching the uneducated, friend tells friend, nationalist comrade tells nationalist comrade."[143] This oscillation of the meaning of the term *Volk* (people) between "the masses" and "nation" was transferred to Toynbee Hall itself, which functioned simultaneously as a social and nationalist institution. Its invention as an all-Jewish institution is confirmed by the following phrasing in a report on its success: "As paradoxical as it may sound, he [Kellner, the founder of the Viennese Toynbee Hall] has almost transformed a beautiful, modern institute into an old Jewish custom."[144] The "old Jewish custom" alludes to the biblical period idealized in the Zionist movement. The modern institution fulfilled the Zionist idea of a historical cyclical movement: through progress back to the ideal of tradition.

What the Jewish Toynbee Halls offered was largely a blend of musical and literary performances as well as lectures on the latest fields of knowledge:

> Here they could obtain instruction in all sorts of branches of human knowledge; here they could entertain their ears at musical, vocal, and declamatory productions, and for a change laugh during humorous talks.[145]

The Veritas association in Stryj described its activities—amateur performances, lectures, a literature society, a society for Jewish history, and a legal circle providing legal advice—as "a kind of modest Toynbee Hall."[146] A report about the Toynbee Hall in L'viv mentioned that one lecture was attended by 414 people (267 women and 147 men), another 50 having to be turned away because of the lack of room. The lecture was entitled "From the Field of Hygiene" and accompanied by music and declamation. Other lectures covering aspects of technology, law, medicine, and Jewish history were to follow, while two Yiddish readings from the work of Josef Perl[147] were planned.[148] The repertoire of the Polish educational elite was also integrated into the program, such as compositions by Frédéric Chopin and the play *Wesele* (The Wedding) by Stanisław Wyspiański first performed in 1901—a new, not yet familiar play by this Kraków writer who rose to fame in his lifetime.[149] The lectures and plays were mainly in Polish, occasionally in German. Hebrew and Yiddish lectures, songs, recitations, and declamations were mostly marked as such.[150] In linguistic terms, too, it was a program that both presupposed and demonstrated a high level of education. Nevertheless, efforts were made to achieve integration. The L'viv Toynbee Hall planned a Yiddish-language booklet aimed at those unable to read the German and Polish languages mainly used in education, and regretted in its 1903 report that there were insufficient people to read aloud in Yiddish.[151]

Overall, the program did not differ significantly from the various other educational associations or reading rooms. Classical and recent works, literature, biblical Jewish history, and talks on the history of the Jews in Poland were presented and performed. Philosophical questions, current topics such as Darwinism and hysteria, and practical topics such as hygiene and law were discussed, usually in the form of lectures.[152] Hebrew and Polish language courses were also mentioned for the Toynbee Hall in Drohobycz, while in 1903, an event campaigning against trafficking in girls took place at the Toynbee Hall in L'viv which provided information not only on causes and forms but also on initiatives in Galicia.[153] By and large, the education program was geared to the canon; the avant-garde at the turn of the century was less suited to demonstrating establishment. It (still) lacked exchange value as cultural capital.[154] Nevertheless, the lecture programs also included themes that did not belong to the established culture, yet were highly topical and much discussed. The program can be interpreted as the direction of social reputation and the claim to advancement; current topics, popularized academic knowledge as a signal for political orientation—progressive, national, and modern. As with Wysłouchowa's magazine concept, social integration and the habitus of an educational elite were not mutually exclusive.

For one thing, the Galician Toynbee Halls had the character of adult education centers. Cultural and popular scientific performances clearly predominated. Second, the settlement house aspect was missing, not just geographically and socially, but also architecturally. Some Toynbee Halls did not have their own building and instead hired halls from other Zionist or educational associations.[155] There are no indications of their being set up in impoverished or neglected areas, nor of members of the middle classes or the intelligentsia residing in these institutions. The fact that socio-topographical localization was evidently not essential for a Toynbee Hall may have something to do with the fact that the whole of Galicia was seen as a squalid region, especially for the Jewish population.[156] Moreover, the polysemantic sense of identity of the institutions played a role: the connection between self-help for a Jewish nation and help for the others, the lower classes, Jewish poverty, the uneducated masses. The Toynbee Halls can be understood as an integration project consisting in the creation of a modern Jewish people. They taught Jewish history and literature, high culture, and in general subjects of contemporary discussion; the play was "The Modernization of Judaism."[157] These kinds of educational projects were not bound to the term "Toynbee Hall." Occasionally, they were presented as people's houses:

> On Sunday, October 3 last year, the inauguration of the Jewish people's house Bet Haom was celebrated with the enormous participation of the local Jewish population. ... In this building—said the speaker among other things—a library is to be founded in order to train the people, so that there is no difference between poor and rich. A Hebrew school is to be established to educate young people to become good Jews. A bank has been founded in this building in order to be able to help the poor small trader with bonds and to make him politically independent.[158]

Like the institutions known as Toynbee Halls, the Jewish people's houses consisted of a library and a Hebrew school. In addition, there was a bank, probably a savings bank, which became a Jewish one simply by virtue of its location.[159]

Instead of Toynbee Halls, the Polish national, peasant and labor movement used the term *domy ludowe* (people's houses). On the one hand, they also referred to the model of the settlement houses without fulfilling all their aspects; on the other, they came from the workers' education movement.[160] These institutions were propagated in several booklets in Galicia around the turn of the century. The accounts provide an insight into their conception by taking stock and discussing ways in which they could be organized. The booklet *Setlementy angielskie a praca oświatowa wśród robotników w Polsce* (The English Settlements and Educational Work among Workers in Poland) published in L'viv in 1907 identified a close connection between settlement houses and people's houses.[161] The author dedicated his outline "to the academic youth working in the circles of the Association of People's School," thus emphasizing the elite and the common people coming together, the settlement house aspect.[162]

Like the Jewish Toynbee Halls, the conceptual plans for the people's houses emphasized the connection between education and social offerings. They reflected the various contexts in which people's houses emerged, i.e., socialist and nationalist politics. They saw themselves as self-help schemes for the working class and as institutions for everyone,[163] and provided the necessary premises for both aspects. The addressees were "the broadest social strata of the people," an expression containing the double connotation of the term "people": people as distinguished from the elite, and people as an entire ethnic group. This was something the Polish people's houses had in common with the Zionist Toynbee Halls.

In an effort to highlight their usefulness, many booklets referred to international models. They presented the first people's house in Great Britain, which had the character of an adult education center, while the People's House (Maison du Peuple/Volkshuis) built in Belgium in 1899 used its architectural splendor to demonstrate the cultural and political significance of the labor movement there.[164] The diverse programs of the various institutions were described in detail, partly to spark ideas elsewhere: washing facilities, theatre groups, gymnastics courses, concerts, medical, and hygiene advice, and of course lectures. Some people's houses contained consumer cooperatives, soup kitchens, professional organizations, kindergartens, day nurseries, and overnight accommodation.[165]

In 1903, Kazimiera Bujwidowa called for a people's house geared to social work in Kraków to promote adult education.[166] Her main objective was to make use of the qualities of the workers' training centers.[167] Referring to the people's houses of the labor movement, she emphasized the aspect of self-help and self-organization, not the welfare concept of the settlement houses. She mentioned the importance of people's houses for workers' level of education and criticized their being equated with socialism. She provided a detailed description of people's house in Berlin as an exemplary model, which brought together inexpensive accommodation, instruction in the rules of everyday hygiene, a library, meeting rooms, cultural and popular scientific offerings, and plenty more besides under one roof. Kraków urgently needed such an institution (she stated) which united the various activities, especially since the city was a destination for peasants from all over Poland attending nationalist commemorative events. She added that every village ought to contain a similar building for educational and reform initiatives, i.e., combining material support, cultural events, hygienic instruction, and meeting facilities in a fixed place. Bujwidowa explicitly distinguished the concept based on the people's houses of the labor movement from the Polish people's houses beyond the borders of the partitions, saying the latter served the struggle against the enemies, in particular to "defend the nationality."[168] The fact that she was concerned with their different functions rather than evaluating people's houses was confirmed by her plan to found a Polish House (*Dom Polski*) in Moravian Ostrava as a school for illiterate people and workers' children which was to contain a lecture hall, a reading room, and a theatre space.[169] Wysłouchowa was also involved in this type of people's house; together with the editorial staff of *Kurjer Lwowski*, she made a donation for the first Polish House opened in Cieszyn Silesia in 1901.[170]

In 1913, the economist, eugenicist, and socialist Zofia Daszyńska-Golińska[171] explicitly used the term "democratic" to describe the people's houses:

> The achievements in the field of people's houses and workers' homes in Poland testify to the fact that we are making progress and that the creation of cultural milieus for the rural and urban population has become dynamic and is taking place in parallel to the development of our democratic ideas.[172]

For Daszyńska-Golińska, people's houses were a place for the "emancipation of the will and demands" of all social and age groups as well as for both sexes.[173] In contrast to Bujwidowa, who was keen to separate the people's houses from their socialist connotations, she used the connection with the labor movement to associate its watchwords—socialism, democracy, emancipation—with adult education.

Most of the people's houses in Galicia emerged from educational associations such as the Ruthenian association Enlightenment, the Association of People's School and the Association of People's Enlightenment, or emerged in the context of the workers' and peasants' movement.[174] In terms of their multifunctionality as well as their architectural and spatial presence, they did not differ from the settlement houses, even though traditional projects like Toynbee Hall and Hull House stemmed from the social work movement and not the workers' movement.[175]

Many of the smaller people's houses as well as the Zionist Toynbee Halls hardly differed from reading rooms. Most of them, however, played with the ambiguity of the concept of the term "people": they served as halls for meetings and rallies, provided facilities for cultural activities such as drama groups and nationalist festivities, organized libraries and series of lectures. Some were inspired by larger institutions to offer training courses and in some cases childcare (assuming women could be encouraged to take on this work), despite not being institutionalized kindergartens or day nurseries. Many people's houses gave this program a nationalist framework; like the Women's Reading Room in L'viv, they emphasized the nationalist orientation of the lecture and cultural program.

In contrast to the Toynbee Halls, the center founded by Pomeranz was more focused on social work and thus reflected more closely the British and American models. Nevertheless, the Jewish Women's Circle, the Toynbee Halls, and the people's houses resembled each other. The people's houses centralized more or less diverse projects in the same building—in both the labor and the peasant movement.[176] The concepts ranged from adult education centers to the more socially reformist concept of the settlement houses. Moreover, they provided a local presence in the province, their functions similar to those of the Zionist Toynbee Halls. The Jewish Women's Circle with its accumulation of projects in L'viv, on the other hand, fulfilled the function of presenting the diversity and potential of women in the Zionist movement, similar to the labor movement's people's house in Berlin and the Women's Reading Room in Kraków.

What these different centers with different names had in common was that they united and concentrated a wide variety of facilities and functions. In addition to the rooms for libraries and lectures, these included care for orphans, early childcare, vocational training for youngsters and adults, placing people in employment, meeting and organizational facilities, and cultural events. The movements were run by association-based initiatives, which on the one hand were dependent on voluntary work and donations, and encouraged the participation of their clientele—by not only offering meeting facilities but also through association membership as well as affordable fees for their services. They combined their architectural presence with multiple activities. The spatial concentration of various initiatives—such as Pomeranz's umbrella association and above all the purchase of buildings—was geared not only to centralization as a pragmatic practice but also to a vision: the centers represented the possibilities of focused change.

Attempts to politically localize the people's houses—or to claim them for a certain direction—also point to similarities rather than differences as to how closely progress, education, participation, culture, and the people or nation were intertwined. Even though Bujwidowa advocated Galicia adapting the Berlin model, the requirements for such an institution—reading rooms, libraries, lectures, and cultural events—had long been in place in Kraków. Nevertheless, or precisely because of this, distinguishing criteria were established and essentialized, such as Bujwidowa's differentiation between objectives in Galicia and in regions of the Polish-speaking diaspora or Daszyńska-Golińska's democratic-socialist focus. The centers were not typical of a specific political position; instead, they were to be found in all movements striving for reforms in society as a whole. The self-help aspect featured more prominently in the movements' activities than at the first Toynbee Hall in London or at Hull House. Accordingly, the reform centers—like the kindergartens and reading rooms—contained both aspects of reform movements: the creation of a separate collective by means of the creation of "others." They were associated with different political demands and aims, with the goal of higher women's or adult education as well as with intervention in lower class families and enabling political participation.

The institutions could be transferred from one context to another because they were similar in their practices, programs, and conception of offering help to their own collective and help for others. They brought together the usual educational institutions, made great use of lectures, and organized social projects. In this amalgamation of activities, they outlined a new vision of society that was intended to resolve the contradiction between the participation of an entire collective—the nation or the people—and the claim to leadership of the elites of the movements, the educated intelligentsia, who saw themselves as politically progressive. They complemented the model of a modern society by establishing practices of social differentiation and simultaneous inclusion or participation. It was only women's politics and education programs that made Zionism a concept for modern Judaism. Similarly, it was only the presence of cultural and popular scientific performances in conjunction with the possibility of assembly and social work, which was a concept for a modern Polish nation.

The activities in the centers were simultaneously presentations and enactments. They were both a performative speech act and a performance. They presented the hardship, deprivation, and inequality, and outlined a new society, because everyone believed or was supposed to believe in this directed production. In addition, they constituted the possibilities of change. The audience was the subject and object of the movement, i.e., the centers represented a model of participation in which hierarchies and differences were redefined. Regardless of whether they were called Toynbee Hall, people's house, or league, the centers were stages on which a diverse, nuanced commitment to a better society was performed. Just as the ritual of the lecture combined participation with hegemony, so did the ambiguous concept of "people."

***

All the projects discussed were based on the conviction that education was the key to success, the key to a better society. Education was intended to grant women access to male-dominated institutions and employment. It was seen as a way of improving the situation in the countryside and guiding Jews to a nation. Education was regarded as a way out of poverty, religious or cultural isolation, and as a path to a better society, be it Christian, Jewish, nationalist, bourgeois, urban, or socialist. It was used in the movements as a medium or tool to create access to new spaces. Above all, however, education was central to the political movements' visions of progress because it functioned not only as a tool but also as a language constituting the outcome and goal of the transfer itself. This is why education and social work were so closely linked in the organizations of the movements. They altered the content of knowledge, the forms of reception, and the manners of participation by rehearsing performative practices.[177] They thus propagated changing society as both feasible and legitimate, and at the same time constituted new knowledge elites.

The ideas, projects, and contacts that shaped political practice were widespread across state frontiers.[178] Their origin was not specific to Galicia, nor was there a west–east divide. Projects such as kindergartens and settlement houses quickly found their way to Galicia. Therefore, what is relevant is not the idea of the origin of a project, but rather that of transnational contexts and local presence, which could be described by the term "diffusion."[179] Local translations diffused from transnational concepts. One pathway of this diffusion was the ritualization of participation in advancement knowledge, another was the rehearsal of "women" as a collective, and a third the combination of rituals and rehearsals, the outlining of a vision of society. Reading rooms can be understood as ritualizations of Wysłouchowa's women's policy in the peasant movement, kindergartens as the key to Kobryns'ka's policy of autonomy, and reform centers as models for Pomeranz's organizational practice. Kobryns'ka endeavored to unite women from different social strata. Pomeranz made the integration of women's politics into Zionism and Wysłouchowa the village the objective of a participatory nation.

Reading rooms, kindergartens, and centers were projects that molded the political movements: they were their guiding ideas and organizations. They were performative, self-referential, and reality-constituting. Being miniature utopias, the centers perhaps best reflected the sense of identity of the Galician movements as nations without their own state. They offered new visions of a society in which the nation was a metaphor for these different socialist, feminist, or Zionist utopias—which is why it was ubiquitous and lacking in substance. Above all, however, these kinds of projects represented concrete spaces where people came together to participate in the ritual of a lecture, to rehearse new connections among women, where not only the professionalization of early childcare but also their "own" language functioned as a link.

Organizing: The Stages 191

They were stages on which the various participants were brought together, on which a new society was presented as a utopia and heterotopia. The enactments—the interaction between the participants—are examined in the following chapter.

Notes

1 For an overview, see Hackmann, "Vereinskultur"; Hüchtker, "Bewegungen"; Veidlinger, *Culture*, XI–XVIII.
2 Janowski, "Galizien," 819–27. Although according to Janowski the density of associations was significantly lower than, for example, in Bohemia or Bukovina, all these projects and initiatives were nevertheless present. The membership of multiple associations, which he described as a "problem" and regarded as an indication of low development, can equally be interpreted as networking and a sign of a flourishing association landscape. See Nitsch, *Wohltätigkeitsvereine*, 316–49. Generally speaking, studies on social work and education initiatives in Galicia have hardly been included in the political and social history of the region. Regarding the state of research, see for example Wierzbieniec, "Dobroczynności"; Barnaś-Baran, "Dobroczynny nurt."
3 Regarding the symbolic significance of material conditions, see also the example of infrastructure in van Laak, "Infra-Strukturgeschichte," 385–86; for an analysis of the significance of space in politics, see the observations of Epstein, *Practice*, especially 106–25.
4 Wysłouchowa to Orzeszkowa, October 27, 1890, PAN Warsaw, 800.
5 Although female peasants could not join due to the restrictive legislation governing associations, they were permitted to attend events.
6 Wysłouchowa, *O życiu*.
7 Szczepanowski, *Nędza*.
8 For the Ruthenian educational associations Enlightenment (*Prosvita*) and Mychajlo Kačkovs'kyj Association (*Obščestvo ymeny Mychayla Kačkovskoho*), the fee in 1877 was one guilder. Struve, *Bauern*, 146.
9 Wysłouchowa to Orzeszkowa, October 27, 1890, PAN Warsaw, 800.
10 Struve, *Bauern*, 139.
11 For an overview, see Czajecka, "Działalność"; Potoczny, *Od alfabetyzacji do popularyzacji*; Terlecki, *Oświata*.
12 Potoczny, *Oświata*, 137–232. Struve, *Bauern*, 148–90. References to Jewish reading rooms are contained in Gaisbauer, *Davidstern*, 288–98; Berichte: Krakau. 1903. *Die Welt* VII (44): 12, mentions a Jewish-nationalist Reading Room for Girls "Ruth" (*Leseverein jüdischnationaler Mädchen "Ruth"*); Kronika. 1897. *Przyszłość* V (10): 70, states that the Zion association ran a reading room with a considerable number of periodicals. A Zionist Academic Reading Hall (*Zionistische Academische Lesehalle*) in L'viv was reported in 1898. Vereinsnachrichten: Lemberg. 1898. *Die Welt* II (21): 4.
13 According to Struve, *Bauern*, 159, there were about 400 reading rooms in the Association of People's Enlightenment by 1900. However, their number then declined rapidly, mainly due to its competitor Association of People's School founded in 1882. Meanwhile, the Enlightenment association had just five reading associations in 1891, but as many as 2,944 in 1914. Struve, *Bauern*, 177. According to Potoczny, *Rozwój*, 174, 176, in 1900 there were 813 reading rooms in the Association of People's Enlightenment and 131 in the Association of People's School.

192   Organizing: The Stages

14 Dieter Hein, "Formen."
15 See Chapter 1, Heroic narrating. For an overview, see Struve, *Bauern*, 160.
16 See also Lieske, *Arbeiterkultur*, 219–25; Veidlinger, *Culture*, 37–39.
17 Potoczny, "Wkład towarzystw oświatowych"; Dieter Hein, "Formen."
18 See Chapter 2, Writing collectives.
19 Parush, "Women Readers"; see also Parush, *Jewish Women*, 57–70; for indications of the high proportion of women using these services, see Veidlinger, *Culture*, 56.
20 See Kałwa, "Bujwidowa"; Dormus, *Kazimiera Bujwidowa*, 61; Hulewicz, "Bujwidowa."
21 Bujwidowa to Wysłouchowa, January 31, 1900, BO, 7187/II, 285–87, here: 285–86. Emphasis in the original.
22 Bujwidowa to Wysłouchowa, January 31, 1900, BO, 7187/II, 285–87, here 287.
23 Bujwidowa to Wysłouchowa, January 31, 1900, BO, 7187/II, 285–87 here: 287.
24 The Adam Mickiewicz Association for Adult Education Center was particularly active in the development of didactic ideas, such as visits to museums, excursions, and encouraging critical thinking. See Potoczny, "Wkład galicyjskich towarzystw," 43–45.
25 Adam Mickiewicz Association for Adult Education Center to Wysłouchowa, February 14, 1900, BO, 7190/II, 283–85, signed by Bujwidowa.
26 Aus der Bewegung: Bericht: Bielitz. 1903. *Die Welt* VII (14): 11 reports on a festivity hosted by the women's and girls' section of the Zionist association "Dawn" (*Haschachar*). Regarding the significance of the speech situation, see also Epstein, *Practice*, 124.
27 Ruch syoński: Kołomyja. 1899. *Przyszłość* VII (13): 106–07, here: 106.
28 See Turner, "Period." Turner develops the concept of liminality in relation to Arnold van Genep's "rites of passage," who distinguished three ritual phases through which a change in the social status of individuals or groups takes place: separation, liminality, and incorporation. Turner emphasizes in particular that the liminal phase is an intermediate stage whose outcome is uncertain.
29 For an overview, see Dormus, "Galicyjskie stowarzyszenia," 336.
30 Women's Reading Room to Wysłouchowa, undated, BO, 7187/II, signed by Siedlecka.
31 Siedlecka was the chair of the Association of People's School's "Women's Circle" (*Koło Pań*) set up in 1892, under the auspices of which she launched the first free book-lending service for youngsters in Kraków in 1895. Wawrzykowska-Wierciochowa, *Wysłouchowa*, 314, 322f.; Bujak, "Siedlecka," 530.
32 Dormus, *Bujwidowa*, 49–50.
33 The corresponding contemporary term might also be "out-of-control children."
34 Czytelnia dla kobiet w Krakowie, *Sprawozdanie*.
35 Gawin, "Moszczeńska"; Rzepecki, "Moszczeńska."
36 Tadeusz Stanisław Grabowski, "Feldman."
37 Czytelnia dla kobiet w Krakowie, *Sprawozdanie*, 7; Weininger, *Sex*.
38 Czytelnia dla kobiet w Krakowie, *Sprawozdanie*, 1.
39 Czytelnia dla kobiet w Krakowie, *Sprawozdanie*, 9–10.
40 Schröder, *Welt*, 333; Schüler, *Frauenbewegung*, 352.
41 Dormus, *Bujwidowa*, 50. The section demanded the reform of civil law, called for the right to vote, and joined the morality campaigns of other women's movements. The background to the campaign was debates in

women's movements about sexuality, prostitution, and marriage. Under the term "morality movement," reforms of marriage morality and gender relations were demanded, and a campaign was launched against the prevailing double standards of marital and extramarital sexuality as well as the common practice of tolerating supervised prostitution. More radical groups addressed female sexuality, contraception, and extramarital motherhood. See Meyer-Renschhausen, *Kultur*, 271–372.

42 As the report notes, speaking in public about these events was permitted everywhere, even on the market square in Kraków. Only women were barred from talking publicly about the Revolution because they were forbidden to engage in politics. Czytelnia dla kobiet w Krakowie, *Sprawozdanie*, 7–8.

43 Czytelnia dla kobiet w Krakowie, *Sprawozdanie*, 7–8. Regarding the Revolution, see Hüchtker, "'Politics.'"

44 This is in contrast to Pestalozzi-Fröbel-Haus in Berlin, which offered a large number of training courses in the field of "caring professions for women," from kindergarten and nursery teachers to courses on housekeeping and seminars for home economics teachers, etc., to name just one example. See Nitsch, *Wohltätigkeitsvereine*, 57–58.

45 See Chapter 2, Writing collectives.

46 *Sprawozdanie z czynności wydziału czytelni dla kobiet.*

47 [Wechslerowa and Czemeryńska], *Historyja*.

48 Wawrzykowska-Wierciochowa, *Wysłouchowa*, 203–04.

49 [Wechslerowa and Czemeryńska], *Historyja*.

50 Regarding the legitimation of women's politics through the campaign for independence, see for example Stegmann, "Kampf," 21.

51 Malančuk-Rybak, *Ideolohija*, 415–16; Czajecka, *Z domu w szeroki świat*, 75.

52 Malančuk-Rybak, *Ideolohija*, 391–426; [Franciška Kobryns'ka et al.], "Ruch." As well as raising money for school scholarships, the Association of Ruthenian Ladies organized its own educational events. See Chapter 1, Dramatic directing.

53 The founders were a woman and several men. Ruch syoński: Kraków. 1899. *Przyszłość* VIII (8): 67. In 1903, the association celebrated its second anniversary—which is puzzling, given that it had been founded in 1899. Kronika: Kraków. 1903. *Wschód* IV (157): 7. An account of the second general assembly of the Sulamith Reading Room for Jewish-nationalist Women (*Czytelnia kobiet narodowo-żydowskich "Sulamith"*) in Rzeszów in 1903 is to be found in Kronika: [E. Weintraub], Rzeszów. 1903. *Wschód* III (135): 13–14. In addition to the introduction of new officials, it contains the lecture program featuring exclusively Jewish and Zionist topics.

54 Ruch w kraju: Jarosław. 1903. *Wschód* IV (152): 7.

55 Ruch w kraju: Jarosław. 1903 *Wschód* IV (152): 7.

56 Ruch w kraju: Jarosław. 1904 *Wschód* V (49): 4.

57 Ruch w kraju: Stanisławów. 1904. *Wschód* V (40): 5.

58 Berichte: Krakau. 1903. *Die Welt* VII (27): 20. The association is probably identical with the Jewish-nationalist reading room.

59 For an overview of reporting on events of high culture as a demonstration of elite positions, see Beresnevičiūtė-Nosálová, "Öffentlichkeit"; Beresnevičiūtė-Nosálová, *Artists*.

60 However, there were also efforts toward autonomy among women's organizations in the Zionist movement. See Chapter 1, Theatrical enacting.

61 One of the honorary members was Odon Bujwid, a professor at the Jagiellonian University and the husband of Kazimiera Bujwidowa. Czytelnia dla kobiet w Krakowie, *Sprawozdanie*, 16.

194   Organizing: The Stages

62 For sharp journalistic criticism of the exclusion of men, see P. de C., "Zjazd."
63 See Chapter 4, Recitations.
64 See Dormus, *Problematyka*, 200–01.
65 Balukiewicz, "Rozwój," 51, in general Bergler, *Von Armenpflegern*.
66 See for example the lists of church childcare facilities in Meissner-Łozińska, "Placówki"; regarding the change in the conservative structures of Jewish orthodoxy, for example Hödl, *Bettler*, 84–98; regarding Polish conservatives, Ustrzycki, "Pomiędzy konserwatyzmem a nacjonalizmem."
67 "Statut tovarystva 'Ochoronka.'"
68 Nahirna, "Ochoronky"; [Francïška Kobryns'ka et al.], "Ruch," 94–95.
69 [Vid redakcyï], "Vidozva."
70 [Kobryns'ka], *Promova*; see Bohachevsky-Chomiak, *Feminists*, 82; 340, footnote 40.
71 Kobryns'ka, "Perša včyteľka." She wrote this story in 1892; it was first printed in 1900 in *Dilo*; see Kobryns'ka, *Vybrani tvory*, 1958, 395.
72 Allen, "Children," 18. The negative connotation of the German term *Anstalt* (institution) results from the contemporary polemics of the liberal, secular kindergarten movement, which criticized the existing facilities as religiously indoctrinating, repressive places where children were simply left under supervision with no educational concept. To reflect the distinction between supervision and educationalization relevant to my argumentation, I employ the term "infant care institution" based on the contemporary term *Kleinkinderbewahranstalt* commonly used in German language research into the history of social work and early childcare. Whenever the nature of a childcare center is undefined, I use "kindergarten" as a term, which captures the spreading educationalization of early childcare. Educationalization took place in Galicia, too, regardless of how children were occupied by individual childcare centers. The terms *ochronka* in Polish and *ochoronka* in Ukrainian, in which "shelter" and "protection" resonate more strongly than in the German *Kleinkinderbewahranstalt*, are not confined to specific eras.
73 Nitsch, *Wohltätigkeitsvereine*, 57–69. Although the kindergarten is often regarded as a German invention, there were other similar ideas and other "inventors" of professional early childcare. Fröbel may not have been the only one, but he became one of the best-known reformers. Allen, "Children," 17–19.
74 In 1836, at the same time as Fröbel, Theodor Fliedner founded the first seminary for female infant teachers in his deaconesses' association in Kaiserswerth. Jacobi, "Erwerbsfleiß," 274.
75 For the German context, see Nitsch, *Wohltätigkeitsvereine*, 51; Reyer, *Mütter*, 17.
76 See Balukiewicz, "Rozwój," 57.
77 See Chapter 4, Dialogues.
78 Regarding differences in the various regions and states, see Allen, "Mutterschaft."
79 Wollons, "Introduction," 2.
80 Haratyk, *Rozwój*, especially the lists in the appendix, 195–207.
81 Balukiewicz, "Rozwój," 57–58.
82 Szmyd, "Z dziejów zakonnej opieki," 137–38; see also Mayer, "Kindergarten."
83 Sandler, "System," 199, 211; Lorence-Kot and Winiarz, "Education."
84 Szczęsny-Parasiewicz, "Nowe pole," *Szkoła* XXI (1884): 27, quoted after Sandler, "System," 215.

85 Sandler, "System," 219.
86 The characteristics of professionalization which most childcare facilities aspired to were the recognition of preschool education as an important task for society, the development of specific training, qualified individuals working together to monitor practice and remuneration within the monopoly situation, and a political campaign to have the system of childcare protected by the government. Allen, "Mutterschaft," 11; Nitsch, *Wohltätigkeitsvereine*, 252, 469–511; regarding the demand for professional training in educational professions for women in the Polish context focusing on Warsaw and the Kingdom of Poland, see Kempa, *Edukacja*, 25–30.
87 Weryho, "Zadanie," 271.
88 Sandler, "System," 208.
89 Jacobi, "Erwerbsfleiß," 273–74.
90 Wollons, "Introduction," 2, 10.
91 For an overview, see Sachße and Tennstedt, *Sicherheit;* Sachße, *Mütterlichkeit*.
92 Or, *Vorkämpferinnen*, 62–63; Balukiewicz, "Rozwój," 58.
93 Korespondencye: Stanisławów. 1903. *Wschód* IV (106): 8.
94 Ruch w kraju: Ze Stanisławowa. 1904. *Wschód* V (4): 6.
95 Ruch w kraju: Kraków," *Wschód* V (1904): 18, 5; Ruch w kraju: Kraków. 1904. *Wschód* V (20): 6. Kindergartens were also discussed at the first conference of the umbrella organization of Zionist women's organizations founded by Pomeranz in 1910. See N. M. Gelber, "Stryj."
96 [Von unserem galizischen Berichterstatter], "Landeskonferenz," 71. The particular relevance of early childcare and training for women is also highlighted in Montel, "Women." Various studies have emphasized that building a modern society in the first Jewish communities in Palestine required school and education policies, including kindergartens for language acquisition and nationalist education. Shilo, "Transformation"; Sitton, "Struggle."
97 Haratyk, *Rozwój*, 203–07.
98 [Francïška Kobryns'ka et al.], "Ruch," 90.
99 "Statut tovarystva 'Ochoronka,'" 94.
100 [Kobryn'ska], *Promova*, 10.
101 "Statut tovarystva 'Ochoronka,'" 98.
102 "Statut tovarystva 'Ochoronka,'" 94.
103 [Kobryn'ska], *Promova*, 10.
104 [Kobryn'ska], *Promova*, 6.
105 Nahirna, "Ochoronky," 51.
106 Nahirna, "Ochoronky," 54.
107 [Vid redakcyï], "Vidozva," 140.
108 For an analysis of thse dichotomies of progress and regression, see Chapter 4, Monologues.
109 [Vid redakcyï], "Vidozva," 142. Emphasis in the original.
110 [Vid redakcyï], "Vidozva," 141.
111 [Kobryn'ska], *Promova*, 9–10.
112 Schönflies and Morgenstern, *Kongress*.
113 Kobryns'ka, "Feleton," 129–31.
114 [Kobryn'ska], *Promova*, 8, 10; Kobryn'ska, "Žinoča sprava," 1–2.
115 Pacholkiv, *Emanzipation*, 288.
116 Kobryns'ka, "Žinoča sprava," 18. However, the reader is reminded that Kobryns'ka had spoken out against an elementary school for rural girls in 1885 in the dispute with the Stanislav association over the financing of a

196   *Organizing: The Stages*

  publication for women. Her positions changed over time, above all with regard to her goals. See Chapter 1, Dramatic directing.
117 Bohachevsky-Chomiak, *Feminists*, 72, 91, 340 footnote 30; Malančuk-Rybak, *Ideolohija*, 406. The kindergarten association was founded by the Club of Ruthenian Women in L'viv which, like the Women's Reading Room in Kraków, pursued various social work and educational projects.
118 Dučymins'ka, *Natalija Kobryns'ka*, 26; Knyš, *Smoloskyp*, 294.
119 Meissner, "Społeczeństwo," 129.
120 See Chapter 4, Dialogues.
121 Allen, "Mutterschaft," 11.
122 "Zionistische Frauenarbeit."
123 It was also decided to support all Zionist institutions, especially the National Fund. Two reports were published about the conference and the projects: [Von unserem Berichterstatter], "Konferenz"; "Zionistische Frauenarbeit." See also Chapter 1, Theatrical enacting.
124 "Eine Versammlung jüdischer Frauen."
125 "Zionistische Frauenarbeit."
126 Schorrowa, "Plon," 35.
127 See Chapter 1, Theatrical enacting.
128 In her view, the concrete work of associations and institutions was not to be discussed. See Chapter 4, Dialogues.
129 Nitsch, *Wohltätigkeitsvereine*, 57–58.
130 Twarecki, *Domy*, 15. Emphasis in the original. See also Potoczny, *Oświata*, 273.
131 Wietschorke, *Arbeiterfreunde*, 53–62.
132 Melcerowa, "Pani."
133 Alexander, "Hull-House"; Schüler, *Frauenbewegung*, 39–125.
134 Weber, "Toynbee Hall"; Meacham, *Toynbee Hall*, X.
135 Schüler, *Frauenbewegung*, 58.
136 See also Shanes, *Nationalism*, 178–80.
137 For an overview, see Malleier, *Settlement*.
138 S-m, "Toynbeehala."
139 "Jüdische Toynbee-Halle"; D.S., "Toynbee-Halle."
140 F., "Landeskonferenz," 6. Not all Jewish nationalist organizations were founded within the Zionist movement. This meant that, as already discussed for the debates concerning the founding of a women's association, they did not subordinate themselves to the Basel Resolutions—for example, they did not actively pursue the collection of shekels for the acquisition of land in Palestine.
141 E. F. Wz., "Toynbee-Hall." Moreover: "The Toynbee Hall founded by us [the association "Bar Kokhba'] last year and run by us has become a necessity of the Jewish masses." Berichte: Tarnopol. 1904. *Die Welt* VIII (5): 11.
142 Kronika: Kołomya. 1901. *Wschód* I (59): 9.
143 Dr. K., "Fragen," 8. This person writing from Vienna confirms, however, the widespread prejudices against the Jewish population in Eastern Europe. "In the eastern lands, at any rate, the need for adult education is the greatest, and here, where the foundations of a healthy adult education are the weakest, ... lecturing will have to consist more in courses of an educational character." The Jewish population from Eastern Europe was perceived on the one hand as those who had preserved their tradition and sense of identity, and on the other as the object of socio-Darwinian projections. The article is an example of the ambivalence inherent in the construction of a Jewish nation in the Zionist movement. Gilman, "Rediscovery."
144 Dr. K., "Fragen," 8.

Organizing: The Stages   197

145 E. F. Wz., "Toynbee-Hall."
146 Kronika: Stryj. 1901. Wschód I (59): 9.
147 Perl was a pioneer of the Jewish Enlightenment in Galicia. "Perl."
148 Kronika: Lwów. 1901. Wschód I (59): 8. In 1909, a free library, a literacy course, and events for children organized by a women's committee were all mentioned. See "Galizien."
149 Rędziński, Żydowskie szkolnictwo, 27–28.
150 The mix of languages continued across the board, for instance at the festival of Hanukkah and other celebrations. See the example of a celebration of Purim in Stanislav at which both Polish and German were spoken and recited. Vereinsnachrichten: Stanislau. 1900. Die Welt IV (11): 12.
151 Kronika: Lwów. 1901. Wschód I (59): 8; E. F. Wz., "Toynbee-Hall." This is also interesting given the language dispute repeatedly emphasized in the literature. Although Hebrew was *the* language of Zionism, people were evidently willing pragmatically to use Yiddish in order to reach the Yiddish-speaking "masses." Polonsky, Jews, 137. The intense language dispute between Yiddish and Hebrew among Zionists in the Kingdom of Poland and the Russian Empire was not reflected in Galicia because a movement which, although Jewish, was directed against Zionism such as the General Jewish Labor Bund in Lithuania, Poland, and Russia (*Algemeyner Jidisher Arbeterbund in Lite, Poyln un Rusland*) founded in 1894, which advocated a socialist, Jewish nationalist, and Jewish cultural policy, was weak until after the turn of the twentieth century. For this reason, the Jewish nationalist and Zionist side demanded for example that Yiddish be recognized as a colloquial language in order to make the Jewish section of the population visible in the Habsburg language statistics. Polonsky, Jews, 124.
152 See for example the list for the Toynbee Hall in Brody: Berichte: Brody. 1904. Die Welt VIII (8): 7.
153 Drohobycz. 1901. Die Welt V (4): 14; [Waldman], "Zwalczanie." This was prompted by conferences held by Jewish organizations in London and Hamburg. See Chapter 4, Monologues.
154 Langewiesche, "Wissensbestände."
155 For example, the newly founded Toynbee Hall in Kołomyja. Kronika: Kołomyja. 1901. Wschód I (59): 9.
156 E. F. Wz., "Toynbee-Hall."
157 Malleier, "Toynbee-Halle"; Schüler, Frauenbewegung, 64–69.
158 Aus der Bewegung: Galizien: Brody. 1909. Die Welt VIII (44): 965; see also Aus der Bewegung: Österreich: Drohobycz. 1913. Die Welt XVII (19): 601; regarding Tarnów "Konstituierung," 125.
159 Regarding ethnically connoted cooperatives and savings banks, see also Magocsi, History, 442–43.
160 See also Niess, Volkshäuser, 105–09, 145–49.
161 Stępowski, Setlementy.
162 Stępowski, Setlementy, 55. The author was full of praise for settlement houses.
163 Gliksman, Domy, 5–6.
164 Gliksman, Domy, 6–11; Kosmowska, Domy, 11–21. The prestigious nature of these buildings is apparent from the illustrations in these booklets.
165 Potoczny, Oświata, 273; Potoczny, Od alfabetyzacji do popularizacji, 104–10.
166 Bujwidowa, Domy.
167 Her careful nuancing is also evident in the polyvalence of *ludowy*, which she used in the sense of both nation and the masses.

168 Bujwidowa, *Domy;* see also Stopińska-Pająk, "Polska oświata," 245.
169 Dormus, *Bujwidowa*, 162.
170 Bryll, "Śląskie kontakty," 55.
171 Krzywiec, "Daszyńska-Golińska"; Red., "Golińska."
172 Daszyńska-Golińska, "Domy," 383.
173 Daszyńska-Golińska, "Domy," 373.
174 Potoczny, *Oświata*, 274–75, regarding the extensive educational program of the peasant movement, also Potoczny, "Problematyka."
175 See Stępowski, *Setlementy*, 51; Gliksman, *Domy*, 13.
176 Regarding centralization efforts, see also Nitsch, *Wohltätigkeitsvereine*, 253–309.
177 See also Veidlinger, *Culture*, 141–64.
178 Rupp, *Worlds*.
179 For example Wollons, "Introduction," 2.

4 Mobilizing
The Enactments

Raphael Samuel analyzed history as an organic form of knowledge encompassing life experience, yet also fantasy, myth, memory, and desire. Above all, he described it as social, with many different people involved in its production.[1] In his view, history should be imagined as the activity of countless actors rather than the result of professionalism.[2] In the same way that Samuel understood history politics can also be understood as a practice of many people. The rhetorical figures and ritual forms, the logics of argumentation and modes of presentation only arise in communication and competition; they are the product of many authors in a communicative field of wide-ranging networks and local contexts.[3] As already stated more than once, if an appearance on stage is to become an enactment, an audience is required. The audience expresses approval or criticism, and the performers react to this encouragement or disapproval, altering the further course of the enactment. Whatever is said or done must be understood; what is understood changes the meaning of not only the new but also the old context.[4] Accordingly, an enactment emerges from the interaction between action and reaction. Being an audience is a role, part of the enactment. Therefore, the analysis of politics as a performance focuses less on the effect of actions, projects, or demands (i.e. the reaction of passive addressees) and more on the importance of reception for the production of politics.

As I have shown, the movements claimed to represent a specific collective while also promising a historically legitimized transformation of society as a whole. In the following, I will explore the narrative strategies with which women's political concepts were simultaneously presented as competing and universally valid, how they positioned themselves vis-à-vis opponents and competitors, and how the significance of the movements was underscored by the construction of networks and their localization in relevant contexts. The strategies presupposed the existence of different roles and questioned the notion of clear separation between authorship and reception. Enactment is regarded as the conception and appearance of various roles: fellow campaigners, competitors, addressees—the implementation of the policy conceived in the plays and their stages.

The presence of fellow campaigners, addressees, references, and rivalries is examined by analyzing the way in which the three female "heroes" communicated. First, the intertextuality of narratives about the historical origins of women's movements is explored. The starting point is a short story by Wysłouchowa in which she connected her own educational pathway to the demand for female employment. The narrative strategies created by an imagined collective on the basis of experience and history have already been examined on the basis of the three protagonists' literary works. However, the collectives also needed a narrative creating common ground, a common history. Using the example of the conception of historiographies about the women's movements, I will show how this was achieved through the repetition of narrative structures. Historical narratives were, I argue, enacted—and were performative because they conceived the movements as movements by imagining a fundamental change for the collective in writing. The narratives functioned like an intertextual recitation.

Second, Kobryns'ka's placement of Ruthenian women's policy in the field of competing movements is explored. Her campaign for autonomy and her claim to prerogative of interpretation were set out in her biography. Now her conflict techniques are analyzed: her struggle for the "power of establishment," the establishment of gender as the central difference and the central common feature—and against the Radicals, against the women who preferred community work. The rhetorical presence of the audience is identified as the addressee of a monologue. I argue that exclusions and inclusions of the collective or positioning and differentiations were only created and established by the presence of the audience. The narrative-strategic imagination of the addressees turned Kobryns'ka's positions into a political performance.[5]

Third, two published debates on the practice of the Zionist movement are analyzed with regard to their argumentative logics. Based on the analysis of how Pomeranz and the Zionist movement used the creation of spaces, and based on the rituals, illustrations, and constructions, the following considerations start from the observation that Pomeranz, although she herself was involved, refused to engage in public debate about the practices of politics. Instead, she insisted on fundamental assumptions of Zionism, on the national home, and nationalist teaching. The specific space she created, the center of women's social work policy, could therefore be described as a stage set for her. I argue that a play about political truth was performed against its background. The rhetoric of this truth unfolded in keeping silent about the stage set, in the direction of Zionism as a matter of course.

Recitations about Role Models

In one of her many letters to Sokolová-Seidlová, Wysłouchowa wrote about her experience with Orzeszkowa's novel *Marta*:

> *Marta* is a very beautiful, albeit somewhat old work among those dealing with the woman question. It is the story of a young woman

who has received a worldly [geared to trivialities/prestige], superficial education and who, after her husband's death, is forced to earn a living for herself and her young child. She cannot cope and dies miserably after a desperate, tragic struggle. This novel, written about twenty years ago, made an overwhelming impression. I have heard of several women who blessed the author and said that after reading the book they felt encouraged to fundamentally perfect themselves in order to find the means for an independent life. Even to myself—a very young girl at the time—Marta opened my eyes to the fact that my studies at home, where the main focus was on flawless French, playing the piano, and so on, were not enough, and so I struggled (over twenty years ago!) with the prejudice of my environment until I was permitted to attend a high school.[6]

Wysłouchowa tells the story of a struggle against discrimination. Roused by a socio-critical novel addressing the lack of employment opportunities for women from the middle classes, she successfully campaigned for the right to attend high school. The hero (of the letter) has an experience and broadens her opportunities. This experience is collectivized, for apart from her, many other women were encouraged by reading *Marta* to aspire to an education that would make an "independent life" possible: the female hero makes history. Wysłouchowa localized herself in an important context of the women's movement whose central demands included secondary education and employment opportunities. The letter shimmers both as a genre and with regard to its narrative style between a historical, collective narrative, and an individual, experiential one. By writing a historical interpretation of the women's movement in the form of a letter, Wysłouchowa reinforced the connection between history, experience, and politics. Marta's story, the demands of the movement, and the women's reactions substantiated each other. Interestingly, Wysłouchowa did not refer to her mother who was forced to provide for her family, who would also have fitted into the feminist interpretation of the letter, and who would have made a suitable initiation narrative.

Eliza Orzeszkowa, the author of the novel, was one of the female writers and journalists in the nineteenth century who, after initial difficulties, were able to make a living from their work. By writing *Marta,* she laid the foundations for her material independence. During her lifetime, she became one of the best-known female representatives of Warsaw positivism (a status she retains to this day), despite not belonging to this circle of (male) intellectuals who drove the debate on social and political reforms.[7] Born near Grodno, she was privately tutored on the family estate before attending boarding school in Warsaw. At the age of 16, she was married off by her mother. To evade this unwanted marriage, she began studying intensively. In 1861, acting against the express wishes of her husband, she founded a village school just as the Tsar began the abolition of serfdom. Her first literary works also date from this period. When her husband was exiled to Siberia after taking part in the 1863/64 uprising, Orzeszkowa only managed to keep the marital estate for a year. She moved back to Grodno, where she died.

The novel *Marta* was first published in *Tygodnik Mód i Powieści* (Weekly Magazine for Fashions and Novels) and that same year as a book.[8] The topic of *Marta* is the plight of unmarried women from well-to-do backgrounds who lack vocational training and are unable to earn a living by themselves. The plot centers on a civil servant's widow who has been left penniless, forcing her to try and earn a living in order to provide for herself and her child. She is turned down everywhere because, although she has undergone education typical for girls, she has no training, professional experience, or expertise. Refusing to accept charity, she becomes increasingly impoverished, her child falls ill, and in the end, she kills herself out of desperation. The novel starts with a prologue dealing with the pointlessness of planning one's life around marriage. It begins: "A woman's life is an eternal burning flame of love... is motherhood... is ... amusement."[9] And it concludes: "[I]f we do not love anyone, then we long to love... We dry up, we develop consumption."[10] In the course of the explanations about the emptiness and hollowness of female life plans, the collective singular "the woman" is transformed into "we." It is, therefore, not just the following story about Marta's misfortune which is presented as a social problem in Orzeszkowa's prologue. The transition from the collective singular to "we" also constructs a social category "woman" and then incorporates the female readership into this collective: "we women."

The prologue makes the transition to Marta's story with the words: "Perhaps a page from a woman's life will tell."[11] The purpose of the narrative is thus defined. The term "page" indicates a biographical background and so the story promises to be readable as an experience. It is said that this experience explains the problem raised in the prologue. In accordance with the aesthetic criteria of realism, the story is constructed as a "rebirth of the real," developed from reality.[12] Philippe Lejeune's autobiographical pact could be adapted and applied such that a pact is agreed between author and reader by the "we" in the prologue to read Marta's story as an experience shared by women.[13] It is, therefore, not the book of life that "reveals" something, but the prologue, namely this specific interpretation.

Marta was viewed by contemporaries as a vivid account of the problem of making an independent living.[14] Shortly after publication, it was translated into multiple languages and acclaimed by European women's movements.[15] At a women's congress in Warsaw in 1907 held to mark Orzeszkowa's 40 years of work, Kuczalska-Reinschmit emphasized how influential the novel had been on the demands of the women's movement, persuading many girls to fight for "educational opportunities or professional specializations" in their families.[16] In her obituary for Wysłouchowa, Sokolová-Seidlová repeated the story about Wysłouchowa's reception of the novel.[17] Movement chronicler Cecylja Walewska described *Marta* as one of the first impulses in the emergence of the women's movement in the second half of the nineteenth century.[18] She stated that the narrative expressed women's experiences: "Marta's cry struck a painful wound in society; it was the result of severe hardships of life kept secret for so long that its echo could be heard not only throughout our country, but also in neighboring German Empire, where a translation of Orzeszkowa's novel spread unusually quickly."[19] The book was decisive, not just in general, but also for women's concrete plans: "If the confessions of our first female doctors, scientists, philosophers, important directors of institutes of higher scholarship were to be heard, it would become apparent that the majority had sought perfection in some professional field under the influence of Marta."[20]

As far as the message of the story was concerned, it was not just that women identified with Marta as someone whose fate they might have shared; they also seized the novel as an opportunity to change the expectations placed on them. The story kindled their imagination and encouraged them to make changes in their lives.[21] Although Kobryns'ka's stories had also been interpreted as an initiation into feminist activities,[22] hardly any of the enthusiastic women personally "shared" the dramatic experiences of Marta or Halya from "For a Crust of Bread". It was not social misery per se that led to political action, but the narratability of suffering. This is not to say that a lack of vocational training or that legal and financial dependence were not social problems, merely that the significance of the stories for the political demands for a livelihood and education was based not on experience but on insight. What Koselleck and Scott called the break-up of experience and expectation or imagination[23] was described by the women, including Kobryns'ka in her autobiography, as reading experience. Research literature occasionally falls short of this interpretation of experience as an occasion for or anticipation of change when it considers Marta's fate to be a mirror of Orzeszkowa's initial difficulties in providing for herself after her husband's banishment and even concludes that the novel was a success because of this similarity.[24]

The claim that the reception history of *Marta* did not simply reflect the experiences of a generation of women in the partitions of Poland or in Europe, but functioned as a narrative that aroused new expectations is supported by the structural similarity of the narratives of initiation that arose in various contexts of the women's movements. Marianne Hainisch, one of the leading representatives of the Austrian women's movement,[25] described the emergence of the women's movement in the reference work and report published in 1930 by the League of Austrian Women's Associations (*Bund österreichischer Frauenvereine*) titled *Frauenbewegung, Frauenbildung und Frauenarbeit in Österreich*

(Women's Movement, Women's Education and Women's Work in Austria) as follows:

> On a beautiful summer's day, a young friend came to see me whose sick husband could no longer support her family. She wanted to be the breadwinner and came to me for advice. But although we both racked our brains from morning to night, we could not find any job opportunities for this woman who spoke several languages and was very musical. This shook me. After all, our female workers could provide for themselves and their children when they were widowed. Why were we in the middle classes unable to earn a living? Admittedly, I have in mind openings with a substantial salary and a position corresponding to a husband's social status. It suddenly became clear to me that middle-class girls had to be given preparation to earn a living. I was deeply moved and on that day I became an advocate for women.[26]

According to Hainisch, this experience had led her to fight for women's education. Several aspects of this story are striking since they correspond to the theme in *Marta* and in Wysłouchowa's letter. Like Orzeszkowa, Hainisch told a tragic story about a talented, educated middle-class woman whose breadwinner could not work and for whom there were no professional opportunities. As with Wysłouchowa, the story became a profound experience when heard or read. Both described the story as a kind of emotional awakening.

The parallelism between the stories is interesting, given that they were used in different genres and came from different contexts: the realistic novel first published in 1873 as a contribution to the need for reform discussed in positivism, the 1894 letter as a mediator between personal and general experiences, and the 1930 handbook documenting the achievements of the Austrian women's movement. One could speak of a veritable topos that conceived hardship or disadvantage both as a personal experience and as a social fact. Hardship was not rooted in the character or story of an individual, but instead in the socially given situation of a collective, in this case women. In the appropriate context, the experience of hardship becomes expectation or fantasy. As the history of its reception shows, *Marta* was read as social fact despite its fictional genre.

The audience also saw the story as a means of identification and legitimation for their dedication to female causes, as a foundation narrative of women's movements. In all three narratives, that of the letter, the handbook, and the novel, the collectivization and politicization of experience were constituted by a personal story. The tension between individual experience and collective interpretation arose not only from the positioning of the autobiographical self in the historically relevant context, but also from the spread of the topic. It is not claimed that *Marta* was the original narrative of it; on the contrary, it shows—especially its presence in a handbook—the intertextuality of the narratives and the virtual networking of the movements.[27] It should be pointed out that Hainisch created a periodization with herself at the head of the movement, and that this kind of mediation of experience and history also implied the claim to personal prerogative of interpretation.

Another very similar topos also frequently encountered in articles and belles-lettres is "waiting." In Kobryns'ka's story "For a Crust of Bread," the daughters are waiting for "Mr. Right"; they are at the mercy of their family's marriage policy and its reputation. "The years speed by like an arrow, and, the farther they go, the less hope a girl has of getting married."[28] And in "Yadzya and Katrusya," Yadzya is also waiting and grows a little odd—as claimed in Orzeszkowa's prologue. Alice Salomon, one of the best-known representatives of women's social work projects and the founder of the Social Women's School (*Soziale Frauenschule*) in Berlin,[29] also emphasized waiting in her report *Zwanzig Jahre soziale Hilfsarbeit* (20 years of social work): "The girls therefore just stayed at home and lay fallow. They fed canaries, watered flowerpots, embroidered tray covers, played the piano, and 'waited.'"[30] According to Salomon, the only thing that saved women from their boredom was their activities in social work associations. In literary as well as in historical and political discourse, the metonymy "waiting" represents a phase of life preceding marriage that is perceived as empty and senseless.[31] This proclaimed meaninglessness legitimized the claim to professional training and employment opportunities for middle-class women.

Both topoi, hardship and boredom, are not simply stereotypes, nor do they reflect facts. Instead, they are figures of a political rhetoric based on historical argumentation. Above all, they constructed similar historical explanations for the emergence of women's movements. These were derived from an experience of awakening turned into expectation. How historicization and collectivization took place is examined in the following on the basis of the women's movements' descriptions of themselves. I argue that the experiences of awakening enter these accounts as a historical watershed and at the same time—as shared topoi—create a kind of virtual network of ideas among women. The network and the watershed make connections between an essentialization of the collective "women" into a movement, its historicization as history, and its potential for change. It is not a question of the extent to which boredom and the lack of employment represented sociohistorical structures of a similar development in European societies, nor of the relevance the accounts had or have for historical historiography. It is about how historical thinking steered the creation of rhetoric geared towards the future and established a transnational network of ideas among the movements.[32]

The above-mentioned Austrian account from 1930 was preceded by a series of handbooks in which the chroniclers of the women's movements introduced their female heroes and summarized their work. The multi-volume *Handbuch der Frauenbewegung* (Handbook of the Women's Movement) published in 1901 by Helene Lange and Gertrud Bäumer, the leading figures of the German women's movement, introduced in the first volume the movements in the European and American states.[33] The article on Poland was written by Iza Moszczeńska, a journalist and activist living in Warsaw who hailed from the Province of West Prussia, while Gertrud Bäumer herself wrote about Germany.[34] *Głos kobiet w kwestyi kobiecej* (The Voice of Women in the Woman Question), which came out in 1903 in Kraków, published a series of lectures organized by the J. I. Kraszewski Association for Scientific Support for Polish Women (*Stowarzyszenie pomocy naukowej dla Polek imienia J. I. Kraszewskiego*), in which well-known women had participated with all the topics discussed in women's movements at that time from education and earning a living to law and gender relations, trafficking in women, and art.[35] The article on history was written by Kuczalska-Reinschmit.[36] In 1887, Wysłouchowa wrote an article about the women's movement in the democracy-focused magazine *Ruch* (Movement).[37] Kobryns'ka also wrote several historical texts dealing with the origins of the Ruthenian women's movement. Two articles appeared in *Peršyj vinok*: "Rus'ke žinoctvo v Halyčyni v našych časach" (The Ruthenian Women in Galicia in Our Times)[38] described the social, family, and cultural circumstances of Ruthenian women in Galicia and their historical origins, while "Pro ruch žinočyj v novijšych časach" (On the Women's Movement in Recent Times)[39] discussed the historical reasons for the advent of women's movements in general. The article "Žinoča sprava v Halyčyni" (The Female Question in Galicia) in *Naša dolja* dealt with the emergence and significance of the woman question in Galicia.[40]

All these works were self-descriptions which aroused public interest and created their own traditions for the movements.[41] The addressees were named in the prefaces. In the *Handbuch der Frauenbewegung*, Helene Lange referred to *Fernerstehende* ("outsiders"), i.e. men, as well as the "women standing inside and outside the movement."[42] The handbook on the Austrian women's movement combined the desire to provide information and share experiences with the younger generation.[43] Kobryns'ka meant by her "we" both "we women" and "we female activists." She thus assumed the readers of the volumes to be women and also part of the movement. Bujwidowa's intention was to inform men supporting the women's movement so that they could become active together. She stressed in the preface: "But we are not doing all this [explaining the inequality of the sexes in law, education, the choice of occupation, morals] in order to declare war on men."[44] Bujwidowa's "we" specifically meant the female authors of the book, yet also alluded to a collectivizing "we activists," especially since the book was written as a collection of groundbreaking, fundamental themes of the movement.

A complex ensemble of rhetorical figures was used in these introductions. The inside and outside of a collective were formulated, belonging and not belonging were mentioned, and the presence of an audience was implied to whom one turned; the audience was not simply the recipient, but both fixed and opened the boundaries between inside and outside, and was part of the enactment. It can therefore be assumed that the reception desired by its female authors and editors consisted in mobilization, in the enactment of the addressees as participants. The accounts of the history of women's movements (or of the woman question) did not usually make the audience as present as the prefaces. They told the story of a collective as the history of mankind, as part of natural and anthropological developments or diverging national histories.[45] In order to explain the emergence of the women's movements from these far-reaching narratives, the texts drew on similar rhetorical figures: in one way or another, they all formulated the motif of a fundamental historical watershed.[46]

According to Wysłouchowa, gender equality was the natural state of a civilized society, the women's movement stepping up to achieve this by removing the "artificial brakes." She saw the woman question embedded in the history of European ideas and connected to the "democratization of society"; the treatment of the woman question was a "criterion of civilization."[47] Wysłouchowa referred to John Stuart Mill, Montesquieu and Henry Thomas Buckle (echoing Kobryns'ka), yet also less well-known women such as the mathematician Sophie Germain and the astronomer Caroline Lucretia Herschel, as well as Joan of Arc and Emilia Plater as evidence of female bravery. The French Revolution had been a decisive development towards a real women's movement, conquering "far-reaching civil rights, if not always in practice, then at least in theory[48] It was in this context that Wysłouchowa placed the Polish women's movement which, due to the "difficult conditions of society" (i.e. the partitions) could not "develop in all its fullness."[49] The writings of Tańska-Hoffmanowa (she continues), who around 1820 had established the need for extensive women's education, and the female enthusiasts who had demanded freedom and happiness in the 1840s were important steps towards the emergence of the movement. The economic changes triggered by the Tsar's reforms of the 1860s were decisive.[50] It was assumed that gainful employment was now necessary for a substantial proportion of women, especially those from the intelligentsia. In this way, Wysłouchowa was hence adding the economic factor to ideas that had previously been decisive regarding the emancipation of women. The Polish women's movement with its demands had emerged from the need for gainful employment, including against the plethora of resistance facing it across Europe. Wysłouchowa considered Napoléon Bonaparte to be an example of such resistance:

> The "Little Corporal," who shed the blood of Europe and enchained the free nations, remained true to himself in this respect, too. In

the 1804 Napoleonic Code, married women lost independence and autonomy with all their rights and privileges. Thanks to the idea of justice raped by him, the nearest drunkard on the street is considered worthier than the noblest and wisest woman before the law.[51]

Wysłouchowa saw in the women's movement a struggle against opponents and obstacles, including the Napoleonic Code, which she criticized for not abolishing guardianship over women as well as regulating marriage law to the detriment of women.[52] Despite resistance to women's independence—as well as to the independence of nations—Wysłouchowa firmly believed that progress would prevail:

> [The great ideas] defeated and oppressed by the enemies of progress will soon raise their white foreheads, full of memories of the pain of last night, but also full of great hope for the pink dawn of the breaking day.[53]

In her very own style, she vividly described progress in dramatic metaphors. For her, the women's movement had emerged from a struggle for civilization and justice. The prerequisite for her was fundamental changes in the history of ideas and in socioeconomic structures, and she saw a connection between the history of the women's movement in general and the Polish women's movement in particular. She, therefore, identified two fundamental watersheds: the French Revolution and Alexanders II's reforms.

Kobryns'ka developed the emergence of women's movements against the background of an economic-historical dash through the history of mankind:

> In previous centuries, men had no other task than the sword. Caring for the field, the house and the cattle was left to women who, together with their children and servants, were in charge of farming.[54]

Even before the man had become a fieldworker and skilled trades businesses had broken away from the closed circuit of domestic housekeeping, much of the work required to meet the family's needs and livelihood had remained in the hands of women. In Kobryns'ka's view, the decisive turning point was the formation of the "modern capitalist order," which had differentiated the division of labor and shifted the production of food outside the home. "The needs of life, the economic condition of society began to force women out of their homes and to define a different role for them in joint human work."[55] As well as identifying changes in the role of women due to a new form of work organization resulting from this historical change, with her critical attitude towards capitalism she also implicitly defined the previous state, domestic work, as historical normality, even though this was not her intention.

However, she attributed the emergence of women's initiatives in Galicia not to a historical change in the organization of work, but to the Habsburg constitution and the Polish uprising of 1863/64, which was therefore political rather than socioeconomic. The exacerbation of the Ruthenian–Polish contrast had shaken up the women of the Ruthenian intelligentsia, the women and daughters of the Greek Catholic clergy, and prompted them to launch the first initiatives for secondary education for girls. In her opinion, the Ruthenian women's movement began with the foundation of her Stanislav association. Like Hainisch, she placed herself at the head of the movement.[56]

Both Wysłouchowa and Kobryns'ka combined analyses of a general history of humanity with national narratives. Both described the emergence of women's movements and increased engagement with the woman question as a consequence of a fundamental historical change; both emphasized the obstacles that prevented women's awakening. At first glance, the cause-and-effect relationships appear different: Wysłouchowa argued in terms of the history of ideas while Kobryns'ka argued socio-economically. When it came to the specifically Polish or Ruthenian situation, however, both changed levels: Wysłouchowa emphasized economic change in the awakening of Polish women while Kobryns'ka claimed political changes for Ruthenian women in Galicia. This divergent but intersecting thinking resulted from a fundamental similarity: both texts initially constructed women as a collective by giving them a common history, drawing a line of continuity between the gender-based division of labor from tribal societies to that of the intelligentsia, or between ideas from Montesquieu to Tańska-Hoffmanowa. They legitimized the women's movements and their demands by placing them in a historical context and assuming the legitimacy of historical progress. And they both emphasized the emergence of a women's movement as a historical turning point by changing the level of argumentation.

Gertrud Bäumer also searched for precursor currents, for traces in the "depths" of history in her handbook article "Die Geschichte der Frauenbewegung in Deutschland" (The History of the Women's Movement in Germany). The Renaissance had brought about an individualization of the human being, a new relationship between subject and world that enabled criticism of social conditions.[57] However, the actual women's movement had been a consequence of the "intellectual and economic hardship" of women in the nineteenth century, who lacked meaningful employment and money. Bäumer viewed the history of the women's movement as part of a pan-European development whose independent significance resulted from a specific combination of various factors (critical ideas and economic conditions). The teleological outline of a development between the Renaissance and the nineteenth century not only connected past and present, inscription and tradition-building, but also eliminated differences and contradictions between women of different origins as well as between women's and general history. Nevertheless, it ultimately remains as inconsistent as Wysłouchowa's and Kobryns'ka's change to Polish or Ruthenian history, for it shifts the level of argumentation from the "depths of history" to the "external achievements" based on economic and social history.[58] Bäumer herself introduced the transition as follows:

> If one assesses the history of the German women's movement in the nineteenth century as a whole, all the phenomena touched on so far belong to it only to the extent that they have a certain symptomatic meaning; however, they are not directly related to each other by cause and effect.[59]

She saw a shift from symptomatic significance to a direct connection in the 1860s, when the woman question had become an economic one. Bäumer not only translated the experience topoi "boredom" and "lack of income" into historical arguments; like Kobryns'ka and Wysłouchowa; she also changed from a transnational level of a European intellectual history to a national narrative. All three transferred the awakening experience into a narrative rift.[60]

Kuczalska-Reinschmit's "Z historyi ruchu kobieciego" (History of the Women's Movement) also contains such a rift. It consists of a shift from oppression to participation. Similarly to Kobryns'ka, Kuczalska-Reinschmit assumed a historical development governed by natural law. First of all, she compiled a series of ethnological and anthropological-historical findings on the diverse fields of work and skills of women in order to counter stereotypical gender dichotomies with scientific arguments:

> Previous stereotypical views on a homogeneous psycho-physical personality of mankind are corrected by the discoveries of biology. They show that the sexes fulfilled another, divergent role in different periods of development.[61]

Kuczalska-Reinschmit stated that irrefutable scientific findings had shown that women were not confined to the home, stove and sexual services. While Kobryns'ka used tribal society to illustrate the fundamental change in the gender-specific division of labor, Kuczalska-Reinschmit related history to ethnological and anthropological arguments to prove the "unnaturalness" of the ideal of female domesticity. In her opinion, the oppression of women was the result of coercion and violence, was historical and not a natural fact, while the emergence of a woman question lay in the development of civilization and the division of labor since industrialization. In Kuczalska-Reinschmit's account, the actual turning point to the European women's movements was the participation of women in fundamental social reforms, in the French Revolution, in the struggle for the abolition of slavery in the USA, in the 1848 revolution in Germany, "here" (meaning in the Kingdom of Poland, which is equated with Poland as a whole) in the abolition of serfdom in 1861. Kuczalska-Reinschmit also changed the level to a context of reasoning caused by political events. She constructed political watersheds throughout Europe into which she inscribed the women's movements. By doing so, she constituted them as historically significant.

"Die Geschichte der Frauenbewegung in Polen" (The History of the Polish Women's Movement) published in the 1901 *Handbuch der Frauenbewegung* begins with the observation that women's movements in all countries had emerged from political, social, and economic changes. The author Iza Moszczeńska Europeanized the Polish women's movement in a joint history of all women's movements before emphasizing immediately afterwards the extraordinary importance of the partitions of Poland. She argued that women were driven by the harshness of the partition policy "to stand by the man as a companion of his misfortune, his banishment, his loneliness in foreign parts."[62] This referred to the 1863/64 uprising in the Russian partition and the deportation of the families involved to Siberia. This simultaneity of two "primal scenes," one European and the other Polish, proves to be a narrative-strategic paradox similar to Wysłouchowa's turning points: Moszczeńska placed the Polish women's movement in the European context and at the same time created a difference from it by means of the second scene. This ambivalence made tradition-building more difficult. Although the term "companion" suggests that women enjoyed equal status with men, only the men remained historical subjects: they acted and suffered while women stood by them—a lack of independence that Wysłouchowa would probably have frowned upon. Given the repression prevailing in the Kingdom of Poland, Moszczeńska assumed that there had been no real women's movement there; instead, she placed it in Galicia with its far greater publication and organizational possibilities. The territorial shift resolved the dilemma of two primal scenes, for the history of the women's movement could thus be told independently from the narrative of uprising and with its own meaning.

Moszczeńska's narrative is unusual in the sense that the history of the Polish women's movement usually starts with Tańczka-Hoffmanowa and the Warsaw enthusiasts; the turning point is located either in the Tsar's reforms, as with Wysłouchowa, or in the post-uprising policy of repression. The 1863/64 uprising, its suppression, the subsequent exiles and confiscations of goods decimated the number of male breadwinners and destroyed the basis of people's livelihoods, forcing women (above all from the middle and lower nobility) to struggle to earn a living.[63] The shift of the origin of the women's movement to Galicia gave Moszczeńska the opportunity to simultaneously embed it in a European history of movements and in the Polish struggle for independence.

The fact that the visions of historical legitimation referred to contemporary works of historiography, philosophy, or natural history is not surprising; nor is it surprising that the considerations were well-founded and that some arguments have not lost their validity to this day. However (and this is decisive here), these explanatory contexts did not reflect Polish, Ruthenian, or European social or historical conditions, they were not reflections of a given reality, but constituted, like the topoi of experience, a fundamental shift towards new expectations. They characterized a European play "Women's Movement," in which the respective authors were actors and audience rolled into one for each other. The authors both watched and created. They used dominant and marginal perspectives to construct periphery and center, within both Polish and Ruthenian as well as European history. The potential of the narratives about the emergence of women's movements lay precisely in the ambiguities. They performed an enactment whose outcome was uncertain, and which took as its theme historical narratives of meaning.[64]

The various narratives—historical justifications, the construction of female heroes and victims—legitimized the movements and their engagement. They united their members across international borders and at the same time *embedded* them in their respective nations. Their common structure consisted in telling the emergence of the women's movement as a fundamental rift, making it a legitimate historical development. The audience was not just the imagined female readers, but also the other movements and the women of intelligentsia with similar interests and narratives. The connections between the audience and the narrators resulted from traveling recitations, from a network of nodes of discourse. A cognitive network was performed that linked past, present, and future via an individual experience of awakening and a collective turning point.[65] The outcome of the enactment, however, was liminal, for placing the narratives in a consistent historical story with far-reaching influence remained contradictory and uncertain.

Monologues about Competition

Kuczalska-Reinschmit, who lived in Warsaw, shared with Moszczeńska the uncertainty about the historical classification of women's policy in Galicia. She expressed the contradiction already characterizing the contemporary perception of the region in a letter to Wysłouchowa:

> It is a quiet little project, but it does bear a grain of usefulness—because from the mere mentions in general correspondence we here know almost nothing about the current state of development of the woman question in Galicia—I can almost hear the answer: because it is not developing at all—but nevertheless rallies have taken place there—a petition for high schools has been introduced in the *Sejm*—all interesting things.[66]

Kuczalska-Reinschmit's "quiet little project" consisted in requesting Wysłouchowa to report on the women's movement in Galicia. With her assumption that "we," the politically active women in the Kingdom of Poland, knew nothing because nothing was happening in Galicia, she was alluding to the widespread assumption that a conservative mood characterized by noble hostility to progress and by Catholic traditionality prevailed in the province. The fact that Wyłouchowa shared a similar view was shown by her accusation of the Kraków editorial board of *Przodownica* of being influenced by clerical-conservative forces.[67] But as Kuczalska-Reinschmit obviously knew, this view was contradicted by the activities there, such as the petition to the Imperial Council calling for academic education for girls and women.

Kobryns'ka also spoke differently about the political possibilities in the province. On the one hand, she noted that dedication to the woman question had developed well despite the adverse circumstances in Galicia.[68] On the other hand, she stressed the backwardness of women in Ruthenian society:

> So this was the unfortunate fate of our Galician Rus', that all healthy, clear, progressive ideas arrived there last and only weakly, whereas everything dark and reactionary arrived first and strongest. It was the same with our women.[69]

Galicia represented backwardness, provinciality, marginality. The title of Szczepanowski's book *Nędza Galicyi,* in which the author described its social structures and relations of production as outdated, became a widely held view.[70] Backward, traditional, unenlightened, conservative and dark on the one hand, progressive, modern, enlightened, radical, bright on the other were terms that structured and ordered contemporary analyses, aims, and depictions of active women and men in Galicia, but which sometimes led to contradictions. Kazimiera Bujwidowa identified in her article "O postępowym i niepostępowym ruchu kobiecym w Galicji" (On the Progressive and Reactionary Women's Movement in Galicia) a ballast which Galician women in particular dragged around with them and which hampered progressive positions.[71] In the Zionist context, too, it was found that "in the atmosphere at that time of the life of Jewish women from the Galician intelligentsia, [they were] strangers to the lively current of national rebirth."[72]

Nevertheless, a diverse publishing landscape of political parties and associations had developed; there were assemblies, elections, petitions, and rallies. The province was also a place of exile for Polish politicians threatened with repression like the Wysłouchs, as well as for Ukrainian-language publications from the Russian Empire. Kuczalska-Reinschmit herself resided in L'viv from 1895 to 1897.[73] Rarely, however, did contemporaries express themselves like Iza Moszczeńska or one of the activists in the education movement, Helena

Radlińska,[74] who in 1910 emphasized that in contrast to the other partitions, there were opportunities in Galicia for popular enlightenment and educational policy.[75]

Being politically active meant reflecting on the presence of others and placing oneself in the context of different interests and groups in society. One of the principles by which the movements campaigning for change organized their perception of the world was, as outlined above, the vision of a future society implying a historical time axis from worse to better. Progress was therefore a key concept for them.

According to Reinhart Koselleck, progress was a genuinely modern idea. In the nineteenth century, it had become a "political slogan and … an unquestioned, ubiquitous guiding concept."[76] It articulated a temporalization; Koselleck argued that transcendent future expectations had shifted to a notion of a historical development for the better. Koselleck's reflections on the use of the term reveal its political mobilizability as a generally used slogan, as an ideological weapon.

> In this respect, "progress" is one of the modern movement concepts that compensate for their lack of experience with projections of the future that remain specific to a particular class or political party. The progressive space of expectations needs to be filled, which in turn invites critical-ideological questioning by the other parties.[77]

Progress implies the need for action and the irrefutability of one's own viewpoint. Thus it was that the simultaneity of the non-simultaneous, namely the experience that different factors of change were in different positions on the imagined time axis, came into view; there were precursors, progress, standstill, retrograde steps, and catching-up. This resulted in competing future plans, opponents and advocates, role models and imitations, in short: the presence of all the participants.

Kobryns'ka placed her own policy by arranging and evaluating competing positions. This required rhetorical figures which could be used to present these debates in the Galician context. As has been shown, one of these figures consisted in enshrining women's movements in history, another in constructing their own narratives. Kobryns'ka began her article "Žinoča sprava" with the observation: "It will not be without interest—including for the history of our cultural development—to present some of the characteristic features in our society [to show] how it relates to the woman question."[78] She made its significance in society—in concurrence with Wysłouchowa—an assessment criterion and established that the woman question was barely on the agenda in Galicia. For example, for centuries Ruthenian men had been accustomed to dealing with women as if they were of lower status and ignoring their reason. Their lack of seriousness in dealing with women's initiatives resulted from this traditional attitude.[79] In order to constitute and demonstrate the significance of the woman question, Kobryns'ka wrote a whole series of articles which she published in *Peršyj vinok* and the three volumes of *Naša dolja*. They included the articles "Rus'ke žinoctvo v Halyčyni v našych časach," "Pro ruch žinočyj v novijšych časach" and "Žinoča sprava v Halyčyni," which have already been analyzed with regard to the construction narratives of the women's movement. Her two-part article "Stremlinja žinočoho ruchu" (The Aspirations of the Women's Movement)[80] is also revealing. All these texts dealt with various opponents, difficulties and conflicts, and presented achievements, demands, and fellow campaigners; they placed Ruthenian women's policy in the political public as well as in the context of the women's and socialist movements. In other words, they aimed to lend the woman question the significance conjured up by Kobryns'ka in the social context. This was done, I argue, by imagining the different roles: as opponents and supporters.

In the following, the texts mentioned are analyzed with regard to their narrative strategies. As I will show, they used different figures of a political rhetoric: appellative, logical-argumentative, polemical, and historicizingly narrative. Their use of direct speech underlines the appellative nature of the texts, the logical argumentation justifies demands, and the historical report proves their reason. According to the thesis, the rhetorical figures turn the texts into a monological enactment, they create positions in conflict-laden fields contextualized by historical reports and narratives, and they imagine an audience before whom logic and narrative bring about legitimation. A central structure of legitimation comprises progress and backwardness, which as development concepts arrange goals and demands on a time axis and thus historically underpin them.

At first glance, judging by their places of publication—*Peršyj vinok* and *Naša dolja*—the addressees of Kobryns'ka's articles were women: Ruthenian women, to be precise. Occasionally, they were directly addressed. "And that doesn't scare us [women] either!"[81] She also wrote of "our people." The direct address lends the texts the character of a speech: speaker and audience are present and united, and the text is a speech act, which is occasionally strengthened by emotional language and a call to action. The rhetoric underlines the political impetus of the texts. Female readers should not be able to escape the collective and the common cause.

The imagined readership of the article "Stremlinja žinočoho ruchu" goes beyond a female audience. Published in 1895 and 1896, this article presents the debates about the key demands of the women's movements: academic education and equal rights in both the European and Galician contexts. Kobryns'ka was concerned with classifying supporters and opponents. She addressed the conflicts between socialist and independent women's movements, criticized positions that did not recognize or acknowledge the importance of women's policy for society as a whole, and

216 *Mobilizing: The Enactments*

underlined the achievements of women's policy in Galicia with various concrete examples, such as Teofil' Okunevs'kyj's campaign for academic education for women and girls in the *Sejm* as well as a lecture by Odon Bujwid, Kazimiera Bujwidowa's husband, about opening up universities to women. Kobryns'ka dealt with the subject of women's suffrage by discussing organizations in France, Norway, the Netherlands, Germany, and the Habsburg Empire in depth. Although the examples from the different states are in some aspects very detailed (for example, the exact date of a petition in Germany as well as the number of participants of a rally in Copenhagen), there is a lack of information about general contexts of the respective associations' policies and the related movements. Instead, Kobryn'ska referred to some historical conditions on which the demands for suffrage were based such as the Napoleonic Code in France. Kobryns'ka reported that women in Denmark fought for local suffrage, while in Great Britain they campaigned for national suffrage. However, there is no justification or strategic assessment of the different demands and conditions. The main function of such a passage is therefore to unite the electoral initiatives embedded in historically different contexts and to present them as components of *one single* movement.[82] By listing the details following basic introductions to the women's movements, a virtual network of demands and movement initiatives is established. Known (and shared) positions are confirmed and initiatives (examples) are united into a single entity. A convinced readership equipped with information literature is implied.[83]

The second part of the article, which deals with the demand for women to be admitted to university degrees and the exclusion of the woman question from social democratic congresses, is even more detailed, with Kobryns'ka providing information for her disputes with the Radicals. This section contains detailed reports on the articles and arguments of individual members of the Imperial Council, the *Sejm* and the Hungarian parliament, journalists and academics on women's education and the women's movement. The various positions on secondary education for girls in the Imperial Council and the positions of international social democrats on claim to independent representation and publication for female workers are presented in surprising detail.[84] In particular, the report on the debate in the Council reads like a protocol of the delegates' speeches, although sometimes, a deputy's argument is neither made clear nor attributed to a political group or direction. This detail and immanence of representation implied an informed public and a presumed discussion circle of intellectual activists who, despite not knowing each other personally, were familiar with each other's arguments. Phrases such as "our nation" and the latently paternalistic "our women" further underline the formation of this circle.[85]

The texts are more or less direct answers to contributions to the debate on the woman question in the intellectual circles of Galicia. They do not always seem to have been understood by the uninitiated; instead, given their presuppositional style, they are evocative of a conversation or correspondence. Just as Pavlyk's published assertion that he had had no sexual relations with women crossed the line between the private or personal and the public or societal, these texts represent a semi-public space. Both refer to the transgression between genres, between literary and journalistic texts and correspondence, and thus also to the close connections between personal and political relations in a small group of the Ruthenian intelligentsia at the turn of the century.

Considering Kobryns'ka's difficulties when it came to continuously finding supporters and her repeated complaints about women's traditionality, this immanence may come as a surprise. However, in these articles she imagined a strong, informed, and interested readership, and demonstrated the relevance of the woman question. The texts constituted different attitudes in discussions and conversations as well as an audience whose interjections and positions were taken into consideration: the mobilization of the collective, (ideological) competition with opponents, and information for fellow campaigners. They document Kobryns'ka's broad knowledge and extensive reception of the (everyday) political press. Kobryns'ka's rhetoric included preparing knowledge and argumentation with figures from a speech or even more so from a conversation. Her appellative figures include not only direct address, but also the imagination of a conversation or a direct confrontation. She was well aware of the importance of the public for a movement. And she also had the positive effect of negative press in mind when she wrote that the newspaper *Dilo,* despite its criticism of her dedication to women's policy, had at least raised awareness of the woman question.[86]

Kobryns'ka presented another part of her articles as an exchange of words with the various positions on women's policy in the context of the Ruthenian intelligentsia. In particular, she addressed their publications, *Dilo* and *Pravda* of the Young Ruthenians as well as *Narod*, the organ of the Radicals.[87] Debate with the latter was particularly important to her, probably because she felt she received too little support from those with whom she agreed the most and felt badly let down, but probably also because the Radicals and Kobryns'ka basically took similar approaches to the primacy of economics, but set different priorities, the economic inequality of the classes versus that of the sexes. This resulted in competing political demands and organizational forms.

Especially in the article "Žinoča sprava v Halyčyni," Kobryns'ka dealt at length with texts, arguments, and positions concerning women's policy with wit and irony. For example, she reacted to an article in *Dilo* that emphasized the domesticity of women as a national task and opposed their public appearance: "Even women who work at kindergartens really prove to be far greater patriots despite not knowing how to sing in

Ruthenian or dress in the Ruthenian style."[88] With this ironic reduction of national domesticity to singing and traditional garb, she elevated kindergartens to genuine patriotic dedication. This account reinforced her position that the magazine had behaved conservatively towards women's policy and did not share progressive, advanced positions such as patriotic childhood care and education. This assessment has a certain irony unintended by Kobryns'ka, since she called for kindergartens to enable Ruthenian-language early childhood education, for which singing would certainly have been expedient. The difference between Kobryns'ka's position and that of the article therefore lay less in the question of how Ruthenian singing should be evaluated and far more in the difference between the places of female activity: in domesticity or in the public sphere. What Kobryns'ka rhetorically achieved with this ironic intensification was a clear separation between conservative and progressive policy on women's issues.

She accused *Narod* (and thus the Radicals) of deeming the Ruthenian women in Galicia uneducated and underdeveloped. For example, she claimed that "telling female Ruthenians ... 'how dark [unenlightened] you are' [is] generally the most popular phrase among our men."[89] She added that in Galicia, women obviously could not expect anything from progressive parties: "If the Radicals, the most progressive party in the country, [already] behave towards us in this way, even less can be expected from other, more conservative parties."[90] Implicitly, Kobryns'ka denied *Narod*, and thus the Radicals, the right to be progressive unless they recognized the importance of Ruthenian women's policy. Although *Narod*, like the socialist parties in general, reported on women's politics and emancipation, it ignored the independent initiatives of Ruthenian women. It also failed to support their most important concerns: petitions, kindergartens, and communal kitchens. Instead, Kobryn'ska set out, it deliberately printed conservative articles disparaging her and her allies. Bujwidowa took a similar tack in her article about the progressive and reactionary women's movement, writing that as long as the social democratic parties did not support the demands of women, they were not progressive, while conversely, all those who did support these demands were progressive, regardless of whether they viewed themselves as conservative.[91] Both authors used a distinction between progressive and conservative politics as a yardstick to lend weight to their criticism of the socialist parties, accusing them of treating women's policy as irrelevant, despite including equal rights in their manifestos. The weight of this argumentative structure resulted from the importance that progressiveness had for social democratic politics in general and hence for the Radicals in particular.

Kobryns'ka not only distanced herself and her politics from the Radicals and the socialist movements, but also distinguished herself within women's political currents. For example, she described the conflict in the Association of Ruthenian Women (which she herself had founded) in her article "Rus'ke žinoctvo v Halyčyni," as follows:

> [C]onservative elements have tried from the outset to turn this association for education into a philanthropic one. How the association will emerge from the spiritual crisis it is currently going through—whether fresh, progressive elements or the spirit of patriarchy and obscurantism will prevail—remains to be seen.[92]

Kobryns'ka judged the association's activities as "conservative"—it participated, as mentioned above, in honoring the bishop and also preferred to invest in schools instead of Kobryns'ka's publications.[93] Philanthropic engagement—probably referring to the girls' school project, which she equated with elementary education for the needy—is associated with "patriarchy and obscurantism." Education, on the other hand, is classified under "fresh, progressive elements." Kobryns'ka rated the different goals of the association as conservative and progressive. The concepts established an argumentative-logical order. They functioned as rhetorical weapons in the arena of women's policy.

To explain these arguments, it was necessary to embed them historically. The starting point for Kobryns'ka's reflections was the observation that Galicia was conservative and its structures rigid, especially regarding gender conventions. It has already been suggested that she was not alone in this attitude. She described the conditions in the Galician villages as traditional and unenlightened, the women in particular being uneducated and poor. She paid special attention, as so often, to the situation of women among the Greek Catholic clergy. She pointed out that unmarried daughters or widows had no opportunities to earn a living, and that even female farmhands and peasants could earn more. She thus corroborated her fundamental view that gender inequality was rooted in economic factors, and inscribed Ruthenian history into that of the European women's movements, for this argument clearly reminds us of the initiation narratives already analyzed. Kobryns'ka explained the historical circumstances in Galicia as follows: the reason why the peasantry making up the majority of Ruthenian-speaking society was characterized by the oppression of women and the villages were unenlightened was because the Ruthenian elite had for centuries been assimilated into other societies (nations):

> The history of our nation is sad, the fate of its women is sad. This poor nation can be compared to a felled tree whose roots have not dried up and which produces strong sprouts. Everything that was once capable and rich has switched to other camps, and what remained was the common people, who alone preserved the language and beliefs of their parents.[94]

Kobryns'ka meant by "camps" the Polish- and Russian-speaking ruling elites, while the "common people" preserving language and beliefs referred to the peasantry. The metaphor of the tree constructed history as natural growth; the loss of elites is presented as an unnatural, violent act. Kobryns'ka concretized and updated this loss with her analysis of the conduct of the male intelligentsia:

> A student attending a secular faculty, on the other hand, draws the last sap for his education from his home and later marries a Polish or German woman, and he abandons his sisters to the will of fate and God and without money and without any training for paid employment ... Such a man is doubtless aware of his national rights, accuses the Ruthenians of lacking in patriotism, but marries a Polish woman himself. A soulmate relationship with his girlfriend is evidently superfluous for him.[95]

By "secular faculty," Kobryns'ka was referring to the milieu from which the patriotic intelligentsia, the grassroots of Ukrainophiles and Radicals, came. She considered them nationalist and progressive, yet conservative in their relations with women. By experiencing secular education in towns and cities, men had alienated themselves from their origins and thus also from the women who had remained in the countryside and were unable to participate in the new urban habitus. They did not seek a "soulmate relationship" implying a modern ideal of equal marriage of the type aspired to by Kobryns'ka. This transferred the history of the Ruthenian people to relations between the sexes, tying them to an analysis decisive for her politics: their inequality. She went on to elaborate:

> [T]he cause of this unfortunate fact is to be seen in a fundamental error of our social order, in the division between man and woman, both in the type of occupation and in the corresponding training, which is nowhere more evident than in the middle classes. This woman depends almost entirely on her husband's occupation and therefore every family tries to give above all the boys a crust of bread by means of study and hence the ability to feed their family in future. He knows from an early age that he is a boy, that he must be reasonable and eat this bread, that his sisters will never master as much as he does ... Women are only seen at home and at pleasure, which is why their needs are only respected in terms of housework or momentary distraction.[96]

The reference to the argumentation of women's movements is clear. Kobryns'ka was referring to criticism of the separate spheres of middle-class families, in which women depended entirely on their husbands for material support and there was no spiritual connection between spouses. The message was that women were married as providers of housework and (sexual) pleasure. Kobryns'ka transferred the women's movement's criticism of marriage and male chauvinism to the situation in Galicia, especially in the families of the rural Greek Catholic clergy. There, investment primarily took place in the urban education of sons, where they became alienated from rural conditions and succumbed to the attractiveness of urban women—Polish or German—and then got married there.[97] Consequently, there was a lack of suitable marriage candidates for the daughters of the Ruthenian rural clergy, and all they could do was work in their family. Kobryns'ka's political demands followed logically from her brief sociological-historical analysis of gender relations: the demands for women's material independence, the right to an academic education for girls, a unanimity of spirit in gender relations, and respect for the female sex. Kobryns'ka, however, relocated Galician circumstances to Europe and, conversely, transferred concepts that were widespread throughout Europe to Galicia, an example of her transnational mindset and cultural translations.

With her historical-narrative figure, Kobryns'ka placed her appellative and analytical language in a context. In order to understand and interpret a statement such as "the fate of its women is sad" as political, we need to release it from the speech act. The sentence is not performative. What is needed is a historical report that transforms the arguments into a narrative structure and thus gives them meaning. A sentence is transformed by a historical report from a detached statement into an embedded argument.[98] The report—for example the embedding of Galician situation in history—turns specific observations into well-founded facts as opposed to partiality or interests. By historicizing the situation, it also becomes changeable. The history of women is classified within an orderly mindset about historical processes (in Hegelian, Marxist, or Darwinian traditions).

Kobryns'ka was extraordinarily well-informed and analytically brilliant.[99] She used the topos of the historical backwardness of the region and women's lack of enlightenment[100] to explain a historical change and to position the Ruthenian initiatives in the arena of women's policy. She countered an essentializing policy of exclusion of the type she believed the socialists pursued when they regarded Galician women as uneducated with a historical perspective. But she also positioned the Galician women's initiatives in the context of European women's movements—not at the forefront, but certainly at eye level.

For Kobryns'ka, a women's movement meant guiding women along the road to progress. Above all, she was concerned with presenting achievements and refuting positions that hindered, disavowed and criticized women's initiatives. Therefore, terms that implied and simultaneously evaluated a temporal development such as "progress" and "backwardness," were key for her. Campaigning for women's rights denoted progressiveness and modernity. Galicia, on the other hand, represented a backward province, the provincial audience, moral and religious conventions, traditionality and dullness of thought.[101] On such a line, demands—and this led to the massive conflicts between Kobryns'ka and the Radicals—were replaceable and hierarchizable. Autonomous feminist policy—Kobryns'ka's publications, for example—could be placed "before" or "after" the demands of the labor movements. Backwardness was therefore not insurmountable for her, nor was it part of a discourse about the "other," which was contrasted with the "European" or "western."

Backwardness, traditionality and conservatism were not specifically Galician experiences, but forms of presentation that became a "translated" meaning in their respective contexts, be they differing national references, gender politics, local conditions, regional or state peculiarities, or merely individuals who thought and worked differently. The terms were not used in an essentializing way, but relationally, as a lever to deal with the dilemma that lay in the simultaneity of engagement for the future and its historical legitimation. Progressiveness and backwardness functioned as links between the different modes of the texts: they connected historical context with logical argumentation and thus kept indignation and experience alive at the same time. They united legitimate logic with the claim to shape change and combined structure and agency.[102] Kobryns'ka's manner of depiction differed little from the general narrative strategies used in movement journalism. Like the reports on the activities of the Zionist associations, it was performative in that it generated, positioned, and classified a movement. Nevertheless, the province repeatedly represented the unattainability of ambitious goals; it ironized the demands and made them appear as satire.[103]

The appellative rhetoric in Kobryns'ka's texts imagined competitors and fellow campaigners and made them visible; whether the appeals were heard or read is relatively irrelevant. The texts implied both the notion of a collective "women" and of the intelligentsia, both those close to them and opponents. They reflected a debate between the addressees and the different groups in the audience respectively. With a change of figure, those addressed could become those depicted—the audience became part of the enactment. The use of direct speech emphasized the importance of the speaker and those addressed. In order to guide them in a certain direction, a change of mode was required. The logical argumentation formed and explained the content, the aims of the movements, presented the participants, and assigned the roles. A large number of these positions and their languages were classified, for example within a gender order. Their inequality—in Kobryns'ka the economic dependence of women—could then be addressed. The historical report contextualized the arguments and bound them to historical legitimacies. The imagination of an audience constructed on the one hand argument and debate, and on the other hand the political context, the reference to competition and contact. The next part deals with the question of how competition became convictions in the debating game.

Dialogues about Practice

In 1898, Pomeranz published her propaganda booklet *An die jüdischen Frauen! Ein Appell zur Umkehr* (To Jewish Women! An Appeal to Turn Back).[104] It was praised in *Die Welt* for its combination of emotion and popularity, yet also its sense of reality:

> In the pamphlet we hear the splendid echo of the appeal made to Jewish woman at the Congress. Genuine love for the Jewish people and a clear view of present-day conditions are combined to create a booklet in which the principles of Zionism are discussed in warm tones and a popular form.[105]

The booklet's appellative effect, similar to Pomeranz's speeches, was highlighted. By being referred to as an "echo," the booklet was also integrated into the central organization of the movement, the Congress in Basel. But the appeal did not go uncommented. A voice calling itself a female Zionist criticized it in *Przyszłość* for lacking sophistication.[106] This condemnation was rejected by Pomeranz in the very next issue.[107] The conflict between Pomeranz and the anonymous critic calling herself a female Zionist concerned what constituted Zionist women's policy and what activities the movement required.

The propaganda booklet is an appeal; in fact, the form and addressees are named in the title. It was aimed at Jewish women who had not previously joined the Zionist movement. In line with her entreating tone, Pomeranz addressed the female readership with direct speech and rhetorical questions: "and now you noble, God-fearing Jewish women, why do you shut yourselves off?"[108] Owing to the direct address, the speech act remains visible—and the addressee, the audience therefore also remains part of the enactment. Pomeranz divided the Jewish women she was addressing into orthodox and assimilated. To the orthodox women skeptically opposed to Zionism, she proffered interpretations of the Bible which said that the Jews would return to the Promised Land before the arrival of the Messiah. And she also held out "the spiritual heritage of the nineteenth century," "achievements" which could not be discarded, which were expressed in "a powerful urge for modern education."[109] These arguments were intended to encourage support for Zionism as a form of protection against the danger of becoming alienated from Judaism. Pomeranz accused the assimilated Jewish women of "self-denial," "obduracy" and "sin"[110] as well as ignorance about the greatness of Jewish history and literature, which had often been ahead of Christianity.[111] She claimed that assimilation was doomed to failure because Jewish women always remained Jewish women and would never be fully accepted by non-Jewish society.

Despite considering the number of "emancipated Jewish women"—by which she meant activity for the (non-Jewish or non-Zionist) women's movement[112]—and female socialists insignificant, she nevertheless took the trouble to refute their positions, too. She wrote that, from a Jewish perspective, modern achievements such as law, educated literature, public welfare and justice were by no means new, dating back instead to biblical times. She therefore regarded Jewish women as the first and most active women to resist oppression because "'Jewish' and 'socialist'... [are] synonyms, so to speak, since the boldest, most far-reaching socialism was created more than three thousand years ago by your ancestors."[113] The dedicated Jewish women regarded freedom, equality and fraternity as achievements of the French revolutions, yet the legislation of the biblical period was the "most socialist ... of all past and future peoples."[114] Pomeranz noted a parallelism of ideals and thus associated the Zionist vision with contemporary notions of progressiveness. In addition, she assigned the authorship of these visions to Judaism. The latent message of the text is clear: for Pomeranz, these two groups were the strongest competitors of the Zionists due to their similar visions for a better future. Although this was a problem that she shared with Kobryns'ka, Pomeranz responded to it differently.

Signed "A female Zionist" (*Syjonistka*), the above-mentioned review of the booklet appeared in *Przyszłość* in 1899. The author put forward two points of criticism. First, the brochure dealt insufficiently with female socialists and emancipated women; second, it concealed the goals of Zionist women's associations. Female socialists and emancipated women had to be won over to Zionism precisely because their positions were so similar. Therefore, a clear program was required for the women's circles of the movement. By insisting on teaching history, literature, and Hebrew in order to be able to educate children in the Jewish nationalist spirit, Pomeranz (claimed the review) only granted women an inadequate, indirect influence: "If women's activities are limited to teaching, the question arises of what those women who don't teach should do."[115] Finally, the author reiterated her criticism with the assertion that the spread of Zionist women's circles was stagnating, this being due to the lack of concrete goals and activities. The reason for the female Zionist to express herself was obviously the fear that Zionist women's policy was not attractive enough in the face of socialist and feminist offerings.[116] Moreover, she criticized, albeit relatively cautiously, the view that the task of Zionist woman was the Zionist home, above all the Zionist upbringing of children (expressed for example in Pomeranz's story *Im Lande der Noth* and by no means confined to her) as patently unappealing.[117] Social work and educational tasks can be assumed behind the mentioned "activities," which were associated in particular by the women's movements with emancipation, participation and the professionalization of women's work.

In her reply, Pomeranz repeated that Jewish women's closeness to socialism was not surprising, for:

> Likewise, it was a natural consequence that Jewish women intensely preoccupied themselves with the old truth in a new form. Everything that is sublime, noble, humanitarian always finds a powerful echo in the heart and mind of the Jewess.[118]

She emphasized even more clearly than in the *Appell* that socialism should be understood as a preliminary form of Zionist principles, adding that the activities and convictions of female socialists had been correct and important before Zionism existed. She thus presented Zionism as a more sophisticated form of a better future on an imaginary time axis instead of competing with socialism. The fact that Pomeranz was not alone in this view of female socialists is shown by a somewhat spiteful report in *Wschód:* in 1903, the Zionist women's association Miriam from Tarnów had organized a meeting for female Jewish workers which drew 30 women with various occupations; a rival event hosted by female Jewish socialists at exactly the same time had been attended by just "three, precisely three."[119]

In addition, Pomeranz defended herself against the accusation of not presenting a Zionist program. First, early childhood education did not mean only exerting an indirect influence. Second, the Zionist movement had granted women the right to vote at the Zionist World Congress and the right to equal work, which could appeal to emancipated Jewish women and female socialists. The concrete activities, however, were the daily business of the movement behind the scenes, without which political work would be impossible. However, shouting it from the rooftops would be a strategic mistake. In addition, people had to decide what needed to be done on a case-by-case basis—and so Pomeranz remained unspecific until the end of the article: "This mysterious program only for 'women' consists of the proverbial 'grain by grain'... from which a full, considerable amount accumulates over time."[120] In her vision of a Zionist women's program, Pomeranz—interestingly with a theatrical metaphor—distinguished between tasks in front of and behind the scenes, the latter above all requiring diligence and patience.

For Zionism—and thus for its vision of a better future—nation-building was the essential goal. It viewed the nation as both (with regard to other peoples) a contemporary, modern phenomenon and (with regard to Jews) a reference back to biblical history, to the era of a Jewish state. Socialism, secular education, and other ideological attitudes were not presented as competing concepts of modernity, but rather as part of a historical time axis. For Pomeranz, Zionism represented a developed form of socialism rooted in history and national law, and also a cyclical development heading back to the values of biblical times. The intelligentsia had the "sacred duty" to study Zionism: "After one has thought long and hard, sooner or later one must come to accept the rationality of Zionism."[121] The fact that competition continued to latently exist was proven by its moral, not rational undertone: when Zionism is developed, socialism becomes betrayal.

Just as nineteenth-century liberals assumed that public welfare was sufficiently persuasive as a concept by virtue of pure logic,[122] Pomeranz assumed that Zionism was convincing due to its very existence and the rationality of a time axis. Therefore, her manifest ignorance of the fiercest, namely socialist and feminist, competition had an argumentative logic based not on the contrast between a Zionist ideal of the family and feminist connotations of gainful employment or participation, but on the assumption of historical development. Pomeranz repeatedly used such arguments. In her lecture "Stanowisko kobiety żydowskiej" (The Status of Jewish Woman) printed in 1903,[123] she also described women's path to Zionism in a cyclical, historical model: whereas in the Middle Ages women had been the most active with regard to the nation, owing to assimilation they had been alienated from Judaism from the first half of the nineteenth century onwards.[124] In the second half, other ideals such as emancipation and socialism had been added, which had been taken up by the Jewish woman with her "specifically Jewish energy." Yet she had always been distanced from these ideals, and only as a Zionist—as a Jewess working for her people—could she establish something new and lasting.[125]

Her silence about the Zionist work of the women's circles resulted from fierce competition with similarly arguing movements with similar practices. The logic behind her refusal to name concrete projects was that Zionism was a further development of socialism and feminism. It represented a higher form, higher values. Historical values rather than practical work formed the core of Pomeranz's Zionism and were supposed to persuade others. Her refusal to comment on Zionist women's work could therefore be regarded as defensive rhetoric in an intra-Zionist dispute over women's political objectives[126]—if Pomeranz had not also been very guarded with regard to concrete projects in the debate about a problem discussed in Jewish as well as Zionist circles in 1903, namely trafficking in women. Her opponents this time were two social work feminists who belonged to the "emancipated Jewish women" she criticized.

In 1902, the social work activist Bertha Pappenheim[127] and the national economist Dr. Sarah Rabinowitsch[128] were sent to Galicia by the Frankfurt Israelite Benevolent Society (*Israelitischer Hilfsverein*) and the Jewish Branch Committee for Combating Trafficking in Women

(*Jüdisches Zweigkomitee zur Bekämpfung des Mädchenhandels*) to investigate the causes of trafficking in women and girls and to develop proposals to combat the situation.[129] They also paid a visit to Pomeranz, which was evidently not very pleasant for either side. Headed "Ein Besuch aus Frankfurt a. M." (A Visit from Frankfurt am Main), Pomeranz criticized the two travelers in *Die Welt* with cutting words:

> The, incidentally, very distinguished ladies, who (especially Miss Pappenheim) were apparently experienced in people's welfare and poor relief ... appeared ... as the mouthpiece of the western high patrons of miserable eastern Judaism.[130]

Pomeranz expressed an ironic view of the activities of the two women as an arrogant presentation of a power imbalance between western and eastern Judaism. She characterized the social work viewpoint advocated by Pappenheim and Rabinowitsch as colonial and paternalistic by the spatial contrast on the one hand and the use of "ladies" and "high patrons" on the other and rejected it.

At the end of the nineteenth century, trafficking in girls and women was addressed—or scandalized—internationally. The social work policies of the women's movements focused on the lack of education and training, labor migration, and the economic hardship of women and girls, and corresponding projects were launched, ranging from aid centers at railway stations to training facilities such as the Home of the League of Jewish Women (*Heim des Jüdischen Frauenbunds*) in the German Empire founded and run by Pappenheim. Above all, the radical wings of the women's movements criticized men's double standards and the tolerance of prostitution by the police as causes, and propagated a new ethics of gender relations.[131] The socialist movements emphasized the plight of female workers and denounced the morality of the middle classes, who protected their own women but exploited lower-class females materially and sexually.[132] In connection with the scientification of society, the rise of medicine and doctors (including a few female doctors), and debates about health policy interventions by the state as well as the emergence of eugenics, measures to tackle trafficking in women were seen in connection with activities to combat the spread of sexually transmitted diseases.[133] Shaken by the stereotype of the Jewish trafficker[134] selling girls and women from the east, especially from Galicia, the "poorhouse of Europe," to the west and overseas, Jewish organizations entered the debate, first in Great Britain and then in Germany.[135] For Jewish community leaders and rabbis' assemblies, the main issue was to counteract the stereotype, to establish whether an above-average proportion of Jewish women really were involved and, if necessary, to take action.[136] In addition, stories about trafficked girls, abducted and unwittingly forced into prostitution and held captive in brothels, filled the columns of the up-and-coming sensationalist press, whose reports contained sociological, psychological, and political analyses, and above all exploited the fascination of sex and crime.[137] "Trafficking in women" was a topos subject to diverse interpretation at the turn of the century.

Given this presence among the politically interested public, the vehemence of Pomeranz's criticism is surprising since one would have expected her to act, too. Even more surprising, however, was the consistency with which she rejected and debased concrete proposals. She received an answer to her dismissive attitude when, just two issues later, Pappenheim rebuffed Pomeranz's polemics. She insisted on being true to herself and not being regarded as a representative of large organizations or "the Jewry of the west." Rabinowitsch also published her position regarding the visit.[138] I understand the arguments and polemics exchanged in *Die Welt,* as did the authors, as a continuation of the debate and thus as an example of the creation of an enactment with multiple participants.

What the conflict between the three women basically amounted to seems clear at first. Pappenheim regarded Zionism as a "castle in the air," as "buildings without foundations," despite the presence of "liberating and invigorating elements" and the fact that it addressed women. But she qualified this by stating that women in Zionism had to be content with the "spirit of ancient Jewish women" instead of being able to tackle the new social tasks.[139] Pomeranz's aim, meanwhile, was of course to defend Galician Zionism. She adopted a dual approach: on the one hand, Zionism had long since devised and carried out various sociopolitical projects, and on the other hand, any action taken was merely window dressing given the scale of Galician misery. Only by encouraging emigration could the situation of Jews be expected to be improved.[140] "Away from here! A different place to live and work—our own home—is our only hope."[141]

Polemically, she asked:

> What were [the non-Zionist organizations] striving to achieve all that time? For the dehumanized anti-Semitic hordes in Persia, Algiers, Romania, Galicia, and Russia not to murder Jewish *illiterates*? For "educated" Jewish women to fall victim to them?"[142]

Given this sharpness, it is not surprising that the three women could not agree on a common policy, since this was obviously a dispute between fundamentally divergent points of view, between a Jewish women's movement and women's policy in Zionism. Can the rejection of joint action against trafficking in women therefore be regarded as political positioning, a reaction to Pappenheim's and Rabinowitsch's anti-Zionist attitude?[143] This view is supported by Pomeranz's sharp distinction between organizations like "Alliance, Ica, B'nai B'rith etc. on the one hand,

Zionism on the other hand!"[144] She explained exactly what the differences were as follows:

> "Charitable deeds" embrace the present, individuals or strata whom one seeks to help, evils that one seeks to eliminate. "Charitable deeds" have an ethical value, in nearly all cases a cultural value. ... "*Deeds*" that should emerge from a people ... have historical significance. They reach into the distant future and embrace the whole in all its aspects, with all its shortcomings and requirements, its causes and consequences, thus unhinging the present itself.[145]

Pomeranz described the social work of non-Zionist organizations as a short-term "charitable deed" that only addressed individual problems, whereas Zionist work had "historical significance," i.e. it was dedicated to "the whole," the general public, society as a whole, and therefore led to fundamental changes. Incidentally, this distinction sheds more light on her silence regarding the activities of women's circles. Pomeranz operated with polemics and cited acute hardship to linguistically convey the urgency of Zionist politics. She presented this as not just the only possible answer, but also as the only one that could attain historical significance, that combined past, present, and future into a policy for and with the whole Jewish people. The text was aimed at the two women, but of course in addition (which is why it appeared in *Die Welt*) at the Zionist public, and doubtless also "western Jewry" among them.

In her response, Pappenheim turned the polemics around:

> "Charitable deeds" in the traditional sense are a religious and therefore a private matter. I distinguish between deeds which are an undeniable general social duty and omissions which are often concealed behind resounding words. Therefore, I contrast the Zionist future plan with a contemporary program in which I describe *the fight against tuberculosis, the personal influence of Jewish women on youth, and strict moral discipline among Jewish men* as more important themes for public discourse than the study of the Hebrew language, the study of ancient Jewish history, the strengthening of self-awareness, and similar pleasant results.[146]

Pappenheim worked in the argumentative field of the social work movement and the women's movement, as indicated by the reference to her key projects such as treating tuberculosis and morality training for men. She explicitly distinguished her approach from religious charity, alluding to the difference between traditional poor relief and a social welfare system based on prevention and professionalism. By sharpening the distinction between "charitable deeds" and "deeds" to "deeds" and "omissions," and distinguishing it from a "contemporary program" of social work, she placed social work above the national educational program of the Zionist movement. The fact that she drew a distinction between a future plan and a contemporary program can doubtless be seen as an ironic sideswipe at the intra-Zionist debate about *Gegenwartsarbeit*.[147] Apart from her polemics such as the insinuation of "hollow gossip," "laziness" and "omissions," her remarks served above all to present the social work she advocated as an indispensable demand from the general public. She reversed Pomeranz's distinction between superficial charity and profound Zionism.

Rabinowitsch also argued in the same manner. It was not the social work projects that would solve short-term problems, but Zionism, which she referred to as a political "party," while "the matter"—the problem of trafficking in women—

> can never be solved in the sense of a party ... The popularity of an institution depends by no means on the political views of its founders, but on whether this institution is conducive to the general prosperity of the people."[148]

All three women contrasted a short-term, party-based interest policy with measures serving the general public. However, while Pappenheim and Rabinowitsch made social work a universal truth, for Pomeranz it was Zionism. Both sides dominated the rhetorical style of the already repeatedly identified connection between truth and emotionality as well as the polemicizing defamation of their opposing positions.

Universal validity and developmental logic were rhetorical figures with which the political movements connected and legitimized the construction of a collective with the vision of a better society. In the arena of women's policy, different interests or movements—and thus different (claims to) truths—competed with each other. The audience of the performances was therefore not just the respective grass roots, even if they were concretely addressed as an object of politics, but also the female activists of the other movements, the polemics being directed against the competition. Even though Pappenheim insisted on her individuality, the context of the conflicts was the divergent political discourses on social work.[149]

The silence regarding concrete action to improve the living standards of Jewish women can be explained by the competition from different yet very similar political directions.[150] This prompted Pomeranz to confront social work, socialist and women's policy and uphold biblical history, the emigration argument and Jewish teaching as symbols of Zionist politics.[151] In her radicalism, keeping silent was probably above all her strategy of communication and the presentation of truths. Pomeranz's example shows that the Zionist movement did not pursue different aims but used different rules of depiction from the women's or socialist movements.[152]

This example is revealing because the need to combat trafficking in women highlighted the requirement for different groups, directions, and interests to pull together. This did indeed take place, and the Zionist movement in Galicia was certainly involved. The L'viv congress on combating trafficking in women in 1903 received benevolent attention, while the three social workers dispatched by the B'nai B'rith Lodge in Hamburg to Galicia in order to initiate social work initiatives over the next two years were emphatically welcomed in *Wschód*.[153] One of the three women was the Zionist and trained social worker Marta Baer.[154] In one of her articles, she evaluated Zionist women's policy somewhat differently from Pomeranz. Although she began to describe the tasks of Zionist women with self-education and Jewish teaching, i.e. nurturing language and history in Jewish homes, she also mentioned social work projects, namely Toynbee Halls and girls' homes. However, a few years later, Pomeranz herself also put her faith in social work, in girls' schools, in the professionalization of women working in housekeeping, in literacy courses, and in caring for the disabled. She even founded centers for the concentration of such activities. Nevertheless, she used her silence about the everyday work of the associations and the refusal of pragmatic cooperation in the matter of "combating trafficking in women" to establish a logic with which Zionism could be propagated as a teleological development towards a better society.

Although her ideas—emigration as a solution and the reference to biblical history—were part of Zionist ideology and were not of course first formulated by Pomeranz, these ideas only developed their effective logic in the movement in debates with a commenting, constructing audience. It was only when arguing about the different priorities of other fellow campaigners and opponents that interests became "competing truths" and thus political goals. Truth was a rhetorical means to make one's own variant of competing political options and future plans plausible.[155] Truth was generated in competition with other truths.[156] The rift between Pomeranz's positions before and after the First World War, as stated in the biographical part, can now be interpreted against the background of the demands placed on an enactment. Her views developed in the context of notions of modernity and feasibility in the Zionist movement. The appearance of the audience, deconstructing the truths of others as dominant master narratives and opposing them with the true interests (because they were her own) belonged to the performance in the arena, to an enactment with scenery topped by large rooftops.

***

Politics is an enactment, and as such includes various roles as well as an audience. In contrast to a traditional play, when politics was involved, it was more of a performance. The audience was part of it, helped to create it, and was not just a passive observer; the course and outcome, although regulated, were not certain; and the performance claimed performativity, i.e. the shaping of reality. The performativity of the applause turned an event into a political one, as shown by the reports concerning Pomeranz's charismatic appearances.[157] A political movement aimed, on the one hand, at the participation of the addressees, while on the other hand, it competed with other movements. The prerogative of interpretation and leadership claimed by dedicated female politicians—such as the three women—required recognition by fellow campaigners inside and outside the movements. Politics, therefore, arose from the interaction of many authors. This banal-sounding insight derives its relevance from having revealed the different levels of such interaction.

The recitation of conversion or arousal motifs, the similarity of the topoi, and the narrative structure in the historicization of women's movements made clear the intertextuality of political rhetoric—intertextuality that established a virtual network. The women wrote depictions of the movements that constructed the moment of integration as an experience of awakening. Wysłouchowa obviously drew her versions of women's policy from this virtual network and contributed to its creation. Kobryns'ka's accounts of Galician women's politics were integrated into the discourse on Galician backwardness, which was not only taken up and shared by the intelligentsia but also repeatedly put forth. The rhetorical means of communication with an informed circle of the intelligentsia, the appeal, the message, and historical contextualization made the texts political, inviting participation and legitimizing the goals and practices of the movements. In this structure, progress and backwardness functioned as strategies for shaping political positions. The participation of the audience in the movement, the garnering of dedication, conviction, and support, were part of the plot presented.[158] Pomeranz's refusal to communicate, her assertion that the practical work of the Zionists need not be discussed further, can be regarded as a strategy for gaining the prerogative of interpretation over nation, truth, and gender. It was possible above all because of the emptiness and overdetermination of the signifiers. Pomeranz presented moments of "fixation" in a permanent movement of differentiation and distinction.

Acting in the arena of women's policy initially required carving out one's own role, i.e. distinguishing oneself from other visions of a better future. The audience to whom narratives and spaces were presented was won over again and again by each individual vision and encouraged to participate. Each movement presented its own play about progressiveness, cast the roles of heroes and victims, enemies and supporters, listeners, addressees, competitors, and participants. In her articles on the politics of the Ruthenian intelligentsia, Kobryns'ka dealt with the difficulties of positioning, the casting of main and secondary roles as well as extras, and the construction of her own stage set—for example,

Mobilizing: The Enactments 233

economic dependencies as a class or gender struggle. Truth and competition, the relationality of backwardness and progress, the intertextuality of stories: all these narrative strategies are rituals that performed the authors' claim to the prerogative of interpretation, competition with other movements and concepts, as well as the audience as performing and observing entities. In the performance revolving around truths and "fixations," the authors and audience, performers, interpreters, and observers permanently changed places and exchanged roles.

Notes

1 "From this point of view textual exegesis, of the kind practiced by Hayden White in *Metahistory* or Steven Bann in The *Inventions of History*; i.e. the close reading of a limited number of well-thumbed books, would be less germane than a study of readership, or what is called in literary criticism 'reception theory.'" Samuel, *Theatres*, 8.
2 Samuel, *Theatres*, 17.
3 "Using the rich conceptual insights of Roger Chartier, the book historian can investigate reading as a cultural practice, to examine what readers bring to their texts, and how they 'appropriate' meaning through the act of reading." Lyons, *Culture*, 7–8.
4 See Eisenberg, "Kulturtransfer"; Hüchtker, *WerkstattGeschichte*.
5 "Texts are accessible to understanding in two ways: as language and as action. ... The understanding of a text as an action is rooted in the understanding of a text as speech." Stierle, "Geschichte," 348.
6 Wysłouchowa to Sokolová-Seidlová, June 5, 1894, PNP, 33/44. Wysłouchowa wrote a very similar story to Kuczalska-Reinschmit which was printed in a publication in honor of Eliza Orzeszkowa: "When I was 13 years old, secretly reading *Marta* made such a powerful impression on me that I didn't stop asking and demanding until, despite the indignation of the whole neighborhood, I was sent to high school." Walewska, "Ankieta," 8.
7 Stegmann, *Töchter*, 65.
8 Orzeszkowa, "Marta. Powieść," *Tygodnik*, 1873; Orzeszkowa, *Marta*, (1873) 1885. First published in 1860 in Warsaw, *Tygodnik* was devoted to practical advice, literature, fashion, popular scientific, social, and educational topics. See Dormus, *Problematyka*, 59; Franke, *Polska prasa*, 79–91.
9 Orzeszkowa, Marta, 2018, 1. (Polish: Orzeszkowa, *Marta*, 1949, 5).
10 Orzeszkowa, Marta, 2018, 2–3. (Polish: Orzeszkowa, *Marta*, 1949, 6–7).
11 Orzeszkowa, Marta, 2018, 3. (Polish: Orzeszkowa, Marta, 1949, 7).
12 Balzer, *Einführung*, 44; Becker, *Realismus*, 124–44.
13 Lejeune, "Pakt."
14 See Stegman, *Töchter*, 170–79.
15 *Marta* first appeared in Russian in 1886, in German under the title *Ein Frauenschicksal* in 1887, in Swedish in 1888, in Dutch in 1898, in Czech in 1906, in Esperanto in 1910, and in Yiddish and Hebrew in 1927. See Gacowa, *Eliza Orzeszkowa*, 22.
16 *Ster*. 1907. I (4): 174, quoted after Stegmann, *Töchter*, 172.
17 Sokolova-Seidlova, Wilma. 1905. "[Obituary]." *Ženský Svět*, reprinted in [Dalecka et al.], *Marja Wysłouchowa*, 69–78, here: 70.
18 Walewska, *Ruch*, 15.

19 Walewska, *Ruch*, 16.
20 Walewska, *Ruch*, 17. See also Walewska, *W walce*, 10: "With Marta, Orzeszkowa aroused women from their sleep as if with a large bell."
21 See also the reference in Hrytsak, "Cycle," 189. Franko's stories are additionally mentioned in various autobiographies of Ukrainian left-wing activists (including Kobryns'ka) as particularly impressive initiations.
22 See Chapter 2, Composing experience.
23 Koselleck, "Spaces"; Scott, "Phantasie."
24 Pietrow-Ennker, "Women," 21; Scholze, Nachwort to Orzeszkowa, *Marta*, 257.
25 Bader-Zaar, "Hainisch."
26 Hainisch, "Geschichte," 14–15.
27 See also Suchmiel, "Books." Suchmiel highlights above all the reception of internationally relevant texts.
28 Kobryns'ka, "Crust," 56.
29 For her biography, see Schüler, *Frauenbewegung*, 187–348.
30 Salomon, *Jahre*, 3.
31 See also Kessel, *Langeweile*, 118–22.
32 In other words, it is not a matter of identifying textual content with political directions within or outside the movements. This is the tack taken using the example of Ruthenian textbook historiography in Galicia by Hofeneder, "Sprach- und Geschichtsmythen"; Hüchtker, *"Cross-mapping."*
33 Lange and Bäumer (eds.), *Handbuch*. Regarding the biographies of the two authors, see Schaser, *Helene Lange*, 29–76.
34 Moszczeńska, "Geschichte"; Bäumer, "Geschichte."
35 *Głos*; Bujwidowa, Przedmowa to *Głos*, V.
36 Kuczalska-Reinschmit, "Z historyi."
37 Wysłouchowa, "Ruch."
38 Kobryns'ka, "Rus'ke žinoctvo."
39 Kobryns'ka, "Pro ruch žinočyj."
40 Kobryns'ka, "Žinoča sprava."
41 Cowman, "Activists," 146.
42 Lange, Vorwort to Lange and Bäumer (eds.), *Handbuch*, V.
43 Hainisch, Geleitwort to Braun et al. (eds.), *Frauenbewegung*.
44 Bujwidowa, Przedmowa to *Głos*, VII.
45 Regarding the historical development of radical theories and ideas, see also McKay, *Leftists*, 13–77.
46 Hüchtker, "Vergangenheit."
47 Wysłouchowa, "Ruch," 25–26.
48 Wysłouchowa, "Ruch," 156.
49 Wysłouchowa, "Ruch," 26.
50 The "Great Reforms" of Tsar Alexander II in the 1860s aimed at modernizing the country and included the abolition of serfdom as well as the introduction of administrative, judicial, military, and educational reforms. See L[öwe], "Reformen."
51 Wysłouchowa, "Ruch," 157. Napoleon's policy of conquest was not initially rejected in partitioned Poland since it was hoped that he would re-establish an independent state. Disapproval was only brought about by the failure of the Duchy of Warsaw, the rump state established by Napoleon in 1807. See Jaworski, Lübke, and Müller, *Geschichte*, 256–57.
52 The civil codes influenced by the legal discourses of the Enlightenment (e.g. the Napoleonic Code and also the General State Laws for the Prussian States and the Civil Code of Austria) regulated matters such as the legal capacity of women and guardianship as well as matrimonial property law.

Mobilizing: The Enactments   235

None of the codes gave women the status of citizens; the Napoleonic Code lagged behind the Austrian code. See Holthöfer, "Geschlechtsvormundschaft," 429–32; Vogel, "Gleichheit."
53 Wysłouchowa, "Ruch," 156.
54 Kobryns'ka, "Pro ruch žinočyj," 7.
55 Kobryns'ka, "Pro ruch žinočyj," 7.
56 Kobryns'ka, "Žinoča sprava," 1–2.
57 Bäumer, "Geschichte," 4.
58 Bäumer, "Geschichte," 165.
59 Bäumer, "Geschichte," 33.
60 To sum it up in Hayden White's terminology, we could speak of a change from an Organicist to a Formist argumentation. White, *Metahistory*, 29.
61 Kuczalska-Reinschmit, "Z historyi," 233.
62 Moszczeńska, "Geschichte," 350.
63 For example Walewska, *W walce*, 5–6; see also Stegmann, "Kampf," 20 on the "barely questioned basic figure of numerous accounts of the genesis of Polish feminism."
64 Regarding the potential of the ambiguity of feminist historiography in relation to history as the past and history as historiography, see Friedman, *Mappings*, especially 199–203.
65 Regarding the performance metaphor in relation to narrations of the movements, see also Welskopp, "Clio," 318.
66 Kuczalska-Reinschmit to Wysłouchowa, no year, BO, 7189/II, folio 99.
67 See Chapter 2, Writing collectives. Wysłouchowa also claimed, for instance, that no one in Galicia was interested in the story of Emilia Plater. Wysłouchowa to Sokolová-Seidlová, no year (probably 1892), PNP, 33/44. Regarding Bujwidowa's assessment of Galician women as passive, see Stegmann, *Töchter*, 84.
68 Kobryns'ka, "Žinoča sprava," 1.
69 Kobryns'ka, "Rus'ke žinoctvo," 79.
70 Szczepanowski, *Nędza*. The title paraphrased for example Frostig, "Nędza." See also Kuberski, "Nędza," 427; Śliwa, "Nędza."
71 Bujwidowa, "O postępowym i niepostępowym ruchu," AOB, 8. The background of the text was Bujwidowa's final break with the Women's Reading Room in Kraków, which at that time was undergoing a nationalization push and distanced itself from demands of the women's movement. The text appeared in *Kurjer Lwowski* at about the same time as a meeting of women's organizations was held in Kraków, which Bujwidowa did not attend.
72 Buchstab Awi-Jonah, "Pamięci," 15. Regarding the Zionist attacks on women, see also Rose, "'Familie,'" 189.
73 Hulewicz, "Kuczalska-Reinschmit," 69.
74 Konarski, "Radlińska"; Lepalczyk and Maraynowicz-Hetka, "Helena Radlińska."
75 Radlińska, "Uniwersytety," 438.
76 Koselleck and Meier, "Fortschritt," 407.
77 Koselleck and Meier, "Fortschritt," 417.
78 Kobryns'ka, "Žinoča sprava," 1.
79 Kobryns'ka, "Žinoča sprava," 7. Although Kobryns'ka's irony is unmistakable, it, too, contains a historicizing perspective.
80 Kobryns'ka, "Rus'ke žinoctvo"; Kobryns'ka, "Pro ruch žinočyj"; Kobryns'ka, "Žinoča sprava"; Kobryns'ka, "Stremlïnja," 1895, 1896.
81 Kobryns'ka, "Žinoča sprava," 35.
82 With regard to a symbolic unification of difference in the women's movement, see also Bosch, "Representations."

83 Kobryns'ka, "Stremlïnja," 1895, 12–14. The article "Pro ruch žinočyj v novijšych časach" has a similar structure: an argumentative, fundamental first part followed by detailed examples. See Kobryns'ka, "Pro ruch žinočyj."
84 Kobryns'ka, "Stremlïnja," 1896, 1–7.
85 Kobryns'ka, "Rus'ke žinoctvo," 68, 79.
86 Kobryns'ka, "Žinoča sprava," 26–27; see also Veidlinger, *Culture*, 164.
87 Regarding Ruthenian periodicals, see Binder, "Das ruthenische Pressewesen," 2113–19.
88 Kobryns'ka, "Žinoča sprava," 31–32.
89 Kobryns'ka, "Žinoča sprava," 4.
90 Kobryns'ka, "Žinoča sprava," 23.
91 Bujwidowa, *O postępowym i niepostępowym ruchu*, AOB, 4–5.
92 Kobryns'ka, "Rus'ke žinoctvo," 102.
93 See Chapter 1, Dramatic directing.
94 Kobryns'ka, "Rus'ke žinoctvo," 68.
95 Kobryns'ka, "Rus'ke žinoctvo," 90, 92.
96 Kobryns'ka, "Rus'ke žinoctvo," 91–92. See also Leszczawski-Schwerk, "Grenzüberwindungen," 40, regarding Kobryns'ka's criticism of marriage.
97 Recent research has highlighted the considerable proportion of mixed-denomination marriages in towns and cities, especially in L'viv, although no distinction by gender is made. Kosyk, "Geschichte," 103–08.
98 Stierle, "Geschichte," 352–53.
99 The fact that Kobryns'ka demonstrated considerable analytical foresight may be illustrated by the similarity displayed by current syntheses regarding conflicts in European women's movements. See for example Paletschek and Pietrow-Ennker, "Emancipation," 324–27.
100 This notion, too, is not genuinely Galician. Regarding its ambiguity, see for example Bock, *Women*, 154–55.
101 For example, Drahomanov wrote in a letter to Kobryns'ka regarding the Galician readership of "our provincial audience of both sexes." Drahomanov to Kobryns'ka, January 2, 1894, reprinted in Pavlyk, *Perepyska*, 19–20, here: 20.
102 Hüchtker, "Rückständigkeit, Fortschritt"; Hüchtker, "Rückständigkeit als Strategie."
103 White, *Metahistory*, 40–41.
104 Pomeranz, *An die jüdischen Frauen*.
105 Bücherwelt: Rosa Pomeranz. *An die jüdischen Frauen! Ein Appell zur Umkehr*. Tarnopol: Verlag des Vereines "Ahawath Zion." 1899. *Die Welt* III (1): 13. The appeal was first advertised in 1898. Büchereinkauf. 1898. *Die Welt* II (51): 14.
106 Syonistka, "O kobiecie."
107 Pomeranz, "Kilka uwag."
108 Pomeranz, *An die jüdischen Frauen*, 8.
109 Pomeranz, *An die jüdischen Frauen*, 9–10.
110 Pomeranz, *An die jüdischen Frauen*, 21–22.
111 Pomeranz, *An die jüdischen Frauen*, 21–22.
112 Pomeranz, *An die jüdischen Frauen*, 6–7.
113 Pomeranz, *An die jüdischen Frauen*, 20.
114 Pomeranz, *An die jüdischen Frauen*, 20.
115 Syonistka, "O kobiecie," 52.
116 Polonsky, *Jews*, 136–38. However, no Jewish women's movement was established in Galicia as happened in, say, the German Empire. A Jewish social democratic party also emerged only very late. It was not until 1904

that a Jewish group was formed within the Polish Socialist Party (*Polska Partia Socjalistyczna*), a separate party being founded in 1905. Regarding the Jewish women's movement see Kaplan, *Movement*; regarding the Bund see Polonsky, *Jews*, 33; regarding Jewish social democracy see Wistrich, "Social Democracy," 111; Wróbel, "Jews," 125–29; in general see Hüchtker, "Bewegungen."

117 See Chapter 2, Enacting history.
118 Pomeranz, "Kilka uwag," 80.
119 Kronika: Tarnów. 1903. *Wschód* IV (159): 6.
120 Pomeranz, "Kilka uwag," 81.
121 Pomeranz, "Kilka uwag," 80.
122 See for example Judson, *Revolutionaries*, especially 267–72; see also Janowski, *Thought*.
123 She gave this speech at the Toynbee Hall in Tarnopol and the women's association Moriah in Drohobycz. Ruch w kraju: Drohobycz. 1903. *Wschód* IV (164): 6–7; Kronika: Tarnopol. 1903. *Wschód* IV (135): 13.
124 She was by no means alone in this; see for example Gutmann, "Weib."
125 Ruch w kraju: Drohobycz. 1903. *Wschód* IV (164): 6–7, here: 7.
126 One could refer her to the different currents of Zionism: Herzlian political Zionism, regional politics (cultural Zionism), and practical Zionism geared towards the settlement of Palestine. As stated in Chapter 1, Theatrical enacting, Pomeranz had in mind the Basel program which, although a compromise between all the factions, was not supported always and everywhere in Galician politics, and also in her rhetoric practical Zionism, which she strongly supported over regional politics (i.e. politics on the ground or *Gegenwartsarbeit*). See for a bit more concrete aims Melzer, "Pflichten."
127 Bertha Pappenheim became active in the German-Jewish women's movement after moving from Vienna to Frankfurt am Main, founded the League of Jewish Women (*Jüdischer Frauenbund*) in the German Empire in 1904, and in 1907 opened a home for Jewish girls, especially migrants from Eastern and Central Europe. Brentzel, *Anna O.*; Guttmann, *Enigma*.
128 Rabinowitsch (Rabinowitsh/Rabinovich) was probably the daughter of the Hebrew writer Shaul Pinhas Rabinovich (Pinkhas Rabinovitsh). She studied economics in the German Empire, was a Bundist and active in the European left; she published for instance a socio-economic study of the Jewish population in Mahilyow, her native city. See Greenbaum, "Heder," 62, footnote 25; "Rabinowich"; Brentzel, *Anna O.*, 106–07. According to Kozińska-Witt, "Bertha Pappenheim," 76, Rabinowitsch was a doctor of medicine. Denz, "'Steppenfurie,'" 28, points to the confusion surrounding two women named Sarah Rabinovitsh, making it impossible to be conclusive about her biography.
129 Guttmann, *Enigma*, 137–40.
130 Pomeranz, "Besuch," 4.
131 Stegmann, "Paradygmaty," 39–41; Kaplan, "Prostitution."
132 For an overview, see also Walkowitz, *City*, 1–13, 121–34; regarding prostitution policy in Galicia, see Wingfield, *World*, especially 171–208; regarding the migration context, see Stauter-Halsted, *Chain*, 137–68.
133 See Sikorska-Kulesza, "Prostytucja."
134 Polonsky, *Jews*, 92–94. Polonsky does not believe the percentage of Jewish prostitutes and brothel-owners to have been disproportionate compared to the percentage of Jews in the population. Staudacher, "Aktion," 97, estimates from police and court records that about 90% of the 1,000 young women abducted from Galicia every year came from poor Jewish families.

238 Mobilizing: The Enactments

Bristow, *Prostitution*, 85–108, does not give any further details. The figures in Wingfield, *World* are all based on individual court cases. The main question, however, concerns the relevance of figures in the scandalization of social phenomena. See Walkowitz's brilliant analysis of the impact of the Jack the Ripper case on politics in London as an example. Walkowitz, *City*, 191–228.

135 Bristow, "Fight."
136 See the notes on the relevance of the topos in Jewish politics and women's movements in Hecht, *Feminismus*, 33–34; Wingfield, *World*, 172–78.
137 Jazbinsek, *Mädchenhandel*.
138 Pappenheim, "Besuch"; Rabinowitsch, "Erwiderung."
139 Bertha Pappenheim. 1904. "Zur Lage der jüdischen Bevölkerung in Galizien: Reiseeindrücke und Vorschläge zur Besserung der der Verhältnisse." In Bertha Pappenheim and Sarah Rabinowitsch. *Zur Lage der jüdischen Bevölkerung in Galizien: Reiseeindrücke und Vorschläge zur Besserung der Verhältnisse*. Frankfurt am Main: Neuer Frankfurter Verlag, reprinted in Pappenheim, *Sisyphus*, 43–106, here: 82–83. Only Pappenheim's part is printed.
140 Pomeranz, "Besuch," 5.
141 Pomeranz, "Besuch," 6.
142 Pomeranz, "Besuch," 5. Emphasis in the original.
143 Regarding Pappenheim's anti-Zionism, which she justified with its misogyny, see Mark H. Gelber, *Pride*, 161.
144 Pomeranz, "Besuch," 5: This means the large international Jewish charitable and cultural organizations: Alliance Israélite Universelle, founded in France in 1860, the secret lodge B'nai B'rith (Independent Order of B'nai B'rith) founded in New York in 1843 by 12 German immigrants, and the Jewish Colonization Association founded in 1891 by Baron Maurice de Hirsch to purchase land for Jews from Eastern Europe. All these organizations pursued Jewish cultural and social policy, The Jewish Colonization Association also conducted settlement policy, albeit focusing on South America, not Palestine. However, none of the organizations belonged to the Zionist movement as set out in the Basel program.
145 Pomeranz, "Besuch," 4. Emphasis in the original.
146 Pappenheim, "Besuch," 15.
147 Shanes, *Nationalism*, 150–64.
148 Rabinowitsch, "Erwiderung," 11–12.
149 Regarding disputes over a Zionist policy towards Alliance Israélite Universelle, see for example Starck, "Kampf."
150 Regarding the similarity of Pappenheim's ideas, see also Konz, *Bertha Pappenheim*, 206.
151 Similarly, see also in Pomeranz, "Bedeutung."
152 Koschorke, *Fact*, 152–55.
153 Ruch w kraju: Stanisławów. 1904. *Wschód* V (48): 4–5; Ruch w kraju: Stanisławów (Z komitetu dystrykcyjnego—Zwalczanie handlu dziewczętami). 1904. *Wschód* V (45): 5; Kronika: Kongres dla zwalczania handlu dziewczętami. 1903. *Wschód* IV (151): 7–8.
154 Since Marta Baer underwent a sex reassignment after her return from Galicia, as documented in contemporary medical studies and current works on the history of medicine, and wrote an autobiography, much research has been conducted into her in transsexuality and transgender studies. Therefore, this should be noted here. See the autobiography Body, *Memoirs* (Body, *Aus eines Mannes Mädchenjahren*); from a medical-historical

Mobilizing: The Enactments 239

perspective Hartmann, "Geschlecht"; for a reconstruction of the life of Marta/Karl Baer see Simon, "Afterword." Whether Martha Baer-Issachar, a Zionist publisher, is Marta Baer could not be proved. See Baer-Issachar, "Frauen."
155 "Competing truths" comes from Griesebner, *Wahrheiten*. The concept of situated knowledges by Donna Haraway is stimulating with regard to the conceivability of "competing truths." Developed for an epistemologically similar problem of gender history, namely the deconstruction of essentialized genders with a simultaneous feminist reference to women, this image combines historical conditionality with the existence of "truths." Haraway, "Knowledges"; see also Kinnunen, "History."
156 Kleeberg and Suter, "Truth."
157 See Chapter 1, Theatrical enacting; Chapter 3, Ritualizing education.
158 See also Wöller, "'Fortschritt.'"

Conclusion

Sure, history must be told, yet it must also be enacted. Political movements formulated demands for participation and recognition, they constructed narratives about historical experiences, action, and visions, and last but not least they presented enactments in order to rehearse for a better society. Movements' narratives are superimposed by the historian with other narratives about performativity, ritual, and transnationality. To help convey the creativity and performativity of narratives and practices of political activity as well as the connections between historical change and historical analysis, I have examined the history of political movements as performance. Performance can be described as a performative enactment which follows rules, whose end is unknown, and which may bring about change. It draws attention to the simultaneity of potency and presentation, to the performativity of theatricality.

During the nineteenth century, class, gender, and nation became essential, self-evident categories of difference, and for this very reason, they also became politicizable and changeable. Specific manners of political activity emerged throughout Europe: political movements. They took these differences and molded them into capable collectives (i.e. *the* women, *the* workers, *the* peasants, *the* Jews, Ukrainians, and Poles), formulated their oppression or discrimination, and legitimized their claim to forge a better future. The weighting of the politicized collectives and the central social, national, or gender-specific oppression or discrimination was the subject of fierce debate—between socialist and feminist movements, and among women's groups of different nationalities. The movements were mostly headed by small groups of activists, mainly intellectual women and men, some of whom had ascended from the peasantry, skilled tradespeople, or the proletariat, while others came from the impoverished nobility or the secularized clergy. The movements were based on social work and educational associations which, apart from alleviating current, specific problems, sought to improve the basic conditions of society.

The study, focused on the biographies of three women and structured according to the aspects of performance, examined the rules and potential for change of political involvement. A performance includes participants, plays (i.e. a plot), a stage, a venue, and the audience. The concept of performance enabled temporal and spatial contexts, the actors, and movements' narratives and practices being interlinked. The biographical perspective brought together the motivations of the participants, emotional ties, the connection between friendship and involvement, the contingency and randomness of some decisions, yet also the similarities between activities, writing, organizing, and communicating. The plays of the women's, peasant, or Zionist movements about collectives, experiences, and history were presented at different stages and repeatedly performed. In the organizations, education and social work were ritualized as a means or media of progressive politics; the practices were performative and constructed the movements as simultaneously participatory and hierarchical. The enactments established narrative motifs, presentation strategies, and conflict management. The aims of this direction were to present the respective movement as authentic, as the source of truth, as well as to guide the participants to political involvement.

The Participants: Author, Artistic Director and Actor

At the end of the nineteenth century, three women took to the political scene stage in search of tasks and recognition: Maria Wysłouchowa, Natalja Kobryns'ka, and Rosa Pomenanz. All three wrote literary and journalistic texts, organized educational and social work associations, and presented themselves to the public—as authors, artistic directors, and actors. Despite being particularly dedicated to a specific movement or identifying with its aims, they worked in multiple political contexts. Wysłouchowa was one of the initiators of the Polish peasant movement and devoted herself to female peasants. However, she also cultivated ties with the women's movement and was organizationally and journalistically networked with the initiatives campaigning for people's education. Kobryns'ka served a Ruthenian women's movement. On the one hand, she moved within the socialist sphere, while on the other, she operated within the European-American context in her pursuit of feminist goals. Before the First World War, Pomeranz campaigned for a role for women in Zionism; after the war, she sought to translate feminist demands for the national movement. Despite their different goals, all three women made use of forms and structures that were very similar regarding narratives and practices. They organized mainly (but not only) women's associations, they wrote a lot, albeit not just for fellow campaigners and the political grassroots, but also for literary success. Above all, they were dedicated to their own nationalities, founding their projects and initiatives within a national narrative. None of the women argued for a consistently transnational collective.

Politics is based on communication. As well as serving debate, dialog, and explanation, communication also creates professional, political, and personal networks, virtual spaces of dialog, friendships, and emotional ties. Although all three women cultivated networks, Pomeranz's are only indirectly visible because her letters could not be found. The letters, yet also their travels—Kobryns'ka's trip to Prague, Pomeranz's across Europe, and Wysłouchowa's to the mountains—connected friendships with political activity, demands with affection, propaganda with relaxation. The movements' associations forged international alliances and constituted journalistic communication spaces transcending national and state borders. The biographical perspective allowed the movements' structural parallelism to be shown in a transnational communication space of politics—unspoken networks and entanglements between all the movements geared towards social work and ideals of progress. This means more than the observation that the movements pursued similar objectives. The three women's activities and trajectory in their political lives were determined by more than gender or nationality. The political and societal conditions, their social background, their professional and material opportunities, family relationships and conditions, and their personal environment were all closely intertwined.

The patterns of life plans include the contingency of historical processes. The three women's political activities were motivated and shaped by their families and environment as well as by death, exile, and illness, and personal and political conflicts: their activities flowed into the history of the movements and the historiographical narratives about them. Even though the educational pathways taken by the women and the movements in which they were involved were limited by gender, nation, and constitution, there were still options; their course was determined by not just structures but also coincidences. Wysłouchowa was able to attend school and teacher seminar (a typical educational pathway for middle-class females at the time), even though her mother had had to earn a living. Kobryns'ka's education at home resulted from the similarly common discrimination of girls, and yet she became a well-known, highly reflective Ukrainian writer whose fame lives on to this day. Pomeranz's formal education was not so much nationalist Jewish as middle class, to put it in socio-historical terms—and hence similar to the Zionist association culture. Her domestic socialization, on the other hand, politicized her—like the other two women—for nationalist involvement. Her family and personal circumstances provided opportunities and directions, and also opened up new prospects. Kobryns'ka's involvement in politics was triggered by the early death of her husband. Wysłouchowa had to go into exile in Galicia with her husband when he was persecuted for socialist activities in the Kingdom of Poland. Despite her limited strength as a result of a heart condition, she was also active outside Galicia, for example in Cieszyn Silesia, where she went for convalescence. She was especially dedicated to the Silesian peasantry, whom she also admired as a special role model.

All three women were married or widowed, and declared that they pursued their professional and political ambitions with the support of their husbands; their extensive activities may also have been facilitated by the fact that none of them had any children. Nevertheless, Kobryns'ka wrote about the effort and lack of mobility entailed by caring for her parents. While her political and professional activities as a writer, teacher, journalist, and organizer overlapped and complemented each other, looking after family members was more of an obstacle. All three women emphasized the support and encouragement from their spouses, who helped shape a politically active marriage as a way of life and utopia. Love, marriage, sexuality, and relations between the sexes were central themes of active policy around 1900, signals in the enactments of modernity. Criticism of marital relations, marriage law, and marriage conventions was part of the movements' narratives, regardless of how different the models they propagated may have been. Their diverging views on free love—as a utopian model of free relationships, as a countermodel to arrangement and convention, as entitlement and dependence, as an expression of patriarchal gender relations—not only represented different notions of a gender-equitable world but symbolized different political directions.

The connection between life and politics is clearly shown by love for the people in its double meaning: love for the nation and for the lower classes, which all three women shared and nurtured. However, the form they gave to this love differed. Wysłouchowa cultivated the romantic love of unity between people and politics, Kobryns'ka nurtured love as a redesigned practice of relations between the sexes (especially in rural areas), while Pomeranz understood love as charisma creating a link between the intelligentsia and the people. The interplay or entanglement of historical logic and historical contingency resulted in the historiographical patterns of their biographies: the author's love, the artistic director's books, and the actor's charisma.

The Plays: Collectives, Experience, and History

In order to form political movements and propagate their ideas, the three women wrote plays about collectives, experience, and history. Political involvement meant writing texts which established meaningful coherence and, at the same time, propagated new perspectives or approaches. These petitions, appeals, and magazines as well as stories, poems, and novels were meant to be read as political, as plays about movements' aims, involvement, and motivation. They were also to be read as historical, i.e. as plots about phenomena tied to a certain era that were changeable rather than (just) about general problems of humanity. The three women considered fiction and popular-history stories to be especially conducive. Rhetorical means and narrative strategies

244 Conclusion

involved the readers and conveyed a sense of community. The stories were about characters who could be viewed as typical of a collective. They described experiences of oppression and deprivation, anti-Semitic prejudice, and the restrictions faced in rural settings by women from the clergy, and collectivized these experiences into a shared history and a common desire for change. They told of female heroes, new occupations, or a new world in Palestine. They offered the possibility of a vision, a concept of the past, present, and the future.

The fact that these narratives were and could be read in a political context was due to their places of publication: movements' organs and collections of texts presented accordingly. By means of their place of publication, introduction, and language, the texts made a pact with the readers to be considered political. It is occasionally pointed out in the research that movements' publications served inward self-assurance rather than propaganda. This can certainly not be ruled out, as long as self-assurance is not solely understood as the repetition of familiar matters. The politically readable narratives also tested new ways of presentation, new narrative structures, and argumentative contexts. Wysłouchowa's magazines with their combination of instruction and the neoromantic presentation of female and male heroes sought ways of rhetorical participation and paternalistic care, the inclusion of the rural population in a knowledge connoted as modern, and the veneration of peasant women as objects of a formative policy. Kobryns'ka's narratives on the misery and plight of the Ruthenian clergy were based on explanatory patterns of women's movements and opened up to female readers in Galician villages and towns not just a European perspective but also examples of changes, whereas Pomeranz set out the options for modern Judaism in a narrative, logical sequence of historical (sometimes misguided) pathways.

The Stages: Education, Nation, and Society

The visions of a better future were not just told and propagated. The women organized stages on which education, nation, and society could be performed. The movements required concrete spaces in order to translate their visions into practices and to perform them. It could be said that the many social work and educational initiatives represented decisive means for a calculated, moldable future. Initiatives included kindergartens and school projects with specific programs, such as teaching Jewish history and culture, enabling external baccalaureate examinations for girls, reading rooms, libraries, and adult education centers, yet also contact centers, accommodation, and training courses for young adults who had migrated from the countryside to the city. The central form of mediation was the lecture. A series of lectures on issues of the day such as hygiene, Darwinism, and the legal position of women were forms of media for all movements. The social work projects defined new relationships with a modern, progressive connotation: enlightened infant care and childcare described as rational or national; the protection of young people, especially girls, from seduction and impoverishment; training courses to improve opportunities on the labor market, etc. The projects legitimized intervention in the family and personal relationships.

Reading rooms were concrete spaces that enabled decentralized networking and also served the presentation of new knowledge. Books and newspapers were distributed; lectures were given there. A lecture combined the presentation of knowledge and the establishment of new hierarchies of those in the know and those not, of lecturers and listeners, activists, and grassroots. It ritualized this relationship and can be seen as symptomatic of the movements' sense of identity. This is shown by both Wysłouchowa's notions of instruction and reports about Pomeranz's appearances at Zionist meetings which described the speaker's charisma, the welcome she received, the audience's emotionalization and applause, yet hardly mentioned anything about the actual content of her talk. Kobryns'ka's kindergarten project, which was intended not just to look after and bring up children but also to unite women from all walks of life and form a national, complete society, can be regarded as an example of attempts to deliver enlightenment and improved organization. In addition, all the movements supported the establishment of centers with educational and social work opportunities which demonstrated the feasibility of a better society and can be seen as representing the movements' power. Pomeranz was so successful at organizing the movement that she was one of the first women and the first Jewish woman to be elected to the *Sejm* of the Second Republic of Poland and was also involved in the conception of state social policy in national and international organizations. The movements' organizations were places where the new field of hierarchical participation was mapped out, demonstrated, and rehearsed. This applied both to the grassroots to be recruited and to the activists, the actors of politics. The participation did not simply mean democratization but also the establishment of new hierarchies, new ways of distinction, and new power relationships, which had to be not just formulated but also put into practice.

The associations served as spaces where the practices of political action could be tested and rehearsed. In addition, the organizations formed an imagined community through concrete places, concrete tasks, and concrete individuals. The social work and educational projects directed the deficits of the past, the action of the present, and the visions of the future in equal measure. Above all, however, they conveyed new knowledge and new relationships between activists and the grassroots, i.e. they established participation in politics, in the collective, in the achievements of a better society, and in the rise of a new (academically) educated and (politically) informed elite. Education was (and remains) the central medium not only of advancement but also of the vision of society on which it is based, a prerequisite of participation and success that can hardly be eschewed.

The Enactments: Role Models, Competition and Practice

The mediation of narratives, as well as practices for their implementation, served to mobilize. The women communicated with the audience, their fellow-campaigners, and opponents about prerogatives and patterns of interpretation. Communication had to take place publicly in order to be political, i.e. to mobilize it; it was part of the imagined collective and helped construct it. Communication, therefore, refers to not just direct debate at events, but also to the virtual networks of ideas created by intertextuality. The legitimation narratives of the women's movements thus shared the patterns of initiation and basic narrative structures. The two-pronged strategy of dissolving the hegemonic historical master narrative and enhancing one's own story through integration into this narrative is apparent in the rhetorical rifts in a series of texts on the emergence of women's movements. The structural similarity of these rifts and the intertextuality of the topoi refer especially clearly to the overlaps between national, international, and transnational communication spaces constructed by the movements, and by means of which they constituted themselves as movements in the first place.

Political legitimation required dealing with competition. Kobryns'ka wrote about her conflicts with women's associations, the Radicals, and others in long articles on the lack of support for feminist projects. She monologized and allowed an imagined audience to perform; the roles between audience and opponents were interchangeable. Kobryns'ka arranged her arguments in this way and legitimized them as the logic of a better society. But above all, by embedding them in historical narratives, the demands became the results of development processes. Backwardness and progress were a means to turn a chronicle into a narrative. Presenting nation as a medium and metonymy of progress and Galicia as a stronghold and metonymy of backwardness were strategies that shaped and promoted the movements' policies.

Above all, the policies of the movements, legitimized by collectively shared and historicized experience, instituted a claim to "truth." For this reason, they established their own criteria of difference as irrefutable and inescapable. Pomeranz's curious strategy of keeping silent about the Zionist movement's social-work projects and thus about her own activities elevated the nation to the most important category, an inclusive and exclusive, border-forming notion and collective identification in a field of ongoing differentiation processes. In this way—and this is the decisive goal of the rhetorical maneuvers—similarities with other movements were obscured: one's own truth became the only truth.

Historicization is, to summarize the enactments, a process of sensemaking that runs through different arenas corresponding to yet also competing with each other. Conflicts served the constitution of truths that not only legitimized but also essentialized the desire for the prerogative of interpretation.

The Performance

While recent research into Galicia emphasizes the "special modernity" of the periphery, from the viewpoint of political movements it appears more like European normality. This is related to the constitutionality of the Habsburg Empire which, despite its censorship and repression, permitted journalism, associations, and political parties, and made participation in representation conceivable through elections which, although unequal, were at least possible. Above all, however, it is connected to the approach of analyzing the "big world" in the periphery and "general history" in the "history of women," as in a microstudy. Each movement formulated its own truth underpinned by rationality, legitimacy, and history. The movements competed with each other for the prerogative of interpretation and practical success. Although they emphasized their differences from other movements, they were not clear-cut organizations or currents that were clearly distinguishable from each other; as well as their campaigning and organizational methods being similar, their imagined collectives also overlapped. Different currents, different notions of the better society to be aspired to, and the ways to get there existed within movements and on their fringes.

In this respect, Galicia was no different from other parts of Europe. Starting from educational initiatives and rural associations, the peasant movements campaigned for the mobilization of villagers, participation, and socially more just society. The women's movements, which at congresses and rallies represented women's demands for university access, equal rights, and changes in gender relations, were also based on a number of associations pursuing educational and social work projects. Similarly, the movements with nationalist concerns, the nation being the driving force of their activity, took a very similar tack. They too put their energies into corresponding projects in order to forge an awareness of an imagined collective with a common history of oppression or discrimination. The movements spread knowledge about culture and history, yet also offered kindergartens, literacy courses, and people's houses to improve networking and their own attractiveness, and also to spread their views in order to recruit the grassroots and shape their way of life and thought.

The socialist-orientated Polish peasant movement shared with other Polish movements and political organizations, including the women's movement, the national narrative of the illegally partitioned state, the

Polish history of suffering and insurrections. The women's movement set slightly different priorities by combining gender and nationalist politics with varying degrees of success. The Ruthenian women's movement focused on the Ukrainian-speaking population in Galicia and Eastern Ukraine and faced the challenge of contributing to the formation of a Ukrainian nation. There was a disagreement among Ruthenian women over whether a more community-based, autonomously organized women's policy or one under the aegis of the socialist-orientated Radicals would be more promising. Zionism pursued the goal of a modern Jewish society based on tradition and competed with other Jewish and non-Jewish movements. Contentious issues included the concentration on a nationalist policy in the Habsburg Empire, emigration to Palestine, and the presentation of ideas and projects of the women's movement. In none of the movements was national difference questioned or relativized. The nation was used as a synonym for society that was both exclusive and inclusive, as a metonymy for modernity, future, and progress, and as a fundamental difference ranging from distinction and competition to aggressiveness and hatred. As the petitions by the women's groups campaigning for the right to be awarded university degrees showed, collaboration was therefore mostly viewed as cooperation or an alliance between different nationalities.

The reason why politics in Galicia was transnational was not that the nation was called into question in this polyethnic region, but because the political concepts diffused throughout Europe, and national movements employed rituals, practices, and interpretations which were structurally very similar to those of the women's and peasant movements. On the one hand, the communication spaces extended far beyond Galicia or East-Central Europe; on the other hand, they were local. The narratives and practices of the movements constructed different spaces, concrete and abstract or metaphorical: the village, intellectual women, the Imperial Council and the laws of the monarchy, the Polish nation, and the Jewish people, the diaspora, Palestine or Europe. The associations and reform centers maintained networks that connected the representatives and activists, yet also conveyed topoi, mindsets, and arguments. Conversely, these abstract and concrete spaces shaped national and transnational collectives: the Jewish nation as an equally transnational and national collective, the women's movements linked together across borders by friendships and publications and representing the collective of "women," and the peasantry as the basis of a Polish nation and as a social group against the feudal Galician elite.

The movements claimed to speak for an essentialized collective and, at the same time, to be agents of historically explained progress towards a better society. They sought not only the enlightenment of passive addressees but also participation, while, at the same time, presenting themselves as the intellectual elite of the movement. Several dilemmas resulted from this concept: on the one hand, the movements saw themselves as participatory, on the other, their activists claimed the prerogative of interpretation; on the one hand, they represented group-specific interests; on the other hand, they propagated an improvement of society as a whole. On the one hand, they spoke on behalf of a collective; on the other hand, this identity presumed to be "natural" collided with other such identities. On the one hand, the historical argumentation of natural change made agitation appear superfluous; on the other hand, it was supposed to signal the need for action in order to make circumstances presumed to be natural and timeless changeable. The truth concepts of the collectives and their political orientations were able to co-exist without curtailing their respective claims to validity.

With their discursive networks permeating Europe in terms of both personnel and organization, with their ability to create collectives that were understood as essentialist and simultaneously a historically explained inevitability of change, with their practices that caught on despite all contradictions and shortcomings—the organization of associations, self-education and intervention, knowledge popularization, emotional politicization—the movements were extraordinarily successful at shaping identity politics right down to the narratives of contemporary history, despite not always (or even only rarely) achieving their concrete goals. Through their rhetoric and practice, they devised new symbolic systems by connecting past, present, and future—or history, politics, and society.

The nub of this connection consisted of the experience of oppression or discrimination and the knowledge of how society functioned, be it rooted in science, ethics, morality, emotion, or logic. The celebration of academic knowledge did not just result from its popularization or the scientification of everyday life but also constituted and confirmed the teleological notion of a collective presumed to be natural and its change in a given direction. Both science and experience meant truth. The growing relevance attributed to experience in political concepts is doubtless related to the fact that, from the late-eighteenth century onwards, the "discovery of the individual"[1] encountered a dynamization of political visions for the future requiring new rationales. The recourse to experience brought individuals to the fore and at the same time made the justifications for the political options appear authentic and therefore to be unquestionable facts (and at the same time a possible option).

The analysis of women's policy as a performance with participants, plays, stages, and enactments has identified precisely these aspects: the art of creating collectives, positionings, and truths in communication with the addressees, opponents, and fellow-campaigners, the ritualization of political practices, and the performativity of political speech acts. The narratives of identity politics forged new political ideas and practices, they created spaces in which the leading heads of the movements met as political subjects and in which marital partnership and political action, as well as the family and the public sphere, were united. Above all, the movements presented a relationship between leadership and grassroots, which was both participatory and hierarchical. Considering the participants, plays, stages, and enactments together, the performance is revealed: a hierarchical participation in a political arena. It deals with the politicization of education and social work as a proposal to shape and test the future, with knowledge bound to institutions and academically based, with the feasibility of a society considered better, with ways of inclusion and exclusion as well as the distribution of power and shifts in interpretation. The performance paved the way for activists to a new elite legitimized with academic knowledge as transformers of the world. Despite their ideological differences, in terms of narration and formulation, the movements were therefore extraordinarily similar. They differed in their political collectives—women, peasants, Jews—against whose discrimination they campaigned. They also differed in their relationships between leadership and grassroots. While the intellectuals in the women's movement and Zionism were part of the underprivileged collective (i.e. self-help and help for others were intertwined), the social distance between the rural population and the intelligentsia in the peasant movement was greater, yet overcome by the ideological exaltation of the rural population as the core of the nation. Seen from this angle, Galicia becomes a place of European history instead of a periphery or a peculiarity.

Changes are embedded in the thoughts and deeds of individuals and in the ritualization of social, material, and practical contexts. A nation may be an imagined community, a movement also arises through the activities of concrete actors and emotional practices, and above all, it required authenticity or experience as a form of credibility regarding the collective community and the promise of a better future which could be conveyed in media. Political movements depended on credibility and presenting it was also their specific ability. The performance concept has enabled this complexity to be made plausible. Plausibility requires an integrative logic. A context of sensemaking must be established. This sensemaking includes writing about politics—not just contemporary political texts but also the historicization of the movements up until today's research. The notion of a stage of reality can make the layering of different sensemaking, its continuation, and its change particularly striking. The limits of the performance concept appear where historical contexts emerging from contingent decisions taken by the women and from chance finds by the historian rule out other contexts and become historical truths.

Note

1 See van Dülmen, *Entdeckung*, 136, especially regarding experience.

Appendix of Names

This appendix is for guidance only and lists the historical figures mentioned in this book along with a brief biography. It does not include the three main characters, literary heroes, scholars, or names included in the titles of institutions.

Addams, Jane (1860–1935): American feminist, philosopher and social reformer, founder of the social work profession, established the famous Hull House (a settlement house) in Chicago

Alexander II (1818–1881): Tsar of the Russian Empire from 1855, carried out far-reaching reforms in the 1860s including the abolition of serfdom, suppressed the January Uprising in 1863/64, was assassinated

Arc, Joan of (1412–1431): French national female hero

Badeni, Kazimierz Feliks Graf (1846–1909): Galician governor, co-initiator of Ruthenian–Polish rapprochement

Baer, Karl: See → Baer, Marta

Baer, Marta (1885–1956): Zionist and social worker from Germany, underwent a sex change and took the name Karl M. Baer, published the autobiography *Memoirs of a Man's Maiden Years* under the pseudonym N. O. Body. It is not known whether she is identical to Marta Baer-Issachar.

Baer, Marta-Issachar: See → Baer, Marta

Balicka, Gabriela: member of the *Przodownica* editorial committee in Kraków

Barnett, Henrietta (1851–1936): Founded the first Toynbee Hall with her husband → Barnett, Samuel in London in 1884

Barnett, Samuel (1844–1913): Anglican clergyman, founded the first Toynbee Hall with his wife → Barnett, Henrietta in London in 1884

Barvinok, Hanna (1828–1911): Originally Bilozers'ka-Kuliš, Oleksandra, Ukrainian writer, married to → Kuliš, Pantelemon

Bäumer, Gertrud (1873–1954): Left-liberal politician, teacher, and writer, one of the leading figures in the women's movement in the German Empire together with → Lange, Helene

Bilozers'ka-Kuliš, Oleksandra: see → Barvinok, Hanna

Błotnicka, M. T.: member of the *Przodownica* editorial committee in Kraków

252   Appendix of Names

Bouffałówna, Maria: Maiden name of Wysłouchowa

Broda: reader of Zorza

Büchner, Georg (1813–1837): German writer, physician and natural scientist

Buchstab Awi-Jonah, Thamar: Co-founder and long-term campaigner in the Jewish Women's Circle in L'viv, emigrated to Palestine in the early 1920s where she is thought to have worked as a journalist and writer

Buckle, Henry Thomas (1821–1862): British historian, known for his book *History of Civilization in England*

Bujwid, Odon (1857–1942): Polish bacteriologist from Vilnius, pioneer of microbiology in Poland, professor at the Jagiellonian University in Kraków, married to → Bujwidowa, Kazimiera

Bujwidowa, Kazimiera (1867–1932): Polish journalist from Warsaw, lived in Kraków from 1893, one of the leading figures in the Polish women's movement, married to → Bujwid, Odon

Byron, George Gordon (1788–1824): British poet of the romantic movement, known as Lord Byron

Chopin, Frédéric (1810–1849): Fryderyk Chopin, Polish–French pianist and composer, born in Warsaw, died in Paris

Chrzanowska, Zofia: Originally Anna Dorota, changed her first name to Zofia, fought in the Defence of Trembowla in 1675 during the war between the Polish–Lithuanian Commonwealth and the Ottoman Empire (1672–1676)

Darwin, Charles (1809–1882): British naturalist, evolutionary theorist

Daszyńska-Golińska, Zofia (1866–1934): Polish economist, historian, eugenicist and socialist from Warsaw, studied in Zurich

De Hirsch, Maurice, Baron (1831–1896): Originally Moritz Freiherr von Hirsch auf Gereuth, entrepreneur and philanthropist, came from an ennobled Jewish family

De Saint-Simon, Henri (1760–1825): Originally Claude-Henri de Rouvroy, Comte de Saint-Simon, French sociologist and philosopher, founder of early-socialist Saint-Simonism

Drahomaniv-Kosač, Ol'ha: See → Pčilka, Olena

Drahomanov (Drahomaniv), Mychajlo (1841–1895): Ukrainian politician, historian, and philosopher, taught at Kiev university until forced into exile, developed approaches to rural socialism, brother of → Pčilka, Olena

Dučymins'ka, Ol'ha (1883–1988): Ruthenian writer, teacher, and feminist from Galicia

Dulębianka, Maria (1861–1919): Polish painter, writer and feminist from Kraków

Ellmann, Rozia: Leading representative of the Zionist movement from Romania

Empress Frederick: See → Victoria

Feldman, Wilhelm (1868–1919): Polish politician, journalist, writer and literary critic of Jewish origin from Galicia

Appendix of Names 253

Flama-Płomienski, Wilhelm: Professor of singing
Flaubert, Gustave (1821–1880): French writer
Fliedner, Theodor (1800–1864): Lutheran pastor and founder of deaconess training in Kaiserswerth
Fontane, Theodor (1819–1898): German writer and pharmacist
Fourier, Charles (1772–1837): French philosopher, early-socialist thinker, coined the term 'feminism'
Franko, Ivan Jankovyč (1856–1916): Ruthenian journalist and politician, wrote in Ruthenian, German and Polish, joined the Young Ruthenians, then co-founded the Ruthenian-Ukrainian Radical Party, later joined the national democrats, came from a village in Eastern Galicia
Frederick III (1831–1888): German Emperor and King of Prussia for fourteen weeks in 1888, from the House of Hohenzollern, husband of Empress → Victoria
Freud, Sigmund (1856–1939): Austrian neurologist, founder of psychoanalysis
Fröbel, Friedrich (1782–1852): German teacher, founder of the concept of kindergartens
Germain, Sophie (1776–1831): French mathematician, physicist and philosopher from Paris
Gogol, Nikolai (1809–1852): Writer from Eastern Ukraine
Haeckel, Ernst (1834–1919): German zoologist and philosopher, spread Darwinism in Germany
Hainisch, Marianne (1839–1936): Lived in Vienna, one of the leading representatives of the Austrian women's movement
Herschel, Caroline Lucretia (1750–1848): British-German astronomer from Hanover, discovered several comets
Herzl, Theodor (1860–1904): Jewish writer and journalist, born in Hungary, died in Austria, pioneer of political Zionism, founded *Die Welt* in 1897 as an organ of the Zionist movement, president of the World Zionist Organization until his death
Ibsen, Henrik (1828–1906): Norwegian writer whose play *A Doll's House* was particularly influential on women's movements
Jack the Ripper: Pseudonym of an unidentified serial killer who is thought to have murdered five prostitutes in London's East End in 1888
Jadwiga (1373/74–1399): Anjou Hedvig (Jadwiga Andegaweńska), queen of Poland, national saint, her marriage to → Jogaila, Grand Duke of Lithuania in 1386 established the Polish–Lithuanian Commonwealth
Jarošyns'ka, Jevhenija (1868–1904): Ruthenian teacher, writer and translator from Bukovina
Jogaila (1362–1434): Grand Duke of Lithuania, his marriage to → Jadwiga in 1386 established the Polish–Lithuanian Commonwealth, whereupon he was known as Władysław II Jagiełło, King of Poland
Joseph II (1741–1790): Holy Roman Emperor and King of Bohemia, Croatia and Hungary, introduced far-reaching reforms

254 Appendix of Names

Kellner, Leon (1859–1928): Jewish teacher and Zionist from Tarnów, Galicia, specialist in English lexicography and grammar, literary historian, founder of the Toynbee Hall in Vienna

Kobryns'kyj, Teofil' (1852–1882): Ruthenian seminary graduate and musician, married to Kobryns'ka

Kobyljans'ka, Ol'ha (1863–1942): Prominent Ruthenian feminist and writer from Bukovina

Konopnicka, Maria (1842–1910): Polish writer from northeast Poland, Podlasie, separated from her husband in 1877, worked as a writer and tutor, died in L'viv

Kosač-Kvitka, Larysa: See→ Ukraïns'ka, Lesja

Kościuszko, Tadeusz (1746–1817): Polish nobleman and general, led the 1794 uprising named after him against the partitioning powers the Habsburg Empire, the Russian Empire and Prussia

Krásnohorská, Eliška (1847–1926): Czech writer, translator and feminist from Prague

Kravčenko, Uljana (1860–1947): Ruthenian teacher, feminist and writer from Galicia

Kremer, Josef (1806–1875): Historian and philosopher, rector of the Jagiellonian University

Kuczalska-Reinschmit, Paulina (1859–1921): Journalist, activist in the Polish women's movement from Warsaw

Kulikowska, Kasylda (1841/44–1894): Polish teacher from Warsaw, campaigner for women's education

Kuliš, Pantelejmon (1819–1897): Ukrainian writer, journalist, and translator, married to → Barvinok, Hanna

Kysilevs'ka, Olena (1896–1956): Ruthenian writer, editor, and journalist, member of the Association of Ruthenian Women in Stanislav

Landau, Saul Raphael (1870–1943): Jewish lawyer, journalist and Zionist from Kraków, first editor-in-chief of the Zionist organ *Die Welt* founded by → Herzl, Theodor

Lange, Helene (1848–1930): Teacher from Oldenburg, one of the leading figures in the German women's movement alongside → Bäumer, Gertrud, founded a number of secondary schools for girls

Lassalle, Ferdinand (1825–1864): Jurist, philosopher and socialist, founded the General German Workers' Association (*Allgemeiner Deutscher Arbeiterverein*) in 1863

Limanowski, Bolesław (1835–1935): Polish historian, sociologist, and politician, member of the Polish Socialist Party

Longfellow, Henry Wadsworth (1807–1882): American poet and translator

Maeterlinck, Maurice (1862–1949): French-speaking writer from Belgium, winner of the Nobel Prize in Literature in 1911

Makovej, Osyp (1867–1925): Ruthenian writer, literary scholar, and translator from Galicia, publications include *Literaturno-naukovyj vistnyk*

Appendix of Names 255

Marx, Karl (1818–1883): German philosopher and economist, the main source of ideas for communist and socialist theories

Melzer, Isaak (died 1933): Official in the railway directorate in L'viv, Zionist, married to Pomeranz

Mickiewicz, Adam (1798–1855): Essayist, and activist, national poet and figurehead of Polish Romanticism

Mill, John Stuart (1806–1873): British philosopher and economist, one of the most influential liberal thinkers, known for his work *The Subjection of Women*

Montesquieu (1689–1755): Originally Charles de Secondat, Baron de Montesquieu, French writer and philosopher of the Enlightenment, formulated the idea of the separation of powers

Moraczewski, Wacław Demian (1876–1950): From Warsaw, studied medicine and chemistry in Zurich, appointed professor at the Academy of Veterinary Medicine in L'viv in 1921, married to → Okunevs'ka, Sofija

Moszczeńska, Iza (1864–1941): Journalist from Warsaw, active in the Polish national and women's movement

Nahirna, Maryja (died 1920): Ruthenian teacher from Galicia, ran a kindergarten with her husband

Napoleon Bonaparte (1769–1821): French general, First Consul of France, then Emperor Napoleon I of France, enacted a series of important legal reforms including in civil law, the Napoleonic Code

Nečuj-Levyc'kyj, Ivan (1838–1918): Ukrainian writer and translator

Nordau, Max (1849–1923): Jewish doctor, writer and co-founder of the World Zionist Organization, regarded as one of the pioneers of political Zionism

Nossig, Alfred (1864–1943): Jewish writer, journalist and artist from Kraków, originally supported assimilation but later became a convinced Zionist

O., Anna: See → Pappenheim, Bertha

Ohonovs'kyj, Omeljan (1833–1894): Ruthenian writer and journalist, professor of Ruthenian language and literature at L'viv university

Okunevs'ka, Sofija (1865–1926): Studied in Zurich, first female doctor in Galicia, came from Bukovina, cousin of Kobryns'ka, married to → Moraczewski, Wacław

Okunevs'ka, Teofilja: Mother of Kobryns'ka, married to → Ozarkevyč, Ivan

Okunevs'kyi, Teofil' (1858–1937): Politician and jurist in Galicia, co-founder of the Ruthenian-Ukrainian Radical Party, deputy in the Imperial Council and the Galician *Sejm,* related to Kobryns'ka

Orkan, Władysław (1875–1930): Originally Smaciarz, Franciszek Xawery, later Smreczyński, Polish writer with a rural background

Orzeszkowa, Eliza (1842–1910): Polish writer from the Eastern Borderlands, representative of Warsaw positivism, spent many years in Grodno

256 Appendix of Names

Owen, Robert (1771–1858): Social reformer and founding father of early socialism and the cooperative movement

Ozarkevyč, Ivan (1826–1903): Ruthenian pastor and politician, member of the Imperial Council, father of Kobryns'ka

Ozarkevyč, Volodymyr (1853–1922): Ruthenian priest and politician, married to → Roškevyč, Ol'ha, brother of Kobryns'ka

Pappenheim, Bertha (1859–1936): Jewish women's rights activist and writer from Vienna, patient (Anna O.) of Josef Breuer and → Freud, Sigmund, lived from 1888 in Frankfurt am Main where she ran social work projects and founded the Jewish Women's Association, travelled through Galicia with → Rabinowitsch, Sarah

Pavlyk, Anna (1855–1928): Ruthenian writer, socialist and feminist, convicted in the L'viv socialists' trial alongside her brother → Pavlyk, Mychajlo, → Franko, Ivan and → Terlec'kyj, Ostap

Pavlyk, Mychajlo (1853–1915): Ruthenian writer, journalist and politician, member of the Ruthenian-Ukrainian Radical Party, brother of → Pavlyk, Anna

Pčilka, Olena (1849–1930): Originally Drahomaniv-Kosač, Ol'ha, Ukrainian journalist, writer, translator and ethnologist, sister of → Drahomanov, Mychajlo, mother of → Ukraïnka, Lesja

Perl, Josef (1773–1839): Jewish writer from Galicia, campaigned for enlightenment and reform

Plater, Emilia (1806–1831): Polish aristocrat from Lithuania, fought in the Polish November Uprising in 1830/31

Pomeranz, M.: Zionist activist, delegate of the executive of the World Zionist Organization

Potocki, Andrzej Graf (1861–1908): Governor of Galicia, Polish politician, murdered by Ruthenian nationalist Miroslav Sičyns'kyj

Rabinovich, Shaul Pinhas (1845–1910), also Rabinovitsh/Rabinovich, Pinkhas: Hebrew writer from the Russian Empire, probably father of → Rabinowitsch, Sarah

Rabinovitsh, Sarah: See → Rabinowitsch, Sarah

Rabinowitsch, Dr Sarah (1880–1918), also Rabinovich/Rabinovitsh: Jewish economist and sociologist from the Russian Empire, studied to doctorate level in Germany, travelled to Galicia with → Pappenheim, Bertha in 1903, thought to be the daughter of → Rabinovich, Shaul, dates of life are may be mixed up with another Rabinovitsh

Radlińska, Helena (1879–1954): Polish teacher from Warsaw, campaigner in the educational movement

Řehoř, František (1857–1899): Czech ethnographer

Renan, Ernest (1823–1892): French philosopher and writer

Romančuk, Juljan (1842–1932): Ruthenian politician in Galicia, co-founder of the educational association Enlightenment, co-initiator of Ruthenian–Polish rapprochement

Rosenheck, Dr.: Zionist activist

Roškevyč, Ol'ha (1857–1935): Ruthenian translator from Galicia, and lover of → Franko, Ivan, married to → Ozarkevyč, Voloymyr

Rothfeld, Flora (1877–1942): Zionist, travelled through Europe with Pomeranz after the First World War, in the Second World War deported and murdered

Salomon, Alice (1872–1948): One of the best-known German representatives of social work activists and founder of the Social Women's School in Berlin

Schach, Mirjam (1867–1956): Feminist and Zionist from Lithuania, emigrated to first the German Empire and then France, delegate at several Zionist congresses

Schapira, Professor: Campaigned for women's policy at the Zionist World Congress, probably married to Jewish mathematics professor Hermann Schapira (1840–1898) who was also active in the World Zionist Organization

Sczaniecka, Emilia (1804–1896): Polish patriot and feminist, took part in the 1830/31 Uprising, devoted herself to people's education

Siedlecka, Maria (1856–1942): Polish journalist, active in the women's, education and peasant movements

Sienkiewicz, Henryk (1846–1916): Polish writer and Nobel laureate in literature

Smaciarz, Franciszek Xawery: See → Orkan, Władyslaw

Smaciarz, Katarzyna, née Smreczak (1846–1936): Published under Smreczyńska, of rural origin, mother of → Orkan, Władysław

Smreczyńska: See → Smaciarz, Katarzyna

Smreczyński: See → Orkan, Władyslaw

Sokolová-Seidlová, Vilma (1859–1941): Activist in the Czech women's movement, writer

Sommerstein, Emil (1883–1957): Jewish lawyer, philosopher and deputy in the Polish *Sejm*

Stapiński, Jan (1876–1946): Polish journalist from the Carpathian foothills, activist in the peasant movement, co-founder of the Polish Peasant Party

Šuchevyč, Mykola (1862–1942): Ruthenian lawyer

Světlá, Karolína (1830–1899): Czech writer from Prague, activist in the women's and national movements

Szczepanowski, Stanisław (1846–1900): Polish liberal, petroleum industrialist, deputy in the Galician *Sejm*, known for *Nędza Galicji w Cyfrach*

Tańska-Hoffmanowa, Klementyna (1789–1845): Polish writer and teacher from Warsaw, published on the woman question and patriotic education, co-founder of an institute for women's higher education

258 Appendix of Names

Taubes, Löbel (1863–1933): Zionist, from Bessarabia, published the first Yiddish-language newspaper in Galicia *Di Yidishe Folkstsaytung*

Terlec'kyj, Ostap (1850–1902): Ruthenian philologist, co-founder of the Ruthenian student organization The Cossack Camp, active in the Ruthenian-Ukrainian Radical Party, convicted in the L'viv socialists' trial alongside the → Pavlyk siblings and → Franko, Ivan

Tisch, J.: Published in *Wschód*

Tolstoy, Lev (1828–1910): Russian writer and social reformer

Toynbee, Arnold (1852–1883): British philanthropist, economist and cultural theorist

Turgenev, Ivan (1818–1883): Russian writer and translator

Ukraïnka, Lesja (1871–1913): Originally Larysa Kosač-Kvitka, from Eastern Ukraine, one of the most famous Ukrainian poets, daughter of → Pčilka, Olena

Van Beethoven, Ludwig (1770–1827): Famous composer and pianist

Victoria (1840–1901): German Empress, daughter of Queen Victoria of the United Kingdom and Prince Albert of Saxe-Coburg and Gotha, married to → Frederick III, often called Empress Frederick

Walewska, Cecylja (1859–1940): Polish writer, journalist, activist in the women's movement

Wantuła, Jan (1877–1953): Polish journalist in the peasant movement, from Cieszyn Silesia

Wechslerowa, Stefania: Polish teacher and women's rights activist, chair of the Women's Reading Room in L'viv

Weininger, Otto (1880–1903): Philosopher of Jewish origin, famous for his controversial work *Sex and Character*

Werhyo, Maria (1858–1944): Polish teacher and author

Wolffsohn, David (1856–1914): Merchant in Cologne, originally from the Eastern Borderlands, president of the World Zionist Organization

Wolfsthal, C.: Activist in the Zionist movement

Wysłouch, Bolesław (1855–1937): Polish politician, activist in the peasant movement, co-founder of the Peasant Party, married to Wysłouchowa

Wyspiański, Stanisław (1869–1907): Polish artist from Kraków, also wrote several plays including *Wesele*

Zweig, Stefan (1881–1942): Austrian writer and journalist

Bibliography

Manuscripts and Archival Documents

Archiv der Hochschule für Musik und Theater "Felix Mendelssohn Bartholdy", Leipzig

A, I. 1, 5586.
A, I. 2, 5586.
A, I. 3, 5586.

Archiwum Odon Bujwid, Kraków

Bujwidowa, Kazimiera, *O postępowym i niepostępowym ruchu kobiecym w Galicji: Przedruk z "Kurjera Lwowskiego."* L'viv 1913 [MS].

Biblioteka Jagiellońska, Kraków

Franciszek Smreczyński (Władysław Orkan), korespondencja:

10465/III, part I: listy wysyłane, do druku przygotował Stanisław Pigoń, kopie maszynowe brulionów listów z lat 1893–1930, vol. 3: 1904–1910.
10471/III, part II: listy odbierane, do druku przygotował Stanisław Pigoń, kopie maszynowe listów z lat 1897–1930, vol. 1: 1897–1899.
10472, part II: listy odbierane, do druku przygotował Stanisław Pigoń, kopie maszynowe listów z lat 1897–1930, vol. 2: 1900–1903.
10473, part II: listy odbierane, do druku przygotował Stanisław Pigoń, kopie maszynowe listów z lat 1897–1930, vol. 3: 1904–1910.

Biblioteka Narodowa, Warsaw

7601, Korespondencja Jana Wantuły, vol. VI: Maria Wysłouchowa do Jana Wantuły, 1901–1905.

Biblioteka Ossolineum, Wrocław

Papiery Bolesława i Marii Wysłouchów:

7185/II, korespondencja Bolesława Wysłoucha, 1787–1937, listy od różnych osób: Wysłouchowa Maria, 1884–1903 and n.d.

7187/II, korespondencja Marii Wysłouchowej, 1895-1903, listy od różnych osób:
———. Bouffałowa Zofia (matka M. W.), 1892-1914 and n.d.
———. Czytelnia dla kobiet w Krakowie, n.d., Bujwidowa Kaz., 1900.
7188/II, korespondencja Marii Wysłouchowej, 1881-1905, listy od różnych osób:
———. Komitet Wiecu Kobiet w Krakowie, 1900.
———. Komitet Redakcyjny "Przodownicy" w Krakowie, 1900.
———. Kółko Roln. w Istebnej, 1898-1901.
———. Kobryńska Natalia, 1901.
7189/II, korespondencja Marii Wysłouchowej, 1891-1904, listy od różnych osób:
———. Reinschmitt-Kuczalska Paulina, 1892 and n.d.
7190/II, korespondencja Marii Wysłouchowej, 1890-1904, listy od różnych osób:
———. Tow. Uniwersytetu ludowego im. Adama Mickiewicza w Krakowie 1900.
———. Wysłouch Bolesław, 1898 and n.d.
7191/II, listy różnych osób i instytucyi do redakcji "Kuriera Lwowskiego," 1887-1919:
———. Czytelnia dla Kobiet w Krakowie, 1897 and n.d.
7193/II, listy różnych osób do "Przyjaciela Ludu" i do "Zorzy," 1892-1911, II: listy do "Zorzy":
———. Broda Jan, 1901.
———. Boner Władysław, n.d.
———. Baron Karol, 1902.
12009/II, Korespondencja Walerego i Stanisława Eliaszów Radzikowskich, 1859-1914, listy do Walerego Eliasza:
———. Wysłouchowa Maria, 1898-1900 and n. d.
12295/III, Autografy różnych osób, 1698-1951:
———. Orkan Wadysław.
———. Wysłouchowa Maria, 1900.

Central Zionist Archives, Jerusalem

Z2/191, Protokoll über die Wahl der Delegierten zum Zehnten Zionistenkongreß, Landesorganisation Galizien 1911.
Z3/813.

Central'nyj Deržavnyj Istoryčnyj Archiv u L'vovi

f. 381, 1, 3, Vesolovs'kyj Jaroslav—žurnalist, 1902-1912.

Instytut literatury im. T. H. Ševčenka nacional'na akademija nauk Ukraïny, Kiev

f. 3, Franko, I. Ja., lysty do Ivana Franka, 1603; 1608; 1618; 1631.
f. 3, Franko, I. Ja., 3366, Kobryns'ka Natalja, Prohrama tovarystva rus'kych ženščyn.

f. 13, Kobryns'ka N. I., lysty N. Kobryns'koï do O. Kuliš (Hanny Barvinok).
f. 14, Kobyljans'ka O. Ju, lysty do O. Kobyljans'koï, 1887–1899.
f. 19, Barvinok Hanna, lysty N. Kobryns'koï do O. M. Kuliš (Hanny Barvinok).
f. 100, Belej I. M., 1801, Kobryns'ka, N. I., Lysty do red. hazetu "Dilo."
f. 101, Pavlyk M. I., lysty Kobryns'koï N. do Jarošyns'koï Je., 1891–1904.

L'vivs'ka nacional'na naukova biblioteka Ukraïny imeni V. Stefanyka

f. NTŠ, 475/III, Natalja Kobryns'ka, Avtobiohrafija.
f. NTŠ, 824, lysty do Šuchevyča Mykola, 1891.

Památník národního písemnictví, Prague

f. Sokolová-Seidlová Vilma 33/40, Kobrinská Natalija [to] Sokolové-Seidlové Vilmě, 1891–1911.
f. Sokolová-Seidlová Vilma 33/44, Wyslouchowa Marja [to] Sokolové-Seidlové Vilmé, 1891–1904.

Polska Akademia Nauk, Instytut literacki, Warsaw

800, listy Marii Wysłouchowej do Elizy Orzeszkowej.

Polska Akademia Nauk, Kraków

4527, fragment korespondencyj Marii Wysłouchowej, 1890–1900, listy od Orzeszkowej Elizy, 1890–1893.
5591, listy różnych osób do różnych adresatów, 1713–1912, Eliza Orzeszkowa do Marii Wysłouchwej, 1897–1898.

Contemporary Literature

Aus der Bewegung: Berichte: Bielitz. 1903. *Die Welt* VII (14): 11.
———. Berichte: Podwoloczyska. 1902. *Die Welt* VI (41): 13.
———. Galizien: Brody. 1909. *Die Welt* VIII (44): 965.
———. Makkabäerfeiern: Brody. 1904. *Die Welt* VIII (53): 12.
———. Österreich: Drohobycz. 1913. *Die Welt* XVII (19): 601.
———. Tarnopol. 1903. *Die Welt* VII (12): 13; (17): 11.
Baer-Issachar, Marta. 1905. "An unsere Frauen." *Die Stimme der Wahrheit: Jahrbuch für wissenschaftlichen Zionismus* 1:334–35.
Bäumer, Gertrud. 1901. "Geschichte der Frauenbewegung in Deutschland." In *Handbuch der Frauenbewegung*, edited by Helene Lange and Gertrud Bäumer. Vol. 1, 1–166. Berlin: Moeser.
Berichte: Brody. 1904. *Die Welt* VIII (8): 7.
———. Kolomea. 1900; 1901. *Die Welt* IV (16): 12; V (16): 12.
———. Krakau. 1903. *Die Welt* VII (27): 20; (44): 12.
———. Podwoloczyska. 1902. *Die Welt* VI (41): 3
———. Tarnopol. 1905. *Die Welt* VIII (5): 11.
Body, N. O. (1907) 1993. *Aus eines Mannes Mädchenjahren*. Reprint Berlin: Edition Hentrich.

———. 2005. *Memoirs of a Man's Maiden Years*, translated by Deborah Simon. Philadelphia: University of Pennsylvania Press. (German original 1907).
"Bohaterskie dzieci." 1901. *Zorza* II (12): 190.
Brodacki, Grzegorz, ed. 1993. "Listy Władysława Orkana do Marii Wysłouchowej w zbiorach biblioteki zakładu narodowego im. Ossolińskich." *Czasopismo Zakładu Narodowego im. Ossolińskich* 3:87–144.
Bryll, Irena. 1978. "Listy Marii Wysłouchowej do Jana Wantuły z lat 1901–1904." *Kwartalnik Opolski* 24:81–93.
———. 1978. "Listy ze Śląska do Marii Wysłouchowej z lat 1884–1906." *Kwartalnik Opolski* 24 (3): 56–101; (4): 82–101.
Büchereinkauf. 1898. *Die Welt* II (51): 14.
Bücherwelt: Rosa Pomeranz. *An die jüdischen Frauen! Ein Appell zur Umkehr.* Tarnopol: Verlag des Vereines "Ahawath Zion." 1899. *Die Welt* III (1): 13.
Buchstab Awi-Jonah, Thamar. 1936. "Pamięci wielkiego człowieka." In *Pamięci Róży Melzerowej*, [edited by Sabina Feuersteinowa, Berta Jegerowa, and Henryka Schreiberowa], 15–19. L'viv: printed by Koło Kobiet Żydowskich.
Buckle, Henry T. 1864. *History of the Civilization in England*. London: Longmans Green.
Bujwidowa, Kazimierza.1903. *Domy ludowe (Przedruk z N-ru I-ego "Krytyki" 1903)*. Kraków: Wydawnictwo "Krytyka."
Bujwidowa, K[azimiera]. 1903. Przedmowa to *Głos kobiet w kwestyi kobiecej*, V–VII. Kraków: printed by Stowarzyszenie Pomocy Naukowej dla Polek imienia J. I. Kraszewskiego.
Chołoniewski, Antoni. 1898. *Nieśmiertelni. Fotografie Literatów Lwowskich*. L'viv.
Czytelnia dla kobiet w Krakowie, ed. 1906. *Sprawozdanie wydziału towarzystwa za r. 1905*. Kraków. Printed by Czytelnia dla kobiet w Krakowie.
D. S. 1901. "Jüdische Toynbee-Halle in Lemberg." *Die Welt* V (44): 12.
Dalecka, Wanda, Zygmunt Fryling, Feliks Gwiżdż, Franciszek Jaworski, Bronisław Laskownicki, Zygmunt Poznański, and Władyław Wąsowicz, eds. 1905. *Marja Wysłouchowa: Wspomnienie pozgonne*. L'viv: no pub.
Daszyńska-Golińska, Zofja. 1913. "Domy ludowe." *Praca oświadowa, jej zadania, metody, organizacja: Podręcznik opracowany starannie uniwersytetu ludowego im. A. Mickiewicza*, 371–83. Kraków: Wydawnictwo Michała Arcta w Warszawie.
"Delegiertenmandate." 1913. *Die Welt* XVII (23): 733–34; (25): 802–03
"Der X. Kongreß." 1911. *Die Welt* XV (29): 686–87.
"Der X. Zionisten-Kongress. Präsenz-Liste" 1911. *Die Welt* XV (32): 799–800.
Di yidishe froyenvelt. 1902 (1).
"Die IX. Landeskonferenz der galizischen Zionisten." 1910. *Die Welt* XIV (14): 312–14.
Die zionistische Bewegung: Kolomea. 1899. *Die Welt* III (10): 12–13; (13): 13.
Die zionistische Bewegung: Wien. 1898. *Die Welt* II (46): 12.
Dr. K. 1901. "Die Fragen der körperlichen, geistigen und wirtschaftlichen Hebung der Juden." *Die Welt* V (4): 8–9.
Drohobycz. 1901. *Die Welt* V (4): 14.
Dučymins'ka, Ol'ha. 1934. *Natalija Kobryns'ka jak feministka*, Kolomyja: no pub.
Dvě populární přednášky z cyklu ve prospěch "Minervy" spolku pro ženské studium v Praze, který pořádal spolek českých učitelek u Praze v letnu a

únoru 1891 ve velké dvoraně měšťanské besedy. 1891. Prague: printed by Minerva. Accessed November 27, 2019. www.literature.at/viewer. alo?objid=11487&page=1&viewmode=fullscreen.

"Dzieci polskie." 1902. *Zorza* III (2): 29.

E. F. Wz. 1903. "Lemberger Toynbee-Hall." *Die Welt* VII (6): 7.

"Eine Versammlung jüdischer Frauen in Lemberg." 1914. *Die Welt* XVIII (9): 223–24.

Emes [Julius Uprimny]. 1901. "Zwei jüdische Romane." *Die Welt* V (23): 8.

Estermann, L. 1910. "Ost und West im Zionismus." *Die Welt* XIV (11): 235–36.

F. 1904. "Oesterreichisch-zionistische Landeskonferenz." *Die Welt* VIII (26): 5–6.

[Feuersteinowa, Sabina, Berta Jegerowa, and Henryka Schreiberowa, eds.] 1936. *Pamięci Róży Melzerowej*. L'viv: printed by Koło Kobiet Żydowskich.

Franko, Ivan. 1957. *Boa Constrictor and Other Stories*, translated by Fainna Solasko. Moscow: Foreign Language Public House.

Franzos, Karl E. 1876. *Aus Halb-Asien: Culturbilder aus Galizien, der Bukowina, Südrußland und Rumänien*. 2 vols. Leipzig: Duncker & Humblot.

———. 1877; 1878. *Vom Don zur Donau: Neue Kulturbilder aus Halb-Asien*. 2 vols. Leipzig: Duncker & Humblot.

Frostig, Mojżesz. 1910. "Nędza Żydów galicyjskich i plan akcyi, zmierzającej do poprawy ekonomicznych stosunków Żydostwa galicyjskiego." In *Almanach Żydowski*, edited by Leon Reich, 174–87. L'viv: Juffy.

"Galizien: Zionistische Kulturarbeit." 1909. *Die Welt* XIII (44): 968.

Gliksman, Ignacy. 1923. *Domy ludowe: Ich organizacja i znaczenie dla rozwoju kultury narodowej*. Warsaw: Nakładem "Przewodnika Ubezpieczniowego".

Głos kobiet w kwestyi kobiecej. 1903. Kraków: printed by Stowarzyszenie Pomocy Naukowej dla Polek imienia J. I. Kraszewskiego.

Gutmann, Elise. 1906. "Das jüdische Weib." *Jüdische Rundschau* XI (2): 11–14.

Hainisch, Marianne. 1930. Geleitwort to *Frauenbewegung, Frauenbildung und Frauenarbeit in Österreich*, edited by Martha Stephanie Braun, Ernestine Fürst, Marianne Hönig, Grete Laube, Bertha List-Ganser, and Carla Zaglits, 7. Vienna: printed by Bund österreichischer Frauenvereine.

———. 1930. "Zur Geschichte der österreichischen Frauenbewegung: Aus meinen Erinnerungen." In *Frauenbewegung, Frauenbildung und Frauenarbeit in Österreich*, edited by Martha Stephanie Braun, Ernestine Fürst, Marianne Hönig, Grete Laube, Bertha List-Ganser, and Carla Zaglits, 13–24. Vienna: printed by Bund österreichischer Frauenvereine.

Hoffmann, Camill. 1902/03. "Im Lande der Not: Von Rosa Pomeranz." *Das litterarische Echo* 5: col. 209.

"Jej życiorys." 1936. In *Pamięci Róży Melzerowej*, [edited by Sabina Feuersteinowa, Berta Jegerowa, and Henryka Schreiberowa], 3–10. L'viv: printed by Koło Kobiet Żydowskich.

"Jubileusz Sienkiewicza." 1901. *Zorza* II (1): 2–9.

"Jüdische Toynbee-Halle in Drohobycz." 1901. *Die Welt* V (6): 12.

[Kobryns'ka, Franciška, Natalija Kobryns'ka, N. N., and Germina Šuchevyčeva]. 1895. "Ruch žinočych tovarystv." In *Naša dolja: Zbirnyk prac' riznych avtoriv*, [edited by Natalja Kobryns'ka], 85–96. L'viv: no pub.

Kobryns'ka, Natalija. 1890. "Na przebój." In *Dla głodnych: Pismo zbiorowe z utworów kobiecego pióra*, 36–38. L'viv: printed by Towarzystwo Oszczędności Kobiet.

———. 1893. "Žinoča sprava v Halyčyni." In *Naša dolja: Zbirnyk prac' riznych avtoriv*, [edited by Natalja Kobryns'ka], 1–35. Stryj: no pub.

———. 1895. "Slivce pro peršyj vypusk 'Žinočoï dolï.'" In *Naša dolja: Zbirnyk prac' riznych avtoriv*, [edited by Natalja Kobryns'ka], 97–106. L'viv: no pub.

———. 1895, 1896. "Stremlïnja žinočoho ruchu." In *Naša dolja: Zbirnyk prac' riznych avtoriv*, [edited by Natalja Kobryns'ka], 3–17; 1–16. L'viv: no pub.

———. 1896. "Feleton." In *Naša dolja: Zbirnyk prac' riznych avtoriv*, [edited by Natalja Kobryns'ka], 116–37. L'viv : no pub.

———. 1897. "Zhadka pro Kuliša." *Zorja* XVIII (22): 438.

———. (1893) 1958. "Avtobiohrafija N. Kobryns'koï." In *Vybrani tvory*, edited by Oleg N. Moroz, 373–80. Kiev: Deržavne Vydavnictvo Chudožn'oï Literatury.

———. (1899) 1958. "Duch času." In *Vybrani tvory*, edited by Oleg N. Moroz, 31–44. Kiev: Deržavne Vydavnictvo Chudožn'oï Literatury.

———. (1893) 1958. "Jadzja i Katrusja." In *Vybrani tvory*, edited by Oleg N. Moroz, 126–86. Kiev: Deržavne Vydavnictvo Chudožn'oï Literatury.

———. (1884) 1958. "Zadlja kusynka chliba." *Vybrani tvory*, edited by Oleg N. Moroz, 45–76. Kiev: Deržavne Vydavnictvo Chudožn'oï Literatury.

———. (1900) 1958. "Perša včytel'ka." In *Vybrani tvory*, edited by Oleg N. Moroz, 200–15. Kiev: Deržavne Vydavnictvo Chudožn'oï Literatury.

———. 1958. *Vybrani tvory*, edited by Oleg N. Moroz. Kiev: Deržavne Vydavnictvo Chudožn'oï Literatury.

———. 1980. *Vybrani tvory*, edited by I. O. Denysjuk and K. A. Kril'. Kiev: Deržavne Vydavnictvo Chudožn'oï Literatury.

———. (1887) 1984. "Pan Suddja: Obrazok z žyttja." In *Peršyj vinok: Žinočyj al'manach*, edited by Natalija Kobryns'ka and Olena Pčilka, 376–94. L'viv: Drukarnja im. T. Ševčenka. Reprint New York: Zoroz Ukraïnok Ameryky.

———. (1887) 1984. "Pro pervisnu cil' tovarystva rus'kych žinok u Stanislavovi." In *Peršyj vinok: Žinočyj al'manach*, edited by Natalija Kobryns'ka and Olena Pčilka, 457–62. L'viv: Drukarnja im. T. Ševčenka. Reprint New York: Zoroz Ukraïnok Ameryky.

———. (1887) 1984. "Pro ruch žinočyj v novijšych časach." In *Peršyj vinok: Žinočyj al'manach*, edited by Natalija Kobryns'ka and Olena Pčilka, 5–23. L'viv: Drukarnja im. T. Ševčenka. Reprint New York: Zoroz Ukraïnok Ameryky.

———. (1887) 1984. "Rus'ke žinoctvo v Halyčyni v našych časach." In *Peršyj vinok: Žinočyj al'manach*, edited by Natalija Kobryns'ka and Olena Pčilka, 68–102. L'viv: Drukarnja im. T. Ševčenka. Reprint New York: Zoroz Ukraïnok Ameryky.

———. (1887) 1984. "Pani Šumins'ka (Obrazok z žyttja)." In *Peršyj vinok: Žinočyj al'manach*, edited by Natalija Kobryns'ka and Olena Pčilka, 177–95. L'viv: Drukarnja im. T. Ševčenka. Reprint New York: Zoroz Ukraïnok Ameryky.

———. 1990. *Duch času: Opovidannja, povist'*, edited by O. M. Kozakevyč. L'viv: "Kamenjar."

Kobryns'ka, Natalija z Ozarkevyč. 1899. *Duch času: Opovidannja*. L'viv: Vydavnyctvo Spilky.

[Kobryns'ka, Natalija and Jevhenija Jarošyns'ka]. 1892. "Žinočyj Al'manach." *Zorja* XIII (14): 279.

Kobryns'ka, Natalija and Olena Pčilka, eds. (1887) 1984. *Peršyj vinok: Žinočyj al'manach.* L'viv: Drukarnja im. T. Ševčenka. Reprint New York: Zoroz Ukraïnok Ameryky.

Kobrynska, Nataliya. 1998. "For a Crust of Bread." In Nataliya Kobrynska, Olena Pchilka, Lyubov Yanovska, Olha Kobylianska, Yevheniya Yaroshynska, Hrytsko Hryhorenko, and Lesya Ukrainka. *For a Crust of Bread: Selected Prose Fiction,* translated by Roma Franko, edited by Sonia Morris, 36–68, Saskatoon: Language Lanterns Publications. (Ukrainian original 1884).

——. 1998. "The Judge." In Nataliya Kobrynska and Olena Pchilka. *The Spirit of the Times: Selected Prose Fiction,* translated by Roma Franko, edited by Sonia Morris, 254–69. Saskatoon: Language Lanterns Publications. (Ukrainian Original 1887).

——. 1998. "The Spirit of the Times." In Nataliya Kobrynska and Olena Pchilka. *The Spirit of the Times: Selected Prose Fiction,* translated by Roma Franko, edited by Sonia Morris, 238–53, Saskatoon: Language Lanterns Publications. (Ukrainian Original 1887).

——. 1998. "Yadzya and Katrusya." In Nataliya Kobrynska and Olena Pchilka. *The Spirit of the Times: Selected Prose Fiction,* translated by Roma Franko, edited by Sonia Morris, 310–81. Saskatoon: Language Lanterns Publications. (Ukrainian original 1893).

Kobryns'ka, Natalja. 1884. "Zadlja kusynka chliba." *Zorja* V (20): 161–65; (21): 173–74; (22): 181–85.

——. 1890. "Petition der ruthenischen Frauen aus Galizien und Bukowina um Zulassung der Frauen zu den Universitätsstudien und Creirung wenigstens eines weiblichen Gymnasiums in Galizien." *Stenographische Protokolle: Haus der Abgeordneten, 405. Sitzung der X. Session am 8. Mai 1890,* 15269–70; 15230–31. Accessed November 27, 2019. http://alex.onb.ac.at/cgi-content/anno-plus?apm=0&aid=spa&datum=00100003&zoom=2&seite=00015269&x=13&y=14.

——. 1891. "Spomyny z prohul'ky do Prahu." *Zorja* XI (22): 438–39; (23): 455–56; (24): 477–78.

——. 1893. "Jadzja i Katrusja." *Zorja* XIV (1): 1–4; (2): 21–26; (3): 41–48; (4): 61–63; (6): 105–07.

——. 1901. *Promova Nataliï Kobryns'koï na zahal'nych zborach ruskoï ochoronky.* L'viv: printed by Tovarystvo ruska ochoronka.

[Kobryns'ka, Natalja, ed.] 1893, 1895, 1896. *Naša dolja: Zbirnyk prac' riznych avtoriv.* Stryj, L'viv: no pub.

Kobyljans'ka, Ol'ha and N[atalja] K[obryns'ka]. 1893. "Zvistky z zahranyci i kraju." In *Naša dolja: Zbirnyk prac' riznych avtoriv,* [edited by Natalja Kobryns'ka], 79–92. Stryj.

Komitet redakcyjny. 1899. "Do sióstr z pod wiejskiej strzechy." *Przodownica* I (1): 1–2.

"Konstituierung des zionistischen Arbeitskomitees." 1910. *Die Welt* XIV (6): 124–25.

Korenec', Ol'ha. 1930. "Natalija Kobryns'ka." *Literaturno-naukovyj vistnyk* XXIX:523–32.

Korespondencye: Stanisławów. 1903. *Wschód* IV (106): 8.

Kosmowska, I. W. 1918. *Domy ludowe u obcych i u nas.* Lublin: Wydawnictwo Michała Arcta w Warszawie.

"Krajowa konferencya syonistów galicyjskich we Lwowie dnia 16 i 17 czerwca 1901 roku (Oryginalne sprawozdanie)." 1901. *Wschód* II (35): 3–8.
Kremer, Josef. 1843. *Listy z Krakowa.* Kraków.
Kronika. 1897. *Przyszłość* V (10): 70.
———. 1900. *Zorza* I (2): 29–30.
———. [B.], Stanisławów w grudniu 1902. 1902. *Wschód* III (114): 11.
———. [E. Weintraub], Rzeszów. 1903. *Wschód* III (135): 13–14.
———. Kołomyja. 1901. *Wschód* I (59): 9.
———. Kongres dla zwalczania handlu dziewczętami. 1903. *Wschód* IV (151): 7–8.
———. Kraków. 1903. *Wschód* IV (157): 7.
———. Lwów. 1901. *Wschód* I (59): 8.
———. Stryj. 1901. *Wschód* I (59): 9.
———. Tarnopol. 1903. *Wschód* IV (135): 13.
———. Tarnów. 1903. *Wschód* IV (159): 6.
Kuczalska-Reinschmit, P[aulina]. 1903. "Z historyi ruchu kobiecego." In *Głos kobiet w kwestyi kobiecej*, 232–341. Kraków: printed by Stowarzyszenie Pomocy Naukowej dla Polek imienia J. I. Kraszewskiego.
"Landesconferenz der galizischen Zionisten in Lemberg (16. und 17. Juni 1901)." 1901. *Die Welt* V (25): 2–6.
Lange, Helene, Vorwort to *Handbuch der Frauenbewegung*, edited by Helene Lange and Gertrud Bäumer. Vol. 1, V–X. Berlin: Moeser.
Lange, Helene and Gertrud Bäumer, eds. 1901–1906. *Handbuch der Frauenbewegung.* Vol. 1–5. Berlin: Moeser.
Listy do "Zorzy": [Józefa Jarorzówna]. 1900. *Zorza* I (4): 62–63.
Litterarisches. 1901. *Israelitische Rundschau: Centralblatt für die jüdischen Vereine* VI (39): 4–5.
M. 1899. "Pierwszy zjazd kobiet polskich." *Nowa Reforma* XVIII (188): 2–3; (189): 3–4; (190): 1–2; (192): 1–2.
———. 1900. "Rady gospodarskie." *Zorza* I (1): 15.
Makkabäer-Feiern: Stanislau. 1899. *Die Welt* III (51): 12.
Mayer, Ottilie. 1930. "Der Kindergarten." In *Frauenbewegung, Frauenbildung und Frauenarbeit in Österreich*, edited by Martha Stephanie Braun, Ernestine Fürst, Marianne Hönig, Grete Laube, Bertha List-Ganser, and Carla Zaglits, 107–12. Vienna: printed by Bund österreichischer Frauenvereine.
Melcerowa, Róża. 1928. "Jeszcze o kontroli urodzeń." *Ewa* I (10): 2.
———. 1930. "Dlaczego milczą kobiety? (W kwestji populacyjnej)." *Ewa* III (52): 2.
———. 1930. "Uświadomienie." *Ewa* III (18): 1.
———. 1931. "Jak to zrobić?" *Ewa* IV (49): 2.
———. Róża. 1931. "Kobieta przyszłości." *Ewa* IV (37): 2.
———. 1931. "Niezgoda między kobietami (dalszy ciąg dyskusji o istocie nowoczesnego feminismu)." *Ewa* IV (23).
———. 1932. "Miłość dawnej i dziś. (Przeciw reformie obyczajowej) (Ciąg dalszy dyskusji)." *Ewa* V (28): 1, 6.
———. 1932. "Pani w Hull-House." *Ewa* V (4): 2.
Melzer, Rosa. 1910. "Nationale Pflichten der jüdischen Frau." *Die Welt* XIV (39): 937–38.

Mill, John S. 1869. *The Subjection of Women*. London: Longmans, Green, Reader & Dyer.

Moszczeńska, I[za]. 1901. "Die Geschichte der Frauenbewegung in Polen." *Handbuch der Frauenbewegung*, edited by Helene Lange and Gertrud Bäumer. Vol. 1, 350–60. Berlin: Moeser.

———. 1903. "Mężczyzna i kobieta." In *Głos kobiet w kwestyi kobiecej*. 121–42. Kraków: printed by Stowarzyszenie Pomocy Naukowej dla Polek imienia J. I. Kraszewskiego.

Nacht, Albert. 1910. "Ost- und Westzionismus." *Die Welt* XIV (13): 280–82.

Nahirna, Maryja. 1895. "Ochoronky." In *Naša dolja: Zbirnyk prac' riznych avtoriv*, [edited by Natalja Kobryns'ka], 51–54. L'viv: no pub.

Nordau, Max. 1910. "Über den Gegensatz zwischen Ost und West im Zionismus." *Die Welt* XIV (11): 231–32.

"O mowę ojczystą." 1902. *Zorza* III (3): 47.

Obchody Machabeuszowskie: [Israeil Halevi], Tarnopol. 1895. *Przyszłość* III (6): 44–45.

———. Korespondencya: Lwów. 1895. *Przyszłość* III (6): 43.

Ochs, Saul. 1934. "Rosa Pomeranz-Melzer." *Jüdische Rundschau* XXXIX (86): 14.

Ohonovskij, Om[eljan]. 1893. "Natalja Kobryn'ska." In Ystorija literaturŷ ruskoy. *Zorja* XIV (4): 75–78; (7): 137–39; (8): 155–58; (9): 174–78.

Ohonovs'kyj, Omeljan. (1891) 1992. "Natalja Kobryns'ka." In *Istorija literatury rus'koï (ukraïns'koï)/Geschichte der ukrainischen Literatur III, 1/2: vik XIX (proza)/XIX. Jahrhundert (Prosa)*, edited by Olexa Horbatsch, 1263–1305. Reprint Munich: Ukraïns'kyj Vil'nyj Universytet.

Orkan, Władysław, "[Obituary]." 1905. *Marja Wysłouchowa. Wspomnienie pozgonne*, [edited by Wanda Dalecka, Zygmunt Fryling, Feliks Gwiżdż, Franciszek Jaworski, Bronisław Laskownicki, Zygmunt Poznański, and Władyław Wąsowicz], 5–13. L'viv: no pub.

Orzeszkowa, Eliza. 1873. "Marta. Powieść." *Tygodnik Mód i Powieści*: 8–28.

———. (1873) 1885. *Marta*. Warsaw: S. Lewental.

———. 1949. *Marta*. Warsaw: Książka i Wiedza. (Eliza Orzeszkowa. Pisma zebrane VIII).

———. 1976. *Listy zebrane*. Vol. VIII, edited by Edmund Jankowski, Wrocław: Zakład Narodowy im. Ossolińskich.

———. 2018. *Marta: A Novel*, translated by Anna Gąsienica-Byrcyn and Stephanie Kraft. Athens: Ohio University Press. (Polish original 1873).

P. de C. 1899. "Zjazd kobiet polskich w Zakopanem." *Przegląd Zakopiański*, August 24, 1899: 4, 7.

Pappenheim, Berta. 1903. "Ein Besuch aus Frankfurt: Erwiderung." *Die Welt* VII (27): 15.

Pappenheim, Bertha, die Anna O. 1992. *Sisyphus: Gegen den Mädchenhandel—Galizien*, edited by Helga Heubach. Freiburg: Kore.

Pavlyk, Mychajlo. 1905. "Peredne slovo." In *Perepyska M. Drahomanova z N. Kobryns'koju 1893–1895*, edited by Mychajlo Pavlyk, 3–13. L'viv: no pub.

———. (1879) 1995. "Rebenščukova Tetjana." In *Proza, publicystyka, lystuvannja (z malovidomoï spadščyny)*, edited by Volodymyr Kačkan, 23–37. L'viv: "Svit."

Pavlyk, Mychajlo, ed. 1905. *Perepyska M. Drahomanova z N. Kobryns'koju* 1893–1895. L'viv: no pub.
"Petycja kobiet do Sejmu." 1893. *Przedświt. Dwutygodnik dla kobiet* I (10): 89–90.
"Pogrzeb." 1905. *Marja Wysłouchowa: Wspomnienie pozgonne,* [edited by Wanda Dalecka, Zygmunt Fryling, Feliks Gwiżdż, Franciszek Jaworski, Bronisław Laskownicki, Zygmunt Poznański, and Władyław Wąsowicz], 14–27. L'viv: no pub.
Pomeranz, Rosa. 1897. "Die Frauen und der Zionismus." *Die Welt* I (12): 7.
———. 1897. "'Oci'—agitatorami syonizmu." *Przyszłość* V (18): 130–35.
———. 1898. *An die jüdischen Frauen! Ein Appell zur Umkehr.* Tarnopol: Verlag des Vereines "Ahawath-Zion".
———. 1900. "Eine offene Frage." *Die Welt* IV (33): 12–13.
———. 1900. "Jüdische Dienstboten." *Die Welt* IV (38): 2–3.
———. 1901. *Im Lande der Noth:* Breslau: S. Schottlaender.
———. 1903. "Ein Besuch aus Frankfurt a. M." *Die Welt* VII (25): 4–6.
———. 1905. "Die Bedeutung der zionistischen Idee im Leben der Jüdin." *Die Stimme der Wahrheit: Jahrbuch für den wissenschaftlichen Zionismus* 1:329–33.
Pomeranz, Rózia. 1899. "Kilka uwag do artykułu 'O kobiecie żydowskiej' zawartego w numerze 7 'Przyszłości.'" *Przyszłość* VII (10): 80–81.
Rabinowitsch, Sara. 1903. "Eine Erwiderung." *Die Welt* VII (37): 11–12.
Radlińska, Helena. 1910. "Uniwersytety ludowe w Polsce. Referat przedłożony III. Międzynarodowemu Kongresowi Oświatowemu w Brukseli (przekład z francuskiego)." *Przewodnik Oświatowy: Organ Towarzystwa Szkoły ludowej, poświęcony sprawom oświaty pozaszkolnej i narodowego wychowania ludu Polskiego* 10 (12): 437–43.
"Rady gospodarskie: [Maryna Glajcarowa], Sposób wypiekania smacznego chleba." 1900. *Zorza* I (2): 31–32.
Redakcja Przyjaciela Ludu. 1905. "Marja Wysłouchowa." *Przyjaciel Ludu* XVII (13): 1.
Redakcja "Zorzy." 1900. "Słówko do Czytelników i Czytelniczek!" *Zorza* I (1): 1.
Reichensteinowa, Ada. 1936. "Pozgonne dla Róży Melzerowej." In *Pamięci Róży Melzerowej,* [edited by Sabina Feuersteinowa, Berta Jegerowa, and Henryka Schreiberowa], 49–51. L'viv: printed by Koło Kobiet Żydowskich.
Rothfeld, Flora. 1936. "Wspomnienia współpracy z Różą Melzerową." In *Pamięci Róży Melzerowej,* [edited by Sabina Feuersteinowa, Berta Jegerowa, and Henryka Schreiberowa], 20–30. L'viv: printed by Koło Kobiet Żydowskich.
Rozmaitości: Nie wyrządzajcie krzywdy ptakom. 1900. *Zorza* I: 14.
———. Tytułowy obrazek naszej gazetki. 1900. *Zorza* I: 14.
Ruch syoński: Drohobycz. 1898 *Przyszłość* VII (3): 23.
———. Kołomyja. 1899. *Przyszłość* VII (10): 82–83; (13): 106–07.
———. Kraków. 1899. *Przyszłość* VIII (8): 67.
Ruch w kraju: Drohobycz. 1903. *Wschód* IV (164): 6–7.
———. Jarosław. 1903. *Wschód* IV (152): 7; V (49): 4.
———. Kraków. 1904. *Wschód* V (18): 5; (20): 6.
———. Stanisławów. 1904. *Wschód* V (40): 5; (48): 4–5.

———. Stanisławów (Z komitetu dystrykcyjnego—Zwalczanie handlu dziewczętami). 1904. *Wschód* V (45): 5.
———. Ze Stanisławowa. 1904. *Wschód* V (4): 6.
"Ś. p. Mariya Wysłouchowa." 1905. *Przodownica* VI (4): 56–57.
Salomon, Alice. 1913. *Zwanzig Jahre Soziale Hilfsarbeit*. Karlsruhe im Breisgau: G. Braun.
Schaff, Maks. 1936. "Wspomnienie." In *Pamięci Róży Melzerowej*, [edited by Sabina Feuersteinowa, Berta Jegerowa, and Henryka Schreiberowa], 52–56. L'viv: printed by Koło Kobiet Żydowskich.
Schönflies, Rosalie and Lina Morgenstern, eds. 1897. *Der internationale Kongress für Frauenwerke und Frauenbestrebungen in Berlin 19. bis 26. Sept. 1896: Eine Sammlung der auf dem Kongress gehaltenen Vorträge und Ansprachen*. Berlin: Walther.
Schorrowa. 1936 "Plon znojnego życia." In *Pamięci Róży Melzerowej*, [edited by Sabina Feuersteinowa, Berta Jegerowa, and Henryka Schreiberowa], 34–37. L'viv: printed by Koło Kobiet Żydowskich.
Schreiber, Dawid. 1936. "Wspomnienia." In *Pamięci Róży Melzerowej*, [edited by Sabina Feuersteinowa, Berta Jegerowa, and Henryka Schreiberowa], 10–14. L'viv: printed by Koło Kobiet Żydowskich.
S-m. 1901. "Żydowska Toynbeehala." *Wschód* I (50): 4.
Smerzyńska, K[atarzyna]. 1900. "Pierwsze kroki: Opowiadanie." *Zorza* I (4): 54–56; (5): 70–72.
Sommerstein, Emil. 1936 "Krzewicielka żydowskiej idei narodowej—działaczka o najwyższej kulturze serca." In *Pamięci Róży Melzerowej*, [edited by Sabina Feuersteinowa, Berta Jegerowa, and Henryka Schreiberowa], 31–33. L'viv: printed by Koło Kobiet Żydowskich.
Sprawozdanie z czynności wydziału czytelni dla kobiet we Lwowie za rok 1892/93. 1893. L'viv: Czytelnia dla kobiet.
"Statut tovarystva 'Ochoronka.'" In *Naša dolja. Zbirnyk prac' riznych avtoriv*, [edited by Natalja Kobryns'ka], 94–100. Stryj: no pub.
Statut Towarzystwa Oszczędności Kobiet. 1892. [L'viv]: no pub.
Stenographisches Protokoll der Verhandlungen des II. Zionisten-Congresses gehalten zu Basel vom 28. bis 31. August 1898, 1898. Vienna: Verlag des Vereines "Erez Israel."
Stenographisches Protokoll der Verhandlungen des X. Zionisten-Kongresses in Basel vom 9. bis inklusive 15. August 1911, 1911. Berlin: Jüdischer Verlag.
Stępowski, Maryan. 1907. *Setlementy angielskie a praca oświatowa wśród robotników w Polsce*, L'viv: printed by Towarzystwo Szkoły Ludowej.
Syonistka. 1899. "O kobiecie żydowskiej." *Przyszłość* VIII (7): 50–52.
[Syonistka lwowska]. 1898. "Słów kilka odpowiedzi na 'Odezwę' syoistek [sic!] stanisław." *Przyszłość* VII (2): 16.
[Syonistki stanisławowskie]. 1898. "Odezwa do kobiet żydowskich." *Przyszłość* VII (1): 1.
Szczepanowski, Stanisław. 1888. *Nędza Galicyi w cyfrach i program energicznego rozwoju gospodarstwa krajowego*, L'viv: Gubrynowicz i Schmidt.
Tisch, J. 1901. "'Im Lande der Noth' v. Rosa Pomeranz." *Wschód* I (58): 6–7.
Towarzystwo Oszczędności Kobiet, ed. 1890. *Dla głodnych: Pismo zbiorowe z utworów kobiecego pióra*. L'viv: printed by Towarzystwo Oszczędności Kobiet.

Twarecki, Leon. 1919. *Domy ludowe, ich znaczenie i potrzeba*. Kraków: printed by Zarząd Główny Towarzystwa Szkoły Ludowej.
Ukraïnka, Lesja. (1887) 1984. "Ljubka." In *Peršyj vinok: Žinočyj al'manach*, edited by Natalija Kobryn'ska and Olena Pčilka, 176. L'viv: Drukarnja im. T. Ševčenka. Reprint New York: Zoroz Ukraïnok Ameryky.

———. (1887) 1984. "Na zelenomu horbočku." In *Peršyj vinok: Žinočyj al'manach*, edited by Natalija Kobryn'ska and Olena Pčilka, 176. L'viv: Drukarnja im. T. Ševčenka. Reprint New York: Zoroz Ukraïnok Ameryky.

———. 1887) 1984. "Pole (virš)." In *Peršyj vinok: Žinočyj al'manach*, edited by Natalija Kobryn'ska and Olena Pčilka, 230. L'viv: Drukarnja im. T. Ševčenka. Reprint New York: Zoroz Ukraïnok Ameryky.

———. (1887) 1984. "Rusalka (poema)." In *Peršyj vinok: Žinočyj al'manach*, edited by Natalija Kobryn'ska and Olena Pčilka, 56. L'viv: Drukarnja im. T. Ševčenka. Reprint New York: Zoroz Ukraïnok Ameryky.

Vereinsnachrichten: Lemberg. 1898. *Die Welt* II (21): 14.

———. Kolomea. 1899. *Die Welt* III (10): 14.

———. Stanislau. 1900. *Die Welt* IV (11): 12.

"Versammlung zionistischer Frauen." 1911. *Die Welt* XV (4): 854–55.

[Vid redakcyï "Našoï doli"]. 1896. "Vidozva do ruskoho žinoctva v spravi ochoronok." *Naša dolja: Zbirnyk prac' riznych avtoriv*, [edited by Natalja Kobryns'ka], 138–42. L'viv: no pub.

[Von unserem Berichterstatter]. 1910. "Die I. Konferenz jüdisch-nationaler Frauen Galiziens und der Bukowina." *Die Welt* XIV (10): 212.

[Von unserem galizischen Berichterstatter]. 1914. "Die XI. Landeskonferenz der Zionisten Galiziens." *Die Welt* XVIII (3): 70–71.

[Waldman, A.] 1903. "Zwalczanie handlu dziewczętami." *Wschód* IV (132): 4–8; (133): 7–9.

Walewska, Cecylja. 1909. *Ruch kobiecy w Polsce*. Vol. 1. Warsaw: Skład główny Gebethner i Wolff.

———. [1912]. "Ankieta dla uczczenia Orzeszkowej." In *Ich spowiedź: Wyniki ankiety dla uczczenia Orzeszkowej*, 7–11. Warsaw: Komisja do Spraw Kobiecych przy Towarzystwie Kultury Polskiej.

———. 1930. *W walce o równe prawa: Nasze bojownice*. Warsaw: "Kobieta Współczesna."

Wechslerowa, Stefania and Anna Czemeryńska. 1894. *Historya rozwoju i działalności czytelni dla kobiet we Lwowie*. L'viv: no pub.

Weryho, Marya. 1904. "Zadanie ogródka dziecięcego." In *Kobieta współczesna, praca zbiorowa wydana nakładem tygodnika "Bluszcz,"* 270–71. Warsaw: Tygodnik "Bluszcz."

Weininger, Otto. [1906]. *Sex and Character*. London: G. Putnam's Sons. (German original 1903).

Whistling, Karl W., ed. 1883. *Statistik des Königl. Conservatoriums der Musik zu Leipzig 1843–1883: Aus Anlaß des Vierzigjährigen Jubiläums der Anstalt*. Leipzig: Breitkopf & Härtel.

"Wiec kobiet wielkopolskich w Poznaniu." 1900. *Zorza* I (3): 40–42.

Wieczorki Machabeuszowskie: Grzymałów. 1898. *Przyszłość* VII (5): 39.

———. Tarnopol. 1901. *Wschód* I (17): 7.

Wittlin, Józef. 2018. *Salt of the Earth*, translated by Patrick John Corness. London: Pushkin Press. (Polish original 1935).

Wurzel, Juliusz. 1898. "Kobieta żydowska a emancypacya." *Przyszłość* VII (3): 21-22.
Wysłouchowa, Maria. 1887. "Ruch kobiecy." *Ruch* I:25-26, 156-57.
———. 1890. *O życiu i pismach Adama Mickiewicza*. L'viv: Wydawnictwo Towarzystwa Przyjaciół Oświaty.
———. 1892. "Emilja Platerówna." *Kurjer Lwowski* X (333): 2-3; (334): 2-3.
———. 1896, 1897. "Ze śląskiej ziemi." *Tydzień* IV (47): 376; (48): 383-84; (50): 399-400; (51): 406-08; (52): 415-16; V (4): 31-32; (5): 39-40; (6): 47-48; (10): 78-79; (11): 86-87; (12): 93-94; (13): 103-04; (14): 112; (15): 119-20; (16): 127-28; (17): 135-36.
———. 1898. "Z Wisły do Izdebnego." *Tydzień* VI (41): 322-24; (42): 330-34.
———. 1899. "Dni świąteczne." *Przodownica* I: 2-3.
———. 1899. "O przezacnej Polce Emilii Sczanieckiej." *Przodownica* I (1): 4-7.
———. 1899. "Z wędrówek po świecie." *Przodownica* I (1): 12.
———. 1900. "Nasze obrazki." *Zorza* I (1): 12-14.
———. 1900. "Zofja Chrzanowska." *Zorza* I (2): 21-22.
———. 1901. "Z ziemi śląskiej." *Zorza* II (7): 106-09; (8): 118-22; (9): 132-34; (10): 154-57; (11): 168-71; (12): 187-88.
———. 1902. "Bohaterka." *Zorza* III (12): 182-84.
Wysłouchowa, Marja. 1891. "Z pobratymczej ziemi." *Kurjer Lwowski* IX (191): 2-3; (193): 1-2; (194): 2-3; (195): 2-3.
———. 1898. *Adam Mickiewicz, jego życie i dzieła opowiedziała w setną rocznię urodzin poety*. L'viv: Wydawnictwo im. K. Kulikowskiej.
———. 1900. "Racławicka bitwa." *Zorza* I (1): 5-7.
Wysłouchowa, Marya. 1892. *Za wolność i lud: Opowiadania z lat 1861-1864*. L'viv: printed by Zjednoczenie Towarzystw Młodzieży Polskiej.
———. 1894. *O Kościuszkowskiem powstaniu z roku 1794*. L'viv: Wydawnictwo im. Tadeusza Kościuszki.
———. 1899. "Chłopi—bohaterowie." *Przodownica* I: 2-4.
———. (1891) 1913. *O Konstytucyi Trzeciego Maja i przyczynach, które ją wywołały*. L'viv: "Kurier Lwowski."
"X. Landeskonferenz der galizischen Zionisten in Stanislau." 1912. *Die Welt* XIV (1): 10-12.
"Zakopane." 1899. *Czas*, Kraków, LII (185): 3; (186): 2.
[Zarząd Towarzystwa oszczędności kobiet]. 1892. "Do kobiet polskich." *Kurjer Lwowski* X (1): 1.
Zeitschriften- und Bücher-Rundschau. 1900. *Die Welt* IV (49): 10.
"Zionistische Frauenarbeit." 1910. *Die Welt* XIV (39): 938-39.
[Zlocisti, Theodor]. 1901. "Rosa Pomeranz. Im Lande der Not. Breslau (S. Schottländer)." *Ost und West: Illustrierte Monatsschrift für modernes Judentum* I (10): cols. 781-82.

Secondary Literature

Alcoff, Linda. 1988. "Cultural Feminism versus Poststructuralism: The Identity Crisis in Feminist Theory." *Signs* 13:405-36.
Alexander, Ruth. 1997. "Hull-House in Chicago." In *"Wer in den Osten geht, geht in ein anderes Land": Die Settlementbewegung in Berlin zwischen*

Bibliography

Kaiserreich und Weimarer Republik, edited by Rolf Lindner, 61–77. Berlin: Akademie Verlag.

Allen, Ann T. 1994. "Öffentliche und private Mutterschaft: Die internationale Kindergartenbewegung 1840–1914." In *Frauen zwischen Familie und Schule: Professionalisierungsstrategien bürgerlicher Frauen im internationalen Vergleich*, edited by Juliane Jacobi, 8–27. Cologne: Böhlau.

———. 2000. "Children between Public and Private Worlds: The Kindergarten and Public Policy in Germany, 1840–Present." In *Kindergartens and Cultures: The Global Diffusion of an Idea*, edited by Roberta Wollons, 16–41. New Haven, CT: Yale University Press.

Alpern Engel, Barbara. 1978. "From Separatism to Socialism: Women in the Russian Revolutionary Movement of the 1870s." In *Socialist Women: European Socialist Feminism in the Nineteenth and Early Twentieth Centuries*, edited by Marilyn J. Boxer and Jean H. Quataert, 51–74. New York: Elsevier Science.

Anderson, Benedict. (1983) 2006. *Imagined Communities: Reflections on the Origin and Spread of Nationalism*. London: Verso.

Anderson, Harriet. 1998. "Der Feminismus des Sich-Erinnerns: Zum Verhältnis zwischen dem Persönlichen und dem Politischen in Autobiographien der österreichischen Frauenbewegung um 1900." In *Autobiographien in der österreichischen Literatur: Von Franz Grillparzer bis Thomas Bernhard*, edited by Klaus Amann and Karl Wagner, 61–73. Innsbruck: StudienVerlag.

Anton, Annette C. 1995. *Authentizität als Fiktion: Briefkultur im 18. und 19. Jahrhundert*. Stuttgart: J. B. Metzler.

Appadurai, Arjun. 1994. "Disjuncture and Difference in the Global Cultural Economy." In *Cultural Discourse and Post-Colonial Theory: A Reader*, edited by Patrick William and Laura Chrisman, 324–39. New York: Columbia University Press.

Arni, Caroline. 2009. "Seelengesetze mit Gesellschaftswert: Weibliche Subjektwerdung und die Utopie menschlicher Perfektion in der feministisch-sexualreformerischen Liebesethik um 1900." *Feministische Studien* 27:196–209.

Assmann, Jan. 1988. "Kollektives Gedächtnis und kulturelle Identität." In *Kultur und Gedächtnis*, edited by Jan Assmann and Toni Hölscher, 9–19. Frankfurt am Main: Suhrkamp.

Baasner, Rainer. 1999. "Briefkultur im 19. Jahrhundert: Kommunikation, Konvention, Postpraxis." In *Briefkultur im 19. Jahrhundert*, edited by Rainer Baasner, 1–36. Tübingen: Niemeyer.

Bachmann-Medick, Doris. 1997. "Einleitung: Übersetzung als Repräsentation fremder Kulturen." In *Übersetzung als Repräsentation fremder Kulturen*, edited by Doris Bachmann-Medick, 1–18. Berlin: Schmidt.

———. 2002. "Übersetzung im Spannungsfeld von Dialog und Erschütterung: Ein Modell der Auseinandersetzung zwischen Kulturen und Disziplinen." In *Übersetzung als Medium des Kulturverstehens und sozialer Integration*, edited by Joachim Renn and Jürgen Straub, 275–91. Frankfurt am Main: Campus Verlag.

———. 2008. "Übersetzung in der Weltgesellschaft: Impulse eines 'translational turn.'" In *Kultur, Übersetzung, Lebenswelt: Beiträge zu aktuellen Paradigmen der Kulturwissenschaften*, edited by Andreas Gipper and Susanne Klengel, 141–60. Würzburg: Königshausen u. Neumann.

Bader-Zaar, Brigitta. 1997. "Bürgerrechte und Geschlecht: Zur Frage der politischen Gleichberechtigung von Frauen in Österreich, 1848–1918." In *Frauen in der Geschichte des Rechts: Von der Frühen Neuzeit bis zur Gegenwart*, edited by Ute Gerhard, 547–62. Munich: C.H. Beck.

———. (2006) 2008. "Hainisch, Marianne." In *A Biographical Dictionary of Women's Movements and Feminisms: Central, Eastern, and South Eastern Europe, 19th and 20th Centuries*. Revised edition by Francisca de Haan, Krassimira Daskalova, and Anna Loutfi, 173–77. Budapest: Central European University Press.

Bagłajewski, Arkadiusz. 2007. "Krasiński und die 'Frau der Zukunft,'" translated by Jan Conrad. In *Romantik und Geschichte: Polnisches Paradigma, europäischer Kontext, deutsch-polnische Perspektive*, edited by Alfred Gall, Thomas Grob, Andreas Lawaty, and German Ritz, 348–68. Wiesbaden: Harrassowitz Verlag.

Bal, Mieke. 2002. *Travelling Concepts in the Humanities: A Rough Guide*. Toronto: University of Toronto Press.

Balukiewicz, Małgorzata. 2002. "Rozwój placówek opiekuńczo-wychowawczych dla dzieci i młodzieży we Lwowie." In *Galicja i jej dziedzictwo*, edited by Kazimierz Z. Sowa. Vol. 16: *Opieka nad dzieckiem w Galicji*, edited by Andrzej Meissner, 46–63. Rzeszów: Wydawnictwo Wyższej Szkoły Pedagogicznej.

Balzer, Bernd. 2006. *Einführung in die Literatur des Bürgerlichen Realismus*. Darmstadt: Wissenschaftliche Buchgesellschaft.

Barnaś-Baran, Ewa. 2011. "Dobroczynny nurt opieki, wychowania i kształcenia dzieci i młodzieży w Galicji—stan badań." In *Galicja 1772–1918: Problemy metodologiczne, stan i potrzeby badań*, edited by Agnieszka Kawalec, Wacław Wierzbieniec, and Leonid Zaszkilniak. Vol. 1, 274–95. Rzeszów: Wydawnictwo Uniwersytetu Rzeszowskiego.

"Barvinok, Hanna." *Internet Encyclopedia of Ukraine*. Accessed November 28, 2019. www.encyclopediaofukraine.com/display.asp?linkpath=pages%5CB-%5CA%5CBarvinokHanna.htm.

Bauer, Ingrid, Christa Hämmerle, and Gabriella Hauch. 2005. "Liebe widerständig erforschen: eine Einleitung." In *Liebe und Widerstand: Ambivalenzen historischer Geschlechterbeziehungen*, edited by Ingrid Bauer, Christa Hämmerle, and Gabriella Hauch, 9–35. Vienna: Böhlau.

Bechtel, Delphine. 1997. "Cultural Transfers between 'Ostjuden' and 'Westjuden': German-Jewish Intellectuals and Yiddish Culture 1897–1930." *Leo Baeck Institute Yearbook* 42:67–83.

———. 2002. *La Renaissance culturelle juive en Europe centrale et orientale 1897–1930: Langue, literature et construction nationale*. Paris: Belin.

Bechtel, Delphine and Xavier Galmiche. 2008. Introduction to *Les villes multiculturelles en Europe centrale*, edited by Delphine Bechtel and Xavier Galmiche, 7–14. Paris: Belin.

Becker, Sabina. 2003. *Bürgerlicher Realismus: Literatur und Kultur im bürgerlichen Zeitalter, 1848–1900*. Tübingen: Francke.

Bell, Catherine. 1992. *Ritual Theory, Ritual Practice*. Oxford: Oxford University Press.

Beresnevičiūtė-Nosálová, Halina. 2009. "Kulturelle Öffentlichkeit als Arena der Elitenvergesellschaftung: Wilna und Brünn in der ersten Hälfte des 19.

Jahrhunderts." In *Aufsteigen und Obenbleiben in europäischen Gesellschaften des 19. Jahrhunderts: Akteure—Arenen—Aushandlungsprozesse*, edited by Karsten Holste, Dietlind Hüchtker, and Michael G. Müller, 269–92. Berlin: Akademie Verlag.

———. 2018. *Artists and Nobility in East-Central Europe: Elite Socialization in Vilnius and Brno Newspaper Discourse in 1795–1863*. Berlin: De Gruyter Oldenbourg.

Berger, Ruth. 1998. "Frauen in der ostjüdischen Volkserzählung." *Aschkenas— Zeitschrift für Geschichte und Kultur der Juden* 8:381–423.

Berger, Stefan. 2017. "Labour Movements in Global Historical Perspectives: Conceptual Eurocentrism and Its Problems." In *The History of Social Movements in Global Perspective: A Survey*, edited by Stefan Berger and Holger Nehring, 385–418. London: Palgrave Macmillan.

Berger, Stefan and Holger Nehring, eds. 2017. *The History of Social Movements in Global Perspective: A Survey*. London: Palgrave Macmillan.

Bergler, Andrea. 2011. *Von Armenpflegern und Fürsorgeschwestern: Kommunale Wohlfahrtspflege und Geschlechterpolitik in Berlin und Charlottenburg 1890 bis 1914*. Stuttgart: Franz Steiner Verlag.

Berkowitz, Michael. 1995. "Transcending 'Tzimmes and Sweetness': Recovering the History of Zionist Women in Central and Western Europe, 1897–1933." In *Active Voices: Women in Jewish Culture*, edited by Maurie Sacks, 41–62. Urbana: University of Illinois Press.

Bernhold, Monika and Johanna Gehmacher. 2002. *Auto/Biographie und Frauenfrage: Tagebücher, Briefwechsel, politische Schriften von Mathilde Hanzel-Hübner (1884–1970)*. Vienna: Böhlau.

Biale, David. 1993. "Eros and Enlightenment: Love Against Marriage in the East European Jewish Enlightenment." In *From Shtetl to Socialism: Studies from Polin*, edited by Antony Polonsky, 168–86. London: Littman Library of Jewish Civilization.

Bilec'kyj, Leonid. 1950. *Omeljan Ohonovs'kyj*. Winnipeg: Nakl. Ukraïns'koi Vil'noï Akd. Nauk.

Binder, Harald. 2002. "Politische Öffentlichkeit in Galizien: Lemberg und Krakau im Vergleich." In *Stadt und Öffentlichkeit in Ostmitteleuropa: 1900–1939*, edited by Andreas R. Hofmann and Veronika Wendland, 259–80. Stuttgart: Franz Steiner Verlag.

———. 2005. *Galizien in Wien: Parteien, Wahlen, Fraktionen und Abgeordnete im Übergang zur Massenpolitik*. Vienna: Verlag der Österreichischen Akademie der Wissenschaften.

———. 2006. "Das polnische Pressewesen." In *Die Habsburgermonarchie 1848–1918*. Vol. VIII: *Politische Öffentlichkeit und Zivilgesellschaft*. Fascicle 2: *Die Presse als Faktor der politischen Mobilisierung*, edited by Helmut Rumpler and Peter Urbanitsch, 2037–90. Vienna: Verlag der Österreichischen Akademie der Wissenschaften.

———. 2006. "Das ruthenische Pressewesen." In *Die Habsburgermonarchie 1848–1918*. Vol. VIII: *Politische Öffentlichkeit und Zivilgesellschaft*. Fascicle 2: *Die Presse als Faktor der politischen Mobilisierung*, edited by Helmut Rumpler and Peter Urbanitsch, 2091–126. Vienna: Verlag der Österreichischen Akademie der Wissenschaften.

Bock, Gisela. 2000. "Poverty and Mothers' Rights in the Emerging Welfare States." In *The History of Women in the West*, edited by Georges Duby and

Michelle Perrot. Vol. 5: *Toward a Cultural Identity in the Twentieth Century*, edited by Françoise Thébaud. Cambridge, MA: The Belknap Press of Harvard University Press, 402–32. (Italian original 1992).

———. 2002. *Women in European History*, translated by Allison Brown. Oxford: Blackwell Publishers.

Bock, Gisela and Margarete Zimmermann. 1997. "Die Querelle des femmes in Europa: Eine begriffs- und forschungsgeschichtliche Einführung." *Querelles: Jahrbuch für Frauenforschung*. Vol. 2: *Die europäische Querelle des Femmes: Geschlechterdebatten seit dem 15. Jahrhundert*, edited by Gisela Bock and Margarete Zimmermann, 9–38.

Bödeker, Hans E. 2003. "Biographie. Annäherungen an den gegenwärtigen Forschungs- und Diskussionsstand." In *Biographie schreiben*, edited by Hans E. Bödeker, 9–63. Göttingen: Wallstein Verlag.

Bohachevsky-Chomiak, Martha. 1982. "Natalia Kobryns'ka: A Formulator of Feminism." In *Nationbuilding and the Politics of Nationalism: Essays on Austrian Galicia*, edited by Andrei S. Markovits and Frank E. Sysyn, 196–219. Cambridge, MA: Harvard University Press.

———. 1988. *Feminists Despite Themselves: Women in Ukrainian Community Life, 1884–1939*. Edmonton: Canadian Institute of Ukrainian Studies, University of Alberta.

———. 2000. "How Real Were Nationalism and Feminism in 19th Century Galicia?" In *Geschlecht und Nationalismus in Mittel- und Osteuropa 1848–1918*, edited by Sophia Kemlein, 143–52. Osnabrück: fibre.

Borkowska, Grażyna, Małgorzata Czermińska, and Ursula Phillips. 2000. *Pisarki polskie od średniowiecza do współczesności: Przewodnik*. Gdańsk: Słowo/obraz terytoria.

Borodziej, Włodzimierz. 2010. *Geschichte Polens im 20. Jahrhundert*. Munich: C. H. Beck.

Bosch, Mineke. 2006. "Representations of Peasant Women in the Spectacle of International Suffrage Feminism: Recollections from a Dutch Perspective." In *Das Jahrhundert des Feminismus: Streifzüge durch nationale und internationale Bewegungen und Theorien*, edited by Anja Weckwert and Ulla Wischermann, 153–69. Königstein, Taunus: Ulrike Helmer Verlag.

———, ed. 1990. *Politics and Friendship: Letters from the International Woman Suffrage Alliance, 1902–1942*. Columbus: Ohio State University Press.

Bourdieu, Pierre. 1998. *Practical Reason: On the Theory of Action*. Stanford, CA: Stanford University Press. (French original 1994).

Bovermann, Christine. 2017. "Gegenwartsarbeit als frauenpolitisches Konzept in der zionistischen Bewegung in Deutschland." PhD diss, Martin Luther University Halle-Wittenberg.

Boxer, Marilyn J. 1978. "Socialism Faces Feminism: The Failure of Synthesis in France, 1879–1914." In *Socialist Women: European Socialist Feminism in the Nineteenth and Early Twentieth Centuries*, edited by Marilyn Boxer and Jean H. Quataert, 75–111. New York: Elsevier Science.

Braidotti, Rosi. 1994. *Nomadic Subjects: Embodiment and Sexual Difference in Contemporary Feminist Theory*. New York: Columbia University Press.

———. 2002. "Identity, Subjectivity and Difference: A Critical Genealogy." In *Thinking Differently: A Reader in European Women's Studies*, edited by Rosi Braidotti and Gabriele Griffin, 158–80. London: Zed Books.

Braungart, Wolfgang. 2004. "Irgendwie dazwischen: Authentizität, Medialität, Ästhetizität: ein kurzer Kommentar." In *Sprachen des Politischen: Medien und Medialität in der Geschichte*, edited by Ute Frevert and Wolfgang Braungart, 356–68. Göttingen: Vandenhoeck & Ruprecht.

Brentzel, Marianne. 2002. *Anna O.—Bertha Pappenheim: Biographie*. Göttingen: Wallstein Verlag.

Brinker-Gabler, Gisela. 1996. "Metamorphosen des Subjekts: Autobiographie, Textualität und Erinnerung." In *Autobiographien von Frauen: Beiträge zu ihrer Geschichte*, edited by Magdalene Heuser, 393–404. Tübingen: De Gruyter.

Bristow, Edward J. (1982) 1983. *Prostitution and Prejudice: The Jewish Fight against White Slavery 1870–1939*. New York: Oxford University Press.

———. 1983. "The German-Jewish Fight against White Slavery." *Leo Baeck Institute Year Book* 28:301–28.

Brix, Emil. 1982. *Die Umgangssprachen in Altösterreich zwischen Agitation und Assimilation*. Vienna: Böhlau.

Brock, Peter. 1954. "Maria Wysłouchowa—wielka nauczycielka ludu polskiego." *Wiadomości* 39 (443): 16.

———. 1958. "Maria Wysłouchowa (1858–1905) and the Polish Peasant Movement in Galicia." *Canadian Slavonic Papers* III:89–102.

Brodzki, Bella and Celeste Schenck, eds. 1988. *Life/Lines: Theorizing Women's Autobiography*. Ithaca, NY: Cornell University Press.

Brower, Daniel R. 1975. *Training the Nihilists: Education and Radicalism in Tsarist Russia*. Ithaca, NY: Cornell University Press.

Bryll, Irena. 1978. "Śląskie kontakty Marii Wysłochowej." *Kwartalnik Opolski* 24 (1): 47–76.

———. 1984. *Maria Wysłouchowa: Pisarstwo dla ludu i zainteresowania ludoznawcze*. Opole: Wyższa Szkoła Pedagogiczna Imienia Powstańców Śląskich w Opolu.

B[rzoza], C[zesław]. 1994. "Pomeranc-Melcerowa Róża." In *Kto był kim w drugiej Rzeczypospolitej*, edited by Jacek M. Majchrowski, 90. Warsaw: Polska Oficyjna Wydawnicza "BGW".

———. 2003. *Żydowska mozaika polityczna w Polsce 1917–1927*. Kraków: Księgarnia Akademicka.

Brzozowski, Stanisław M. 1976. "Moraczewski Wacław Damian." In *Polski Słownik Biograficzny*, edited by Polska Akademia Nauk and Polska Akademia Umiętności. Vol. XXI, 691–92: Wrocław: Wydawnictwo Polskiej Akademii Nauk.

Bujak, Jan. 1995/96. "Siedlecka Maria Joanna." In *Polski Słownik Biograficzny*, edited by Polska Akademia Nauk and Polska Akademia Umiętności. Vol. XXXVI, 530–31. Warsaw: Wydawnictwo Polskiej Akademii Nauk.

Buszko, Józef. 1996. "Ludowcy w parlamencie wiedeńskim." In *Działalność polityczna ruchu ludowego*, edited by Stanisław Dąbrowski, 111–28. Rzeszów: Wydawnictwo Wyższej Szkoły Pedagogicznej.

———. 1999. "The Consequences of Galician Autonomy after 1867." In *Focusing on Galicia: Jews, Poles, and Ukrainians 1772–1918*, edited by Israel Bartal and Antony Polonsky, 86–99. London: Littman Library of Jewish Civilization.

Butler, Judith. 1993. *Bodies that Matter: On the Discursive Limits of "Sex."* New York: Routledge.

Canning, Kathleen. 1994. "Feminist History after the Linguistic Turn: Historicizing Discourse and Experience." *Signs* 19:368–404.

———. 2002. "Problematische Dichotomien: Erfahrung zwischen Narrativität und Materialität." *Historische Anthropologie* 10:163–82.

Casanova, Pascal. 2004. *The World Republic of Letters*, translated by M. B. DeBevoise. Cambridge, MA: Harvard University Press. (French original 1999).

Caumanns, Ute. 2019. "Organische Arbeit und staatsgesellschaftliche Integration." In *Polen in der europäischen Geschichte: Ein Handbuch in vier Bänden*, edited by Michael G. Müller. Vol. 3: *Die polnisch-litauischen Länder unter der Herrschaft der Teilungsmächte 1772/1795–1914*, edited by Michael G. Müller, Karsten Holste, Igor Kąkolewski, and Robert Traba, 401–20. Stuttgart: Anton Hiersemann.

Chartier, Roger and Jean Hébrard. 1991. "Entre public et privé: La correspondance, une écriture ordinaire." In *La correspondance: Les usages de la lettre au XIXᵉ siècle*, edited by Roger Chartier, 451–58. [Paris: Fayard].

Chitnis, Rajenda. (2006) 2008. "Světlá, Karolína." In *A Biographical Dictionary of Women's Movements and Feminisms: Central, Eastern, and South Eastern Europe, 19th and 20th Centuries*. Revised edition by Francisca de Haan, Krassimira Daskalova, and Anna Loutfi, 548–51. Budapest: Central European University Press.

Chwalba, Andrzej. 2001. *Historia Polski 1795–1918*. Kraków: Wydawnictwo Literackie.

Cott, Nancy F. 1997. "The Modern Woman of the 1920s, American Style." In *A History of Women in the West*, edited by Georges Duby and Michelle Perrot. Vol. 5: *Toward a Cultural Identity in the Twentieth Century*, edited by Françoise Thébaud, 76–91. Cambridge, MA: The Belknap Press of Harvard University Press. (Italian original 1992).

Cowman, Krista. 2009. "'There Is So Much, and It Will All Be History': Feminist Activists as Historians, the Case of British Suffrage Historiography, 1908–2007." In *Gendering Historiography: Beyond National Canons*, edited by Angelika Epple and Angelika Schaser, 141–62. Frankfurt am Main: Campus Verlag.

Csáky, Moritz, Johannes Feichtinger, Peter Karoshi, and Volker Munz. 2004. "Pluralitäten, Heterogenitäten, Differenzen: Zentraleuropas Paradigmen für die Moderne." In *Kultur—Identität—Differenz: Wien und Zentraleuropa in der Moderne*, edited by Moritz Csáky, Astrid Kury, and Ulrich Tragatschnig, 13–43. Innsbruck: StudienVerlag.

Čyževs'kyj, Dmytro. 1975. *A History of Ukrainian Literature (From the 11th to the End of the 19th Century*. Littleton, CO: Ukrainian Academic Press.

Czajecka, Bogusława. 1990. *"Z domu w szeroki świat..." Droga kobiet do niezależności w zaborze austriackim w latach 1890–1914*. Kraków: Towarzystwo Autorów i Wydawców Prac Naukowych "Universitas."

———. 1997. "Działalność żydowskich stowarzyszeń kobiecych (zawodowych, oświatowych i charytatywnych) w Krakowie w latach 1869–1939." In *Żydzi i judaizm we współczesnych badaniach polskich: Materiały z konferencji, Kraków, 21–23 XI 1995*, edited by Krzysztof Pilarczyk, 249–56. Kraków: Księgarnia Akademicka.

Dadej, Iwona. 2009. "Czytelnia dla kobiet jako miejsce i przestrzeń krakowskiego ruchu kobiecego: Salon czy własny pokój?" In *Krakowski szlak*

278 Bibliography

kobiet: Przewodniczka po Krakowie emancypantek, edited by Ewa Furgał, Vol. 1, 32–38. Kraków: Fundacja Przestrzeń Kobiet.

———. 2010. "Gebildete Damen im staatlichen Dreieck: Grenzen und Schranken in der polnischen Frauenbewegung um 1900." *Ariadne: Forum für Frauen- und Geschlechtergeschichte* 57: *Über die Grenzen: Wie Frauen(bewegungen) mit Grenzen umgehen*, 32–37.

———. 2010. "Przyjaźnie i związki kobiece w ruchu kobiecym przełomu XIX i XX wieku." In *Krakowski Szlak Kobiet: Przewodniczka po Krakowie emancypantek*, edited by Ewa Furgał, Vol. 2, 39–50. Kraków: Fundacja Przestrzeń Kobiet.

Davidoff, Leonore, "'Adam Spoke First and Named the Orders of the World': Masculine and Feminine Domains in History and Sociology." In *Politics of Everyday Life: Continuity and Change in Work and the Family*, edited by Helen Corr and Lynn Jamieson, 229–55. Houndsmill: Palgrave Macmillan UK.

Davies, Norman. 1981. *God's Playground: A History of Poland*. Vol. II: *1795 to the Present*. Oxford: Oxford University Press.

Davis, Natalie Zemon. 2001. "Heroes, Heroines, Protagonists," introduced by Gabriele Jancke and Claudia Ulbrich. *L'Homme. Z. F. G.* 12:322–28.

De Certeau, Michel. (1984) 1988. *The Practice of Everyday Life*, translated by Steven F. Rendall. Berkeley: University of California Press. (French original 1980).

De Haan, Francisca, Krassimira Daskalova, and Anna Loutfi. (2006) 2008. Introduction to *A Biographical Dictionary of Women's Movements and Feminisms: Central, Eastern, and South Eastern Europe, 19th and 20th Centuries*, revised edition by Francisca de Haan, Krassimira Daskalova and Anna Loutfi, 1–15. Budapest: Central European University Press.

Denz, Rebekka. 2010. "Zwischen 'russischer Steppenfurie' und Idealtyp einer Revolutionärin: Das bewegte Leben der Sozialistin Sarah Rabinovitsh." *Ariadne: Forum für Frauen- und Geschlechtergeschichte* 57: *Über die Grenzen. Wie Frauen(bewegungen) mit Grenzen umgehen*, 28–31.

"Die Jahrhundertwende—eine Epoche? Eine Diskussion zwischen Reinfried Hörl (SDR), August Nitschke, Detlev J. K. Peukert und Gerhard A. Ritter." 1990. In *Jahrhundertwende: Der Aufbruch in die Moderne 1880–1930*, edited by August Nitschke, Detlev J. K. Peukert, Gerhard A. Ritter, and Rüdiger vom Bruch, Vol. 1, 13–24. Reinbek bei Hamburg: Rowohlt.

Dohrn, Verena. 1998. "Abraham Mapus 'Zionsliebe': Die Geburt einer neuen Zionsidee in Osteuropa." In *Der Traum von Israel: Die Ursprünge des modernen Zionismus*, edited by Heiko Haumann, 108–39. Weinheim: Athenaeum.

Dormus, Katarzyna. 2002. *Kazimiera Bujwidowa 1867–1932: Życie i działalność społeczno-oświatowa*. Kraków: Secesja.

———. 2006. *Problematyka wychowawczo-oświatowa w prasie kobiecej zaboru austriackiego w latach 1826–1918*. Warsaw: Wydawnictwo Retro-Art.

———. 2008. "Galicyjskie stowarzyszenia i organizacje kobiece doby autonomicznej jako wyraz kobiecych dążeń do samoorganizacji." In *Działaczki społeczne, feministki, obywatelki ... Samoorganizowanie się kobiet na ziemiach polskich do 1918 roku (na tle porównawczym)*, edited by Agnieszka Janiak-Jasińska, Katarzyna Sierakowska, and Andrzej Szwarc, 323–48. Warsaw: Neriton.

Dunin-Wąsowicz, Krzysztof. 1952. *Czasopiśmiennictwo ludowe w Galicji.* Wrocław: Wydawnictwo Zakładu Narodowego im. Ossolińskich.

———. 1990. "Die sozialen und politischen Bewegungen der polnischen Bauern in Galizien am Ende des 19. und zu Beginn des 20. Jahrhunderts." In *Galizien um die Jahrhundertwende: Politische, soziale und kulturelle Verbindungen mit Österreich,* edited by Karl Heinz Mack, 51–67. Vienna: Böhlau.

Dużyk, Józef. 1973. "Orkan Władysław." In *Polski Słownik Biograficzny,* edited by Polska Akademia Nauk and Polska Akademia Umiętności. Vol. XXIV, 189–93. Wrocław: Wydawnictwo Polskiej Akademii Nauk.

Ebrecht, Angelika and Elfi Bettinger. 2000. Einleitungsessay to *Querelles: Jahrbuch für Frauenforschung.* Vol. 5: *Transgressionen: Grenzgängerinnen des moralischen Geschlechts,* edited by Angelika Ebrecht and Elfi Bettinger, 9–27.

Eickenrodt, Sabine and Cettina Rapisarda. 1998. "Über Freundschaften und Freundinnen—ein Überblick." In *Querelles: Jahrbuch für Frauenforschung.* Vol. 3: *Freundschaft im Gespräch,* edited by Sabine Eickenrodt and Cettina Rapisarda, 9–30.

Eisenberg, Christiane. 2003. "Kulturtransfer als historischer Prozess: Ein Beitrag zur Komparatistik." In *Vergleich und Transfer: Komparatistik in den Sozial-, Geschichts- und Kulturwissenschaften,* edited by Hartmut Kaelble and Jürgen Schriewer, 399–417. Frankfurt am Main: Campus Verlag.

Eisenstadt, Samuel N. 2000. "Multiple Modernities." *Daedalus* 129:1–29.

Epple, Angelika. 2003. *Empfindsame Geschichtsschreibung: Eine Geschlechtergeschichte der Historiographie zwischen Aufklärung und Historismus.* Cologne: Böhlau.

Epstein, James. 2003. *In Practice: Studies in the Language and Culture of Popular Politics in Modern Britain.* Stanford, CA: Stanford University Press.

Evans, Richard J. 1987. *Comrades and Sisters: Feminism, Socialism and Pacifism in Europe 1870–1945.* Brighton: Palgrave Macmillan.

Fastnacht, Adam, ed. 1966. *Inwentarz rękopisów biblioteki zakładu narodowego im. Ossolińskich we Wrocławiu.* Vol. III. Wrocław: Zakład Narodowy im. Ossolińskich.

Favret, Mary A. 1993. *Romantic Correspondence: Women, Politics and the Fiction of Letters.* Cambridge: Cambridge University Press.

Feiner, Shmuel. 1996/97. "The Pseudo-Enlightenment and the Question of Jewish Modernization." *Jewish Social Studies* 3:62–88.

Ferree, Myra Marx and Carol McClurg Mueller. 2004. "Feminism and the Women's Movement: A Global Perspective." In *The Blackwell Companion to Social Movements,* edited by David A. Snow, Sarah A. Soule, and Hanspeter Kriesi, 576–607. Malden: Wiley.

Filipowicz, Halina. 1996. "The Daughters of Emilia Plater." In *Engendering Slavic Literatures,* edited by Pamela Chester and Sibelan Forrester, 34–58. Bloomington: Indiana University Press.

Fischer-Lichte, Erika. 2003. "Performance, Inszenierung, Ritual: Zur Klärung kulturwissenschaftlicher Schlüsselbegriffe." In *Geschichtswissenschaft und "performative turn": Ritual, Inszenierung und Performanz vom Mittelalter bis zur Neuzeit,* edited by Jürgen Martschukat and Steffen Patzold, 33–54. Cologne: Böhlau.

———. 2008. *The Transformative Power of Performance: A New Aesthetics,* translated by Saskya Iris Jain. London: Routledge.

Franke, Jerzy. 1999. *Polska prasa kobieca w latach 1820–1918: W kręgu ofiary i poświęcenia*. Warsaw: Wydawnictwo SBP.
Freidenreich, Harriet Pass. 1991. *Jewish Politics in Vienna, 1918–1938*. Bloomington: Indiana University Press.
———. 2002. *Female, Jewish, Educated: The Lifes of Central European University Women*, Bloomington: Indiana University Press.
———. 2006. "Die jüdische 'neue Frau' des frühen 20. Jahrhunderts." In *Deutsch-jüdische Geschichte als Geschlechtergeschichte: Studien zum 19. und 20. Jahrhundert*, edited by Kirsten Heinsohn and Stefanie Schüler-Springorum, 123–32. Göttingen: Wallstein Verlag.
French, Lorely. 1996. *German Women as Letter Writers: 1750–1850*. Madison, WI: Fairleigh Dickinson University Press.
Frevert, Ute. 2004. "Politische Kommunikation und ihre Medien." In *Sprachen des Politischen: Medien und Medialität in der Geschichte*, edited by Ute Frevert and Wolfgang Braungart, 7–19. Göttingen: Vandenhoeck & Ruprecht.
———. 2005. "Neue Politikgeschichte: Konzepte und Herausforderungen." In *Neue Politikgeschichte: Perspektiven einer historischen Forschung*, edited by Ute Frevert and Heinz-Gerhard Haupt, 7–26. Frankfurt am Main: Campus Verlag.
Friedman, Susan Stanford. 1998. *Mappings: Feminism and the Cultural Geographies of Encounter*. Princeton, NJ: Princeton University Press.
Gacowa, Halina. 1999. *Eliza Orzeszkowa*. Wrocław: Zakład Narodowy im. Ossolińskich.
Gaisbauer, Adolf. 1988. *Davidstern und Doppeladler: Zionismus und jüdischer Nationalismus in Österreich 1882–1918*. Vienna: Böhlau.
Gall, Alfred, Thomas Grob, Andreas Lawaty, and German Ritz. 2007. "Einleitung." In *Romantik und Geschichte: Polnisches Paradigma, europäischer Kontext, deutsch-polnische Perspektive*, edited by Alfred Gall, Thomas Grob, Andreas Lawaty, and German Ritz, 7–17. Wiesbaden: Harrassowitz Verlag.
Gaus, Detlef. 2011. "Dimensionen und Funktionen des Bildungsbegriffs im langen 19. Jahrhundert: Zur Begriffsgeschichte und Begriffsverwendung eines deutschen Synkretismus." In *Bildungskonzepte und Bildungsinitiativen in Nordosteuropa*, edited by Anja Wilhelmi, 15–37. Wiesbaden: Harrassowitz Verlag.
Gawin, Magdalena. (2006) 2008. "Moszczeńska, Iza." In *A Biographical Dictionary of Women's Movements and Feminisms: Central, Eastern, and South Eastern Europe, 19th and 20th Centuries*. Revised edition by Francisca de Haan, Krassimira Daskalova, and Anna Loutfi, 352–55, Budapest: Central European University Press.
Geertz, Clifford. 1973. "Thick Description: Toward an Interpretive Theory of Culture." In *The Interpretation of Cultures: Selected Essays*, 3–30. New York: BasicBooks.
Gehmacher, Johanna. 2005. "Die Nation lieben: Zur Darstellung und Herstellung eines Gefühls." In *Liebe und Widerstand: Ambivalenzen historischer Geschlechterbeziehungen*, edited by Ingrid Bauer, Christa Hämmerle, and Gabriella Hauch, 125–43. Vienna: Böhlau.
———. 2009. "Wenn Frauenrechtlerinnen wählen können... Frauenbewegung, Partei/Politik und politische Partizipation von Frauen—begriffliche und forschungsstrategische Überlegungen." In *Wie Frauenbewegung geschrieben*

wird: Historiographie, Dokumentation, Stellungnahmen, Bibliographien, edited by Johanna Gehmacher and Natascha Vittorelli, 135–80. Vienna: Löcker Verlag.

Gehmacher, Johanna, Elisa Heinrich, and Corinna Oesch. 2018. *Käthe Schirmacher: Agitation und autobiografische Praxis zwischen radikaler Frauenbewegung und völkischer Politik*. Vienna: Böhlau.

Gelber, Mark H. 2000. *Melancholy Pride: Nation, Race, and Gender in the German Literature of Cultural Zionism*. Tübingen: Niemeyer.

Gelber, N. M. 1958. *Toldot ha-tenu'ah ha-tsyonit be-Galitsyah, 1875–1918*. Vol. 2: *1899–1918*. Yerushalayim: Hotsa'at Re'uven Mas.

———. 1962. "The Stryj Community after 1886." In *Book of Stryj (Ukraine)*, edited by N. Kudish. Tel Aviv: published by Former Residents of Stryj in Israel. Accessed December 2, 2019. www.jewishgen.org/yizkor/stryj2/stryj2.html.

———. 1967. "The History of the Jews of Rzeszow." In *Rzeszow Community Memorial Book (Poland)*, edited by M. Yari-Wold. Tel Aviv: published by Former Residents of Rzeszow in Israel and the USA. Accessed December 2, 2019. www.jewishgen.org/Yizkor/Rzeszow/Rzeszow.html.

Gerhard, Ute. 1997. "Grenzziehungen und Überschreitungen: Die Rechte der Frauen auf dem Weg in die politische Öffentlichkeit." In *Frauen in der Geschichte des Rechts: Von der Frühen Neuzeit bis zur Gegenwart*, edited by Ute Gerhard, 509–46. Munich: C. H. Beck.

———. 2001. "Kommentar zu Joan W. Scott." *Feministische Studien* 19:89–94.

Gestrich, Andreas. 1988. "Einleitung: Sozialhistorische Biographieforschung." In *Biographie—sozialgeschichtlich*, edited by Andreas Gestrich, Peter Knoch, and Helga Merkel, 5–28. Göttingen: Vandenhoeck & Ruprecht.

Geulen, Christian. 2001. "Nation als Wille und Wirklichkeit: Historische Anmerkungen zu einer problematischen Unterscheidung." In *Politische Kollektive: Die Konstruktion nationaler, rassischer und ethnischer Gemeinschaften*, edited by Ulrike Jureit, 68–80. Münster: Westfälisches Dampfboot.

Gierl, Martin. 1996. "Gesicherte Polemik: Zur polemischen Natur geschichtswissenschaftlicher Polemik und zu Anthony Graftons 'Die tragischen Ursprünge der deutschen Fußnote.'" *Historische Anthropologie* 4:267–78.

Gillerman, Sharon. 2006. "Jüdische Körperpolitik: Mutterschaft und Eugenik in der Weimarer Republik." In *Deutsch-jüdische Geschichte als Geschlechtergeschichte: Studien zum 19. und 20. Jahrhundert*, edited by Kirsten Heinsohn and Stefanie Schüler-Springorum, 196–213. Göttingen: Wallstein Verlag.

Gillis, John R. 1994. "Memory and Identity: The History of a Relationship." In *Commemorations: The Politics of National Identities*, edited by John R. Gillis, 3–24. Princeton, NJ: Princeton University Press.

Gilman, Sander L. 1979. "The Rediscovery of the Eastern Jews: German Jews in the East, 1890–1918." In *Jews and Germans from 1860 to 1933: The Problematic Symbiosis*, edited by David Bronsen, 338–65. Heidelberg: Carl Winter Universitätsverlag.

———. 1992. "The Jewish Body: A Footnote." In *People of the Body: Jews and Judaism from an Embodied Perspective*, edited by Howard Eilberg-Schwartz, 223–41. Albany, NY: SUNY Press.

Gilmore, Leigh. 1994. "The Mark of Autobiography: Postmodernism, Autobiography, and Genre." In *Autobiography & Postmodernism*, edited by

Kathleen Ashley, Leigh Gilmore, and Gerald Peters, 3–18. Amherst: University of Massachusetts Press.
Gleixner, Ulrike. 2005. *Pietismus und Bürgertum: Eine historische Anthropologie der Frömmigkeit*. Göttingen: Vandenhoeck & Ruprecht.
Glenn, Susann A. 1990. *Daughters of the Shtetl: Life and Labor in the Immigrant Generation*. Ithaca, NY: Cornell University Press.
Gloger, Maciej. 2007. "Modernizowanie pozytywizmu." *teksty drugie* 4: 102–13.
Gmür, Priska. 1997. "'It Is Not up to Us Women to Solve Great Problems': The Duty of the Zionist Woman in the Context of the First Ten Zionist Congresses." In *The First Zionist Congress in 1897: Causes—Significance—Topicality*, edited by Heiko Haumann, translated by Wayne van Dalsum and Vivian Kramer, 292–96. Basel: Karger.
Goldman, Lawrence. 2000. "Intellectuals and the English Working Class 1870–1945: The Case of Adult Education." *History of Education* 29:281–300.
Górnicka-Boratyńska, Aneta. 2000. "Idea emancypacji w literaturze polskiej XIX i XX wieku." In *Nowa świadomość płci w modernizmie: Studia spod znaku gender w kulturze polskiej i rosyjskiej u schyłku stulecia*, edited by German Ritz, Christa Binswanger, and Carmen Scheide, 13–31. Kraków: Towarzystwo autorów i wydawców prac naukowych "Universitas."
Grabowski, Sabine. 1998. *Deutscher und polnischer Nationalismus: Der deutsche Ostmarken-Verein und die polnische Straż 1894–1914*. Marburg: Verlag Herder-Institut.
Grabowski, Tadeusz Stanisław. 1948. "Feldman Wilhelm." In *Polski Słownik Biograficzny*, edited by Polska Akademia Nauk and Polska Akademia Umiętności, Vol. VI, 399–404. Kraków: Polska Akademia Umiejętności.
Greenbaum, Alfred A. 1997. "The Girls' Heder and Girls in the Boys' Heder in Eastern Europe Before World War I." *East/West Education* 18:55–62.
Greenway, Judy. 2002. "No Place For Women? Anti-Utopianism and the Utopian Politics of the 1890s." *Geografiska Annaler Series B: Human Geography* 84:201–09. Accessed December 2, 2019. www.jstor.org/stable/3554316.
Griesebner, Andrea. 2000. *Konkurrierende Wahrheiten: Malefizprozesse vor dem Landgericht Perchtoldsdorf im 18. Jahrhundert*. Vienna: Böhlau.
Groag, Susan and Marilyn Yalom, eds. 1992. *Revealing Lifes: Autobiography, Biography, and Gender*. New York: State University of New York Press.
Grözinger, Karl E. 2009. "Die ostjüdischen Volkserzählungen des 18. und 19. Jahrhunderts als Teil der europäischen Literatur." In *Integration und Ausgrenzung: Studien zur deutsch-jüdischen Literatur- und Kulturgeschichte von der Frühen Neuzeit bis zur Gegenwart: Festschrift für Hans Otto Horch zum 65. Geburtstag*, edited by Mark H. Gelber, Jakob Hessing, and Robert Jütte, 47–56. Tübingen: Niemeyer.
Guesnet, François. 2004. "Chanukah and Its Function in the Invention of a Jewish-heroic Tradition in Early Zionism, 1880–1900." In *Nationalism, Zionism and Ethnic Mobilization of the Jews in 1900 and Beyond*, edited by Michael Berkowitz, 227–45. Leiden: Brill.
Guttmann, Melinda Given. 2001. *The Enigma of Anna O.: A Biography of Bertha Pappenheim*. Wickford, RI: Moyer Bell.
Hacker, Hanna. 1998. *Gewalt ist: keine Frau: Der Akteurin: oder eine Geschichte der Transgression*. Königstein, Taunus: Ulrike Helmer Verlag.

Hackmann, Jörg. 2012. "Vereinskultur und Zivilgesellschaft in Nordosteuropa: lokal, national, regional, europäisch oder global?" In *Vereinskultur und Zivilgesellschaft in Nordosteuropa: Regionale Spezifik und europäische Zusammenhänge/Associational Culture and Civil Society in North Eastern Europe: Regional Features and the European Context*, edited by Jörg Hackmann, 11–36. Cologne: Böhlau.

Hahn, Barbara. 1991. *Unter falschem Namen: Von der schwierigen Autorschaft der Frauen*. Frankfurt am Main: Suhrkamp.

Haid, Elisabeth, Stephanie Weismann, and Burkhard Wöller. 2013. Einleitung to *Galizien: Peripherie der Moderne—Moderne der Peripherie?* edited by Elisabeth Haid, Stephanie Weismann, and Burkhard Wöller, 1–10. Marburg: Verlag Herder-Institut.

Halpern, L. 1933. "Polityka żydowska w Sejmie i Senacie Rzeczpospolitej Polskiej 1914–1933." *Sprawy Narodowościowe* 2 (1): 29–70.

Hämmerle, Christa and Edith Saurer. 2003. "Frauenbriefe—Männerbriefe? Überlegungen zu einer Briefgeschichte jenseits von Geschlechterdichotomien." In *Briefkulturen und ihr Geschlecht: Zur Geschichte der privaten Korrespondenz vom 16. Jahrhundert bis heute*, edited by Christa Hämmerle and Edith Saurer, 7–32. Vienna: Böhlau.

Haratyk, Anna. 2002. *Rozwój opieki nad dziećmi i młodzieżą w Galicji doby autonomicznej*. Radom: Instytut Pedagogiki Uniwersytetu Wrocławskiego.

Haraway, Donna. 1988. "Situated Knowledges: The Science Question in Feminism and the Privilege of Partial Perspective." *Feminist Studies* 14:575–99.

Harmak, Agnieszka. 2001. "Prototypy ról kobiecych w kanonie polskiej literatury dziewiętnastowiecznej." In *Rola i miejsce kobiet w edukacji i kulturze polskiej*. Vol. 2, edited by Wiesław Jamrożek and Dorota Żołądź-Strzelczyk, 255–79. Poznań: Instytut Historii Uniwersytetu im. Adama Mickiewicza.

Hartmann, Andreas. (1995) 2005. "Im falschen Geschlecht: Männliche Scheinzwitter um 1900." In *Der falsche Körper: Beiträge zu einer Geschichte der Monstrositäten*, edited by Michael Hagner, 187–220. Göttingen: Wallstein Verlag.

Haumann, Heiko. 1998. "Zionismus und die Krise jüdischen Selbstverständnisses." In *Der Traum von Israel: Die Ursprünge des modernen Zionismus*, edited by Heiko Haumann, 9–64. Weinheim: Beltz Athenäum.

Hausen, Karin. 1981. "Family and Role Division: The Polarization of Sexual Stereotypes in the Nineteenth Centry: An Aspect of Dissociation of Work and Family Life," translated by Cathleen Catt. In *The German Family: Essays on the Social History of the Family in Nineteenth- and Twentieth-Century Germany*, edited by Richard J. Evans and W. R. Lee, 51–83. London: Croom Helm. (German original 1976).

———. 1992. "Öffentlichkeit und Privatheit: Gesellschaftspolitische Konstruktionen und die Geschichte der Geschlechterbeziehungen." In *Frauengeschichte—Geschlechtergeschichte*, edited by Karin Hausen and Heide Wunder, 81–88. Frankfurt am Main: Campus Verlag.

———. 1998. "Die Nicht-Einheit der Geschichte als historiographische Herausforderung: Zur historischen Relevanz und Anstößigkeit der Geschlechtergeschichte." In *Geschlechtergeschichte und Allgemeine Geschichte: Herausforderungen und Perspektiven*, edited by Hans Medick and Anne-Charlott Trepp, 15–55. Göttingen: Wallstein Verlag.

Häusler, Wolfgang. (1988) 2012. "'Aus dem Ghetto': Der Aufbruch des österreichischen Judentums in das bürgerliche Zeitalter (1780–1867)." In *Conditio Judaica: Judentum, Antisemitismus und deutschsprachige Literatur vom 18. Jahrhundert bis zum Ersten Weltkrieg: Interdisziplinäres Symposium der Werner-Reimers-Stiftung Bad Homburg v. d. H. First Part*, edited by Hans O. Horch and Horst Denkler, 47–70. Tübingen: Niemeyer.

Hébrard, Jean. 1990. "La correspondance au XIXe siècle: approche historique." In *L'épistolarité à travers les siècles: Geste de communication et/ou d'écriture*, edited by Mireille Bossis and Charles A. Porter, 162–68. Stuttgart: Franz Steiner Verlag.

Hecht, Dieter J. 2008. *Zwischen Feminismus und Zionismus: Die Biografie einer Wiener Jüdin, Anitta Müller-Cohen (1890–1962)*. Vienna: Böhlau.

Heczková, Libuše. (2006) 2008. "Krásnohorská, Eliška." In *A Biographical Dictionary of Women's Movements and Feminisms: Central, Eastern, and South Eastern Europe, 19th and 20th Centuries*. Revisited edition by Francisca de Haan, Krassimira Daskalova, and Anna Loutfi, 262–65. Budapest: Central European University Press.

Hein, Dieter. 2003. "Formen gesellschaftlicher Wissenspopularisierung: Die bürgerliche Vereinskultur." In *Wissenskommunikation im 19. Jahrhundert*, edited by Lothar Gall and Andreas Schulz, 147–69. Stuttgart: Franz Steiner Verlag.

Hein, Jürgen. 1980. "Berthold Auerbach: Barfüßele (1856): Dorfgeschichte als Rettung der 'Schönheit des Heimlichen und Beschränkten.'" In *Romane und Erzählungen des Bürgerlichen Realismus: Neue Interpretationen*, edited by Horst Denkler, 173–87. Stuttgart: Reclam.

Heinsohn, Kirsten and Stefanie Schüler-Springorum, eds. 2006. *Deutschjüdische Geschichte als Geschlechtergeschichte: Studien zum 19. und 20. Jahrhundert*. Göttingen: Wallstein Verlag.

Hering, Sabine and Berteke Waaldijk. 2006. *Guardians of the Poor—Custodians of the Public: Welfare History in Eastern Europe 1900–1960*. In cooperation with Kurt Schilde and Dagmar Schulte, Opladen and Farmington Hills: Barbara Budrich Publishers.

Herres, Jürgen and Manfred Neuhaus. 2002. Vorwort der Herausgeber to *Politische Netzwerke durch Briefkommunikation: Briefkultur der politischen Oppositionsbewegungen und frühen Arbeiterbewegungen im 19. Jahrhundert*, edited by Jürgen Herres and Manfred Neuhaus, 7–25. Berlin: Akademie Verlag.

Hettling, Manfred. 1997. "Erlebnisraum und Ritual: Die Geschichte des 18. März 1848 im Jahrhundert bis 1948." *Historische Anthropologie* 5:417–34.

Hettling, Manfred and Stefan-Ludwig Hoffmann, "Der bürgerliche Wertehimmel: Zum Problem individueller Lebensführung im 19. Jahrhundert." *Geschichte und Gesellschaft* 23:333–59.

Heyde, Jürgen. 2019. *"Das neue Ghetto?" Raum, Wissen und jüdische Identität im langen 19. Jahrhundert*. Göttingen: Wallstein Verlag.

Himka, John-Paul. 1983. *Socialism in Galicia: The Emergence of Polish Social Democracy and Ukrainian Radicalism (1860–1890)*. Cambridge, MA: Harvard University Press.

———. 1998. "The Transformation and Formation of Social Strata and Their Place in the Ukrainian National Movement in Nineteenth-Century Galicia." *Journal of Ukrainian Studies* 23:3–22.

———. (1999) 2002. "The Construction of Nationality in Galician Rus': Icarian Flights in Almost All Directions." In *Intellectuals and the Articulation of the Nation*, edited by Ronald G. Suny and Michael D. Kennedy, 109–64. Ann Arbor: University of Michigan Press.

Hödl, Klaus 1994. *Als Bettler in die Leopoldstadt: Galizische Juden auf dem Weg nach Wien*. Vienna: Böhlau.

Hölscher, Lucian. 1999. *Die Entdeckung der Zukunft*. Frankfurt am Main: Fischer Taschenbuch Verlag.

Hofeneder, Philipp. 2009. "Sprach- und Geschichtsmythen der in Galizien publizierten ruthenischen Geschichtslehrbücher in der zweiten Hälfte des 19. Jahrhunderts." In *Galizien: Fragmente eines diskursiven Raums*, edited by Doktoratskolleg Galizien, 143–58. Innsbruck: StudienVerlag.

Hoff, Jadwiga. 2011. "Badania nad dziejami i kulturą Galicji w Polsce." In *Galicja 1772–1918: Problemy metodologiczne, stan i potrzeby badań*, edited by Agnieszka Kawalec, Wacław Wierzbieniec, and Leonid Zaszkilniak, Vol. 1, 49–72. Rzeszów: Wydawnictwo Wyższej Szkoły Pedagogicznej.

Hofmann, Andreas R. 2009. "Utopien der Nation: Landes- und Nationalausstellungen in Ostmitteleuropa vor und nach dem Ersten Weltkrieg." *Zeitschrift für Ostmitteleuropaforschung* 58:5–32.

Holdenried, Michaela. 2000. *Autobiographie*. Stuttgart: Reclam.

Holste, Karsten, Dietlind Hüchtker, and Michael G. Müller, "Aufsteigen und Obenbleiben in europäischen Gesellschaften des 19. Jahrhunderts: Akteure—Arenen—Aushandlungsprozesse." In *Aufsteigen und Obenbleiben in europäischen Gesellschaften des 19. Jahrhunderts: Akteure—Arenen—Aushandlungsprozesse*, edited by Karsten Holste, Dietlind Hüchtker, and Michael G. Müller, 9–19. Berlin: Akademie Verlag.

Holthöfer, Ernst. 1997. "Die Geschlechtsvormundschaft: Ein Überblick von der Antike bis zum 19. Jahrhundert." In *Frauen in der Geschichte des Rechts: Von der Frühen Neuzeit bis zur Gegenwart*, edited by Ute Gerhard, 390–451. Munich: C. H. Beck.

Homola-Skąpska, Irena. 1992. "Galicia: Initiatives for Emancipation of Polish Women." In *Women in Polish Society*, edited by Rudolf Jaworski and Bianka Pietrow-Ennker, 71–89. New York: Columbia University Press.

Hoock-Demarle, Marie-Claire. 2008. *L'Europe des lettres: Réseaux épistolaires et construction de l'espace européen*. Paris: Albin Michel.

Hornowa, Elżbieta. 1968. *Ukraiński obóz postępowy i jego współpraca z polską lewicą społeczną w Galicji 1876–1895*. Wrocław: Zakład Narodowy im. Ossolińskich.

Hroch, Miroslav. (1989) 2007. "Zionism as European National Movement." In *Comparative Studies in Modern European History: Nation, Nationalism, Social Change*, translated by Ruth Morris, 73–81. Aldershot: Routledge.

———. 2015. *European Nations: Explaining their Formation*, translated by Karolina Graham. London: Verso. (German original 2005).

Hrytsak, Yaroslav. 1999. "A Ukrainian Answer to the Galician Ethnic Triangle: The Case of Ivan Franko." In *Focusing on Galicia: Jews, Poles, and Ukrainians 1772–1918*, edited by Israel Bartal and Antony Polonsky, 137–46. London: Littman Library of Jewish Civilization.

———. 2005. "Franko's Boryslav Cycle: An Intellectual History." In *Synopsis: A Collection of Essays in Honour of Zenon E. Kohut*, edited by Serhii Plokhy and Frank E. Sysyn, 169–89. Edmonton: Canadian Institute of Ukrainian Studies Press.

———. 2009. "Nationalizing a Multiethnic Space: The Case(s) of Ivan Franko and Galicia." In *Imperienvergleich: Beispiele und Ansätze aus osteuropäischer Perspektive. Festschrift für Andreas Kappeler*, edited by Guido Hausmann and Angela Rustemeyer, 247–67. Wiesbaden: Harrassowitz Verlag.

———. 2018. *Ivan Franko and His Community*. Boston, MA: Academic Studies Press. (Ukrainian original 2006).

Hüchtker, Dietlind. 2001. "Deconstruction of Gender and Agency of Women: A Proposal for Incorporating Concepts of Feminist Theory into Historical Research, exemplified using Berlin's Poor Relief Policy, 1770–1850." *Feminist Theory* 2 (3): 328–48.

———. 2004. "Der Blick von der Peripherie: Die Erinnerungen an die polnische Frauenbewegung und die galizische Unabhängigkeitsbewegung im geteilten Polen." In *Zwischen Kriegen: Nationen, Nationalismen und Geschlechterverhältnisse in Mittel- und Osteuropa 1918–1939*, edited by Johanna Gehmacher, Elizabeth Harvey, and Sophia Kemlein, 83–103. Osnabrück: fibre.

———. 2004. "Die Bäuerin als Trope: Sprache und Politik in der polnischen Frauen- und Bauernbewegung der Jahrhundertwende." *WerkstattGeschichte* 13 (37): *rhetorik*, 49–63.

———. 2009. "Rückständigkeit als Strategie oder Galizien als Zentrum europäischer Frauenpolitik." Beitrag zum Themenschwerpunkt "Europäische Geschichte—Geschlechtergeschichte." *Themenportal Europäische Geschichte*. Accessed December 6, 2019. www.europa.clio-online.de/Portals/_Europa/documents/B2009/E_Huechtker_Rueckstaendigkeit.pdf.

———. 2011. "'Mädchenbildung' im Dickicht der Narrative über Gesellschaftsreform." In *Bildungskonzepte und Bildungsinitiativen in Nordosteuropa*, edited by Anja Wilhelmi, 378–92. Wiesbaden: Harrassowitz Verlag.

———. 2011. "'The Politics and Poetics of Transgression': Die Revolution von 1905 im Königreich Polen." In *Revolution in Nordosteuropa*, edited by Detlef Henning, 81–104. Wiesbaden: Harrassowitz Verlag.

———. 2012. "Rückständigkeit, Fortschritt und Geschichte: Die Rhetorik der Frauenpolitik in Galizien." *Historyka: Studia metodologiczne* XLII:231–56. Accessed December 6, 2019. http://journals.pan.pl/dlibra/publication/125567/edition/109562/content.

———. 2014. "*Cross-mapping*: Lokale Verankerungen und transnationale Netzwerke in den Narrativen ostmitteleuropäischer Frauenbewegungen um 1900." In *Vergessene Vielfalt: Territorialität und Internationalisierung in Ostmitteleuropa seit der Mitte des 19. Jahrhunderts*, edited by Steffi Marung and Katja Naumann, 164–91. Göttingen: Vandenhoeck & Ruprecht.

———. 2014. "Der 'Mythos Galizien.' Versuch einer Historisierung." In *Die Nationalisierung von Grenzen: Zur Konstruktion nationaler Identität in sprachlich gemischten Grenzregionen*, edited by Michael G. Müller and Rolf Petri, 81–107. Marburg: Verlag Herder-Institut. Accessed December 4, 2019. www.kakanien-revisited.at/beitr/fallstudie/DHuechtker2.pdf.

———. 2019. "Politische und soziale Bewegungen seit der Mitte des 19. Jahrhunderts." In *Polen in der europäischen Geschichte: Ein Handbuch in vier Bänden*, edited by Michael G. Müller. Vol. 3: *Die polnisch-litauischen*

Länder unter der Herrschaft der Teilungsmächte 1772/1795–1914, edited by Michael G. Müller, Igor Kąkolewski, Karsten Holste, und Robert Traba, 421–50. Stuttgart: Anton Hiersemann.

———. 2019. "Vergangenheit, Gefühl und Wahrheit: Strategien der Geschichtsschreibung über Frauenpolitik und Frauenbewegungen in Galizien an der Wende vom 19. zum 20. Jahrhundert." In *Verzicht auf Traditionsstiftung und Erinnerungsarbeit? Narrative der europäischen Frauenbewegungen im 19. und 20. Jahrhundert*, edited by Angelika Schaser, Sylvia Schraut, and Petra Steymans-Kurz, 291–318. Frankfurt am Main: Campus Verlag.

Hüchtker, Dietlind, ed. 2008. *WerkstattGeschichte* 17 (48): *über-setzen*.

Hulewicz, Jan. 1936. *Walka kobiet polskich o dostęp na uniwersytetu*. Warsaw: Drukarnia Polska.

———. 1937. "Bujwidowa Kazimiera z Klimentowiczów." In *Polski Słownik Biograficzny*, edited by Polska Akademia Nauk and Polska Akademia Umiętności, Vol. III, 111–12. Kraków: Polska Akademia Umiejętności.

———. 1939. *Sprawa wyższego wykształczenia kobiet w Polsce w wieku XIX*. Kraków: Polska Akademia Umiejętności.

———. 1971. "Kuczalska-Reinschmit Paulina." In *Polski Słownik Biograficzny*, edited by Polska Akademia Nauk and Polska Akademia Umiętności, Vol. XVI, 69–70. Wrocław: Wydawnictwo Polskiej Akademii Nauk.

Humenjuk, Mychajlo P. 1988. "Peredmova." In *"Zorja" 1880–1897: Systematyčnyj pokažčyk zmistu žurnalu*, edited by O. D. Kizlyk, 3–12. L'viv: L'vivs'ka naukova biblioteka im. V. Stefanyka.

Hundorova, T[amara] I. 1990. "Kobryns'ka Natalija Ivanivna." In *Ukraïns'ka literaturna encyklopedija*, edited by I. O. Dzeverin, Vol. 2, 505–06. Kiev: Vydavnyctvo Ukraïns'ka Radjans'ka Encyklopedija im. M. P. Bažana.

———. 2002. *Femina Melancolica: Stat' i kultura v hendernij utopiï Ol'hy Kobyljans'koï*. Kiev: Krytyka.

Hutnikiewicz, Artur. 2000. *Młoda Polska*. Warsaw: Wydawnictwo Naukowe PWN.

Jacobi, Juliane. 1994. "Zwischen Erwerbsfleiß und Bildungsreligion—Mädchenbildung in Deutschland." In *Geschichte der Frauen*, edited by Georges Duby and Michelle Perrot, Vol. IV, *19. Jahrhundert*, edited by Geneviève Fraisse and Michelle Perrot, 267–81. Frankfurt am Main: Campus Verlag and Paris: Editions de la Fondation Maison des Sciences de l'Homme.

———. 2006. "'Entzauberung der Welt' oder 'Rettung der Welt.' Mädchen- und Frauenbildung im 19. Jahrhundert in Deutschland." *Zeitschrift für Erziehungswissenschaft* 9:171–86.

Janion, Maria. 1998. Vorwort to *Polnische Romantik: Ein literarisches Lesebuch*, edited by Hans-Peter Hoelscher-Obermaier, 9–42. Frankfurt am Main: Suhrkamp.

———. 2014. *Die Polen und ihre Vampire: Studien zur Kritik kultureller Phantasmen*, translated by Bernhard Hartmann and Thomas Weiler. Berlin: Suhrkamp.

Jankowski, Edmund. 1979. "Orzeszkowa z Pawłowskich Eliza." In *Polski Słownik Biograficzny*, edited by Polska Akademia Nauk and Polska Akademia Umiętności, Vol. XXIV, 311–20. Wrocław: Wydawnictwo Polskiej Akademii Nauk.

Janowski, Maciej. 2004. *Polish Liberal Thought before 1918*. Budapest: Central European University Press. (Polish original 1998).
———. 2006. "Galizien auf dem Weg zur Zivilgesellschaft." In *Die Habsburgermonarchie 1848–1918*. Vol. VIII: *Politische Öffentlichkeit und Zivilgesellschaft* Fascicle 1: *Vereine, Parteien und Interessenverbände als Träger der politischen Partizipation*, edited by Helmut Rumpler and Peter Urbanitsch, 805–58. Vienna: Verlag der Österreichischen Akademie der Wissenschaften.
Jansen, Christian. 2008. "Briefe und Briefnetzwerke des 19. Jahrhunderts." In *Briefe in politischer Kommunikation vom Alten Orient bis ins 20. Jahrhundert*, edited by Christina Antenhofer and Mario Müller, 185–204. Göttingen: V & R unipress.
Jarowiecki, Jerzy. 2001. "Prasa ugrupowań politycznych we Lwowie w okresie autonomii galicyjskiej." In *Kraków—Lwów: Książki, czasopisma, biblioteki XIX i XX wieku*, edited by Jerzy Jarowiecki, Vol. V, 395–426. Kraków: Wydawnictwo Naukowe Akademii Pedagogicznej.
Jaworska, Maria. 1939. "Dulębianka Maria." In *Polski Słownik Biograficzny*, edited by Polska Akademia Nauk and Polska Akademia Umiętności, Vol. V, 457. Kraków: Polska Akademia Umiejętności.
Jaworski, Rudolf, Christian Lübke, and Michael G. Müller. 2000. *Eine kleine Geschichte Polens*. Frankfurt am Main: Suhrkamp.
Jaworski, Wojciech. 1996. *Struktura i wpływ syjonistycznych organizacji politycznych w Polsce w latach 1918–1939*. Warsaw: Oficyna Wydawnicza Rytm.
Jazbinsek, Dieter. 2002. *Der internationale Mädchenhandel: Biographie eines sozialen Problems*. Berlin: Wissenschaftszentrum Berlin für Sozialforschung gGmbH (WZB Discussion Paper FS II 02–501). Accessed December 6, 2019. http://bibliothek.wzb.eu/pdf/2002/ii02-501.pdf.
Jedlicki, Jerzy. 1997. "Wiek dziewiętnasty: inteligencja w pojęciu polskim." In *Inteligencja polska XIX i XX wieku, materiały z wystawy i sesji naukowej*, edited by Aleksandra Garlicka and Jerzy Jedlicki, 137–44. Warsaw: Galeria Sztuki Współczesnej Zachęta.
Jobst, Kerstin S. 1993. "Die ukrainische Nationalbewegung bis 1917." In *Geschichte der Ukraine*, edited by Frank Golczewski, 158–71. Göttingen: Vandenhoeck & Ruprecht.
———. 1996. *Zwischen Nationalismus und Internationalismus: Die polnische und ukrainische Sozialdemokratie in Galizien von 1890 bis 1914: Ein Beitrag zur Nationalitätenfrage im Habsburgerreich*. Hamburg: Dölling und Galitz Verlag.
Judson, Pieter M. 1996. *Exclusive Revolutionaries: Liberal Politics, Social Experience, and National Identity in the Austrian Empire, 1848–1914*. Ann Arbor: University of Michigan Press.
———. 2016. *The Habsburg Empire: A New History*. Cambridge, MA: The Belknap Press.
Kačkan, Volodymyr. 1995. "'Ja vid vas nikoly nikudy ne išov ...' (Peredmova)." In *Mychajlo Pavlyk. Proza, publicystyka, lystuvannja (z malovidomoï spadščyny)*, edited by Volodymyr Kačkan, 3–22. L'viv: Vydavnyctvo "Svit."
———. 1995. "Komentari." In *Mychajlo Pavlyk. Proza, publicystyka, lystuvannja (z malovidomoï spadščyny)*, edited by Volodymyr Kačkan, 146–54. L'viv: Vydavnyctvo "Svit."

Kakanien revisited. Accessed December 6, 2019. www.kakanien.at.
Kałwa, Dobrochna. (2006) 2008. "Bujwidowa, Kazimiera." In *A Biographical Dictionary of Women's Movements and Feminisms: Central, Eastern, and South Eastern Europe, 19th and 20th Centuries*. Revisited edition by Francisca de Haan, Krassimira Daskalova, and Anna Loutfi, 85–88. Budapest: Central European University Press.
Kaplan, Marion A. 1979. *Jewish Feminist Movement in Gemany: The Campaigns of the Jüdischer Frauenbund, 1904–1938*. Westport, WA: Greenwood Press.
———. 1982. "Prostitution, Morality Crusades and Feminism: German-Jewish Feminists and the Campaign Against White Slavery." *Women's Studies International Forum* 5:619–27.
Kaps, Klemens. 2009. "Peripherisierung der Ökonomie, Ethnisierung der Gesellschaft: Galizien zwischen äußerem und innerem Konkurrenzdruck (1856–1914)." In *Galizien: Fragmente eines diskursiven Raums*, edited by Doktoratskolleg Galizien, 37–62. Innsbruck: StudienVerlag.
Kaszynski, Stefan H. 1996. "Der jüdische Anteil an der Literatur in und über Galizien." In *Von Franzos zu Canetti: Jüdische Autoren aus Österreich: Neue Studien*, edited by Mark H. Gelber, Hans O. Horch, and Sigurd Scheichl, 129–40. Tübingen: Niemeyer.
Kempa, Grażyna. 1996. *Edukacja dziewcząt i kobiet śląskich*. Katowice: Wydawnictwo Uniwersytetu Śląskiego
Kennedy, Michael D. and Ronald G. Suny. (1999) 2002. "Introduction." In *Intellectuals and the Articulation of the Nation*, edited by Michael D. Kennedy and Ronald G. Suny, 1–56. Ann Arbor: University of Michigan Press.
Kessel, Martina. 2001. *Langeweile: Zum Umgang mit Zeit und Gefühl in Deutschland vom späten 18. bis zum frühen 19. Jahrhundert*. Göttingen: Wallstein Verlag.
Kinnunen, Tiina. 2009. "History as Argument—Alexandra Gripenberg, Ellen Key and the Notion of True Feminism." In *Gendering Historiography: Beyond National Canons*, edited by Angelika Epple and Angelika Schaser, 181–207. Frankfurt am Main: Campus Verlag.
———. 2009. "'Werde, die du bist'—Feminismus und weibliches Lebensgefühl Anfang des 20. Jahrhunderts: Beitrag zum Themenschwerpunkt 'Europäische Geschichte—Geschlechtergeschichte.'" *Themenportal Europäische Geschichte*. 1–10. Accessed December 6, 2019. www.europa.clio-online.de/Portals/_Europa/documents/B2009/E_Kinnunen_Feminismus.pdf.
Kisielewski, Tadeusz. 1977. *Heroizm i kompromis: Portret zbiorowy działaczy ludowych. Part I: Okres zaborów*. Warsaw: Książka i Wiedza.
Kizwalter, Tomasz. 1994. "Ernest Gellners Nationalismustheorie und die polnische Nationalbewegung im 19. Jahrhundert." In *Formen des nationalen Bewußtseins im Lichte zeitgenössischer Nationalismustheorien: Vorträge der Tagung des Collegium Carolinum in Bad Wiessee vom 31. Oktober bis 3. November 1991*, edited by Eva Schmidt-Hartmann, 163–72. Munich: Oldenbourg.
———. 2003. "Demos i ethnos: Kilka uwag o demokratyzacji społecznej w Europie XIX w." In *Społeczeństwo w dobie przemian wiek XIX i XX: Księga jubileuszowa Profesor Anny Żarnowskiej*, edited by Maria Nietyksza, Katarzyna Sierakowska, and Agnieszka Janiak-Jasińska, 325–30. Warsaw: Wydawnictwo "DiG."

Klandermans, Bert. 2001. "Why Social Movements Come into Being and Why People Join Them." In *The Blackwell Companion to Sociology*, edited by Judith R. Blau, 268–81. Oxford: Blackwell Publishers.

Kłańska, Maria. 1994. *Aus dem Schtetl in die Welt 1772–1938: Ostjüdische Autobiographien in deutscher Sprache.* Vienna: Böhlau.

Klausmann, Christina. 1997. *Politik und Kultur der Frauenbewegung im Kaiserreich: Das Beispiel Frankfurt am Main.* Frankfurt am Main: Campus Verlag.

———. 2006. "Die bürgerliche Frauenbewegung im Kaiserreich—eine Elite?" In *Frauen auf dem Weg zur Elite*, 61–77, edited by Günther Schulz. Munich: H. Boldt Verlag im R. Oldenbourg-Verlag.

Kleeberg, Bernhard and Robert Suter. 2014. "Doing Truth: Bausteine einer Praxeologie der Wahrheit." *Zeitschrift für Kulturphilosophie* 8 (2): *Wahrheit*, 211–26.

Kleinau, Elke. 1987. *Die freie Frau: Soziale Utopien des frühen 19. Jahrhunderts.* Düsseldorf: Schwann.

Knyš, Irena. 1957. *Smoloskyp u temrjavi: Natalija Kobryns'ka j ukraïns'kyj žinočyj ruch.* Vinnipeg: Printed by the author.

———. 1958. *Žinka včora j s'ohodni: Vybrani statti.* Vinnipeg: Printed by the author.

Kobchenko, Kateryna. 2008. "Parallele Geschichten: Die Entwicklung der akademischen Frauenbildung in der Ukraine von der Mitte des 19. bis zum Anfang des 20. Jahrhunderts." *Ariadne: Forum für Frauen- und Geschlechtergeschichte* 53/54: Mädchenschulgeschichte(n): Die preußische Mädchenschulreform und ihre Folgen, 110–18.

Kobylińska, Ewa. 1998. "Polens Gedächtnis und seine Symbole." In *erinnern, vergessen, verdrängen: Polnische und deutsche Erfahrungen*, edited by Ewa Kobylińska and Andreas Lawaty, 120–44. Wiesbaden: Harrassowitz Verlag.

Konarski, Stanisław. 1986. "Radlińska z Raichmanów Helena." In *Polski Słownik Biograficzny*, edited by Polska Akademia Nauk and Polska Akademia Umiętności, Vol. XXIX, 696–703. Wrocław: Wydawnictwo Polskiej Akademii Nauk.

Kondracka, Mariola. 2009. "Aktywność parlamentarna posłanek i senatorek Rzeczypospolitej Polskiej w latach 1919–1927." In *Działaczki społeczne, feministki, obywatelki... Samoorganizowanie się kobiet na ziemiach polskich po 1918 roku (na tle porównawczym)*, edited by Agnieszka Janiak-Jasińska, Katarzyna Sierakowska, and Andrzej Szwarc, Vol. II, 49–73. Warsaw: Neriton.

Konstantinovič, Zoran and Fridrun Rinner. 2003. *Eine Literaturgeschichte Mitteleuropas.* Innsbruck: StudienVerlag.

Konz, Britta. 2005. *Bertha Pappenheim (1859–1936): Ein Leben für jüdische Tradition und weibliche Emanzipation.* Frankfurt am Main: Campus Verlag.

Koschorke, Albrecht. 2018. *Fact and Fiction: Elements of a General Theory of Narrative*, translated by Joel Golb. Berlin: De Gruyter. (German original 2012).

Koselleck Reinhart. 2004. "'Spaces of Experience' and 'Horizon of Expectation': Two Historical Categories." In *Futures Past: On the Semantics of Historical Time*, translated by Keith Tribe. 255–76. New York: Columbia University Press. (German original 1976).

———. 2007. "Fiktion und geschichtliche Wirklichkeit." *Zeitschrift für Ideengeschichte* I:39–54.
Koselleck Reinhart and Christian Meier. (1975) 1992. "Fortschritt." In *Geschichtliche Grundbegriffe: Historisches Lexikon zur politisch-sozialen Sprache in Deutschland*, edited by Otto Brunner, Werner Conze, and Reinhart Koselleck, Vol. 2, 351–432. Stuttgart: Klett-Cotta.
Kośny, Witold. 1980. "Der polnische Positivismus." In *Europäischer Realismus*, edited by Reinhard Lauer, 367–90. Wiesbaden: Aula-Verlag.
Kosyk, Ihor. 2009. "To Marry the Other: Zur Geschichte der gemischten Ehen in Galizien und Lemberg in der zweiten Hälfte des 19. Jahrhunderts." In *Galizien: Fragmente eines diskursiven Raums*, edited by Doktoratskolleg Galizien, 99–112. Innsbruck: StudienVerlag.
Kotowski, Albert S. 2000. "Deutsche—Tschechen—Polen—Juden: Über die Bevölkerungsverhältnisse im Teschener Schlesien 1850–1914." *Zeitschrift für Ostmitteleuropaforschung* 49:317–40.
Kozik, J[an]. 1978. "Ohonovs'kyj Omeljan Mychajlovyč." *Österreichisches Biographisches Lexikon 1815–1950*. Vol. 7, installment 33, 220–21. Vienna: Verlag der Österreichischen Akademie der Wissenschaften. Accessed December, 6, 2019. www.biographien.ac.at/oebl/oebl_O/Ohonovskyj_Omeljan-Mychajlovyc_1833_1894.xml?frames=yes.
———. 1978. "Ozarkevyč (Ozarkiewicz), Ivan (Jan)." *Österreichisches Biographisches Lexikon 1815–1950*, Vol. 7, installment 33, 273. Vienna: Verlag der Österreichischen Akademie der Wissenschaften. Accessed December 6, 2019. www.biographien.ac.at/oebl/oebl_O/Ohonovskyj_Omeljan-Mychajlovyc_1833_1894.xml?frames=yes.
Kozińska-Witt, Hanna. 2009. "Städtische Selbstpräsentation auf der Allgemeinen Landesausstellung in Lemberg 1894 am Beispiel der Stadt Krakau." *Zeitschrift für Ostmitteleuropaforschung* 58:162–96.
———. 2011. "Bertha Pappenheim und die Ostjüdinnen." *Scripta Judaica Cracoviensia* 9:69–87.
Kozłowska-Sabatowska, Halina. 1978. *Ideologia pozytywizmu galicyjskiego 1864–1881*. Wrocław: Zakład Narodowy im. Ossolińskich.
Kraft, Claudia. 2009. "Gendering the Polish Historiography of the Late Eighteenth and Nineteenth Centuries." In *Gendering Historiography: Beyond National Canons*, edited by Angelika Epple and Angelika Schaser, 78–101. Frankfurt am Main: Campus Verlag.
Kravtsiv, Bohdan and Oleksa Horbach. (1993). "Nechui-Levytsky, Ivan." *Internet Encyclopedia of Ukraine*. Accessed December 6, 2019. www.encyclopediaofukraine.com/display.asp?linkpath=pages%5CN%5CE%5C-Nechui6LevytskyIvan.htm.
Krischer, André. 2010. "Das Verfahren als Rollenspiel? Englische Hochverratsprozesse im 17. und 18. Jahrhundert." In *Herstellung und Darstellung von Entscheidungen: Verfahren, Verwalten und Verhandeln in der Vormoderne*, edited by Barbara Stollberg-Rilinger and André Krischer, 211–51. Berlin: Duncker & Humblot.
Krzoska, Markus, Kolja Lichy, and Konstantin Rometsch. 2018. "Jenseits von Ostmitteleuropa? Zur Aporie einer deutschen Nischenforschung." *Journal of Modern Europen History* 16 (1): 40–63.

Bibliography

Krzywiec, Grzegorz. (2006) 2008. "Daszyńska-Golińska, Zofia." In *A Biographical Dictionary of Women's Movements and Feminisms: Central, Eastern, and South Eastern Europe, 19th and 20th Centuries.* Revised edition by Francisca de Haan, Krassimira Daskalova, and Anna Loutfi, 102–05. Budapest: Central European University Press.

———. (2006) 2008. "Kuczalska-Reinschmit (Reinschmidt), Paulina Jadwiga." *A Biographical Dictionary of Women's Movements and Feminisms: Central, Eastern, and South Eastern Europe, 19th and 20th Centuries.* Revised edition by Francisca de Haan, Krassimira Daskalova, and Anna Loutfi, 274–77. Budapest: Central European University Press.

Kuberski, Leszek. 2001. "Nędza Galicji Stanisława Szczepanowskiego i jej odbicie w ówczesniej prasie polskiej." In *Kraków—Lwów: Książki, czasopisma, biblioteki XIX i XX w*, edited by Jerzy Jarowiecki, Vol. V, 427–39. Kraków: Wydawnictwo Naukowe Akademii Pedagogicznej.

Kuhn, Bärbel and Christiane Kohser-Spohn. 2001. "Befreite Liebe." In *Entdeckung des Ich: Die Geschichte der Individualisierung vom Mittelalter bis zur Gegenwart,* edited by Richard van Dülmen, 489–516. Cologne: Böhlau.

Kusber, Jan. 2011. "Bildungskonzepte und Bildungsinstitutionen im Nordosteuropa des 19. Jahrhunderts: Ein Problemaufriss." In *Bildungskonzepte und Bildungsinitiativen in Nordosteuropa,* edited by Anja Wilhelmi, 38–56. Wiesbaden: Harrassowitz Verlag.

Labins'ka, H. 1999. "Natalja Kobryns'ka—'Borec' za prava žinky.'" In *Žinka v nauci ta osviti: Mynule, sučasnist', majbutne: Materialy mižnarodnoï naukovo-praktičnoï konferencïi, Ukraïna, Kyïv, 3–4 hrudnja 1999,* edited by Mykola Žulyns'kyj, Nonna Kopystjans'ka, and Jelizaveta Kordjum, 120–22. Kiev.

Labouvie, Eva. 2009. "Zur Einstimmung und zum Band." In *Schwestern und Freundinnen: Zur Kulturgeschichte weiblicher Kommunikation,* edited by Eva Labouvie, 11–31. Cologne: Böhlau.

Landau, Moses. 1932. "Geschichte des Zionismus in Oesterreich-Ungarn." PhD diss, University of Vienna.

Landwehr, Achim. 2010. "Diskurs und Wandel: Wege der Historischen Diskursforschung." In *Diskursiver Wandel,* edited by Achim Landwehr, 11–28. Wiesbaden: Springer.

———. 2016. *Die anwesende Abwesenheit der Vergangenheit: Essay zur Geschichtstheorie.* Frankfurt am Main: S. Fischer.

Langewiesche, Dieter. 2003. "Welche Wissensbestände vermittelten Volksbibliotheken und Volkshochschulen im späten Kaiserreich?" In *Wissenskommunikation im 19. Jahrhundert,* edited by Lothar Gall and Andreas Schulz, 213–41. Stuttgart: Franz Steiner Verlag.

Lawaty, Andreas. 2007. Zur romantischen Konzeption des Politischen: Polen und Deutsche unter fremder Herrschaft. In *Romantik und Geschichte: Polnisches Paradigma, europäischer Kontext, deutsch-polnische Perspektive,* edited by Alfred Gall, Thomas Grob, Andreas Lawaty, and German Ritz, 21–59. Wiesbaden: Harrassowitz Verlag.

Lehmann, Jürgen. 1988. *Bekennen, Erzählen, Berichten: Studien zur Theorie und Geschichte der Autobiographien.* Tübingen: Niemeyer.

Lejeune, Philippe. 1989. "Der autobiographische Pakt." In *Die Autobiographie: Zu Form und Geschichte einer literarischen Gattung,* edited by Günter Niggl, 214–57. Darmstadt: Wissenschaftliche Buchgesellschaft.

Lepalczyk, Irena and Ewa Maraynowicz-Hetka. 2003. "Helena Radlinska—A Portrait of the Person, Researcher, Teacher and Social Activist." In *History of Social Work in Europe: (1900–1960): Female Pioneers and their Influence on the Development of International Social Organizations*, edited by Sabine Hering and Berteke Waaldijk, 71–77. Opladen: Leske + Buderich.
Leszczawski-Schwerk, Angelique. 2009. "Frauenbewegungen in Galizien um 1900–Raum zwischen Kooperation und Konfrontation?" In *Galizien: Fragmente eines diskursiven Raums*, edited by Doktoratskolleg Galizien, 63–81. Innsbruck: StudienVerlag.
———. 2010. "Grenzüberwindungen versus Grenzziehungen: Frauenbewegungen im österreichischen Galizien um 1900." *Ariadne: Forum für Frauen- und Geschlechtergeschichte 57: Über die Grenzen: Wie Frauen(bewegungen) mit Grenzen umgehen*, 38–43.
———. 2015. *"Die umkämpften Tore zur Gleichberechtigung": Frauenbewegungen in Galizien (1867–1918)*. Vienna: LIT-Verlag.
Levi, Giovanni. 1991. "On Microhistory." In *New Perspectives on Historical Writing*, edited by Peter Burke, 93–113. Cambridge: Polity Press.
Liebhart, Karin and Béla Rásky. 2001. "Helden und Heldinnen in nationalen Mythen und historischen Erzählungen Österreichs und Ungarns." *L'Homme. Z.F.G.* 12:239–64.
Lieske, Adina. 2007. *Arbeiterkultur und bürgerliche Kultur in Pilsen und Leipzig*. Bonn: Dietz.
Lindemann, Gesa. 1994. "Die Konstruktion der Wirklichkeit und die Wirklichkeit der Konstruktion." In *Denkachsen: Zur theoretischen und institutionellen Rede vom Geschlecht*, edited by Gesa Lindemann and Theresa Wobbe, 115–46. Frankfurt am Main: Suhrkamp.
Linz, Juan J. and Alfred C. Stepan. 1996. *Problems of Democratic Transition and Consolidation: Southern Europe, South America, and Post-Communist Europe*. Baltimore, MD: Johns Hopkins University Press.
Lionnet, Françoise. 1989. *Autobiographical Voices: Race, Gender, Self-Portraiture*. Ithaca, NY: Cornell University Press.
Loentz, Elizabeth. 2007. *Let Me Continue to Speak the Truth: Bertha Pappenheim as Author and Activist*. Cincinnati, OH: Hebrew Union College Press.
Lorence-Kot, Bogna and Adam Winiarz. 2000. "Preschool Education in Poland." In *Kindergartens and Cultures: The Global Diffusion of an Idea*, edited by Roberta Wollons, 166–94. New Haven, CT: Yale University Press.
———. 2004. "The Polish Women's Movement to 1914." In *Women's Emancipation Movements in the Nineteenth Century: A European Perspective*, edited by Sylvia Paletschek and Bianka Pietrow-Ennker, 206–20. Stanford, CA: Stanford University Press.
Loutfi, Anna. 2009. "Politics and Hegemony in the Historiography of Women's Movements (Nineteenth and Twentieth Centuries): A Call for New Debates." In *Wie Frauenbewegung geschrieben wird: Historiographie, Dokumentation, Stellungnahmen, Bibliographien*, edited by Johanna Gehmacher and Natascha Vittorelli, 81–101. Vienna: Löcker Verlag.
Löw, Martina. 2001. *Raumsoziologie*. Frankfurt am Main: Suhrkamp.
L[öwe], H[einz]-D[ietrich]. 1985. "Große Reformen." In *Lexikon der Geschichte Rußlands: Von den Anfängen bis zur Oktoberrevolution*, edited by Hans Joachim Torke, 139–42. Munich: C. H. Beck.

———. 1985. "Narodniki." In *Lexikon der Geschichte Rußlands: Von den Anfängen bis zur Oktoberrevolution*, edited by Hans Joachim Torke, 244–47. Munich: C. H. Beck.
Lowi, Theodore J. 2009. *Arenas of Power*, Boulder, CO: Paradigm Publishers.
Luckyj, George S. N. (1975) 1997. "An Overview of the Twentieth Century." In Dmytro Čyževs'kyj. *A History of Ukrainian Literature (From the 11th to the End of the 19th Century)*, 2nd extended edition by George S. N. Luckyj, 685–706. New York: Ukrainian Academic Press.
Lüdtke, Alf. 1997. "Alltagsgeschichte: Aneignung und Akteure: Oder—es hat doch kaum begonnen!" *WerkstattGeschichte* 6 (17): *Neue Verhältnisse*, 83–91.
———. 2003. "Alltagsgeschichte—ein Bericht von unterwegs." *Historische Anthropologie* 11:278–95.
Lutman, Roman, Maria Bonarska and Maria Kruczkiewicz. 1967. "Papiery Bolesława i Marii Wysłouchów w zbiorach biblioteki zakładu narodowego im. Ossolińskich." *Z skarbca kultury: Biuletyn informacyjny zakładu narodowego im. Ossolińskich biblioteki Polskiej Akademii Nauk* 19:274–343.
Lyons, Martyn. (1995) 1999. "Die neuen Leser im 19. Jahrhundert: Frauen, Kinder, Arbeiter." *Die Welt des Lesens: Von der Schriftrolle zum Bildschirm*, edited by Roger Chartier and Guglielmo Cavallo, 457–97. Frankfurt am Main: Campus Verlag.
———. 2008. *Reading Culture and Writing Practices in Nineteenth-Century France*. Toronto: University of Toronto Press.
Lyotard, Jean-François. 1984. *The Postmodern Condition: A Report on Knowledge*, translated by Geoff Bennington and Brian Massumi. Mineapolis: University of Minnesota Press.
Magocsi, Paul R. 1996. *A History of Ukraine*. Toronto: University of Toronto Press.
———. 2002. *The Roots of Ukrainian Nationalism: Galicia as Ukraine's Piedmont*. Toronto: University of Toronto Press.
———. 2005. "Galicia: A European Land." In *Galicia: A Multicultured Land*, edited by Christopher Hann and Paul R. Magocsi, 3–21. Toronto: University of Toronto Press.
Makowiecki, Andrzej Z. 1981. *Młoda Polska*. Warsaw: Wydawnictwa Szkolne i Pedagogiczne.
Malančuk-Rybak, Oksana. 1999. "Ukraïns'kyj ta pol's'kyj žinočyj ruch kincja XIX—počatku XX st.: Typolohična identyfikacija i porivnjal'na charakterystyka." *Warszawski zeszyty ukrainoznawcze/Varšavs'ki ukraïnoznavči zapysky*. Vol. 8/9: *Spotkanie polsko-ukraińskie/Polsko-ukraïns'ki zustrič*, 188–200.
———. 2006. *Ideolohija ta suspil'na praktyka žinočoho ruchu na zachidnoukraïns'kych zemljach XIX—peršoï tretyny XX st.: typolohija ta jevropejs'kyj kul'turno-istoryčnyj kontekst*. Černivci: Knyhy XXI.
Malečková, Jitka. 2000. "Nationalizing Women and Engendering the Nation: The Czech National Movement." In *Gendered Nations: Nationalisms and Gender Order in the Long Nineteenth Century*, edited by Ida Blom, Karen Hagemann, and Catherine Hall, 293–310. Oxford: Berg Publishers.
Malleier, Elisabeth. 2005. *Das Ottakringer Settlement—Zur Geschichte eines frühen internationalen Sozialprogramms*. Vienna: Edition Volkshochschule.

———. 2006. "Die Jüdische Toynbee-Halle in der Wiener Brigittenau." *Spurensuche: Zeitschrift für Geschichte der Erwachsenenbildung und Wissenschaftspopularisierung* 17:104–13.
Manekin, Rachel. 2006. "Die hebräische und jiddische Presse in Galizien." In *Die Habsburgermonarchie 1848–1918*. Vol. VIII: *Politische Öffentlichkeit und Zivilgesellschaft*, Fascicle 2: *Die Presse als Faktor der politischen Mobilisierung*, edited by Helmut Rumpler and Peter Urbanitsch, 2341–65. Vienna: Verlag der Österreichischen Akademie der Wissenschaften.
Marakowitz, Ellen. 1996. "Gender and National Identity in Finland." *Women's Studies International Forum* 19:55–63.
Mark, Rudolf A. 1994. *Galizien unter österreichischer Verwaltung: Verwaltung—Kirche—Bevölkerung*. Marburg: Verlag Herder-Institut.
Martinsen, Renate. 1990. *Der Wille zum Helden: Formen des Heroismus in Texten des 20. Jahrhunderts*. Wiesbaden: Deutscher Verlag.
Martschukat, Jürgen and Steffen Patzold. 2003. "Geschichtswissenschaft und 'performative turn': Eine Einführung in Fragestellungen, Konzepte und Literatur." In *Geschichtswissenschaft und "performative turn": Ritual, Inszenierung und Performanz vom Mittelalter bis zur Neuzeit*, edited by Jürgen Martschukat and Steffen Patzold, 1–31. Cologne: Böhlau.
Marung, Steffi and Katja Naumann. 2014. Einleitung to *Vergessene Vielfalt: Territorialität und Internationalisierung in Ostmitteleuropa seit der Mitte des 19. Jahrhunderts*, edited by Steffi Marung and Katja Naumann, 9–44. Göttingen: Vandenhoek & Ruprecht.
Marung, Steffi, Matthias Middell, and Uwe Müller. 2017. "Territorialisierung in Ostmitteleuropa bis zum Ersten Weltkrieg." In *Handbuch einer transnationalen Geschichte Ostmitteleurops*. Vol. 1: *Von der Mitte des 19. Jahrhunderts bis zum Ersten Weltkrieg*, edited by Frank Hadler and Matthias Middell, 37–130. Göttingen: Vandenhoek & Ruprecht.
Mason, Mary G. 1988. "The Other Voice: Autobiographies of Women Writers." In *Life/Lines: Theorizing Women's Autobiography*, edited by Bella Brodzki and Celeste Schenck, 19–43. Ithaca, NY: Cornell University Press.
McClintock, Anne. 1997. "'No Longer in a Future Heaven': Gender, Race, and Nationalism." In *Dangerous Liaisons: Gender, Nation, and Postcolonial Perspectives*, edited by Anne McClintock, Aamir Mufti, and Ella Shohat, 89–112. Minneapolis: University of Minnesota Press.
McKay, Ian. 2008. *Reasoning Otherwise: Leftists and the People's Enlightenment in Canada, 1890–1920*. Toronto: Between the Lines.
Meacham, Standish. 1987. *Toynbee Hall and Social Reform, 1880–1914: The Search for Community*. New Haven, CT: Yale University Press.
Meissner, Andrzej. 1996. "Społeczeństwo Galicyjskie wobec oświaty ludowej." In *Chłopi. Naród. Kultury*. Vol. 4: *Kultura i oświata wsi*, edited by Andrzej Meissner, 119–31. Rzeszów: Wydawnictwo Wyższej Szkoły Pedagogicznej.
Meissner-Łozińska, Justyna. 2002. "Placówki opieki nad dzieckiem w Krakowie w okresie autonomii Galicyjskiej." In *Galicja i jej dziedzictwo*, edited by Kazimierz Z. Sowa. Vol. 16: *Opieka nad dzieckiem w Galicji*, edited by Andrzej Meissner, 94–113. Rzeszów: Wydawnictwo Wyższej Szkoły Pedagogicznej.
Mencwel, Andrzej. 1997. "Poza 'weselem' i 'snem o potędze': Inteligencja polska na progu XX wieku." In *Inteligencja polska XIX i XX wieku, materiały z wystawy i sesji naukowej*, edited by Aleksandra Garlicka and Jerzy

Jedlicki, 145–58. Warsaw: Galeria Sztuki Współczesnej Zachęta: Polskie Towarzystwo Historyczne.
Mendelsohn, Ezra. 1971. "From Assimilation to Zionism in Lvov: The Case of Alfred Nossig." *Slavonic and East European Review* 49:521–34.
Meyer-Renschhausen, Elisabeth. 1989. *Weibliche Kultur und soziale Arbeit: Eine Geschichte der Frauenbewegung am Beispiel Bremens 1810–1927.* Cologne: Böhlau.
Micińska, Magdalena. 2008. *Inteligencja na rozdrożach 1864–1918.* Warsaw: Neriton.
Mickutė, Jolanta. 2014. "Making of the Zionist Woman: Zionist Discourse on the Jewish Woman's Body and Selfhood in Interwar Poland." *East European Politics and Societies and Cultures* 28:137–62. Accessed December 6, 2019. http://erf.sbb.spk-berlin.de/han/505083922/https/journals.sagepub.com/doi/pdf/10.1177/0888325413493113.
Molenda, Jan. 1999. *Chłopi, Naród, Niepodległość: Kształtowanie się postaw narodowych i obywatelskich chłopów w Galicji i Królestwie Polskim w przededniu odrodzenia Polski.* Warsaw: Neriton.
Monakhva, Natalia V. (2006) 2008. "Pchilka, Olena." In *A Biographical Dictionary of Women's Movements and Feminisms: Central, Eastern, and South Eastern Europe, 19th and 20th Centuries.* Revised edition by Francisca de Haan, Krassimira Daskalova, and Anna Loutfi, 416–19. Budapest: Central European University Press.
———. (2006) 2008. "Ukrainka, Lesia." In *A Biographical Dictionary of Women's Movements and Feminisms: Central, Eastern, and South Eastern Europe, 19th and 20th Centuries.* Revised edition by Francisca de Haan, Krassimira Daskalova, and Anna Loutfi, 592–94. Budapest: Central European University Press.
Montel, Angela. 1997. "Women and Zionist Journalism: 'Frauen in der Welt der Männer.'" In *Theodor Herzl and the Origins of Zionism,* edited by Ritchie Robertson and Edward Timms, 87–95. Edinburgh: Edinburgh University Press.
Moroz, Oleg N. 1958. "Natalja Kobryns'ka ta ïï tvory." In Natalja Kobryns'ka, *Vybrani tvory,* edited by Oleg N. Moroz, 3–27. Kiev: Deržavne Vydavnictvo Chudožn'oï Literatury.
Moser, Michael. 2000. "Die Entwicklung der ukrainischen Schriftsprache." *Österreichische Osthefte* 42:483–95.
Mosse, George L. 1985. *Nationalism and Sexuality: Respectability and Abnormal Sexualitity in Modern Europe.* New York: Howard Fertig.
Możejko, Edward. 1999. "Modernizm literacki: Niejasność terminu i dychotomia kierunku." In *Modernizm a literatury narodowe,* edited by Eugenia Łoch, 9–25. Lublin: Wydawnictwo Uniwersytetu Marii Curie-Skłodowskiej.
Müller, Michael G. 2000. "Die Historisierung des bürgerlichen Projekts—Europa, Osteuropa und die Kategorie der Rückständigkeit." *Tel Aviver Jahrbuch für deutsche Geschichte* 29:163–70.
———. 2002. "Wie ethnisch war die Nation? Ethnizität in polnischen und deutschen nationalen Diskursen." *Tel Aviver Jahrbuch für deutsche Geschichte* 30:104–15.
Müller-Funk, Wolfgang. 2002. "Kakanien revisited: Über das Verhältnis von Herrschaft und Kultur." In *Kakanien revisited: Das Eigene und das*

Fremde (in) der österreichisch-ungarischen Monarchie, edited by Wolfgang Müller-Funk, Peter Plener, and Clemens Ruthner, 14–32. Tübingen: Francke Verlag. Accessed December 6, 2019. www.kakanien-revisited.at/beitr/theorie/WMueller-Funk1.pdf.

Munslow, Alun. 2007. *Narrative and History*. Basingstoke: Red Globe Press.

Myśliński, Jerzy. 1991. "Wysłouchowie—twórcy prasy ludwej." *Kwartalnik Historii Prasy Polskiej* XXX:145–52.

Najdus, Walentyna. 1994. "O prawa obywatelskie kobiet w zaborze austriackim." *Kobieta i świat polityki: Polska na tle porównawczym w XIX i w początkach XX wieków*, edited by Anna Żarnowska and Andrzej Szwarc, 99–118. Warsaw: Wydawnictwo "DiG."

Neuman, Shirley. 1991. "Autobiography and Questions of Gender: An Introduction." In *Autobiography and Questions of Gender*, edited by Shirley Neuman, 1–11. London: F. Cass.

Nacionaln'na akademija nauk Ukrainy. Instytut literatury im. T. H. Ševčenka, ed. 1999. *Putivnyk po fondach Viddilu Rukopysiv Instytutu Literatury*. Kiev: Vydavnyčyj Centr "Spadščyna."

Nickisch, Reinhard M. G. 1991. *Brief*. Stuttgart: J.B. Metzler.

Niess, Wolfgang. 1984. *Volkshäuser, Freizeitheime, Kommunikationszentren: Zum Wandel kultureller Infrastruktur sozialer Bewegungen: Beispiele aus deutschen Städten von 1848–1984*. Hagen: Kulturpolitische Gesellschaft.

Nietyksza, Maria. 1995. "Kobiety w ruchu oświatowym: Królestwo Polskie na przełomie wieków." In *Kobieta i edukacja na ziemiach polskich w XIX i XX wieku*. Vol. II, part 2, edited by Anna Żarnowska and Andrzej Szwarc, 63–82. Warsaw: Wydawnictwo "DiG."

Nitsch, Meinolf. 1998. "Die vereinsgetragene Sozialreform im Berlin des Kaiserreichs." *Berlin in Geschichte und Gegenwart: Jahrbuch des Landesarchivs Berlin*, 83–104.

———. 1999. *Private Wohltätigkeitsvereine im Kaiserreich: Die praktische Umsetzung der bürgerlichen Sozialreform in Berlin*. Berlin: De Gruyter.

Nünning, Vera and Ansgar Nünning. 2006. "Making Gendered Selves: Analysekategorien und Forschungsperspektiven einer genderorientierten Erzähltheorie und Erzähltextanalyse." In *Narration und Geschlecht*, edited by Sigrid Niberle and Elisabeth Strowick, 23–44. Cologne: Böhlau.

Offen, Karen. 2000. *European Feminisms 1700–1950: A Political History*. Stanford, CA: Stanford University Press.

———. 2004. "Feminist Criticism and the Context for Women's Movements, 1789–1860." In *Women's Emancipation Movements in the 19th Century: A European Perspective*, edited by Sylvia Paletschek and Bianka Pietrow-Ennker, 11–30. Stanford, CA: Stanford University Press.

Olechowski, Thomas. 2006. "Das Preßrecht in der Habsburgermonarchie." *Die Habsburgermonarchie 1848–1918*. Vol. VIII: *Politische Öffentlichkeit und Zivilgesellschaft*. Fascicle 2: *Die Presse als Faktor der politischen Mobilisierung*, edited by Helmut Rumpler and Peter Urbanitsch, 1493–1533. Vienna: Verlag der Österreichischen Akademie der Wissenschaften.

Onyškevyč, Larysa M. L. Zales'ka. 1984. "Biohrafični informaciï pro avtorok." In *Peršyj vinok: Žinočyj al'manach*, edited by Natalija Kobryns'ka and Olena Pčilka, 465–81. New York: Soiuz Ukraïnok Ameryky.

———. 1984. "Jak sleteno vinok." In *Peršyi vinok: Žinočyj al'manach*, edited by Natalija Kobryns'ka and Olena Pčilka, VII–XIX. New York: Soiuz Ukraïnok Ameryky.
Or, Tamara. 2009. *Vorkämpferinnen und Mütter des Zionismus: Die deutsch-zionistischen Frauenorganisationen (1897–1938)*. Frankfurt am Main: Peter Lang.
Pacholkiv, Svjatoslav. 2002. *Emanzipation durch Bildung: Entwicklung und gesellschaftliche Rolle der ukrainischen Intelligenz im habsburgischen Galizien (1890–1914)*. Vienna: Verlag für Geschichte und Politik.
Paletschek, Sylvia and Bianka Pietrow-Ennker. 2004. "Women's Emancipation Movements in the Long Nineteenth Century: Conclusions." In *Women's Emancipation Movements in the Nineteenth Century: A European Perspective*, edited by Sylvia Paletschek and Bianka Pietrow-Ennker, 301–33. Stanford, CA: Stanford University Press.
Partacz, Czesław. 1996. *Od Badeniego do Potockiego: Stosunki polsko-ukraińskie w Galicji w latach 1888–1908*. Toruń: Wydawnictwo Adam Marszałek.
Parush, Iris. 1997. "Women Readers as Agents of Social Change Among Eastern European Jews in the Late Nineteenth Century." *Gender and History* 9:60–82.
———. 2004. *Reading Jewish Women: Marginality and Modernization in Nineteenth-Century Eastern European Jewish Society*. Hanover: Brandeis.
Pavlychko, Solomea. 1996. "Modernism vs. Populism in Fin de Siècle Ukrainian Literature: A Case of Gender Conflict." In *Engendering Slavic Literatures*, edited by Pamela Chester and Sibelan Forrester, 83–103. Bloomington: Indiana University Press.
"Perl, Josef." 1968. *Leksikon fun der neyer jidischer Literatur*. Vol. 7, cols. 183–84. New York: Congress for Jewish Culture.
Pierson, Ruth Roach. 2000. "Nations: Gendered, Racialized, Crossed with Empire." In *Gendered Nations: Nationalisms and Gender Order in the Long Nineteenth Century*, edited by Ida Blom, Karen Hagemann, and Catherine Hall, 41–61. Oxford: Berg Publishers.
Piesker, Yvonne. 2006. *Die Diskurse zur höheren Mädchen- und Frauenbildung in Deutschand und Russland: Vom ausgehenden 18. Jahrhundert bis zu den Anfängen des Frauenstudiums*. Berlin: sine causa Verlag.
———. 2011. "Die höhere Mädchen- und Frauenbildung in Russland in der zweiten Hälfte des 19. Jahrhunderts." In *Bildungskonzepte und Bildungsinitiativen in Nordosteuropa*, edited by Anja Wilhelmi, 292–308. Wiesbaden: Harrassowitz Verlag.
Pietrow-Ennker, Bianka. 1992. "Women in Polish Society: A Historical Introduction." In *Women in Polish Society*, edited by Rudolf Jaworski and Bianka Pietrow-Ennker, 1–29. New York: Columbia University Press.
———. 1999. *Russlands "neue Menschen": Die Entwicklung der Frauenbewegung von den Anfängen bis zur Oktoberrevolution*. Frankfurt am Main: Campus Verlag.
Piwarski, Kazimierz. 1937. "Chrzanowska Anna Dorota." In *Polski Słownik Biograficzny*, edited by Polska Akademia Nauk and Polska Akademia Umiętności, Vol. III, 458. Kraków: Polska Akademia Umiejętności.
Plach, Ewa. 2005. "Feminism and Nationalism in the Pages of Ewa: Tygodnik, 1928–1933." In *Jewish Women in Eastern Europe*, edited by Chaeran Freeze, Paula Hyman, and Anthony Polonsky, 241–62. Oxford: Taylor & Francis.

Planert, Ute. 2000. "Vater Staat und Mutter Germania: Zur Politisierung des weiblichen Geschlechts im 19. und 20. Jahrhundert." In *Nation, Politik und Geschlecht: Frauenbewegungen und Nationalismus in der Moderne*, edited by Ute Planert, 15–65. Frankfurt am Main: Campus Verlag.
Polonsky, Antony. 2010. *The Jews in Poland and Russia*. Vol. II: *1881 to 1914*. Oxford: Littman Library of Jewish Civilization.
Polowy, Teresa. (2006) 2008. "Kobylianska, Olha." In *A Biographical Dictionary of Women's Movements and Feminisms: Central, Eastern, and South Eastern Europe, 19th and 20th Centuries*. Revised edition by Francisca de Haan, Krassimira Daskalova, and Anna Loutfi, 248–52. Budapest: Central European University Press.
Porter, Brian. 2000. *When Nationalism Began to Hate: Imagining Modern Politics in Nineteenth-Century Poland*. Oxford: Oxford University Press.
Potoczny, Jerzy. 1986. "Wkład galicyjskich towarzystw oświatowych w rozwój praktyki i teorii popularyzacji wiedzy wśród dorosłych." *Rocznik Komisji Nauk Pedagogicznych* XXXVI: 35–50.
———. 1988. *Rozwój elementarnej oświaty dorosłych w Galicji doby autonomicznej, 1867–1918*. Rzeszów: Wydawnictwo Wyższej Szkoły Pedagogicznej.
———. 1990. "Wkład towarzystw oświatowych Galicji doby autonomicznej w rozwój czytelnictwa i czytelni ludowych." *Rocznik Przemyski* XXVII:251–79.
———. 1994. *Od alfabetyzacji do popularyzacji wiedzy: Ruch oświaty dorosłych w Galicji (1867 1918)*. Rzeszów: Wydawnictwo Wyższej Szkoły Pedagogicznej.
———. 1996. "Problematyka oświaty ludowej w programach galicyjskiego ruchu ludowego (1870–1918)." In *Chłopi. Naród. Kultury*. Vol. 4: *Kultura i oświata wsi*, edited by Andrzej Meissner, 133–43. Rzeszów: Wydawnictwo Wyższej Szkoły Pedagogicznej.
———. 1998. *Oświata dorosłych i popularyzacja wiedzy w plebejskich środowiskach Galicji doby konstytucyjnej (1867–1918)*. Rzeszów: Wydawnictwo Wyższej Szkoły Pedagogicznej.
Prestel, Claudia T. 1994. "Frauen und die Zionistische Bewegung (1897–1933)." *Historische Zeitschrift* 258:29–71.
Prunitsch, Christian, ed. 2009. *Konzeptionalisierung und Status kleiner Kulturen: Beiträge zur gleichnamigen Konferenz in Dresden vom 3. bis 6. März 2008*. Munich: Sagner.
Pynchon, Thomas. 2006. *Against the Day*. New York: Penguin Press.
"Rabinowich, Sarah." 2007. *Encyclopaedia Judaica*. Vol. 17, 39. Detroit: Thomson Gale.
Raphael, Lutz. 2009. "Jenseits von Strukturwandel oder Ereignis? Neuere Sichtweisen und Schwierigkeiten der Historiker im Umgang mit Wandel und Innovation." *Historische Anthropologie* 17:110–20.
Reckwitz, Andreas. 2003. "Grundelemente einer Theorie sozialer Praktiken: Eine sozialtheoretische Perspektive." *Zeitschrift für Soziologie* 32 (4): 282–301.
Red. 1959/60. "Golińska l. V. Daszyńska Zofia." In *Polski Słownik Biograficzny*, edited by Polska Akademia Nauk and Polska Akademia Umiętności, Vol. VIII, 223–25. Wrocław: Wydawnictwo Polskiej Akademii Nauk.
Rędziński, Kazimierz. 2000. *Żydowskie szkolnictwo świeckie w Galicji w latach 1813–1918*. Częstochowa: Wydawnictwo Wyższej Szkoły Pedagogicznej.

Bibliography

Requate, Jörg. 1999. "Öffentlichkeit und Medien als Gegenstände historischer Analyse." *Geschichte und Gesellschaft* 25:5–32.

Reyer, Jürgen. 1983. *Wenn die Mütter arbeiten gingen... Eine sozialhistorische Studie zur Entstehung der öffentlichen Kleinkinderziehung im 19. Jahrhundert in Deutschland*. Cologne: Pahl-Rugenstein.

Rezler, Marek. 1995/96. "Sczaniecka Emilia." In *Polski Słownik Biograficzny*, edited by Polska Akademia Nauk and Polska Akademia Umiętności. Vol. XXXVI, 95–97. Warsaw: Wydawnictwo Polskiej Akademii Nauk.

Ricœur, Paul. 1998. *Das Rätsel der Vergangenheit: Erinnern—Vergessen—Verzeihen*, translated by Andris Breitling and Henrik Richard Lesaar. Göttingen: Wallstein Verlag. (French original 1998).

Ritz, German. (1998) 2002. "Młoda Polska a transgresja płciowa," translated by Małgorzata Łukasiewicz. In *Nić w labiryncie pożądania: Gender i płeć w literaturze polskiej od romantyzmu do postmodernizmu*, 111–36. Warsaw: Wiedza Powszechna.

Roberts, Mary Louise. 2002. *Disruptive Acts: The New Woman in Fin-de-siècle France*. Chicago, IL: University of Chicago Press.

Romankówna, Mieczysława. 1984. "Dwa bieguny." In *Literatura Polska: Przewodnik encyklopedyczny*, edited by Julian Krzyżanowski and Czesław Hernas, 217. Warsaw: Państwowe Wydawnictwo Naukowe.

Rose, Alison. 2006. "Die 'Neue Jüdische Familie': Frauen, Geschlecht und Nation im zionistischen Denken." In *Deutsch-jüdische Geschichte als Geschlechtergeschichte: Studien zum 19. und 20. Jahrhundert*, edited by Kirsten Heinsohn and Stefanie Schüler-Springorum, 177–95. Göttingen: Wallstein Verlag.

———. 2008. *Jewish Women in Fin de Siècle Vienna*. Austin: University of Texas Press.

Rosman, Moshe. 2002. "A Prolegomenon to the Study of Jewish Cultural History." *Jewish Studies, an Internet Journal* 1:109–27. Accessed December 8, 2012. https://jewish-faculty.biu.ac.il/files/jewish-faculty/shared/JSIJ1/rosman.pdf.

Rucht, Dieter. 2017. "Studying Social Movements: Some Conceptual Challenges." In *The History of Social Movements in Global Perspective: A Survey*, edited by Stefan Berger and Holger Nehring, 39–62. London: Palgrave Macmillan.

Rudnicki, Szymon. 2004. *Żydzi w parlamencie II rzeczypospolitej*. Warsaw: Wydawnictwo Sejmowe.

Rudnytsky, Ivan L. 1987. "Drahomanov as a Political Theorist." In *Essays in Modern Ukrainian History*, edited by Peter L. Rudnytsky, 203–54. Edmonton: University of Toronto Press.

———. 1989. "The Ukrainians in Galicia under the Austrian Rule." In *Nationbuilding and the Politics of Nationalism: Essays on Austrian Galicia*, edited by Andrei S. Markovits and Frank E. Sysyn, 23–67. Cambridge, MA: Harvard University Press.

Rumpler, Helmut. 2006. "Von der 'bürgerlichen Öffentlichkeit' zur Massendemokratie: Zivilgesellschaft und politische Partizipation im Vielvölkerstaat der Habsburgermonarchie." In *Die Habsburgermonarchie 1848–1918*. Vol. VIII: *Politische Öffentlichkeit und Zivilgesellschaft*. Fascicle 1: *Vereine, Parteien und Interessenverbände als Träger der politischen Partizipation*, edited by Helmut Rumpler and Peter Urbanitsch, 1–14. Vienna: Verlag der Österreichischen Akademie der Wissenschaften.

Rupp, Leila J. 1997. *Worlds of Women: The Making of the International Women's Movement.* Princeton, NJ: Princeton University Press.

Rüthers, Monica. 1996. *Tewjes Töchter: Lebensentwürfe ostjüdischer Frauen im 19. Jahrhundert.* Cologne: Böhlau.

Ryan, Louise. 1997. "A Question of Loyalty: War, Nation, and Feminism in Early Twentieth-Century Ireland." *International Forum* 20:21–32.

Rzepecki, Jan. 1977. "Moszczeńska (Moszczeńska–Rzepecka) Iza." In *Polski Słownik Biograficzny*, edited by Polska Akademia Nauk and Polska Akademia Umiętności, Vol. XXII, 80–85. Wrocław: Wydawnictwo Polskiej Akademii Nauk.

Sachße, Christoph. 1986. *Mütterlichkeit als Beruf: Sozialarbeit, Sozialreform und Frauenbewegung 1871–1929.* Frankfurt am Main: Suhrkamp.

Sachße, Christoph and Florian Tennstedt. 1986. *Soziale Sicherheit und soziale Disziplinierung: Beiträge zu einer historischen Theorie der Sozialpolitik.* Frankfurt am Main: Suhrkamp.

———. 1988. *Geschichte der Armenfürsorge in Deutschland.* Vol. 2: *Fürsorge und Wohlfahrtspflege 1871 bis 1929.* Stuttgart: Kohlhammer Verlag.

Salomon, Richard. 1997. "'A Simulacrum of Power': Intimacy and Abstraction in the Rhetoric of the New Journalism." *Victorian Periodicals Review* 30:41–52.

Samuel, Raphael. 1994. *Theatres of Memory.* Vol. I: *Past and Present in Contemporary Culture.* London: Verso.

Sandler, Bella. 1958. "System Froebla w Galicji." *Rozprawy z Dziejów Oświaty* 1:199–223.

Sarasin, Philipp. (2001) 2003. "Die Wirklichkeit der Fiktion: Zum Konzept der 'imagined communities.'" In *Geschichtswissenschaft und Diskursanalyse,* 150–76. Frankfurt am Main: Suhrkamp.

———. (2001) 2003. "Geschichtswissenschaft und Diskursanalyse." In *Geschichtswissenschaft und Diskursanalyse,* 10–60. Frankfurt am Main: Suhrkamp.

Saurer, Edith. 2006. "Frauenbewegung und soziale Netzwerke: Kommentar zur Karriere eines Begriffs." In *Das Jahrhundert des Feminismus: Streifzüge durch nationale und internationale Bewegungen und Theorien,* edited by Anja Weckwert and Ulla Wischermann, 77–94. Königstein, Taunus: Ulrike Helmer Verlag.

Schaser, Angelika. (2000) 2010. *Helene Lange und Gertrud Bäumer: Eine politische Lebensgemeinschaft.* Cologne: Böhlau.

Schenk, Frithjof Benjamin. 2007. "Das Paradigma des Raumes in der Osteuropäischen Geschichte." *zeitenblicke* 6:1–23. Accessed December 8, 2019. www.zeitenblicke.de/2007/2/schenk.

Schenker, Anatol. 1997. "Zionist Press and Publishing Houses in German-Speaking Countries: A Survey from the Beginning up to the Second World War." In *The First Zionist Congress in 1897: Causes—Significance—Topicality,* edited by Heiko Haumann, translated by Wayne van Dalsum and Vivian Kramer, 324–27. Basel: Karger.

Schieb, Roswitha. 2000. *Reise nach Schlesien und Galizien: Eine Archäologie des Gefühls.* Berlin: Berlin Verlag.

Schiffmann, Minna. 1931. "Die deutsche Ghettogeschichte." PhD diss, University of Vienna.

Schlientz, Gisela. 2002. "Verdeckte Botschaften: George Sands Briefwechsel mit ihren politischen Freunden." In *Politische Netzwerke durch Briefkommunikation: Briefkultur der politischen Oppositionsbewegungen und frühen Arbeiterbewegungen im 19. Jahrhundert*, edited by Jürgen Herres and Manfred Neuhaus, 27–47. Berlin: Akademie Verlag.

Scholze, Dietrich. 1984. Nachwort to Eliza Orzeszkowa. *Marta*, translated by Peter Ball, 256–60. Berlin: Verlag der Nation.

Schröder, Iris. 2001. *Arbeiten für eine bessere Welt: Frauenbewegung und Sozialreform 1890–1914*. Frankfurt am Main: Campus Verlag.

Schüler, Anja. 2004. *Frauenbewegung und soziale Reform: Jane Addams und Alice Salomon im transatlantischen Dialog, 1889–1933*. Stuttgart: Franz Steiner Verlag.

Schulte, Dagmar. 2006. "A History of Social Work in Eight East European Countries from 1900 to 1960—An Overview." In Sabine Hering and Berteke Waaldijk. *Guardians of the Poor—Custodians of the Public: Welfare History in Eastern Europe 1900–1960*. In cooperation with Kurt Schilde and Dagmar Schulte, 83–140. Opladen and Farmington Hills: Barbara Budrich Publishers.

Schulte, Regina. 1995. "Käthe Kollwitz' Opfer." In *Von der Aufgabe der Freiheit: Politische Verantwortung und bürgerliche Gesellschaft im 19. und 20. Jahrhundert: Festschrift für Hans Mommsen zum 5. November 1995*, edited by Christian Jansen, Lutz Niethammer, and Bernd Weisbrod, 647–72. Berlin: Akademie Verlag.

Scott, Joan W. 1988. Introduction to *Gender and the Politics of History*, 1–14. New York: Columbia University Press.

———. 1992. "'Experience.'" In *Feminists Theorize the Political*, edited by Judith Butler and Joan W. Scott, 22–40. New York: Routledge.

———. 1996. *Only Paradoxes to Offer: French Feminists and the Rights of Man*. Cambridge, MA: Harvard University Press.

———. 2001. "Phantasie und Erfahrung," translated by Regine Othmer. *Feministische Studien* 19:74–88.

Sdvižkov, Denis. 2006. *Das Zeitalter der Intelligenz: Zur vergleichenden Geschichte der Gebildeten in Europa bis zum Ersten Weltkrieg*. Göttingen: Vandenhoeck & Ruprecht.

Seidman, Naomi. 2000. "The Modernist Erotics of Jewish Tradition: A View from the Gallery." In *Jews and Gender: The Challenge to Hierarchy*, edited by Jonathan Fraenkel, 156–70. Oxford: Oxford University Press.

Sellin, Volker. 1988. "Nationalbewußtsein und Partikularismus in Deutschland im 19. Jahrhundert." In *Kultur und Gedächtnis*, edited by Jan Assmann and Tonio Hölscher, 241–64. Frankfurt am Main: Suhrkamp.

Senkus, Roman. 1993. "Pavlyk, Mykhailo", In *Internet Encyclopedia of Ukraine*. Accessed December 8, 2019. www.encyclopediaofukraine.com/display.asp?linkpath=pages%5CP%5CA%5CPavlykMykhailo.htm.

Serrier, Thomas. 2005. *Provinz Posen, Ostmark, Wielkopolska: Eine Grenzregion zwischen Deutschen und Polen 1848–1914*. Marburg: Verlag Herder-Institut.

Shanes, Joshua. 2012. *Diaspora Nationalism and Jewish Identity in Habsburg Galicia*. Cambridge: Cambridge University Press.

Shedletzky, Itta. 1996. "Ost und West in der deutsch-jüdischen Literatur von Heinrich Heine bis Joseph Roth." In *Von Franzos zu Canetti: Jüdische Autoren aus Österreich: Neue Studien,* edited by Mark H. Gelber, Hans O. Horch, and Sigurd Scheichl, 189–200. Tübingen: Niemeyer.

Shepherd, Naomi. 1993. *A Price Below Rubies: Jewish Women as Rebels & Radicals.* Cambridge, MA: Harvard University Press.

Shilo, Margalit. 1996. "The Transformation of the Role of Women in the First Aliyah, 1882–1903." *Jewish Social Studies* 2:64–86.

———. 1998. "The Double or Multiple Image of the New Hebrew Woman." *Nashim: A Journal of Jewish Women's Studies* I:73–94.

Shimoni, Gideon. 1995. *The Zionist Ideology.* Hanover: Brandeis University Press, 1995.

Siadkowski, Marcin. 2009. "The Land Exhibition in Lemberg (Lwów, L'viv) in 1894, Galicia and Schlachzizen in the German Political Discourse in Vienna." *Zeitschrift für Ostmitteleuropaforschung* 58:197–222.

Sieder, Reinhard. 2007. Editorial to *Österreichische Zeitschrift für Geschichtswissenschaften* 18 (3): *Liebe: Diskurse und Praktiken,* 5–12.

Sikorska-Kulesza, Jolanta. 2003. "Prostytucja a program reformy obyczajów na początku XX w." In *Społeczeństwo w dobie przemian wiek XIX i XX: Księga jubileuszowa Profesor Anny Żarnowskiej,* edited by Maria Nietyksza, Katarzyna Sierakowska, and Agnieszka Janiak-Jasińska, 119–26. Warsaw: Wydawnictwo "DiG."

———. 2008. "Trójzaborowe zjazdy kobiet na ziemiach polskich na przełomie XIX i XX wieku." In *Działaczki społeczne, feministki, obywatelki... Samoorganizowanie się kobiet na ziemiach polskich do 1918 roku (na tle porównawczym),* edited by Agnieszka Janiak-Jasińska, Katarzyna Sierakowska, and Andrzej Szwarc, 81–95. Warsaw: Neriton.

Simon, Hermann. 2006. "Afterword: In Search of Karl Baer." In N. O. Body. *Memoirs of a Man's Maiden Years,* translated by Deborah Simon. 113–36. Philadelphia: University of Pennsylvania Press.

Simonek, Stefan. 2000. "Ukrainische Literatur und Wiener Moderne." *Österreichische Osthefte* 42:541–51.

———. 2008. "Franko, Przemycki, Wien—Zur Relevanz urbaner Lebenswelten um 1900 als tertium comparationis jenseits von Nationalliteraturen." In *Die Ukrainer (Ruthenen, Russinen) in Österreich-Ungarn und ihr Sprach- und Kulturleben im Blickfeld von Wien und Budapest,* edited by Michael Moser and András Zoltán, 221–45. Vienna: LIT-Verlag.

———. 2011. "Zwischen 'Drittem Raum' und 'pulsierender Region': Mitteleuropa als Schnittstelle 'autochthoner' und 'übersetzter' Theorieangebote." In *Überbringen—Überformen—Überblenden: Theorietransfer im 20. Jahrhundert,* edited by Dietlind Hüchtker and Alfrun Kliems, 163–86. Cologne: Böhlau.

Sitton, Shoshana. 2001. "The Struggle for Professional Recognition: Hebrew-Language Kindergarten Teachers in Palestine, 1899–1920." *Journal of Educational Administration and History* 33:87–101.

Śliwa, Michał. 1994. "Nędza Galicyjska: Mit i rzeczywistość." In *Historia i polityka,* edited by Włodzimierz Bonusiak and Józef Buszko. 145–55. Rzeszów: Wydawnictwo Wyższej Szkoły Pedagogicznej.

Smith, Bonnie G. 1998. *The Gender of History: Men, Women, and Historical Practice*. Cambridge, MA: Harvard University Press.

Smolyar, Lyudmyla. 2006. "The Ukrainian Experiment: Between Feminism and Nationalism or the Main Features of Pragmatic Feminism." In *Women's Movements: Networks and Debates in Post-communist Countries in the 19th and 20th Centuries*, edited by Edith Saurer, Margareth Lanzinger, and Elisabeth Frysak. 397–411. Cologne: Böhlau.

Snoek, Johannes. 2003. "Performance, Performativity, and Practice: Against Terminological Confusion in Ritual Studies." *Paragrana* 12:78–87.

Sohn, Anne-Marie. 2000. "Between the Wars in France and England", translated by Arthur Goldhammer. In *A History of Women in the West*, edited by Georges Duby and Michelle Perrot. Vol. V: *Toward a Cultural Identity in the Twentieth Century*, edited by Françoise Thébaud, 92–119. Cambridge, MA: The Belknap Press of Harvard University Press. (Italian original 1992).

Sokół, Zofia. 1982. "'Przodownica' (1899–1912): Zarys monograficzny." *Rocznik Naukowo-Dydaktyczny* 78:99–124.

———. 1984. "'Zorza' Marii Wysłouchowej (1900–1902)." *Kwartalnik Historii Prasy Polskiej* 23:53–70.

Spurlock, John. 1988. "The Free Love Network in America, 1850 to 1860." *Journal of Social History* 21:765–80.

Stalleybrass, Peter and Allon White. 1986. *The Politics and Poetics of Transgression*. London: Cornell University Press.

Stampfer, Shaul. 2010. *Families, Rabbis, and Education: Traditional Jewish Society in Nineteenth-Century Eastern Europe*. Oxford: Littman Library of Jewish Civilization.

Stanislawski, Michael. 2001. *Zionism and the Fin de Siècle: Cosmopolitanism and Nationalism from Nordau to Jabotinsky*. Berkeley: University of California Press.

Starck, Astrid. 1998. "Kampf gegen Assimilation und gegen die Politik der Alliance Israélite Universelle: Der elsässische Zionist Alfred Elias (1865–1940)." In *Der Traum von Israel: Die Ursprünge des modernen Zionismus*, edited by Heiko Haumann, 274–94. Weinheim: Beltz Athenäum.

Staudacher, Anna. 1990. "Die Aktion 'Girondo': Zur Geschichte des internationalen Mädchenhandels in Österreich-Ungarn um 1885." In *"Das Weib existiert nicht für sich": Geschlechterbeziehungen in der bürgerlichen Gesellschaft*, edited by Heide Dienst and Edith Saurer, 97–138. Vienna: Verlag für Gesellschaftskritik.

Stauter-Halsted, Keely. 1994. "Patriotic Celebrations in Austrian Poland: The Kościuszko Centennial and the Formation of Peasant Nationalism." *Austrian History Yearbook* 25:79–95.

———. 2001. *The Nation in the Village: The Genesis of Peasant National Identity in Austrian Poland 1848–1914*. Ithaca, NY: Cornell University Press.

———. 2015. *The Devil's Chain: Prostitution and Social Control in Partitioned Poland*. Ithaca, NY: Cornell University Press.

Steffen, Katrin. 2004. *Jüdische Polonität: Ethnizität und Nation im Spiegel der polnischsprachigen jüdischen Presse 1918–1939*. Göttingen: Vandenhoeck & Ruprecht.

———. 2005. "Connotations of Exclusion—'Ostjuden,' 'Ghettos,' and Other Markings." *Jahrbuch des Simon-Dubnow-Instituts/Simon Dubnow Institute Yearbook* 4:459–79.

———. 2007. "Für 'bewusste Mutterschaft' und eine 'physische Erneuerung der Judenheit'—die jüdische Frauenzeitschrift Ewa (1928–1933) in Warschau." In *Frauen und Frauenbilder in der europäisch-jüdischen Presse von der Aufklärung bis 1945*, edited by Eleonore Lappi and Michael Nagel, 103–22. Bremen: Ed. Lumière.

Stegmann, Natali. 1999. "Zwischen feministischem Kampf und nationalem Opfer: Weibliche Leitfiguren der polnischen Frauenbewegung vor dem Ersten Weltkrieg." In *Normsetzung und -überschreitung: Geschlecht in der Geschichte Osteuropas im 19. und 20. Jahrhundert*, edited by Carmen Scheide and Natali Stegmann, 19–33. Bochum: Winkler.

———. 2000. *Die Töchter der geschlagenen Helden: "Frauenfrage," Feminismus und Frauenbewegung in Polen 1863–1919*. Wiesbaden: Harrassowitz Verlag.

———. 2000. "Paradygmaty nauk przyrodniczych, ruch kobiecy i kategoria 'sex': O ustaleniu ról płciowych w polskim ruchu na rzecz moralności w przededniu pierwszej wojny światowej." In *Nowa świadomość płci w modernizmie: Studia spod znaku gender w kulturze polskiej i rosyjskiej u schyłku stulecia*, edited by German Ritz, Christa Binswanger, and Carmen Scheide, 33–50. Kraków: Towarzystwo autorów i wydawców prac naukowych "Universitas."

Stierle, Karlheinz. 1973. "Geschichte als Exemplum—Exemplum als Geschichte: Zur Pragmatik und Poetik narrativer Texte." In *Geschichte—Ereignis und Erzählung*, edited by Reinhart Koselleck and Wolf-Dieter Stempel, 347–75. Munich: Fink Verlag.

Stites, Richard. (1978) 1990. *The Women's Liberation Movement in Russia: Feminism, Nihilism, and Bolshevism, 1860–1930*. Princeton, NJ: Princeton University Press.

Stollberg-Rilinger, Barbara, "Was heißt Kulturgeschichte des Politischen?" In *Was heißt Kulturgeschichte des Politischen?* edited by Barbara Stollberg-Rilinger, 9–24. Berlin: Duncker & Humblot.

Stopińska-Pająk, Agnieszka. 1995. "Polska oświata dorosłych w Galicji na przełomie XIX i XX wieku: Kierunki i formy kształcenia." In *Nauka i oświata*, edited by Andrzej Meissner and Jerzy Wyrozumski, 239–51. Rzeszów: Wydawnictwo Wyższej Szkoły Pedagogicznej.

Strasser, Sabine and Gerlinde Schein. 1997. "Intersexions oder der Abschied von den Anderen: Zur Debatte um Kategorien und Identitäten in der feministischen Anthropologie." In *Intersexions: Feministische Anthropologie zu Geschlecht, Kultur und Sexualität*, edited by Sabine Strasser and Gerlinde Schein, 7–32. Vienna: Milena.

Struve, Kai. 2005. *Bauern und Nation in Galizien: Über Zugehörigkeit und soziale Emanzipation im 19. Jahrhundert*. Göttingen: Vandenhoeck & Ruprecht.

Subtelny, Orest. (1988) 1994. *Ukraine: A History*. Toronto: University of Toronto Press.

Suchmiel, Jadwiga. 2006. "Books and Periodicals on the Women's Movement and a Changing Model of Women's Education on Polish Territories at the Turn of the 19th Century." In *Women's Movements: Networks and Debates in Post-communist Countries in the 19th and 20th Centuries*, edited by Edith Saurer, Margareth Lanzinger, and Elisabeth Frysak, 541–57. Cologne: Böhlau.

Swindells, Julia, ed. 1995. *The Uses of Autobiography*. London: Taylor & Francis.

Szmyd, Kazimierz. 2002. "Z dziejów zakonnej opieki nad dzieckiem na Podkarpaciu." In *Opieka nad dzieckiem w Galicji*, edited by Andrzej Meissner, 130–51. Rzeszów: Wydawnictwo Uniwersytetu Rzeszowskiego.
Tatarowski, Lesław. 1991. *Ludowość w literaturze Młodej Polski.* Wrocław: Wydawnictwo Uniwersytetu Wrocławskiego.
Taylor, Barbara. 1983. *Eve and the New Jerusalem: Socialism and Feminism in the Nineteenth Century.* London: Pantheon Books.
Terlecki, Ryszard. 1990. *Oświata dorosłych i popularyzacja nauki w Galicji w okresie autonomii.* Wrocław: Zakład Narodowy im. Ossolińskich.
Turda, Marius. 2010. *Modernism and Eugenics.* Basingstoke: Palgrave Macmillan.
Turner, Victor. 1967. "Betwixt and Between: The Liminal Period in Rites de Passage." In *The Forest of Symbols: Aspects of Ndembu Ritual*, 93–111. Ithaca: Cornell University Press.
———. 1982. *From Ritual to Theatre: The Human Seriousness of Play.* New York City: Performing Arts Journal Publications.
Turska, Jadwiga, ed. 1948. *Inwentarz rękopisów biblioteki zakładu narodowego im. Ossolińskich we Wrocławiu.* Vol. I. Wrocław: Zakład Narodowy im. Ossolińskich.
Ustrzycki, Mirosław. 2000. "Pomiędzy konserwatyzmem a nacjonalizmem: Podolacy wobec kwestii narodowej na wsi wschodniogalicyjskiej na przełomie XIX i XX wieku (do roku 1908)." *Przegląd Wschodni* VI (3/23): 477–98.
Van Dülmen, Richard. 1997. *Die Entdeckung des Individuums 1500–1800.* Frankfurt am Main: Fischer Taschenbuch Verlag.
Van Laak, Dirk. 2001. "Infra-Strukturgeschichte." *Geschichte und Gesellschaft* 27:367–93.
Veidlinger, Jeffrey. 2009. *Jewish Public Culture in the Late Russian Empire.* Bloomington: Indiana University Press.
Velychenko, Stephen. 2000. "Rival Grand Narratives of National History: Russian/Soviet, Polish and Ukrainian Accounts of Ukraine's Past (1772–1991)." *Österreichische Osthefte* 42:139–60.
Venturi, Franco. 1960. *Roots of Revolution: A History of the Populist and Socialist Movements in Nineteenth Century Russia.* New York: Alfred A. Knopf.
Vierhaus, Rudolf. 1972. "Bildung." In *Geschichtliche Grundbegriffe: Historisches Lexikon zur politisch-sozialen Sprache in Deutschland*, edited by Otto Brunner, Werner Conze, and Reinhart Koselleck, 508–51. Stuttgart: Klett-Cotta.
Vilmain, Vincent. 5769/2008. "A Woman within Zionism: The Path of Myriam Schach (1867–1956)." *Nashim: A Journal of Jewish Women's Studies & Gender Issues* 16:174–95.
Vittorelli, Natascha. 2007. *Frauenbewegung um 1900: Über Triest nach Zagreb.* Vienna: Löcker Verlag.
———. 2009. "Wie Frauenbewegung geschrieben wird: Historisierung und Historiographie am Beispiel von Frauenbewegungen der Habsburgermonarchie." In *Wie Frauenbewegung geschrieben wird: Historiographie, Dokumentation, Stellungnahmen, Bibliographien*, edited by Johanna Gehmacher and Natascha Vittorelli, 103–33. Vienna: Löcker Verlag.
Vogel, Ursula. 1997. "Gleichheit und Herrschaft in der ehelichen Vertragsgesellschaft—Widersprüche der Aufklärung." In *Frauen in der*

Geschichte des Rechts: Von der Frühen Neuzeit bis zur Gegenwart, edited by Ute Gerhard, 265–92. Munich: Beck.

Von Glasenopp, Gabriele. 1996. *Aus der Judengasse: Zur Entstehung und Ausprägung deutschsprachiger Ghettoliteratur im 19. Jahrhundert*. Tübingen: Niemeyer.

Von Hammerstein, Katharina. 1996. "Selbst—Geschichte(n)—Schreiben: Dokumente persönlicher Lebensführung und politischen Engagements einer Vormärzlerin: Louise Aston." In *Autobiographien von Frauen: Beiträge zu ihrer Geschichte*, edited by Magdalene Heuser, 285–301. Tübingen: Niemeyer.

Voznjak, Mychajlo. 1937. *Jak dijšlo do peršoho žinočoho al'manacha*. L'viv: Vydavec' Ivan Tyktor.

Wagner, Peter. 1998. "Fest-Stellungen: Beobachtungen zur sozialwissenschaftlichen Diskussion über Identität." In *Identitäten*, edited by Aleida Assmann and Heidrun Friese, 44–72. Frankfurt am Main: Suhrkamp.

Walkowitz, Judith R. 1992. *City of Dreadful Delight: Narratives of Sexual Danger in Late-Victorian London*. Chicago, IL: University of Chicago Press.

Warneken, Bernd J. 1988. "Zur Schichtspezifik autobiographischer Darstellungsmuster." In *Biographie—sozialgeschichtlich*, edited by Andreas Gestrich, Peter Knoch, and Helga Merkel, 141–63. Göttingen: Vandenhoeck & Ruprecht.

Wasserloos, Yvonne. 2004. *Das Leipziger Konservatorium der Musik im 19. Jahrhundert: Anziehungs- und Ausstrahlungskraft eines musikpädagogischen Modells auf das internationale Musikleben*. Hildesheim: Olms.

Wawrzykowska-Wierciochowa, Dionizja. 1960. "Kobiece Koło Oświaty Ludowej (1883–1894)." *Przegląd Historyczno-Oświatowy* III:49–65.

———. 1960. "Maria Wysłouchowa (1858–1905)." *Rocznik Dziejów Ruchu Ludowego* 2:399–417.

———. 1961. *Z dziejów kobiety wiejskiej: Szkice historyczne 1861–1945*. Warsaw: Ludowa Spółdzielnia Wydawnicza.

———. 1971. "Kulikowska Kasylda." In *Polski Słownik Biograficzny*, edited by Polska Akademia Nauk and Polska Akademia Umiętności. Vol. XVI, 154–56. Wrocław: Wydawnictwo Polskiej Akademii Nauk.

———. 1975. *Wysłouchowa: Opowieść biograficzna*. Warsaw: Ludowa Spółdzielnia Wydawnicza.

Weber, Katharina. 1997. "Toynbee Hall in London." In *"Wer in den Osten geht, geht in ein anderes Land": Die Settlementbewegung in Berlin zwischen Kaiserreich und Weimarer Republik*, edited by Rolf Lindner, 51–60. Berlin: Akademie Verlag.

———. 2000. "Galizien: Westen des Ostens, Osten des Westens." *Österreichische Osthefte* 42:389–421.

Wendland, Anna V. 2009. "Eindeutige Bilder, komplexe Identitäten: Imperiale, nationale, regionale Identitätskonzepte und ihre Visualisierung auf der galizischen Allgemeinen Landesausstellung in Lemberg 1894." *Zeitschrift für Ostmitteleuropaforschung* 58:111–61.

Wenk, Silke. 2000. "Gendered Representations of the Nation's Past and Future." In *Gendered Nations: Nationalisms and Gender Order in the Long 19th Century*, edited by Ida Blom, Karen Hagemann, and Catherine Hall, 63–77. Oxford: Berg Publishers.

Weismann, Stephanie. 2017. *Das Potenzial der Peripherie: Leopold von Sacher-Masoch (1836–1895) und Galizien*. Göttingen: V & R unipress and Vienna University Press.

Weißbrod, Bernd. 1986. "'Visiting' und 'Social Control': Statistische Gesellschaften und Stadtmissionen im Viktorianischen England." In *Soziale Sicherheit und soziale Disziplinierung*, edited by Christoph Sachße and Florian Tennstedt, 181–208. Frankfurt am Main: Suhrkamp.
Welskopp, Thomas. 2010. "Clio and Class Struggle in Socialist Histories of the Nation: A Comparison of Robert Grimm's and Eduard Bernstein's Writings, 1910–1920." In *Nationalizing the Past: Historians as Nation Builders in Modern Europe*, edited by Stefan Berger and Chris Lorenz, 298–318. Basingstoke: Palgrave Macmillan.
White, Hayden. 1973. *Metahistory: The Historical Imagination in Nineteenth-Century Europe*. Baltimore, MD: Johns Hopkins University Press.
Wiegandt, Ewa. 1997. *Austria Felix czyli o micie Galicji w polskiej prozie współczesnej*. Poznań: Bene Nati.
Wierzbieniec, Wacław. 2011. "Dobroczynności i opieka społeczna w Galicji w okresie autonomii—stan i perspektywy badań." In *Galicja 1772–1918: Problemy metodologiczne, stan i potrzeby badań*. Vol. 1, edited by Agnieszka Kawalec, Wacław Wierzbieniec, and Leonid Zaszkilniak, 258–73. Rzeszów: Wydawnictwo Uniwersytetu Rzeszowskiego.
Wietschorke, Jens. 2013. *Arbeiterfreunde: Soziale Mission im dunklen Berlin 1911–1933*. Frankfurt am Main: Campus Verlag.
Wingfield, Nancy M. 2017. *The World of Prostitution in Late Imperial Austria*. Oxford: Oxford University Press.
Wistrich, Robert S. 1981. "Austrian Social Democracy and the Problem of Galician Jewry 1890–1914." *Leo Baeck Institute Year Book* 26:89–124.
Wöller, Burkhard. "'Fortschritt' und 'Rückständigkeit' als diskursive Strategien moderner Geschichtsschreibung in Galizien: Polnische und ruthenische Entwicklungsdiagnosen und mentale Verortungen des Fürstentums Halyč-Volyn." In *Galizien: Peripherie der Moderne—Moderne der Peripherie?* edited by Elisabeth Haid, Stephanie Weismann, and Burkhard Wöller, 45–59. Marburg: Verlag Herder-Institut.
Wolff, Larry. 2010. *The Idea of Galicia: History and Fantasy in Habsburg Political Culture*. Stanford, CA: Stanford University Press.
Wollons, Roberta. 2000. "Introduction: On the International Diffusion, Politics, and Transformation of the Kindergarten." In *Kindergartens and Cultures: The Global Diffusion of an Idea*, edited by Roberta Wollons, 1–15. New Haven, CT: Yale University Press.
Wolsza, Tadeusz. 1999. "Organisatorki ruchu oświatowego na wsi: Królestwo Polskie na przełomie wieków." In *Kobieta i edukacja na ziemiach polskich w XIX i XX wieku*. Vol. II, part 2, edited by Anna Żarnowska and Andrzej Szwarc, 83–92. Warsaw: Wydawnictwo "DiG."
Wróbel, Piotr. 1994. "The Jews of Galicia under Austrian-Polish Rule, 1869–1918." *Austrian History Yearbook* XXV: 97–138.
Wulf, Christoph and Jörg Zirfas. 2003. "Anthropologie und Ritual: Eine Einleitung." *Paragrana* 12:11–28.
Wunder, Heide. 1998. *He Is the Sun, She Is the Moon: Women in Early Modern Germany*, translated by Thomas Dunlap. Cambridge, MA: Harvard University Press. (German original 1992).
"Wysłouch Bolesław." 1989. In *Słownik biograficzny działaczy ruchu ludowego*, edited by Józef Dancygier, 445–46. Warsaw: Ludowa Spółdzielnia Wydawnicza.

"Wysłouchowa Maria." 1989. In *Słownik biograficzny działaczy ruchu ludowego*, edited by Józef Dancygier, 447. Warsaw: Ludowa Spółdzielnia Wydawnicza.

Wytrzens, G. 1977. "Okunevs'kyj Theophil." In *Österreichisches Biographisches Lexikon 1815–1950*. Vol. 7, installment 33, 223–24. Vienna: Verlag der Österreichischen Akademie der Wissenschaften. Accessed December, 6, 2019. www.biographien.ac.at/oebl/oebl_O/Okunevskyj_Theophil_1858_1937.xml;internal&action=hilite.action&Parameter=Okunevs*.

Yerushalmi, Yosef H. 1988. *Zachor: Erinnere Dich! Jüdische Geschichte und jüdisches Gedächtnis*. Berlin: Klaus Wagenbach.

Zaleska, Zofia. 1938. *Czasopisma kobiece w Polsce (Materiały do Historii czasopism) Rok 1818–1937*. Warsaw: Wyższa Szkoła Dziennikarska.

Zhurzhenko, Tatiana. 2006. "Ukrainian Women in Galicia: Origins of the Feminist Tradition and the Challenges of Nationalism." In *Frauenbilder, feministische Praxis und nationales Bewusstsein in Österreich-Ungarn 1867–1918*, edited by Waltraud Heindl, Edit Kiraly, and Alexandra Millner, 257–68. Tübingen: Francke.

Zimmermann, Susan. 2005. "The Challenge of Multinational Empire for the International Women's Movement: The Habsburg Monarchy and the Development of Feminist Inter/National Politics." *Journal of Women's History* 17:87–117.

———. 2006. "Reich, Nation und Internationalismus: Kooperationen und Konflikte der Frauenbewegungen der Habsburger Monarchie im Spannungsfeld internationaler Organisation und Politik." In *Frauenbilder, feministische Praxis und nationales Bewusstsein in Österreich-Ungarn 1867–1918*, edited by Waltraud Heindl, Edit Kiraly, and Alexandra Millner, 119–67. Tübingen: Francke.

Żmigrodzka, Maria. 1976. "Probleme des romantischen Umbruchs." In *Positionen polnischer Literaturwissenschaft der Gegenwart: Methodenfragen der Literaturgeschichtsschreibung*, edited by Eberhard Dieckmann and Maria Janion, 39–75. Berlin: Akademie Verlag.

Index

Adam Mickiewicz Association for Adult Education Center (Towarzystwo Uniwersytetu ludowego im. Adama Mickiewicza) 40, 158, 160, 192
adult education 33, 158–60, 163, 186–7, 189, 196; centers 6, 158–9, 182, 185–6, 188, 244; initiatives 158, 169
Advice Centers for Conscious Motherhood (Poradni dla świadomego macierzyństwa) 90
Algiers 228
Alliance Israélite Universelle 146, 238
almanac 22, 58, 60–2, 66, 70, 74, 107–10, 136, 148
America 44–5, 51–2, 71; South 238; United States of 87, 116, 171, 182, 211
arena 3, 9–10, 93, 120, 151, 231, 247, 250; of feminist politics 67; of women's politics/policy 120, 219, 221, 230, 232
assimilation [Jewish] 8, 133–5, 141–2, 144–5, 147, 224, 226, 255
Association of Friends of Education (Towarzystwo Przyjaciół Oświaty) 41, 109, 157–9, 163
Association of Girlfriends (Związek koleżeński) 108
Association of Jewish Women in Eastern Lesser Poland (Związek Kobiet Żydowskich Małopolski Wschodniej) 114
Association of People's Enlightenment (Towarzystwo Oświaty Ludowej) 158, 187, 191
Association of People's School (Towarzystwo Szkoły Ludowej) 158–9, 186–7, 191–2

Association of Ruthenian Ladies (Obščestvo ruskych dam) 59, 193
Association of Ruthenian Women in Stanislav (Tovarystvo ruskich žinok v Stanislavovi) 56, 59, 62, 67, 73, 137, 175, 195, 209, 219, 254
Association of Women of the Kingdom of Poland and Lithuania (Zrzeszenie Kobiet Korony i Litwy) 98
audience 5, 9 11, 15, 24, 26, 42, 53, 74, 77, 79–82, 85, 92, 95, 120, 125, 161–2, 165, 168–9, 189, 199–200, 204, 207, 212, 215, 217, 222–3, 230–3, 236, 241, 245–6
Austria 234, 253
Austro-Hungarian Empire *see* Habsburg Empire
author 3, 26–7, 33–5, 38–9, 43, 53–5, 57, 62, 71–2, 77, 90, 92, 94, 96, 103, 110, 116, 120, 123, 128–9, 137–8, 146–7, 173, 186, 197, 199, 201–2, 207, 211–13, 218, 224, 228, 232–4, 241, 243, 258; female 147, 206–7

Bar Kokhba [Association] 82, 113, 196
Basel 33, 75, 83–5, 93, 196, 223, 237–8
Bavaria 151
Belgium 186, 254
Berlin 6, 88, 115, 150, 178, 181, 187–9, 193, 205, 257
Beskids 41
Bielsko/Bielitz 81
biography 24–6, 33–5, 38–9, 57–8, 69, 79, 93, 96, 105–6, 129, 200, 234, 237, 240, 243, 251; auto-, 22, 26, 34, 54, 56–8, 69, 94, 104, 140, 203, 234, 238, 251

312 Index

B'nai B'rith 86, 228, 231, 238
Bohemia 38, 52, 63, 93, 99, 151, 191, 253
Bojanowo 86–7
Bolechiv/Bolechów 54, 59–60, 63, 66–7, 72–3, 111, 178
Boryslav/Borysław 105
Brazil 150
Breslau *see* Wrocław
Brittany 151
Brody 113, 183, 197
Bukovina 64, 71, 73, 134, 191, 253–5

Carpathian Mountains 139
Central Land Committee for War Orphan Care (Centralny Krajowy Komitet Opieki nad Sierotami Wojennymi) 86
Central Office for Women's Zionist Work (Zentralstelle für die Zionistische Frauenarbeit) 115
Central Office of the World Zionist Organization (Zentralbüro der Zionistischen Weltorganisation) 115
charisma 75, 79, 92, 95, 138, 162, 243, 245
charity 138–9, 170, 172, 202, 229–30
Chernivtsi/Černivci/Cernăuti 58
Chicago 1, 44, 182
childcare 156, 170–6, 178–80, 188, 190, 194–5, 245
Cieszyn Silesia 8, 41–2, 99, 187, 242, 258
Circle of Ukrainian Girls (Kružka ukraïns'kych divčat) 153
Cisleithania 85
Club of Ruthenian Women in L'viv (Klub Rusynok w L'vovi) 71, 167, 196
collective 2, 9, 12, 14–15, 17, 19, 24–7, 39, 58, 61, 90, 93–6, 105, 119–22, 127, 132, 135, 140–1, 143, 145–6, 148–9, 152, 155, 163, 169–70, 177–80, 182, 189, 199–202, 204, 206–7, 212, 215, 217, 230, 240–1, 243–50; identities 15, 132; imagined 26, 120, 200, 246–7; memory 24, 49; national 12, 106, 168, 183, 248; of women 62, 84, 90, 125, 178, 180, 190, 204–5, 209, 222, 240, 248
Cologne 115, 258
Colorado 1

Committee for a Women's Rally in Kraków (Komitet wiecu kobiet w Krakowie) 48
Committee for a Women's Work Section (Komitet Działu Pracy Kobiet) 101, 166
Congress of Polish Women from the Three Partitions in L'viv (Zjazd Kobiet Polskich z trzech zaborów we Lwowie) 43, 52
contemporary work, siehe Gegenwartsarbeit 84, 212, 230
Copenhagen/København 216
correspondence 19, 22–3, 31, 35–6, 40, 48, 52, 68, 70, 73–4, 93–4, 107, 110–11, 127, 212, 217
(The) Cossack Camp (Sič) 56, 105, 140

Dawn Academic Association (Haschachar) 81, 192
Denmark 216
diaspora 1, 7, 41, 84, 87–8, 146, 189, 248
Drohobyč/Drohobycz 84, 104, 114, 174, 183–4, 237

East End (London) 182, 253
Eastern Borderland/Kresy Wschodnie 4, 41, 43, 256, 258
educational association 8, 40, 43, 158, 166, 184–5, 187, 191, 240, 257
educational project 8, 60, 82, 156, 159, 173, 181, 185, 196, 245, 247
educational work 2, 26, 37, 42–3, 59, 75, 86, 165, 169, 180–2, 241, 245
elite 5–6, 20, 27, 40, 42, 50–1, 62, 64, 86, 104, 127, 129–33, 142, 151, 170, 184–6, 189–90, 193, 219–20, 245, 248, 250
emancipation 38, 78, 84, 89, 94, 128, 144–5, 187, 218, 225–6; women's 59, 69, 74–5, 84, 92, 125, 143–4, 146, 207
Enlightenment (Prosvita) [Association] 158, 187, 191, 257
Equality for Women Committee (Komitet Równouprawnienia Kobiet) 65, 101
Europe 1, 17, 46, 49, 74, 87, 89, 118, 181, 203, 207, 211, 221, 227, 240, 242, 247–9, 257; Central 11, 16–17, 111, 237; East-central

Index 313

16–17, 19, 248; Eastern 16–17, 20, 28, 196, 237–8; Southeastern 18; Western 20, 76
expectation 6, 20–1, 70, 137, 139, 141, 203–5, 212, 214
experience 1–2, 13, 20–2, 25–6, 33, 54–5, 57–8, 70, 73, 75, 87, 119, 121, 126, 132–7, 139–43, 145–9, 153, 155, 159, 168, 176, 199–206, 210, 212, 214, 222, 232, 240–1, 243–4, 246, 249–50; construction of 21, 25, 121

Falcon (Sokol) 36
Family Counselling Center (Poradnia dla rodzin) 90
fantasy 16, 70, 141, 199, 204
female peasant/peasant woman 4, 19, 25, 41, 124–7, 130–2, 151, 175–7, 191, 241, 244
Female Teachers' Association (Stowarzyszenie Nauczycielek) 108
femininity 7–8, 17–18, 78, 95, 110, 117, 139, 144–5, 153, 179
feminism 17–18, 30, 74, 89–92, 226, 235, 253; collective 17; individual 17, 30; liberal 74; pragmatic 30; relational 17, 30
feminist movement *see* women's movement
France 17, 61, 85, 103, 109, 150, 216, 238, 255, 257
Frankfurt *see* Frankfurt am Main
Frankfurt am Main 226, 237, 256

Gegenwartsarbeit (contemporary work) 84, 230, 237
General Jewish Labor Bund in Lithuania, Poland, and Russia (Algemeyner Jidisher Arbetersbund in Lite, Poyln un Rusland) 197, 237
Geneva 62, 105
German Empire 17, 44–5, 86, 88, 96, 99, 107, 146, 150, 203, 227, 236–7, 251, 257
Germany 142, 206, 209, 211, 216, 227, 251, 253, 256
Great Britain 17, 85, 118, 171, 186, 216, 227
Greater Poland 127
Greek Catholic clergy/bishop 54, 59, 61, 104, 136, 140, 209, 219, 221
Greenland 164

Grodno/Hrodna 4, 201–2, 256
Grzymałów 113

Habsburg Empire/Austro-Hungarian Empire 1, 6, 16, 31, 33, 45, 62–3, 71, 88, 108, 112, 216, 247–8, 254
Hamburg 197, 231
Health Protection Association (Towarzystwo Ochrony Zdrowia) 90
hero 33–4, 37–8, 51, 53, 78, 97, 127–30, 140, 165, 201, 232, 251; female 7, 36–8, 51, 53–4, 77–9, 88, 129–30, 132, 149, 199–201, 205, 212, 244, 251; male 51, 54, 130, 244
higher education 6–7, 46, 59, 65, 79, 98, 105, 162, 178, 258
historicization 2, 25–6, 135, 141, 205, 232, 247, 250
Horodenka 175
Hull House 182, 187, 189, 251
husband 7, 40–1, 54–6, 59, 69–70, 72–3, 75, 77, 79, 94–5, 99, 128–9, 136–8, 152, 157–8, 165, 193, 201–4, 216, 220, 242–3, 251, 253–5
Husiatyn/Husjatyn 114, 175

identity 11–12, 14–15, 20, 24, 26, 55, 64, 70, 88, 91, 94, 105, 120, 129, 132, 161, 249; politics 2, 8, 12, 95, 249; sense of 161, 185, 190, 196, 245
imagined community 7, 12, 127, 143, 245, 250
intelligentsia 15, 18, 20, 30, 39, 42, 47, 50, 53, 57–8, 68, 73, 95, 97–8, 101, 103–4, 127, 131, 162, 169, 176–7, 185, 189, 207, 209, 212–13, 217, 220, 222, 226, 232, 243, 250
International Congress of Women's Activities and Women's Aims (Internationaler Kongress für Frauenwerke und Frauenbestrebungen) 178
International Council of Women 44, 101
International Woman Suffrage Alliance 65, 101
Ireland 111
Israelite Benevolent Society (Israelitischer Hilfsverein) 226
Istebna/Istebno/Izdebna/Izdebno 100

Jarosław 167
Jerusalem 23
Jewish Association for People's Education (Żydowskie Towarzystwo Oświaty Ludowej) 158
Jewish Branch Committee for Combatting Trafficking in Women (Jüdisches Zweigkomitee zur Bekämpfung des Mädchenhandels) 226–7
Jewish Colonization Association 238
Jewish-nationalist Reading Room for Girls "Ruth" (Leseverein jüdischnationaler Mädchen) 191
Jewish-nationalist Reading Room for Young Women "Ruth" (Narodowożydowska Czytelnia młodieży żeńskiej "Ruth") 167
Jewish People's School Society (Żydowskie Towarzystwo Szkoły Ludowej) 116
Jewish Women's Circle in L'viv (Koło Kobiet Żydowskich we Lwowie) 76–7, 83, 86, 113, 180–1, 188, 252
Jewish World Aid Conference (Jüdische Welthilfskonferenz) 86, 116
Jezierna 114
J. I. Kraszewski Association for Scientific Support for Polish Women (Stowarzyszenie pomocy naukowej dla Polek imienia J. I. Kraszewskiego) 206
Judith (Iudyta) women's association 82

Kaiserswerth 194, 253
Kasylda Kulikowska Publishing House (Wydawnictwo im. Kasyldy Kulikowskiej) 43
Kiev/Kyïv 22, 56, 105, 252
Kindergarten 6–8, 14, 26, 63, 65, 72, 85, 107, 149, 155–7, 167, 170–82, 186, 188–90, 193–6, 217–18, 244–5, 247, 253, 255
Kishinev/Chişinău 85
K. Kulikowska Foundation (Fundusz im. K. Kulikowskiej) 43, 102
knowledge 2, 9–10, 13, 24, 40, 45–6, 49, 54, 56–7, 60–1, 82, 119, 122–3, 125–8, 131–2, 134–5, 139, 149, 157, 159–65, 168–70, 173, 179–80, 182, 184, 190, 199, 217, 244–5, 247, 249–50; academic 126, 159, 165, 168, 185, 249–50; experiential 11, 126–7, 131; historical 61, 126, 148; institutional 11, 126, 131; rural 11, 126; situated 29, 239
Kołomyja/Kolomyja/Kolomea 80, 82, 183, 197
Kraków 6, 22–3, 28, 31, 41, 43, 46–8, 51, 66, 72, 93, 103, 108, 134, 163, 166–8, 172, 174, 184, 186–7, 189, 192–3, 196, 206, 213, 235, 251–2, 254–5, 258
Kresy Wschodnie see Eastern Borderlands

Labor (Trud) [Association] 167
labor movement 2, 105, 181–3, 186–8, 222
League of Austrian Women's Associations (Bund österreichischer Frauenvereine) 203
League of Jewish Women (Jüdischer Frauenbund) 227, 237
lecture 6, 10–11, 40–1, 43, 46, 53, 62–3, 65, 79, 82, 85–6, 103, 156, 158–70, 173, 175, 180–90, 193, 206, 216, 226, 244–5
Leipzig 23, 79, 92, 112
Léopol see L'viv
letter 5, 13, 22, 25, 31, 36–8, 41–2, 44–5, 47–9, 51–2, 54–5, 60–1, 63, 68–70, 72–4, 79, 93, 96, 99, 101–2, 104, 107–11, 124, 126, 132, 151, 157–8, 160–1, 200–1, 204, 212, 236, 242
library 22–3, 41, 63, 68, 73, 120, 155, 158–9, 164, 166–7, 180, 182–3, 185, 187–9, 197, 244
literacy 5, 125, 150–1, 159, 197, 231, 247; il-, 124–5, 150–1
literature 3, 16, 27–8, 33, 38–9, 41, 44, 50–2, 54–61, 72–3, 75, 79, 88, 98–101, 103, 105–6, 109, 112, 116, 119–20, 127, 140–1, 143, 147, 149, 153, 159–60, 164, 166–8, 182, 184–5, 197, 203, 216, 223–4, 233, 254–5, 257; folk 43, 49, 120, 156; ghetto 88, 121, 145; narrative 3, 154
Lithuania 37, 52–3, 93, 126, 253, 256–7
London 85, 182–3, 189, 197, 238, 251, 253
love 35, 37, 39, 49–54, 58, 68, 74, 90–1, 95, 99, 109, 117, 128, 130,

136–7, 140, 144–5, 202, 223, 243; free 7, 69–70, 94–5, 243; story 142–3, 145–6, 154
L'viv/Lwów/Lemberg 1, 4, 6, 9, 22–3, 35, 39–43, 46, 48, 51–3, 58–60, 65, 68, 71–3, 75, 79–80, 82–7, 93, 99, 101–2, 104, 108, 110, 114, 124, 153, 157, 160, 172–3, 175, 178, 183–4, 186, 188, 191, 213, 231, 236, 252, 254–6, 258
L'viv Fighters (L'vôvskij Bojan') 63
Lvov *see* L'viv

Maccabee celebration 80, 112–13
Maccabee festival *see* Maccabee celebration
Mahilyow/Mahilioü 237
marriage 6–7, 46, 68–70, 74, 78, 89, 94–5, 110, 126, 136, 138–40, 142–3, 145, 193, 201–2, 205, 208, 220–1, 236, 243, 253; arranged 59, 62, 137, 140, 143; criticism of 68, 70, 94–5, 221, 236
masculinity 8, 18, 95, 135, 144
memory 24, 78–9, 97, 128–9, 199, 208; collective 24, 49; communicative 24; cultural 127; group 77, 112
middle class 8, 20, 26, 58, 68, 70, 79–80, 87, 89, 112, 173, 181–3, 185, 204, 220, 227, 242; females (*see* women); women 62, 146, 168–9, 174, 178, 201, 204–5, 242
Minerva [Association] 63, 65
Miriam [Association] 225
modernism 72, 111, 118
Moravian Ostrava/Moravská Ostrava/ Ostrava 187
Moriah [Association] 174, 237
mother 7, 17, 39, 41, 46, 51, 78, 89, 96, 98, 106, 108, 128–9, 131, 135, 138, 142, 145, 151, 164, 171, 173–6, 180, 201, 242, 255–7
motherhood 18, 164, 193, 202; conscious 89
Mychajlo Kačkov'skyj Association (Obščestvo ymeny Myhayla Kačkovskoho) 158, 191

Nahujevyči/Nahujowice 104
narrative 2–3, 8–10, 12–13, 24–5, 33–5, 39, 54, 57–8, 77–9, 88, 92–6,

Index 315

105, 121, 125, 129, 133–8, 140–1, 143, 149, 151, 154, 200–5, 207, 210–12, 214–15, 219, 232, 240–4, 246–9; biographical 34–5; historical 1, 15, 25, 51, 129, 200–1, 212, 215, 221, 246; literary 22, 25, 95, 129, 148; master 3, 15, 17, 231, 246; national 2, 15, 21, 33, 209–10, 241, 247; political 1, 54, 92; strategy 25, 133, 137, 140, 199–200, 211, 215, 222, 233, 243; structure 149, 200, 221, 232, 244, 246; style 53, 129, 145, 148–9, 201
narrativity 3, 10, 57
narrator 3, 5, 26, 34, 57, 93, 134, 137, 139, 142, 147, 212
National Jewish Women's League of Galicia and Bukovina (Narodowo-Żydowski Związek Kobiet z Galicji i Bukowiny) 83–5, 94, 180–1
national movement 2, 14, 29–30, 52, 73, 77–8, 91, 97, 112, 124, 129, 135, 144, 146, 151, 158, 164, 186, 241, 248, 257
Nationalism 7, 43, 128, 152
nationality 6, 19, 27, 63, 65, 84, 108, 134, 151, 187, 242; trans-, 8, 14, 26, 28, 156, 178, 240
Netherlands 85, 216
New York 238
Norway 216

Ottoman Empire 129, 252

Palestine 33, 79, 84, 87, 89, 90, 114–15, 117, 142, 172, 195–6, 237–8, 244, 248, 252
Paris 1, 18, 41, 86, 103, 112, 114, 118, 252–3
Patriotism 36, 39–40, 49, 65, 127, 159, 220
peasant movement 2–8, 11, 13, 19, 21, 28, 33, 35–6, 40–2, 47–8, 50, 109, 124, 148, 157–8, 169, 179–80, 186–8, 190, 198, 241, 247–8, 250, 257–8
Peasant Party (Stronnictwo Ludowe) 7, 41, 150, 158, 179, 257–8
peasant woman *see* female peasant
people's house 155, 181–2, 185–9, 247
Peoples House (Maison du Peuple/ Volkshuis) 186

Index

performance 3, 9–14, 16–17, 24–5, 29, 35, 54, 77, 79–80, 82, 86, 92–3, 120, 129, 156, 160, 162, 167, 182, 184–5, 189, 199–200, 230–3, 235, 240–1, 247, 249–50
performativity 3, 9–11, 14, 29, 83, 232, 240, 249
Persia 228
Pestalozzi-Fröbel-Haus 181, 193
petition 8, 64–6, 107–8, 165–6, 168–9, 212–13, 216, 218, 243, 248
Podwołoczyska 113
Pokuttya 139
Poland 7, 33, 41–2, 49–51, 53, 77–8, 85–7, 89–90, 101, 107, 112, 115, 126–7, 129–30, 132, 160, 184, 186–7, 203, 206, 211, 234, 252–4; Kingdom of 4–5, 19, 40–1, 45, 52, 97–8, 103, 127, 150, 164–5, 195, 197, 211, 213, 242; Second Republic of/Second Polish Republic 1, 75, 77, 115, 245
Polish Livonia 39, 42, 52
Polish-Lithuanian Commonwealth 1, 4, 37, 39, 106, 126, 129–30, 140
Polish Socialist Party (Polska Partia Socjalistyczna) 237
positivism 17, 37, 50, 97, 103, 201, 204, 256
Poznań 48, 52; Grand Duchy of 97; Province of 41, 43, 52, 100, 123, 150; voivodeship 86
Prague/Praha 16, 22, 52, 63–5, 73, 107, 170, 242, 254, 257
professionalization 65, 89, 91, 156, 164–5, 169–70, 172–3, 177–8, 180–1, 190, 195, 225, 231
prostitution 193, 227, 237
Prussia 44, 150, 171; Province of West 206, 253–4
Przemyśl 172
Pskov 39

Rachel (Rachela) women's association 82, 174
Racławice 41, 99, 126
radicals 7, 26, 59, 63, 66–9, 71–2, 74, 84, 94–5, 105, 109, 158, 178, 200, 216–18, 220, 222, 246, 248
reader 34–5, 38, 54, 57, 81, 94, 103, 119, 123–9, 132, 137–9, 148, 163, 195, 202, 206, 212, 215, 233, 244, 252; -ship 10, 23, 26, 31, 36, 49–50, 89, 124, 202, 215–17, 223, 233, 236
reading room 26, 40–1, 72, 100, 120, 149, 155–9, 163–4, 167–9, 179–80, 182, 184, 187–91, 193, 244–5, 258
realism 37, 55–6, 58, 106, 121, 140–1, 153, 202
reform center 8, 26, 155–6, 180–2, 189–90, 248
rhetoric 22, 24, 61, 78, 81, 117, 132, 135, 150, 200, 205, 215, 217, 222, 226, 237, 249; political 134, 141, 205, 215, 232
right to vote *see* suffrage
ritual 9–10, 12–14, 132, 156–7, 161–3, 165, 167–70, 180, 189–90, 192, 199–200, 233, 240, 248
ritualization 12–14, 24, 93, 121, 149, 162, 168, 180, 190, 249–50
Romania 78, 228, 252
Romanticism 50, 52, 95, 97, 118, 130, 132, 141, 255; neo-, 50, 88, 103, 121
Russia 44, 197, 228
Russian Empire 4–5, 27, 33, 35, 37, 39, 57, 85, 98, 101, 105–6, 109, 165, 197, 213, 251, 254, 256
Ruthenian Kindergarten Association (Tovarystvo Rus'ka zachoronka) 178
Ruthenian-Ukrainian Radical Party (Rus'ko-Ukraïnska Radykal'na Partija) 59, 104, 253, 255–6, 258
Ruthenian Women's Circle in Kolomyja (Ru'skyj žinočej kružok v Kolomyï) 167
Rzeszów 113–14, 193

Saint Petersburg/Sankt-Petersburg 39, 55, 97–8
Section for the Defense of Women's Rights (Sekcja dla Obrony Praw Kobiet) 165
settlement 87, 115, 181–2, 186, 237–8; house 182–3, 185–8, 190, 197
Shulamit [Association] 114
Siberia 1, 37–8, 98, 202, 211
Silesia 41–2, 52, 124, 127, 151
sister 7, 28, 52, 58, 60–1, 77, 106, 124–5, 128–9, 132, 150, 220, 256
Skilled Trades Association (Towarzystwo Warsztatów Rękodzielnych) 116

social democracy 109, 237
social democratic movement 67
Social Women's School (Soziale Frauenschule) 205, 257
social work 2–3, 5, 8, 14, 21, 26, 37, 44–5, 59, 65, 75, 77–8, 82–3, 85–7, 91–2, 131, 155–6, 166–7, 169–70, 172, 174, 178–83, 186–91, 194, 196, 200, 205, 224, 226–7, 229–31, 240–2, 244–6, 250–1, 256–7
socialism 20, 59, 173, 186–7, 224–6, 256; agrarian (*see* rural); rural 59, 98, 105, 252
socialist movement 7, 17, 67, 136, 158, 172, 215, 218, 227, 230, 240
space 1, 8–9, 13–15, 21–2, 24, 26, 29, 62, 64, 96, 120, 124, 155–6, 164, 168–9, 172, 175, 179–80, 187, 190–1, 200, 214, 217, 232, 242, 244–6, 248–9
speaker 33, 41–2, 50, 53, 71, 80–1, 113, 161–2, 167–9, 185, 215, 222, 245; male 84, 162, 168
Stanislav/Stanisławów/Stanislaviv/Ivano-Frankivs'k 59–61, 80, 84, 86, 174, 197
Stryj 54, 65, 71, 113, 170, 178, 184
suffrage/right to vote 4–6, 40, 45, 63, 65, 78, 84, 165, 192, 216; women's 7, 18, 45, 67, 75, 91, 112, 216, 225
Sulamith Reading Room for Jewish-nationalist Women (Czytelnia kobiet narodowo-żydowskich "Sulamith") 193
Switzerland 62, 85, 125

Tarnopol/Ternopil 80, 82, 85, 112–14, 237
Tarnów 197, 225, 254
Thamar Association for National Jewish Young Women (Stowarzyszenie panien narodowo-żydowskich "Thamar") 167
Toynbee Hall 155, 182–9, 196–7, 231, 237, 251, 254
trafficking in women and girls 6, 184, 206, 226–8, 230–1
Trembowla/Terebowlja 129, 252
truth 2, 26, 34, 42, 81, 134–5, 200, 225, 230–3, 239, 241, 246–7, 249–50

Ukraine 1, 15, 18, 107, 248; Eastern 15, 18, 27, 62, 73, 93, 95, 104–5, 248, 253, 258; Western 1
United League of Zionist Parties (Farajnigter Farband fun di Cionistisze Organizacje in Pojlen/Komitet Zjednoczonych Stronnictw Narodowo-Żydowskich) 115
USA *see* America, United States of

Veritas [Association] 184
Vienna/Wien 6, 15–16, 29, 56, 58–9, 63, 73, 85, 87–8, 106, 112, 115, 182, 196, 237, 253–4, 256
Vitebsk/Vicebsk 39

Warsaw/Warszawa 23, 35, 37, 39–40, 42–4, 48–9, 51–2, 87, 93, 97–8, 101, 103, 110, 116, 128, 150, 164, 195, 201–2, 206, 211–12, 233, 252, 254–6, 258; Duchy of 234
welfare 21, 86–7, 91, 115, 163, 170, 186, 224, 226–7, 229
Whitechapel (London) 182
woman question 56, 60, 62–3, 65, 71, 102, 105, 200, 206–7, 209–10, 212–17, 258
Women's Circle for People's Education (Kobiece Koło Oświaty Ludowej) 39, 42, 100–1, 166
Women's Circle of the Kingdom [of Poland] and Lithuania (Koło Kobiet Korony i Litwy) 46, 100–1
Women's International Zionist Organization 85
Women's Library (Žinočna Biblioteka) 71–3
women's movement/feminist movement 2–4, 6–8, 11, 14, 17–19, 21, 28, 30, 33, 36, 44–5, 49, 52, 56, 59–60, 62, 65, 69, 71, 73, 78, 81, 89, 91, 102, 105, 112, 117, 124–5, 136, 140–1, 143–7, 154, 158, 164–5, 168, 174, 178–81, 192–3, 200–16, 218–21, 224–5, 227, 229, 232, 235–6, 238, 240, 241, 244, 246–8, 250–1, 253, 257–8; Austrian 64, 203–4, 206, 253; Czech 36, 64, 257; French 18, 21; German 31, 64, 206, 210, 254; Jewish 96, 228, 236–7; Polish 17, 35, 44, 46, 90, 117, 160,

163–4, 169, 179, 207–8, 211, 247, 252, 254–5, 257; Ruthenian 74, 121, 177–8, 206, 209, 241, 248; Ukrainian 17
Women's Reading Room in Kraków (Czytelnia dla Kobiet w Krakowie) 46, 163–6, 168–9, 180–1, 188, 196, 235
Women's Reading Room in L'viv (Czytelnia dla Kobiet we Lwowie) 43, 101, 108, 158, 163, 166–9, 188, 258
Women's Savings Association (Towarzystwo Oszczędności Kobiet) 43–4, 108
Women's Scholarly Reading Room (Czytelnia naukowa kobiet) 100
workers' movement *see* labor movement
World Zionist Organization (Zionistische Weltorganisation) 112, 115, 253, 255–8
Wrocław/Breslau 23, 148

Zakopane 46, 51, 101, 168
Zborów 114
Zion Association (Stowarzyszenie Syjon) [L'viv, Brody] 82, 113, 158, 191
Zionism 4, 7–8, 20, 29–31, 77–82, 84, 88–92, 94–5, 112–13, 117, 133–5, 143, 147, 152, 179, 182, 189–90, 197, 200, 223–6, 228–31, 237, 241, 248, 250; cultural 88, 116, 147, 237; political 84, 114, 237, 253, 255; practical 87, 237
Zionist Academic Reading Hall (Zionistische Academische Lesehalle) 191
Zionist movement 3, 6–7, 23, 25, 31, 33, 75, 77–80, 84, 94, 114, 116, 144, 146, 148, 162, 168, 172, 174, 177, 179, 182, 184, 188, 193, 196, 200, 223, 225, 230–1, 238, 241, 246, 252–3, 258
Zionist Organization in Eastern Lesser Poland (Organizacja Syjonistyczna w Małopolsce Wschodniej) 115
Zionist organization in Poland (Histradut ha-Tsyonit be Poloniah/Organizacja Syjonistyczna w Polsce) 86
Zionist World Congress 7, 33, 75, 78, 83–5, 114, 223, 225, 257
Złoczów 114
Zurich/Zürich 62, 110, 252, 255
Żywiec 4